D1298331

Training Guide:
Configuring Windows® 8

Scott D. Lowe
Derek Schauland
Rick W. Vanover

PUBLISHED BY
Microsoft Press
A Division of Microsoft Corporation
One Microsoft Way
Redmond, Washington 98052-6399

Library of Congress Control Number: 2012955627
ISBN: 978-0-7356-7322-9

Printed and bound in the United States of America.

First Printing

Microsoft Press books are available through booksellers and distributors worldwide. If you need support related to this book, email Microsoft Press Book Support at mspinput@microsoft.com. Please tell us what you think of this book at http://www.microsoft.com/learning/booksurvey.

Acquisitions Editor: Anne Hamilton
Developmental Editor: Karen Szall
Project Editor: Karen Szall
Editorial Production: nSight, Inc.
Technical Reviewer: Michael Toot; Technical Review services provided by Content Master, a member of CM Group, Ltd.
Copyeditor: Kerin Forsyth
Indexer: Lucie Haskins
Cover: Microsoft Press Brand Team

Contents at a glance

Contents

What do you think of this book? We want to hear from you!

Microsoft is interested in hearing your feedback so we can continually improve our
books and learning resources for you. To participate in a brief online survey, please visit:

www.microsoft.com/learning/booksurvey/

Chapter 2   Installing and migrating to Windows 8   37

Chapter 7   Administering Windows networking   223

Chapter 8   Configuring security   261

Chapter 9   Working with remote management tools   293

Chapter 12 Administering authentication and authorization   419

What do you think of this book? We want to hear from you!

Microsoft is interested in hearing your feedback so we can continually improve our books and learning resources for you. To participate in a brief online survey, please visit:

www.microsoft.com/learning/booksurvey/

Introduction

This training guide is designed for information technology (IT) professionals who support or plan to support Windows 8 and are ramping up on the latest technology. It is assumed that before you begin using this guide, you have at least an entry-level understanding of Microsoft Windows and common Internet technologies.

This book covers some of the topics and skills that are the subject of the Microsoft certification 70-687 exam. If you are using this book to complement your study materials, you might find this information useful. This book is designed to help you in the job role; it might not cover all exam topics. If you are preparing for the exam, you should use additional study materials to bolster your real-world experience. For your reference, a mapping of the topics in this book to the exam objectives is included in the back of the book.

By using this training guide, you will learn how to do the following:

- Install Windows 8 on a new computer or upgrade to Windows 8 from an earlier version of Windows
- Share network resources, including printers and file storage space on a Windows 8 client
- Navigate the new Windows 8 user interface and perform common administrative tasks in both the new and the earlier interfaces
- Manage the Windows 8 client-side Hyper-V virtualization software
- Configure and manage Internet Explorer 10
- Manage and troubleshoot hardware device drivers
- Secure the Windows 8 operating system environment

System requirements

The following are the minimum system requirements your computer needs to meet to complete the practice exercises in this book. To minimize the time and expense of configuring physical computers for this training guide, it's recommended that you use Hyper-V, which is a feature of Windows Server 2008, Windows Server 2008 R2, Windows 8, and Windows Server 2012. You can use other virtualization software instead, such as Windows Virtual PC or VirtualBox. If you do not have a way to create a virtual environment, have two physical PCs capable of running Windows 8 so that you can take full advantage of the training in this guide.

NOTE REQUIREMENTS FOR A FULL TEST OF HYPER-V

If you want to test the Hyper-V feature in Windows 8 fully, you must use a physical computer that supports Second Level Address Translation or a visualization platform that allows other virtualization platforms to run inside it. Such platforms include VMware Workstation 8 or higher and VMware Fusion 4 or higher.

Hardware requirements

This section presents the hardware requirements for Hyper-V, the hardware requirements if you are not using virtualization software, and the software requirements.

Virtualization hardware requirements

If you choose to use virtualization software, you need only one physical computer to perform the exercises in this book. That physical host computer must meet the following minimum hardware requirements:

- x64-based processor that includes both hardware-assisted virtualization (AMD-V or Intel VT) and hardware data execution protection. (On AMD systems, the data execution protection feature is called the No Execute or NX bit. On Intel systems, this feature is called the Execute Disable or XD bit.) These features must also be enabled in the BIOS. (You can run Windows Virtual PC without Intel-VT or AMD-V.)
- 4.0 GB of RAM (more is recommended)
- 120 GB of available hard disk space
- DVD-ROM drive
- Internet connectivity

Physical hardware requirements

If you choose to use physical computers instead of virtualization software, use the following list to meet the minimum hardware requirements of the practice exercises in this book:

- Three personal computers, each with a 1-GHz processor, 512 MB of RAM, network card, video card, and DVD-ROM drive
- At least 25 GB of disk space available on each computer
- All three computers physically connected to each other and to the Internet

Software requirements

The following software is required to complete the practice exercises:

- Windows 8.   You can download an evaluation edition of Windows 8 at *http://technet.microsoft.com/en-us/windows/windows-8.aspx*.

- The Windows Assessment and Deployment Kit (Windows ADK) for Windows 8.   You can find an overview of Windows ADK at *http://technet.microsoft.com/en-us/library/hh824947.aspx*, and the download is available at *http://www.microsoft.com/en-us/download/details.aspx?id=30652*.

- A web browser such as Internet Explorer 8 or later.

Practice setup instructions

Most of the practice exercises in this training guide require only a single computer, but for full testing, a second computer is often useful. For example, after you learn how to create a file share, you can then test your work by browsing to that file share from the other computer.

Acknowledgments

The authors would like to thank a number of people who helped in the creation of this Training Guide.

SCOTT LOWE

As is the case with everything I do, I dedicate this work to my beautiful wife, Amy, and my life-enriching, wonderful children, Ryan and Isabella. Without you, none of this would matter.

I also thank my coauthors, Derek Schauland and Rick Vanover, for their tireless efforts in getting this work to print.

DEREK SCHAULAND

This project has been one of the largest single writing projects that I have taken on, and although it was quite a bit of work to get to this point, we got it done. I have a newfound understanding of the work that goes into the certification process; for me, no longer is it about exams as much as it is about the entire process, from learning content all the way to the test.

I thank my wife Laura for encouraging me to keep going even when activities were popping up all the time. I also thank my friends and other family members for continuing to show interest in how the writing was going. It amazes me how much this helps the focus stick.

Last but certainly not least, I thank my fellow authors, Scott Lowe and Rick Vanover. Without the two of you, this project wouldn't have crossed my radar.

Thank you for the amazing opportunity.

RICK VANOVER
Rick dedicates his work in this book to his wife Amie and daughter Rilee.

Errata & book support

We've made every effort to ensure the accuracy of this book and its companion content. Any errors that have been reported since this book was published are listed on our Microsoft Press site at Oreilly.com:

http://go.microsoft.com/FWLink/?Linkid=275532

If you find an error that is not already listed, you can report it to us through the same page.

If you need additional support, email Microsoft Press Book Support at mspinput@microsoft.com.

Please note that product support for Microsoft software is not offered through the addresses above.

We want to hear from you

At Microsoft Press, your satisfaction is our top priority, and your feedback our most valuable asset. Please tell us what you think of this book at:

http://www.microsoft.com/learning/booksurvey

The survey is short, and we read every one of your comments and ideas. Thanks in advance for your input!

Stay in touch

Let's keep the conversation going! We're on Twitter: *http://twitter.com/MicrosoftPress.*

CHAPTER 1

Evaluating Windows 8

Windows 8 is a bold undertaking that brings to the Windows product an impressive array of new capabilities and improved features. Indeed, in many ways Windows 8 is a radical departure from earlier versions of Windows and is intended to enable Microsoft to bring the Windows experience to a wider variety of device form factors, from traditional PCs and laptops to portable tablets and smart phones.

Although previous editions of Windows boasted many new features, the sheer level of innovation included in the Windows 8 product will require many Windows administrators to abandon old processes and conventions and embrace new ways to support Windows 8 environments. Whether you are a consumer or an enterprise customer, Windows 8 is full of new capabilities that might change the way you work.

Lessons in this chapter:

Before you begin

To complete the practice exercises in this chapter, you will need two Windows 8 devices. A virtual hard disk (VHD) is optional but will be helpful in performing your practice exercises.

Lesson 1: What's new in Windows 8

To ensure maximum success in your Windows 8 deployment efforts, you need to have a complete understanding of the features and capabilities it includes. Most important, you must become intimately familiar with the new user interface (UI), Microsoft's new foray into revitalizing the interface to make it simpler to use across device platforms.

The new UI, however, is just the beginning. This lesson describes in broad terms how everything fits together, which is essential as a starting point.

Navigating the Windows 8 user interface

The most immediate visual manifestation of Windows 8 is the new Start screen (Figure 1-1), which replaces the Start menu. In Windows 8, Microsoft has even jettisoned the Start button. The new Start screen brings a new paradigm to the user experience. The Start menu gave you access to programs and other tools, but the Start screen brings you a more dynamic and engaging experience.

FIGURE 1-1 The Windows 8 Start screen

 You will notice the change immediately. Gone are mini-icons representing the programs that users launch at the beginning of each workday. Replacing the icons is a series of *live tiles* that display current information related to an application. Although the UI features tiles throughout, a live tile includes information that is dynamically updated, such as a text string, number, or picture. For example, in the Mail app, the live tile displays the number of unread messages and some of the text from the newest message in the inbox. In Figure 1-2, you don't see much personalization yet because Phil Gibbins has just finished a new installation of Windows 8.

FIGURE 1-2 A live tile in action

Touchscreen terminology

Windows 8 operates on a wide variety of devices, including touch-enabled tablets and smart phones. Every action that uses a keyboard and mouse on a non-touch-enabled device has an equivalent for touch-enabled devices that uses a finger or a stylus. Throughout the book, both types of instructions are included, such as "Tap or click the tile." If you are using a touch-enabled device for the first time, here are the descriptions of the most-used actions.

- **Tap**   The same as a mouse button click. Use your fingertip or stylus to tap the indicated area gently and briefly on the screen.
- **Double-tap**   The same as a mouse button double-click. Use your fingertip or stylus to tap the indicated area twice in quick succession.
- **Press and hold**   Tap the indicated area, but instead of removing your fingertip or stylus, keep it in contact with the indicated area for a brief time (about two seconds). Used in place of the mouse-hover technique by which you move the mouse cursor over the indicated area and pause.
- **Slide**   Much like press and hold, but instead of pausing, slide your fingertip or stylus to the desired area. Works like click and drag with a mouse.
- **Swipe**   Slide your fingertip or stylus from the indicated area in the indicated direction, such as "To scroll the Start screen, swipe from the right edge of the screen to the left." The swipe action does not have an exact equivalent with a mouse, but it behaves similarly to using scroll bars, Page Up or Page Down keys, or zoom-in and zoom-out buttons.

Managing the Start screen

In Windows 8, an *app* refers to any application that is launched from the Start screen and runs within the confines of the new *Windows Runtime* (*WinRT*) environment. Apps are written in HTML 5, JavaScript, C++, C#, or Visual Basic. Figure 1-1 displays a number of desktop apps, including Mail, Calendar, and Messaging, but many more apps are available.

Sometimes, acronyms take on a life of their own, much to the dismay of users everywhere. The acronym WinRT is one that might cause confusion because of its similarity to a new Windows 8 edition: Windows RT. Windows RT is a full edition of the Windows 8 operating system; Windows RT has also gone by the name of Windows on ARM. The Windows RT operating system is intended to bring the Windows 8 experience to devices that run on the low-power ARM architecture, which enables Windows 8 deployment across a much wider array of hardware. It is only available pre-installed on PCs and tablets that are powered by ARM processors. WinRT is the set of application programming interfaces (APIs) and the runtime environment that enables programs to run on both ARM and x86-based processor architectures.

Therefore, Windows RT is a full operating system. WinRT is a runtime environment that runs on all Windows 8 editions to support application execution.

The Start screen isn't limited to apps; Microsoft is not ignoring the millions of software applications that have been created over the years. These traditional desktop applications also appear on the Start screen, side by side with the new apps.

As indicated before, a key difference between apps and traditional applications lies in the execution model each type of program uses to operate. Whereas traditional applications continue to run in the way they always have and continue to maintain a complete set of application controls, apps run inside the new WinRT environment. As you might expect from a user-focused product, the Start screen is about as far from "what you see is what you get" as possible. It's eminently customizable so that you can personalize it to meet your individual needs and wants.

Each tile is individually manageable and customizable. You can even completely remove it from the Start screen if it's an app you don't use often. As an alternative, you can resize each tile. There are two tile sizes; the smaller tile size is a square, and the larger is a rectangle.

You can customize each tile to meet your needs. For example, if you find that you don't use the Photo app often but you want to keep it on your Start screen, what are your options? To see the available options to manage this app, tap or right-click the app icon on the Start screen. Figure 1-3 shows the result; three options are available for this app.

FIGURE 1-3 Available app management options

Different apps have different options, so what you see at the bottom of the screen depends on which app you've selected. Here are some of the management options you might see:

- **Unpin From Start**   Remove the app or application from the Start screen. This is useful when you don't use an app and want to reclaim screen space for other tools. If you want to use the app again in the future, just add it back to the Start screen. Instructions on how to do this follow.

- **Uninstall**   Uninstall the app from the system. If you uninstall the app, you must reinstall it as a new app if you want to use it later. You learn more about managing applications in Chapter 4, "Installing and configuring applications."

- **Smaller (or Larger)**   Reduce or increase the size of the app's tile. In Figure 1-3, the Smaller option is available because the tile is already consuming two screen slots.

- **Turn Live Tile Off**   If a tile's automatic update is annoying or isn't useful, you can leave the tile in place and just turn off the tile's ability to display current information.

- **Open New Window**   Some apps can run multiple copies. For example, Microsoft Internet Explorer is an app in which many people keep multiple sites open. Use Open New Window to open another app window.

- **Clear Selection**   When multiple tiles are selected, a check mark appears in the upper-right corner of each selected tile. You generally have only two options: remove the tiles from the Start screen or clear your selection. When you clear your selection, the check mark is cleared from each of the tiles.

- **All Apps**   The All Apps option displays an app list arranged by category so you can select and work with multiple tiles at one time or select an app that you want visible on the Start screen.

NOTE **NOT ALL TILES CAN BE RESIZED**

Apps that include notifications generally can be resized to use multiple tile areas. Other apps can be placed on the Start screen but will take just a single tile space and can't be made larger.

If you remove an app from the Start screen, you can add it back by using a few swipes of the finger or a few clicks of the mouse. Here's how:

1. Tap or right-click anywhere on the Start screen that isn't covered by a tile, and All Apps appears in the lower-right corner of the screen. Tap or click the All Apps icon.

2. A screen that displays all the desktop apps and traditional applications appears, looking much like the one shown in Figure 1-4.

3. Press and hold or right-click the app that you want to place on the Start screen.

4. In the lower-left corner of the screen, tap or click Pin To Start. This places the app on the Start screen.

FIGURE 1-4 Displaying all the programs installed on the computer

You can use the same process to add other applications to the Start screen. In Figure 1-4, notice that a number of applications are to the right of the Apps list. These are traditional Windows applications that are installed on this Windows 8 system. Many of the applications on which administrators have come to depend remain on Windows 8 systems and are still fully supported.

The ability to resize tiles and remove apps from the Start screen and place apps on it is good, but real customization enables you to move items around to suit your needs. With the Start screen, this is a straightforward process. To move a tile, either tap or click the tile and drag it to the desired location on the Start screen.

The Start screen also provides you with a place to handle some basic management functions. By tapping or clicking your account picture, you open a drop-down menu from which you can change your account picture, lock the system, or sign out so that another user can sign in. This drop-down menu is displayed in Figure 1-5.

FIGURE 1-5 Basic account maintenance options available from the Start screen

Quick check

■ How do you add previously deleted apps back to the Start screen?

Quick check answer

■ Start by tapping or right-clicking anywhere on the Start screen that isn't covered by a tile. When All Apps appears in the lower-right corner of the screen, tap or click it to open a screen that displays all apps installed on the system. Press and hold or right-click the app you want to place on the Start screen. In the lower-left corner of the screen, click Pin To Start. This places the app on the Start screen.

Adding Windows administrative programs to the Start screen

Unless you're using the Windows RT edition of Windows 8, explained later in this chapter, it's likely that you won't use just the desktop apps. In fact, you might want to have a way to more quickly access the familiar administrative tools that formerly appeared on the Start menu. These tools include the Resource Monitor, Windows PowerShell, Disk Cleanup, and many more.

To add tiles for the administrative tools:

1. Swipe from the right or hover your mouse in the upper-right or lower-right corner of the screen. A series of small tiles called *charms* appears on the side of the screen. Charms are discussed in "Understanding charms" later in this chapter.

2. Select the Settings charm.

3. Tap or click Tiles.

4. When the Tiles flyout opens, select the slider under Show Administrative Tools so that it displays Yes (Figure 1-6).

FIGURE 1-6 To display icons for installed administrative tools

5. After selecting Yes, the Start screen displays the available administrative tools, as shown in Figure 1-7.

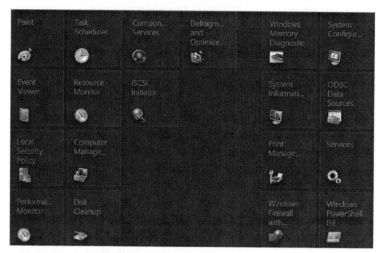

FIGURE 1-7 Administrative tools tiles added to the Start screen

Understanding charms

Although the Start menu is gone, Windows 8 retains quick access to certain system features by using *charms*, which are part of the Edge UI. The *Edge UI* is a narrow strip on the right side of the screen, which is accessible in one of two ways:

- On a touch interface, swipe from the right side of the screen toward the center.
- With a mouse, hover the mouse pointer on one of the hot spots on the right side of the screen. These hot spots are located in the two corners on the right side of the screen. You do not need to click the mouse.

After you open the Edge UI, the five charms appear in a vertical strip (Figure 1-8).

FIGURE 1-8 Charms appearing on the right side of the desktop

Each charm serves a specific purpose:

- **Search** The Search charm enables you to perform a system-wide search for a particular word or phrase. Search also enables you to look for a word or phrase that might exist within an app. For example, suppose you have an email message that contains a particular phrase. Search finds the search phrase in the message and returns it as a result.

- **Share** The Share charm enables applications to participate in bidirectional sharing, both sending and receiving information.

  Windows 8 is steeped in the new paradigm based on collaboration and sharing. Appropriate apps have individual sharing options you can access by selecting the Share charm while the application is open. In Figure 1-9, the Maps app is open; when the Share charm is selected, you can see that the map can be shared with two other apps, Mail and People. Each app carries its own sharing options; learn more about configuring these options in Chapter 10, "Sharing resources."

FIGURE 1-9 Sharing options for the Maps app

- **Start** The Start charm gives you an easy way to return to the Start screen.
- **Devices** By using the Devices charm, you can manage devices such as printers or cameras that are attached to your Windows 8 system.
- **Settings** Every Windows 8 system has a number of configurable settings, including sound levels, network connections, notifications, and more. The Settings charm gives you quick access to these settings. (Application settings are discussed further in Chapter 4.)

Switching between applications

The ability to switch between applications is still available in Windows 8. You can use the traditional Alt+Tab keyboard method to switch between apps, and Windows 8 adds a new, touch-based method. To open the left Edge UI, which contains thumbnail images of running programs, touch the left-side corners of the screen or, if you're using a mouse, hover the mouse pointer over one of those two locations. When you do so, the left Edge UI appears, as shown in Figure 1-10. Here, you can select any open application, and Windows switches to it.

FIGURE 1-10 A list of open applications in the Edge UI

Note also that you can open the Start screen from this list of open applications. If you press and hold or right-click the Start screen option from the list of open applications, a shortcut menu opens (Figure 1-11) that can help you quickly make your way to various system functions.

Programs and Features
Power Options
Event Viewer
System
Device Manager
Disk Management
Computer Management
Command Prompt
Command Prompt (Admin)

Task Manager
Control Panel
Windows Explorer
Search
Run

Desktop

FIGURE 1-11 Opening a shortcut menu

Closing applications

On the web, some bloggers are lamenting that you can't close a desktop app manually; you can. Like much of the functionality in Windows 8, all it takes is a swipe of the finger or a drag of the mouse.

While the application is open, either swipe from the top of the display to the bottom or, if using a mouse, hover the mouse pointer over the top of the screen. When the hand appears, which you can see in Figure 1-12, drag it to the bottom of the window. The app closes, and it no longer appears on the list of running applications.

FIGURE 1-12 Closing a running desktop app

As you progress through this book, you will find much more information about managing apps.

Introducing some new features

Windows 8 is a major operating system release and, with this release, Windows is open to a much wider array of hardware devices. Further, with each new release of Windows, the operating system needs to keep pace with the natural advancement that occurs in technology over time. The following sections outline some key new features that are bundled into Windows 8.

Internet Explorer 10

In Windows 8, you actually get two variations of Internet Explorer 10 in a single product. One variation is tailored for the new touch-optimized UI, whereas the other is an updated version of the desktop application that you've been using for years. Although the two variations look different, they're the same program. In Figure 1-13, you see the touch-optimized version of Internet Explorer 10. In Figure 1-14, you see Internet Explorer for the desktop, which has the traditional appearance of Internet Explorer.

FIGURE 1-13 Internet Explorer 10 featuring touch optimization

FIGURE 1-14 Internet Explorer 10 for the desktop with traditional appearance

You can see that each version renders the same content, but the overall interface is different. In the new UI, Internet Explorer renders the content above the address bar, which appears at the bottom of the screen. In the traditional view, the address bar remains at the top of the window.

When evaluating Windows 8, you should understand some of the high-level differences between the two versions of Internet Explorer 10. One of the critical differences concerns how plug-ins operate or, perhaps, don't operate. Plug-ins are add-ons to Internet Explorer that extend the browser's capabilities. If you've used Flash to view web content in Internet Explorer, you've used a browser plug-in. However, although plug-ins can be wonderful tools, they have two drawbacks. First, they are not touch-friendly. Second, they have been one of the most common vectors by which malware has managed to infect Windows systems. Therefore, the touch-optimized version of Internet Explorer 10 does not support the use of plug-ins, although the Internet Explorer for the desktop version retains this extensibility. Because the new UI in Internet Explorer 10 doesn't support plug-ins, you can have a very different browsing experience as you move between the two versions of the product, and you might not be able to do everything to which you've become accustomed in the traditional UI in the new Internet Explorer UI.

Microsoft continued support for Flash. Many Flash-based sites still work fine in Internet Explorer 10 because Microsoft built Flash support into both versions of the browser. That said, Internet Explorer 10 was designed to stay as close to browser-based standards as possible, and the hope is that more sites will make the move toward HTML5, which provides built-in support for multimedia without requiring plug-ins.

There is much more to Internet Explorer 10 in Windows 8. In fact, there is so much that this book dedicates an entire chapter to the product. You learn more about Internet Explorer 10 in Chapter 5, "Managing Internet Explorer."

Adding applications from the Windows Store

The user experience is being considered increasingly in the computing paradigm, and the application is taking center stage. As a result, various vendors are building application stores that make it simple for you to obtain the tools you need to accomplish your computing goals, whether those goals are to find tools to help you manage your network or to find a new world to explore in the latest online strategy game.

> **IMPORTANT WINDOWS RT AND THE WINDOWS STORE**
>
> If you're using Windows RT (remember, Windows RT is the Windows on ARM version), the Windows Store is the only method by which you can add apps to your device. There are no other supported application installation methods.

As you peruse the Windows Store (Figure 1-15), you will notice that the method by which to move between application categories has moved into the modern, widescreen landscape era. Rather than scrolling up and down to find what you want, you slide left to right, and new application categories appear along with individual applications available for addition (Figure 1-16).

FIGURE 1-15 A look at the Windows Store from within Windows 8

Top free

FIGURE 1-16 Another view of the Windows Store

After you've identified an app that you want to install:

1. Tap or click the app.

   The view you see in Figure 1-17 opens, which provides you with pertinent information about the selected app, including links to a short overview of the app, more in-depth details about the app, and reviews from other people who have installed the app.

FIGURE 1-17 Adding a new app to your device

2. Tap or click the Install button.

3. In the upper-right corner of the screen, a notification that the app is being installed appears.

4. After the app is installed, the app icon briefly appears in the same space. If you tap or click the app, the app opens.

Increasing numbers of people are using more than one computing device in their everyday lives. A Windows 8 work PC might be sitting on your desk while, at home, you might have a laptop and a tablet both running Windows 8. When you combine this device ubiquity with the flexibility of the cloud, a world of new possibilities opens. In this case, it becomes easier than ever to keep your purchased applications in sync across your devices. In the Windows Store, you can see a list of the apps that you've purchased under your Microsoft account by pressing and holding or right-clicking the screen and choosing Your Apps. This Your Apps area is shown in Figure 1-18.

FIGURE 1-18 Windows Store, tracking all the apps you have downloaded

In this Your Apps area, shown in Figure 1-18, four items are displayed because those are the only items that have been purchased so far. Note the drop-down box that currently displays Apps Installed On Win8. By selecting the drop-down arrow in that box, you can choose instead to view just the apps that have been installed on one of the devices associated with the currently logged-on *Microsoft account*, formerly known as Windows Live ID. If you're using a device on which some apps have yet to be installed, being able to select by device makes it much easier to determine which apps a system might need.

From a consumer perspective, the Windows Store is a powerful addition to the Windows product that can make life a lot easier and more enjoyable. For enterprises, however, although the movement toward the democratization of IT is well underway through such initiatives as Bring Your Own Device policies, some companies will not be as accommodating as others. Many, due to regulatory issues, might have to restrict access to the Windows Store to maintain a secure, productive work environment.

Microsoft has always ensured that Windows supports consumers' demand to share while still supporting enterprises' need to restrict how systems are used. This fact has not changed in Windows 8. Enterprises can disable access to the Windows Store. You learn much more about the Windows Store and enterprise control of its use in Chapter 4.

Hyper-V

 In an enterprise environment and from a developer's perspective, perhaps one of the most useful steps taken for Windows 8 is the introduction of *Hyper-V* as a client-side *hypervisor*. A hypervisor is a software layer that abstracts workloads running on the system to enable the introduction of multiple *virtual machines* that share the same physical hardware.

Hyper-V is the Microsoft enterprise-grade virtualization platform that has long been included in the Windows Server platform and has now, for the first time, been brought to the client side of the computing equation. With Windows 8, Hyper-V enables developers to run test systems without having to build a separate lab or use production resources. For other IT professionals, this client-side Hyper-V implementation enables quick and easy testing of new software and of client tools that are intended for deployment. Better yet, these professionals can do their testing within the confines of the virtual environment without risking damage to the production environment.

Although Hyper-V on Windows 8 is derived from Hyper-V on Microsoft Windows Server, a few key differences are important to understand before you begin using Hyper-V in Windows 8:

- Only the 64-bit edition of Windows 8 supports Hyper-V. If you're using the 32-bit edition, Hyper-V is not available. You can run either 32-bit or 64-bit workloads on Hyper-V, but Hyper-V itself must be installed on a 64-bit machine. Don't forget that you must make sure that you have appropriate licenses for any software you might be running inside a virtual machine. You can learn more about the differences between the 32-bit and the 64-bit editions of Windows 8 in Lesson 2 of this chapter.

- The system must have at least 4 GB of RAM.

■ The system on which the 64-bit edition of Windows 8 is installed must support what is called Second Level Address Translation (SLAT). Most modern processors support this performance-enhancing technology.

You might be wondering what happened to the Windows 7 feature that was known as *XP Mode*. Because of the inclusion of Hyper-V in Windows 8, the XP Mode feature from Windows 7 was not moved to Windows 8. Whereas XP Mode was a stopgap intended to address potential backward compatibility issues for certain software titles, Hyper-V is a full-fledged hypervisor product that can do everything XP Mode could do and much more.

Hyper-V includes dozens of features that make it a truly enterprise-grade product. Because the inclusion of Hyper-V in Windows 8 is so important, a full chapter of this book is dedicated to learning how to use this feature. You find this information in Chapter 6, "Using Hyper-V."

Windows desktop administrators don't generally have to manage systems in the company data center, Microsoft Hyper-V Server 2012 is a completely free product and might prove to be useful for your own testing of new Microsoft products. Because they share much of the same functionality, you can use Windows 8 Hyper-V to become familiar with the forthcoming version of Hyper-V in Windows Server 2012.

Cloud connectivity

We've entered a new era of computing in which the computing device has moved beyond the confines of the local area. Whereas in the past people stored files, pictures, and other documents on local hard drives and used the web for basic entertainment and email, today people live in a hyper-connected world. People and systems are always tethered to the ubiquitous computing cloud. Further, as people obtain more devices, the local nature of personal files has become a hindrance that needs to be overcome.

Think about it. Do you carry a smart phone, tablet, or laptop with you? Is that device constantly or very often connected to the Internet? Do you need or want immediate, easy access to your files and folders on an anytime, anywhere basis?

Enter the cloud.

Today, computing device users rely on simple, inexpensive—often free—services to manage their personal and work lives. Important documents are no longer stored only on local PCs; rather, these files are automatically synchronized across a variety of devices by using free and powerful services from companies such as Microsoft.

As a next-generation operating system, Windows 8 embraces cloud computing and takes cloud connectivity to levels heretofore unseen in an operating system. With inclusion and deep integration of such features as SkyDrive and the Windows Store, Windows 8 is also the first version of Windows by which you can log on to the machine by using only a Microsoft account. By using a Microsoft account, you can access many of the resources that are linked to that account. Further, you can easily synchronize important system settings between different devices, thus streamlining the process of personalizing your systems, as Figure 1-19 shows.

Your account

Phil Gibbins
phil.gibbins@1610group.com

You can switch to a local account, but your settings won't sync between the PCs you use.

Switch to a local account

More account settings online

FIGURE 1-19 User using a Microsoft account rather than a local user account

To synchronize settings between Windows 8 devices:

1. Open the Start screen.

2. Open the Charms bar and choose Settings.

3. When Settings opens, click Change PC Settings.

4. From PC Settings, choose Sync Your Settings.

   The window you see in Figure 1-20 opens.

5. Make any desired changes to your synchronization settings.

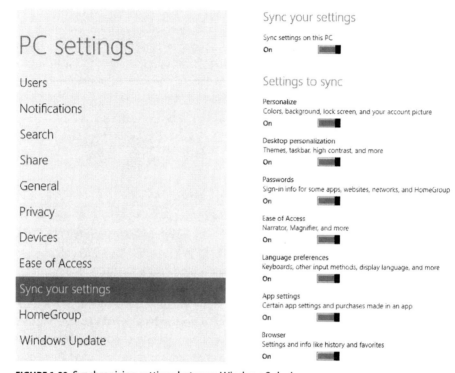

FIGURE 1-20 Synchronizing settings between Windows 8 devices

An important part of the Windows 8 experience in the cloud is the inclusion of SkyDrive, a free Microsoft service that enables cloud-based sharing and synchronization of files and folders. You can share files with other people, and you can ensure that your files and folders are synchronized across your devices.

When you use SkyDrive, Windows 8 is just one option you have for a target device. Microsoft does not require you to use Windows 8 to enjoy the benefits of file and folder synchronization. You can synchronize your files and folders between devices running Windows 8, Windows 7, Windows XP, Windows Phone, Mac OS X, and iOS (iPhone and iPad). This wide support means that Windows 8 users can use a variety of mainstream devices while remaining part of the Microsoft ecosystem. You learn much more about SkyDrive in Windows 8 in Chapter 10, "Sharing resources."

Earlier in this chapter, you learned about the Windows Store and its ability to keep track of the applications that have been installed across all your Windows 8 devices. This is another cloud-supported service that will help Windows 8 customers manage multi-device lives more easily.

Windows To Go

Many of today's enterprises are struggling with a rapidly changing technology landscape and attempting to figure out whether and how so-called bring your own device (BYOD) initiatives fit into the corporate environment. BYOD is a catch-all phrase that describes the ability for workers to bring their own devices to the workplace. Although there are some potential corporate benefits under such arrangements, the initiative also creates a new set of challenges that must be considered.

Employees expect to be able to work from home or access corporate resources when they're not in the office. In addition, enterprises are hiring more contractors every day and need to find ways to quickly provision corporate IT resources to these people so that they can get set up and running as quickly as possible. The challenge for enterprise IT is how to provide these resources in a way that doesn't add undue burden to already overwhelmed IT departments.

Windows To Go is a revolutionary new way for IT departments to provision complete Windows desktops for a variety of clients. Windows To Go enables users to start a complete Windows 8 desktop from a USB storage device, such as a free USB stick from a trade show, or from an external hard drive. Enterprise IT departments can customize the Windows 8 image that is housed on the storage device and supply users with a portable copy of their desktop.

After the user has been provided with the imaged USB device, he or she inserts the device into any Windows 7 or Windows 8 PC and the embedded Windows 8 system starts, complete with copies of his or her applications and files. The newly booted system then uses that USB storage as its local hard drive and avoids modification of the files on the host system.

This is not a Hyper-V or other virtualized edition of Windows. It's a full version of Windows running by using the local hardware. If you're worried about what would seem to be a major weakness in this solution—security—don't be. Windows To Go devices can be protected by using BitLocker Drive Encryption. You learn more about Windows To Go in Chapter 13, "Managing and securing mobility."

 Quick check

  ■ **What are some primary Windows To Go use cases?**

  Quick check answer

  ■ **Most often, Windows To Go will be used by contract employees or by mobile employees who want to or need to work from home.**

Mobile broadband

Today's mobile workforce demands constant, always-on connectivity from anywhere. It's no surprise that more hardware than ever is shipping with WiFi and 3G/4G cellular data capability in the device. Further, for those who don't have a device equipped this way, portable cellular hotspot devices are available on the market.

Making portable cellular data devices work in Windows used to be a challenge because each device and each carrier had its own management software. Windows 8 brings order to the chaos with native inclusion of mobile broadband management in Windows 8. With this native support, Windows 8 no longer needs to rely on specialized driver and third-party software to make cellular data devices operate.

> **REAL WORLD** **THE WORLD IS STILL CATCHING UP**
>
> Windows 8 can support a variety of devices as long as they support the emerging Mobile Broadband Interface Model (MBIM) standard. Although hardware makers are beginning to adopt this standard, it will take some time to make its way through the entire market. In Windows 8, as long as the device supports MBIM, a Windows 8 generic driver can offer support with any mobile chip supporting MBIM.

Because cellular data connections are treated as equal partners in networking in Windows 8, there are new opportunities for application awareness. For example, you can configure Windows 8 to prevent certain activities from taking place when the costs will be particularly high. In Figure 1-21, you see just one example; here, you can choose to turn Windows 8 settings synchronization capabilities on or off, depending on the overall cost of the connection. You learn more about mobile broadband in Chapter 9, "Administering remote management."

Sync over metered connections

Sync settings over metered connections

On

Sync settings over metered connections even when I'm roaming

Off

FIGURE 1-21 Windows 8 enables you to decide how and when to save money

Secure Boot and Trusted Boot

The basic input/output system (BIOS) has been in use for decades. A system's BIOS handles the basic interaction between the operating system and the underlying hardware. Like many earlier technologies, BIOS is being replaced by a new technology known as the *Unified Extensible Firmware Interface (UEFI)*. UEFI carries with it significant enhancements over BIOS. In the context of Windows 8, the most important enhancement that is coming through the UEFI migration is called *Secure Boot*, sometimes referred to as *Trusted Boot*.

Because of limitations found in BIOS, earlier systems are vulnerable to compromised code being inserted into the system during the startup process. When using UEFI and Windows 8 Secure Boot, a computer will not load an operating system that has not been signed by the publisher. In essence, Secure Boot helps prevent unauthorized code from being executed during startup.

Windows 8 implements Secure Boot differently, depending on the kind of device you plan to use and the edition of Windows 8 you select.

- **x86 Windows 8 edition**   You can enable Secure Boot with Windows 8, sign your own operating systems, or completely disable Secure Boot. The latter two options are useful if you want to use your own Linux build or an operating system that doesn't support signing.
- **Windows 8 RT**   These ARM-based devices designed for Windows 8 RT cannot boot to any operating system other than Windows 8.

This might seem restrictive, but it's not. With x86-based computers, you can still do whatever you want. You can enable or disable Secure Boot and run Windows 8 or Linux; it's your choice. For tablets and other ARM-based devices, Microsoft is aligning with other hardware vendors by ensuring that the devices remain clean and free from infection. You learn more about Secure Boot in Chapter 8, "Configuring security."

Refresh your PC and reset your PC

Over time, unruly applications that don't follow the rules can reduce the performance and stability of a Windows PC. By adding shortcuts, new files and associations, and registry keys, Windows accumulates many objects to track, and users aren't always good at maintaining their computers. Wouldn't it be nice if you could just push a button and revert your system to the state it was in the day you brought it home?

Windows 8 makes this possible with features known as Refresh and Reset. You learn more about these features in Chapter 15, "System protection and recovery."

- **Refresh Your PC**   Keep all personal data, apps, and important settings from the PC and reinstall Windows. This is the least disruptive option, and it can bring a barely functioning system back to life in a significant way.
- **Reset Your PC**   Remove all personal data, apps, and settings from the PC and reinstall Windows. A reset is a full reinstallation of Windows 8 but doesn't require you to answer setup questions. Windows 8 just reinstalls.

> *IMPORTANT* **POTENTIAL DATA LOSS**
>
> It's important to note that this is a disruptive process that can result in data loss unless you first back up your data.

Lesson summary

- The Start screen has replaced the Windows Start menu.
- You can customize the Start screen by adding, removing, rearranging, and resizing the live tiles that are displayed. You can also choose whether administrative tool shortcuts are displayed on the Start screen.
- Charms are interface elements that are new to Windows 8. They are often context-sensitive, meaning that the function they perform depends on what you're doing at the time.
- In Windows 8, there are two Internet Explorer 10 versions. One version implements the new UI and does not support the use of plug-ins, and the other is the full, traditional Internet Explorer experience.
- In an effort to streamline the application deployment process and help users track application installations between devices, the Windows Store has been added to Windows 8.
- Microsoft Hyper-V replaces the Windows 7 XP Mode and Windows Virtual PC as the virtualization platform of choice for Windows 8. A client version of Hyper-V is included in the operating system.
- Windows 8 embraces the cloud in a number of ways with the inclusion of Windows Store and through the integration of tools such as the cloud-based SkyDrive service.
- Windows To Go is a new Windows 8 feature by which IT can provide users with a complete Windows 8 system on a USB thumb drive that can be run from any Windows 7 or Windows 8 PC.
- Secure Boot greatly reduces the potential for viruses and other bad code to be executed while the system is starting, thereby improving overall environment security.
- Refresh Your PC and Reset Your PC are two new features in Windows 8 by which you can return your Windows 8 PC to operational condition.

Lesson review

Answer the following questions to test your knowledge of the information in this lesson. You can find the answers to these questions and explanations of why each answer choice is correct or incorrect in the "Answers" section at the end of this chapter.

1. What is the name of the environment in which desktop apps run?

    A. Windows RT

    B. WDDM

    C. WinRT

    D. ARM

2. How do you go back to the Start screen after you've started an app?

   A. Click the Start button.

   B. Find a hotspot to open the Edge UI and then tap or click the Start screen icon or the Start charm.

   C. Press and hold or right-click the screen and choose Start.

   D. Hover the mouse over the upper-left corner of the screen and choose an application thumbnail.

3. With which new Windows 8 feature can you to take a full corporate desktop with you on a USB drive?

   A. Windows To Go

   B. SkyDrive

   C. Sync Settings

   D. Secure Boot

Lesson 2: Understanding product editions, architectures, and hardware requirements

Over the years, Microsoft has created a wide variety of targeted editions of Windows to address emerging technologies and changing customer needs. Between this and an attempt to define the market more granularly, some editions of the Windows client have had as many as six primary editions, with each edition being offered in 32-bit and 64-bit editions.

Microsoft has simplified the editions list in a significant way, but there are still four editions of Windows 8 from which to choose, and you still need to decide whether the 32-bit edition will suffice or a 64-bit operating system is necessary to meet your organization's ongoing workload needs.

In this lesson, you explore the features found in various editions of Windows 8 and learn about what changes when you switch between the 32-bit and 64-bit edition of the product.

After this lesson, you will be able to:

- Explain the differences among the various editions of Windows 8.
- Understand the feature differences between the 32-bit and the 64-bit product architectures.
- Describe the minimum hardware requirements that are necessary to run a Windows 8 PC.
- Understand the hardware requirement differences between the 32-bit and the 64-bit editions of Windows 8.

Estimated lesson time: 30 minutes

Windows 8 product edition differences

Microsoft is offering three editions of Windows 8 for consumers. A fourth edition is targeted squarely at the enterprise space, so there are actually four editions from which to choose. Table 1-1 summarizes the differences among these editions. You learn about the various features throughout this book.

TABLE 1-1 Windows 8 edition comparison

Feature name	Windows 8	Windows 8 Pro	Windows 8 Enterprise	Windows RT
Product target	Consumers	Businesses, enthusiasts, technical professionals	Enterprise customers	ARM-based PCs or tablet devices
Maximum processors	1	2	2	2
Apps (Mail, Calendar, People, Messaging, Photos, SkyDrive, Reader, Music, Video)	●	●	●	●
Application Sideload			●	
AppLocker			●	
BitLocker and BitLocker To Go		●	●	
Boot from VHD		●	●	
BranchCache			●	
Client Hyper-V		●	●	
Connected standby	●	●	●	●
Desktop	●	●	●	●
Device encryption				●
DirectAccess			●	
Domain Join		●	●	
Encrypting File System		●	●	
Enhanced Task Manager	●	●	●	●
Exchange ActiveSync	●	●	●	●
File History	●	●	●	●
Group Policy		●	●	
Installation of x86/64 and desktop software	●	●	●	

Feature name	Windows 8	Windows 8 Pro	Windows 8 Enterprise	Windows RT
Internet Explorer 10	•	•	•	•
ISO/VHD mount	•	•	•	•
Microsoft account	•	•	•	•
Microsoft Office (Word, Excel, PowerPoint, OneNote)				•
Mobile broadband features	•	•	•	•
Multiple-monitor support	•	•	•	•
Picture password	•	•	•	•
Play To	•	•	•	•
Remote Desktop (client)	•	•	•	•
Remote Desktop (host)		•	•	
Reset and refresh your PC	•	•	•	•
SmartScreen	•	•	•	
Snap	•	•	•	•
Start screen, Semantic Zoom, Live Tiles	•	•	•	•
Storage Spaces	•	•	•	
Switch languages on the fly	•	•	•	•
Touch and Thumb keyboard	•	•	•	•
Trusted Boot	•	•	•	•
Updated File Explorer	•	•	•	•
VDI improvements			•	
VPN client	•	•	•	•
Windows Defender	•	•	•	•
Windows Media Player	•	•	•	
Windows Store	•	•	•	•
Windows To Go			•	
Windows Update	•	•	•	•

*Source: Windows Team Blog at *http://windowsteamblog.com/windows/b/bloggingwindows/archive/2012/04/16/announcing-the-windows-8-editions.aspx.*

Perhaps one of the most notable differences becomes obvious in the software deployment process. Although the Standard, Pro, and Enterprise editions of Windows 8 support the deployment of both desktop apps and full x86-based applications, devices running Windows RT can receive new applications only from the Windows Store.

Further, the Pro and Enterprise editions of Windows offer the Microsoft full BitLocker Drive Encryption feature to protect these devices. Windows RT includes its own full device encryption, which is an increasingly important feature for mobile devices that can be easily lost or stolen. Although this consumer-focused edition of Windows 8 does not include any native encryption software, free third-party encryption tools are available that can fill this feature gap.

 Quick check

- Where can you find a list of specific differences among the various editions of Windows 8?

Quick check answer

- You can find a comprehensive list of Windows 8 features on a per-edition basis at *http://windowsteamblog.com/windows/b/bloggingwindows/archive/2012/04/16 /announcing-the-windows-8-editions.aspx.*

Windows 8 product architecture differences

Not long ago, the need for a 64-bit client operating system was limited to media and IT professionals. Today, due to the incredible expansion and feature benefits that 64-bit processors offer, the market is seeing a growing desire for 64-bit client operating systems that can use these benefits.

When you look at the different editions of Windows 8, which were outlined in the previous section, the 32-bit versus 64-bit question pertains only to the Windows 8, Windows 8 Pro, and Windows 8 Enterprise editions. These are the editions of Windows 8 that run on standard x86 hardware. Windows RT runs on ARM processors, which are different from Intel x86.

Note that x86 includes both 32-bit and 64-bit processors; it is just a catch-all term for everyday processors from AMD and Intel.

The 64-bit versus 32-bit question becomes one of scalability. From a compatibility perspective, nearly all 32-bit software sold today runs fine on 64-bit operating systems. However, the reverse is not true. You cannot run 64-bit software on a 32-bit operating system.

In terms of addressable memory, a 64-bit system can scale up to 192 GB of RAM, which is far beyond what nearly anyone needs today on the desktop. A 32-bit system, however, tops out at just 4 GB of addressable memory. A few years ago, 4 GB was a luxury; today, it's commonplace and widely considered a minimum for real work. In addition to the memory limit, the other major difference between 32-bit and 64-bit Windows 8 is the 32-bit edition's lack of support for Hyper-V. Table 1-2 summarizes these differences.

TABLE 1-2 Windows 8 architecture comparison

Feature name	32-bit	64-bit
Maximum memory	4 GB	192 GB
Features	No Hyper-V	Improved scalability, more significant workloads

Windows 8 hardware requirements

The hardware requirements for Windows 8 are extremely modest, especially when you consider the number of new capabilities that have been added to the operating system. In fact, if your current PC can run Windows 7, it can probably run Windows 8, too. Of course, to take advantage of some of the new features in Windows 8, such as touch, you need hardware that supports touch.

The minimum hardware requirements depend on which Windows 8 architecture you're running. There are different hardware requirements for the 32-bit edition and the 64-bit edition. Table 1-3 summarizes the minimum hardware requirements for each architecture.

TABLE 1-3 Windows 8 hardware requirements

Resource	Windows 8 32-bit	Windows 8 64-bit
Processor	1 GHz or faster	1 GHz or faster
RAM	1 GB	2 GB
Disk space	16 GB	20 GB
Graphics card	Microsoft DirectX 9 graphics device with Windows Display Driver Model (WDDM) driver	
Touch interface	A tablet computer or a monitor that supports touch	
Windows Store	Internet connection and a screen resolution of at least 1024 × 768	

If you're wondering what a DirectX 9 graphics device with WDDM driver is, wonder no more. DirectX is a group of technologies that makes Windows-based computers ideal systems for running and displaying applications rich in multimedia elements such as full-color graphics, video, 3D animation, and rich audio.

Windows Display Driver Model (WDDM) 1.0 was originally introduced in the Windows Vista development period and replaced the Windows XP display driver architecture. WDDM introduced to Windows superior graphics performance and new graphics functionality.

Windows 7 built on the WDDM model with the introduction of WDDM 1.1, which included a host of updates that helped make Windows 7 an unqualified commercial success. Included in WDDM 1.1 are technologies that improve the performance and the security of the graphics system. Further, WDDM 1.1 introduced enhanced support for multiple-monitor support in systems with multiple graphics adapters.

In Windows 8, Microsoft has introduced WDDM 1.2, which further improves graphics performance and adds support for stereoscopic 3D rendering and video playback. In addition, WDDM 1.2 includes a preemptive multitasking feature, enabling the graphics processor to interrupt other tasks and suspend currently executing processes to determine which process should execute next. This helps make sure that all processes get some CPU time.

> **MORE INFO LEARN MORE ABOUT WDDM**
>
> A complete description of WDDM is far beyond the scope of this book and not generally applicable in the day-to-day life of a Windows administrator. However, if you'd like to learn more about WDDM, you can read about it at *http://msdn.microsoft.com/en-us/library /aa480220.aspx.*

Do you know what kind of hardware is in your Windows 8 PC? It's easy to find out.

1. From the Start screen, choose the Desktop tile to open the full Windows 8 traditional desktop environment.

2. Open the Settings charm.

3. From Settings, choose PC Info.

   The System page in Control Panel opens (see Figure 1-22), which shows the information for your PC.

In Figure 1-22, you see that the System window displays pertinent high-level information about the local PC. It displays the edition of Windows 8 that is currently installed and the processor type, amount of RAM, and the status of any touch-based hardware that is installed.

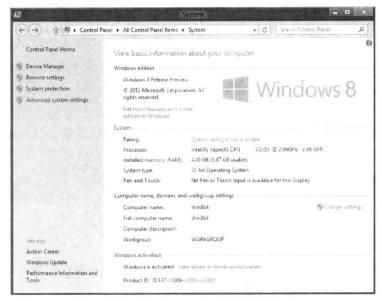

Figure 1-22 The hardware configuration for a Windows 8 computer

Lesson summary

- Windows 8 ships in four editions: Windows 8, Windows 8 Pro, Windows 8 Enterprise, and Windows 8 RT.

- All editions except Windows 8 RT run on Intel/AMD x86-compatible hardware. Windows RT, also known as Windows on ARM, runs on ARM processors.

- The Windows 8 RT edition includes a touch-optimized edition of Microsoft Office.

- Windows RT devices support full encryption.

- If a system can support Windows 7, it can almost certainly support Windows 8.

Lesson review

Answer the following questions to test your knowledge of the information in this lesson. You can find the answers to these questions and explanations of why each answer choice is correct or incorrect in the "Answers" section at the end of this chapter.

1. Which edition of Windows 8 requires a formal corporate license agreement with Microsoft?

    A. Windows 8

    B. Windows 8 Pro

    C. Windows 8 Enterprise

    D. Windows RT

2. Which edition of Windows 8 requires applications to be deployed only from the Windows Store?

   A. Windows 8

   B. Windows 8 Pro

   C. Windows 8 Enterprise

   D. Windows RT

3. Which feature is not available in the 32-bit edition of Windows 8?

   A. SkyDrive

   B. Hyper-V

   C. Windows Store

   D. Windows To Go

Practice exercises

In this practice, you learn about different techniques for managing the Windows 8 Start screen.

Exercise 1: Add an Internet Explorer shortcut to the Start screen

In this exercise, you pin a website to the Start screen. To complete this exercise, perform the following steps:

1. Browse to the website you'd like to pin to the Start screen.

2. Click the Pin icon on the browser bar.

   A window appears that asks you to name the new icon (Figure 1-23). Provide a name or accept the default.

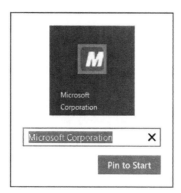

FIGURE 1-23 Pinning a site to the Start screen

3. Click Pin To Start to complete the process. The website now appears as a tile on the Start screen.

Exercise 2: Configure user settings to synchronize between Windows 8 devices

In this exercise, you synchronize two devices. To access the PC settings area, which provides you with access to the selections you need and the ability to enable or disable to synchronize settings between Windows 8 devices, perform the following steps:

1. Open the Start screen and select the Settings charm.
2. Click Change PC.
3. From PC Settings, choose Sync Your Setting.
4. Make any desired changes to your synchronization settings.

Suggested practice exercises

The following additional practices are designed to give you more opportunities to practice what you've learned and to help you successfully master the lessons presented in this chapter.

Because Windows 8 can function so efficiently on virtual hard disks, creating a Windows installation on a VHD will provide skills to help you use the new operating system in your environment.

■ **Exercise 1** Add tiles to and remove tiles from the Windows 8 Start screen.

■ **Exercise 2** Review the Windows 8 editions and associated feature matrix and determine which edition of Windows 8 makes the most sense for you in your situation.

■ **Exercise 3** Peruse the hardware requirements for each edition of Windows 8 to verify that your existing computer can run the operating system.

Answers

This section contains the answers to the lesson review questions in this chapter.

Lesson 1

1. **Correct answer: C**

   A. **Incorrect:** Windows RT is also known as Windows on ARM and uses a full Windows operating system, not just an application runtime environment.

   B. **Incorrect:** Windows Display Driver Model (WDDM) is a set of drivers and an architecture for Windows display devices.

   C. **Correct:** Windows Runtime (WinRT) is the application execution environment used for desktop apps.

   D. **Incorrect:** ARM is a processor architecture.

2. **Correct answer: B**

   A. **Incorrect:** The Start button has been removed from Windows 8.

   B. **Correct:** You will find hotspots in the four corners of the screen.

   C. **Incorrect:** No shortcut menu is available with right-click as a Start option.

   D. **Incorrect:** This enables you to switch between applications only.

3. **Correct answer: A**

   A. **Correct:** Windows To Go is an enterprise-only feature that enables mobile workers to take their desktop with them.

   B. **Incorrect:** SkyDrive is a service that enables files and folders to synchronize between devices.

   C. **Incorrect:** Sync Settings is a new feature that enables settings to be synchronized between devices.

   D. **Incorrect:** Secure Boot is a feature intended to provide additional security to the system while it starts up.

Lesson 2

1. **Correct answer: C**

   A. **Incorrect:** Windows 8 does not require a formal corporate license agreement.

   B. **Incorrect:** Windows 8 Pro does not require a formal corporate license agreement.

   C. **Correct:** Windows 8 Enterprise requires a formal corporate license agreement.

   D. **Incorrect:** Windows RT does not require a formal corporate license agreement.

2. **Correct answer: D**

   A. **Incorrect:** Windows 8 supports the deployment of both desktop apps and full x86-based applications.

   B. **Incorrect:** Windows 8 Pro supports the deployment of both desktop apps and full x86-based applications.

   C. **Incorrect:** Windows 8 Enterprise supports the deployment of both desktop apps and full x86-based applications.

   D. **Correct:** Windows RT can receive new apps only from Windows Store.

3. **Correct answer: B**

   A. **Incorrect:** SkyDrive is not available in the 32-bit edition.

   B. **Correct:** Hyper-V is available in the 32-bit edition.

   C. **Incorrect:** Windows Store is not available in the 32-bit edition.

   D. **Incorrect:** Windows To Go is not available in the 32-bit edition.

CHAPTER 2

Installing and migrating to Windows 8

The installation and migration process is always at the forefront of the minds of informa-tion technology professionals as they consider deploying new operating systems. This chapter is a journey through the Windows 8 installation process, using multiple installation methods. Specifically, you look at the installation process as performed from a blank disk or virtual hard drive (VHD) and as performed by using the upgrade method of installation. Because many organizations remain on versions of Microsoft Windows that are earlier than Windows 7, this chapter also explores the process of migrating to Windows 8 from an older operating system, a process that is accompanied by migrating user data to Windows 8 to enable a smooth transition to the newest version of Windows. You can find additional information about Windows 8 for IT professionals online in "The Springboard Series for Windows" at *http://technet.microsoft.com/windows/hh771457.aspx*.

In addition, this chapter introduces Windows To Go, one of the innovative new features in Windows 8. This new feature is a portable configuration of the operating system that enables many new deployment scenarios and can streamline an organization's implementa-tion of bring your own device (BYOD) initiatives.

Lessons in this chapter:

Before you begin

To complete the practice exercises in this chapter, you will need:

- Removable USB media at least 32 GB in size to configure Windows To Go. This can be a USB flash drive that is attached to a keychain or an external USB hard drive.
- To download the Windows Automated Installation Kit (for Windows 7) from *http://www.microsoft.com/en-us/download/details.aspx?id=5753* to obtain the DISM utility to apply installation images to removable media.

■ Tools from the Windows Assessment and Deployment Kit (for Windows 8), which can be downloaded from *http://www.microsoft.com/en-us/download/details.aspx?id=30652*.

Lesson 1: Installing Windows 8 on a new or formatted system

If you are installing Windows 8 on a new system, you need to be familiar with the concepts and procedures in this lesson. This lesson shows you how to install Windows 8 by starting with a blank disk and formatting that disk during the installation.

After this lesson, you will be able to:

■ Install Windows 8 (32-bit or 64-bit) onto a new computer.

■ Configure Windows To Go on a removable USB device.

Estimated lesson time: 60 minutes

Starting the installation

Installing Windows 8 is similar to installing Windows 7 in that the number of tasks is kept to a minimum and much of the work occurs without user intervention. The Setup Wizard guides you through the installation.

> *NOTE* **WINDOWS 8 INSTALLATION MEDIA**
>
> Windows 8 can use several types of installation media. You can create media on a USB disk, start from an ISO file for virtual installations, start from a VHD, or use traditional DVD media. The media you choose depend on your environment.

To get started installing Windows 8, complete the following steps:

1. Turn on your computer and insert the media for the operating system.

2. In the Windows Setup dialog box that appears, select the language to install, the time and currency formats, and the keyboard or input method, and then tap or click Next.

3. Tap or click Install Now to start the installation of Windows 8.

4. When the Windows Setup dialog box requests a product key to activate Windows, type your product key and tap or click Next to continue.

5. Read the End User License Agreement (EULA), select I Accept The License Terms, and tap or click Next.

6. Windows Setup prompts you to identify the type of installation to perform:
   - Upgrade: Install Windows And Keep Files, Settings, And Applications
   - Custom: Install Windows Only (Advanced)

   Select Custom to advance to the next page of Windows Setup.

7. All the available disks and partitions visible to your computer are listed. When you are prompted to choose a disk for the Windows 8 installation, select the disk you want to use.

8. Select the Drive Options (Advanced) link to add or remove partitions on the selected disks or to create multiple partition systems within your environment.

> **NOTE MULTIPLE PARTITION SYSTEMS**
>
> **Using multiple partition systems can be valuable if you need to run multiple operating systems on your computer or when you want to separate your data from the operating system files and start files for Windows.**

9. Select where you want to install Windows and tap or click Next.

The installer copies, unpacks, and installs the files, features, and updates from the operating system media to your computer, as shown in Figure 2-1. During this process, the system restarts and begins configuring devices. The installation time for Windows 8 varies based on a number of factors, including the type of installation media in use and the speed of the computer.

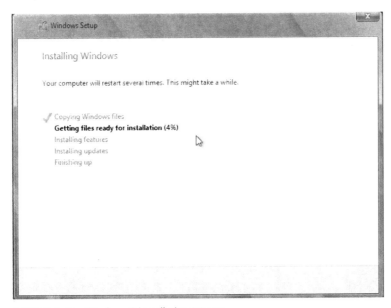

FIGURE 2-1 The Windows 8 installation process

Configuring your account

After the devices have been configured, the system restarts and requests answers to some questions about configuring your account. During the final restart of the installation process, some configuration begins to initialize the computer for first use, which includes the following:

- Getting devices ready
- Getting the system ready

During the initialization process for the system and devices, the computer restarts and continues the configuration process.

1. When prompted, enter the following information, and then tap or click Next:

   - A color for the background and theme
   - A name for your computer

   On the Settings screen, you are given two initial options to configure general settings for your computer: Express Settings or Custom.

2. If you select Use Express Settings (shown in Figure 2-2), the wizard turns on the following options for you:

   - Enabling automatic updates
   - Enabling the phishing and malware filters
   - Opting to participate in the Microsoft Customer Experience program
   - Checking for solutions to issues online
   - Enabling location-based services for personalized content
   - Enabling sharing and connecting to devices on the network

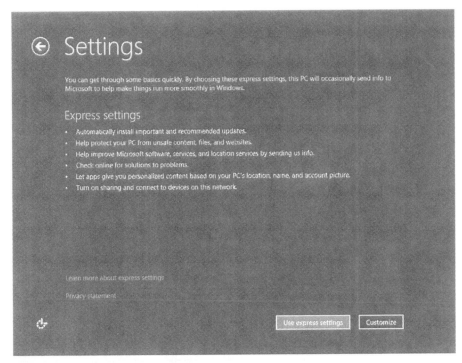

FIGURE 2-2 Selecting how to handle initial settings

Select Customize and the wizard guides you through the available settings.

3. If a network is available, you can select the type of network sharing, depending on the network, on the first page.

   - For home or work networks, select Yes, Turn On Sharing And Connect To Devices.

   - For public networks, such as cafés or libraries, select No, Don't Turn On Sharing Or Connect To Devices.

   You can change these settings later; for now, select the one that best matches your available network.

4. Tap or click Next to configure settings that help protect and update your system, as shown in Figure 2-3.

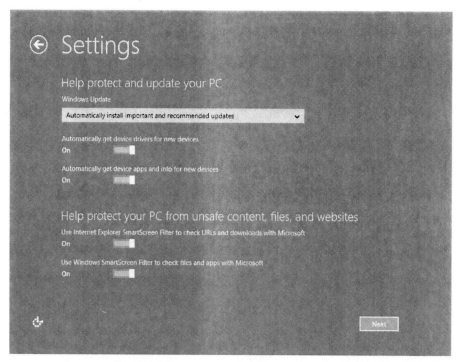

FIGURE 2-3 If you customize installation, a wizard guides you through configuration of initial settings

5. Select the amount of information that is exchanged with Microsoft, such as information about malicious applications or location data when location-aware apps are used and then tap or click Next.

   The next page contains settings for online solution checking and information sharing between apps.

6. After configuring the settings for your computer, sign in, as shown in Figure 2-4. Choose from the following options and then tap or click Next.

   ▪ Sign in with your Microsoft account by typing the email address associated with it.

   ▪ Sign up for a new email address to use with a Microsoft account.

   ▪ Sign in without a Microsoft account.

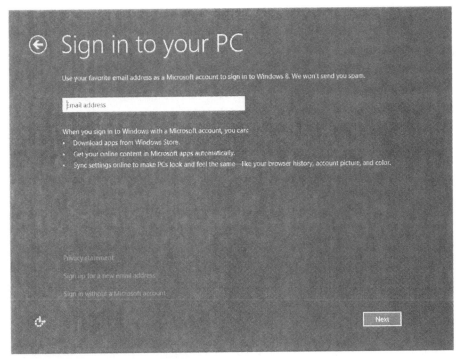

FIGURE 2-4 Signing in with your Microsoft account

There are a number of benefits to using a Microsoft account to access your system. Most notably, your system can take direct advantage of Microsoft services such as Hotmail and SkyDrive directly from the desktop. Because some of these services are built into Windows 8, this configuration seamlessly connects the local desktop to cloud-based services.

> *NOTE* **ACTIVE DIRECTORY DOMAIN ENVIRONMENTS**
>
> If your Windows 8 system will be used in an Active Directory domain environment, selecting a local administrator user name and password is probably better than using your Microsoft account. To use an Active Directory domain account, select Sign In Without A Microsoft Account on the Sign In To Your PC screen shown in Figure 2-4. On the next page, select Local Account. On the next page, type a local administrator account name, confirm the password, enter a password hint, and then click Finish. Windows creates a profile and readies your environment for first use. When this process completes, you see your Start screen, and you can start using Windows 8.

Joining an Active Directory domain

After the local administrator account is created for the computer, it will be a member of the WORKGROUP work group. To join the computer to an Active Directory domain, complete the following steps:

1. On the Start screen, type or search for **system**.
2. Select Settings.
3. Tap or click System from the results.
4. In the Computer Name, Domain, And Workgroup Settings section, select Change Settings.
5. In the System Properties dialog box, tap or click the Change button.
6. Select Domain in Member Of.
7. Enter the name of the domain to join; for example, contoso.com.
8. Tap or click OK in the Computer Name/Domain Changes dialog box.
9. Provide credentials with permission to join a computer to the domain in the form of domain\username or username@domain.com.
10. Tap or click OK twice to save the credentials and close the System Properties dialog box.
11. Restart the computer to complete the process of joining the domain.

You can associate a Microsoft account after initial configuration by completing the following steps:

1. Access the Start screen by selecting the Start charm or by pressing the Windows key on the keyboard.
2. Select the Settings charm.
3. Select Change PC Settings.
4. On the PC Settings screen, select Users.

   You can either switch to a local account if you are using a Microsoft account or add a Microsoft account if you are using a local account.

Installing Windows 8 with Windows To Go

Windows To Go is a new feature in the Windows 8 Enterprise edition. It redefines the concept portability by creating a Windows 8 workspace that runs from removable media. The USB drive becomes your Windows To Go workspace. There are some disadvantages to this new method, but the idea of Windows in your pocket is something that you should consider in the following scenarios:

- Employees frequently share hardware.
- Employees might need to access multiple Windows operating systems.
- Employees travel frequently and do not need to or prefer not to carry a laptop.

Things to consider before deploying Windows To Go workspaces include the following:

- Windows 8 Enterprise is required.
- USB media must be 32 GB or larger.
- Hibernate and Sleep actions are disabled by default. Because the installation is portable and can be moved between PCs by ejecting the USB drive containing the Windows To Go workspace and starting another computer from the device, there is little reason to allow the computer to enter a power-saving state.
- Internal disks are not used and are offline. Windows To Go creates a completely portable Windows workspace; the computer behaves like a docking station for the operating system, bringing USB, keyboard, and screen to the Windows workspace.
- Trusted Platform Module (TPM) is not used because the Windows To Go workspace can move between computer environments. If you encrypt the drive with BitLocker, a password rather than TPM is used at startup.
- Windows Recovery Environment is not available. There is no benefit to including the ability to enter the recovery environment because you can change computers at a moment's notice. The likelihood of hardware causing a problem with the workspace that wouldn't be solved by a restart is minimal.
- Push Button Reset is not available.
- Windows To Go is not available on ARM systems.

To set up a Windows To Go workspace from the GUI, complete the following steps:

1. Connect the USB device to use for your Windows To Go workspace and insert the Windows 8 installation media.

IMPORTANT **SAVE FILES TO ANOTHER DEVICE**

This process will format your USB device. Make sure you have backed up any files or folders you want to keep.

2. In Control Panel, select Windows To Go.
3. Windows searches for removable media. Select the disk found with the appropriate space for Windows To Go and tap or click Next.

   Windows then searches for the installation media. If it is found, the name of the operating system is displayed for selection. If not, you can specify additional search locations to look for media.

4. Select the operating system to install and tap or click Next.
5. On the Set a BitLocker Password page, choose whether to encrypt the USB device with BitLocker. If you want to encrypt the device, tap or click Use BitLocker With My Windows To Go Workspace, type a password, retype the password, and then tap or click Next. If you don't want to encrypt the device, tap or click Skip.

6. Windows formats the target media. When prompted that data on the device will be lost, tap or click Yes to continue or No to cancel.

7. Next, you are asked whether Windows To Go should enable BitLocker on the target drive. If you want to encrypt the information, select Yes and provide a password for encryption. If you do not want to encrypt the information, tap or click Skip.

   Windows creates a Windows To Go workspace on the target media. This can take some time, depending on the size of the media and speed of connection to your computer.

When this completes, the Installation wizard asks whether the computer should restart from the Windows To Go workspace. Tap or click Yes to start from the new workspace automatically or tap or click No if you need to change the BIOS settings on your computer so you can start into the new workspace. Tap or click Save and then Restart to close the wizard and restart your computer or tap or click Save and then Close to close the wizard without restarting.

To set up a Windows To Go workspace from the command line, complete the following steps:

1. Plug your USB device into a computer running Windows 7 or a later operating system and open an administrative command prompt.

2. From the command line, type **diskpart**.

3. At the DISKPART> prompt, type **list disk** and press Enter to see which disks are connected to your system.

> **NOTE A TIP FOR FINDING A DISK NUMBER**
>
> You can run list disk with the USB device unplugged and then run it again with the disk plugged in so that you know which disk number is assigned to the drive for which you are looking.

4. Type **select disk #** at the DISKPART> prompt to select the disk to use.

5. Clean the disk by typing **clean**.

6. When the disk is clean, create a system partition of 350 MB by typing **create partition primary size=350** in the command line and pressing Enter.

7. Type **active** in the command line to mark the partition as active.

8. Format the partition with the Fat32 file system and label it as the system partition by typing **format fs=ntfs quick label=W2G**.

   The quick option speeds up the formatting process slightly.

9. Type **Assign letter=W** in the command line to add a drive letter of S for this partition.

10. To prevent issues when starting up, set the volume being used to have no default drive letter by typing **Attribute volume set NODEFAULTDRIVELETTER** in the command line.

11. Exit DiskPart by typing **Exit**.

> **REAL WORLD** **USING COMPUTER MANAGEMENT TO PREPARE A DISK FOR WINDOWS TO GO**
>
> In addition to DiskPart and the command line, you can use computer management and the GUI to create the partitions on your Windows To Go disk. Creating the partitions in the command line is the same for these as for any other partitions. Use the options indicated in the previous procedure.

12. You need the DISM utility from the Windows Automated Installation Kit (AIK). You can search for and download the kit from either the Microsoft Download Center or TechNet; the URLs are listed in the "Before you begin" section at the beginning of this chapter.

13. When the AIK is downloaded, mount the ISO and Install the kit on your system. Browse to the C:\Program Files\Windows AIK\Tools\Amd64 folder. Locate the Dism.exe file and copy it to an easy-to-remember folder on the C drive, such as C:\Windows\system32.

14. Locate the Install.wim file in the sources directory of the Windows 8 media. If you downloaded an ISO, mount the ISO and browse to the sources directory.

    The Install.wim file will be rather large, 2 to 3 GB.

15. At the administrative command prompt, change to the directory where the C:\Windows\System32 directory is and type the following:

    ```
    dism /apply-image /imagefile:e:\install.wim /index:1 /applydir:f:\
    ```

    where *e:\install.wim* contains the entire path to the Install.wim file, and *f:* is the drive letter of the disk on which the image will reside when the application is complete.

    During this process, expect to wait a good amount of time, given the size of the .wim file, as shown in Figure 2-5.

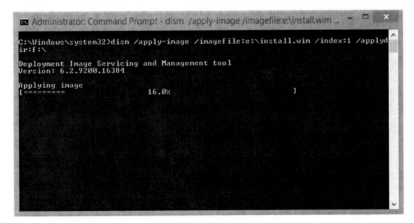

FIGURE 2-5 Progress of copying Install.wim

16. When the application of the .wim file is complete, create the boot files on the Windows To Go installation by typing the following:

```
Bcdboot.exe f:\windows /s f:
```

where *f:* is the drive letter assigned to your Windows To Go device.

> **NOTE** **THE BCDBOOT.EXE COMMAND**
>
> The preceding Bcdboot.exe command assumes that the system on which you are running it is Windows 7. If you are using a Windows 8 system to generate a Windows To Go workspace, the command is **bcdboot.exe g:\windows /s g: /f ALL**, where *g:* is the drive you created on your USB device.

Because the purpose of using Windows To Go is to be hardware-independent, the first time a computer starts from a Windows To Go device, Windows goes through the initial setup process, including asking for a product key. Each time you start on a different system, Windows tries to detect the hardware and install the necessary drivers for the connected environment. You might need to download the necessary drivers for each computer you use with this install.

> **IMPORTANT** **TEST YOUR APPLICATIONS**
>
> Applications used with Windows To Go must be tested to ensure that they can roam between environments. Some applications might not support this because they have dependencies on hardware, which can cause issues with roaming.

Lesson summary

- The process for installation is straightforward and mostly automated.
- When the operating system has been installed, the configuration questions for file sharing, wallpaper personalization, and computer name appear, informing you that everything is nearly ready.
- A Windows To Go workspace is a version of Windows 8 that runs from removable USB media. It can use USB hard drives or flash memory devices if the devices are large enough and fast enough.
- The benefit of a Windows To Go workspace is that it can move between hardware configurations, checking and obtaining the needed drivers for a specific PC on first start. This essentially turns any PC into a vehicle for mouse, keyboard, and screen.

Lesson review

Answer the following questions to test your knowledge of the information in this section. You can find the answers to these questions and explanations of why each is correct or incorrect in the "Answers" section at the end of this chapter.

1. On what types of media can a Windows To Go workspace be configured? (Choose two.)

    A. Optical media, including CDs and DVDs

    B. USB removable hard drives

    C. USB flash removable media

    D. CDs and DVDs only

2. What information can be configured for logon to Windows 8? (Choose all that apply.)

    A. A Microsoft account

    B. User ID and password combination

    C. Domain-based credentials

    D. A smart card

3. You plan to provide members of your organization's IT staff with Windows To Go workspaces on removable media because the members are very mobile and might not always be able to access their primary laptop when out on a call. When a technician uses a Windows To Go workspace, which options are not available for use? (Choose all that apply.)

    A. Sleep and Hibernation features

    B. Device drivers

    C. CD-ROM devices

    D. Internal disks

Lesson 2: Upgrading or migrating from a previous version of Windows

If you are moving from an existing version of Windows to Windows 8, you need to know about the upgrade and migration options that are the topic of this lesson. Although it is likely that some older hardware will not be compatible with Windows 8 and might need to be replaced, there are many occasions when the existing hardware will be more than sufficient to drive Windows 8. From a hardware performance standpoint, nearly every Windows 7–capable system will handle Windows 8 fine, making the upgrade process simple.

To perform an upgrade to Windows 8, you need the media containing the Windows 8 operating system and a current Windows 7–based computer. The format of the media can be either DVD or USB.

Although upgrading from Windows 7 is straightforward, there are scenarios in which you might not want to upgrade or might be unable to upgrade to Windows 8. This lesson also covers migrating from Windows Vista and Windows XP.

After this lesson, you will be able to:

- Plan the appropriate Windows 8 deployment type for your environment.
- Ensure that the appropriate measures are taken to prevent loss of user information.
- Transfer files by using the Windows Easy Transfer (WET) application.
- Migrate data by using the User State Migration Tool.

Estimated lesson time: 60 minutes

REAL WORLD   **CREATING A BOOT DISK**

Microsoft has made the Windows 7 USB DVD Download tool available to create a startup system disk, either on DVD or USB disks, from the downloaded ISO. The name specifies Windows 7, but I had no problems using this tool to create USB media for Windows 8. You can find the download in the Microsoft Store at *http://go.microsoft.com /fwlink/?LinkID=221699.*

Running the Setup Wizard

When you insert the Windows 8 media in your computer and run Setup.exe, the initialization process begins, and the Setup Wizard guides you through the installation. Setup checks for any updates that will help make the installation process smoother. After the updates are installed, Setup guides you through the installation setup process.

1. Type the product key and tap or click Next to continue.
2. Read the End User License Agreement (EULA), select I Accept The License Terms, and tap or click Accept.
3. Select the type of install to perform:
   - Keep Windows Settings, Files, And Apps
   - Keep Personal Files Only
   - Nothing

   If you are unsure which type of install to use, you can select Help Me Decide, and Windows will provide some cases for each type of installation. After you have chosen your path, Windows checks to see whether any configuration items it locates need input from you; if not, the next option is to install. If the installer discovers items that require your attention, it prompts you to provide this information.

After the installation begins, a message appears that informs you that your computer will restart a few times during the process. As the process moves along, a progress bar is displayed. There will be a few restarts during the upgrade, but the installer will continue where it left off each time. Saving your information during the installation process might slow things down, so the upgrade might take slightly longer than a fresh installation. Remember, this is your data that Windows 8 is preserving; patience here will be rewarded with intact data!

Configuring your account

When the installation process is complete, the system restarts, and you need to configure your account.

1. When prompted, enter the following information, and then tap or click Next:
   - A color for the background and theme
   - A name for your computer

   On the Settings screen, you are given two initial options to configure general settings for your computer: Express Settings or Custom.

2. If you select Use Express Settings (shown in Figure 2-2), the wizard turns on the following options for you:
   - Enabling automatic updates
   - Enabling the phishing and malware filters
   - Opting to participate in the Microsoft Customer Experience program
   - Checking for solutions to issues online
   - Enabling location-based services for personalized content
   - Enabling sharing and connecting to devices on the network

   Select Customize and the wizard guides you through the available settings.

3. If a network is available, you can select the type of network sharing, depending on the network, on the first page.
   - For home or work networks, select Yes, Turn On Sharing And Connect To Devices.
   - For public networks, such as cafés or libraries, select No, Don't Turn On Sharing Or Connect To Devices.

   You can change these settings later; for now, select the one that best matches your available network.

4. Tap or click Next to configure settings that help protect and update your system, as shown in Figure 2-3.

5. Select the amount of information that is exchanged with Microsoft, such as information about malicious applications or location data when location-aware apps are used and then tap or click Next.

   The next page contains settings for online solution checking and information sharing between apps.

6. After configuring the settings for your computer, sign in, as shown in Figure 2-4. Choose from the following options and then tap or click Next.

    - Sign in with your Microsoft account by typing the email address associated with it.

    - Sign up for a new email address to use with a Microsoft account.

    - Sign in without a Microsoft account.

    When you have answered these questions, the system does some final housekeeping and then displays the Start screen. When you see the Start screen, your upgrade is complete, and Windows 8 is ready to use.

Upgrading from Windows Vista

With Windows 8, you can keep some aspects of your Windows Vista installation; however, you will need to reinstall your applications to use them on your newly upgraded computer. When migrating from Windows Vista to Windows 8, your system will keep the following items:

- Windows Settings
- User Accounts and Files

All the applications that were installed in Windows Vista will need to be reloaded in Windows 8, but personal settings and user data will be migrated during the upgrade.

Upgrading from Windows XP

When moving from Windows XP to Windows 8, the installation process for Windows 8 migrates user accounts and files from the Windows XP installation. However, your Windows settings will need some reconfiguration, and any installed applications will need to be reinstalled. The computer and Windows settings will be just like new, depending on your hardware, and your user accounts and files will migrate to the new system.

Before beginning this process, check the specifications for Windows 8 and match them against the existing hardware. If the computer running Windows XP does not meet the hardware requirements for the new operating system, it might not be worth attempting the upgrade.

Moving and transferring files by using Windows Easy Transfer

With the Windows Easy Transfer application, you can use several types of media to move files between an existing—or source—computer and a new—or destination—computer. Unlike in previous versions, you can choose from several options for moving your information. If you have an easy transfer cable—a USB-to-USB cable specifically made for this process—you can use it. Otherwise, you can transfer files over your home or business network or use a removable hard drive.

Using removable media

You can start from either your current computer or your new Windows 8–based computer. First, search for the Windows Easy Transfer tool. You begin your search from the Start menu on your current computer or from the Start screen on your Windows 8–based computer.

1. When the Windows Easy Transfer Wizard opens, a Welcome screen describes some of the types of information and files that you can transfer by using this application. Click Next.

2. Choose the medium you want to use for the transfer, as shown in Figure 2-6.

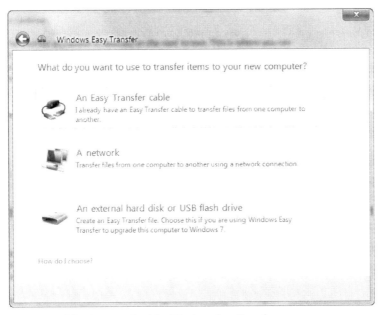

FIGURE 2-6 Selecting a method for Windows Easy Transfer

Your options are to use an Easy Transfer cable, a network connection, or an external hard disk or USB flash drive. If you're not sure which method to use, click How Do I Choose?. The help file discusses each option and provides some frequently asked questions about what can be transferred between systems.

3. After you have selected a transfer option, choose the PC from which you are working. Windows Easy Transfer determines what additional software is needed to complete the process.

   ■ If your old computer is running Windows XP or Vista, you need to install the Windows Easy Transfer application before proceeding. You can find the tool at *http://windows.microsoft.com/en-US/windows7/products/features/windows-easy -transfer*. After you install the tool, you are prompted to choose a media type to use for this installation. At this point, Windows Easy Transfer will copy itself to your chosen media so you can install the application on your old computer.

■ If you are running Windows 7 or a version of Windows 8, the wizard displays instructions on how to launch the Windows Easy Transfer application on your old computer.

When you open the Windows Easy Transfer application, the wizard asks you for information it will use to transfer files.

USING AN EASY TRANSFER CABLE

Using an Easy Transfer cable, if you have one, is the easiest and least time-consuming option in terms of setup. However, the transfer will still take some time, depending on the amount of data you are migrating.

1. Identify the computer on which you are currently working as either the old or the new computer.

2. Complete the Windows Easy Transfer Wizard on the other computer until you have selected to use an Easy Transfer Cable and specified the computer on which you are working.

3. Return to the computer from which you are migrating and click Next to proceed.

The wizard establishes a connection by the cable to the new computer and asks you to select which files and folders should be included in the transfer. When the items are selected, click Next to begin moving the files to the new system.

USING A NETWORK CONNECTION

1. If you select the network option for transferring files, a Windows Easy Transfer key, like the one shown in Figure 2-7, is displayed.

FIGURE 2-7 Windows Easy Transfer key

2. When this key is displayed, on the new computer, start the Windows Easy Transfer tool. Select a network, select This Is My New PC, select the appropriate operating system, click Next, enter the Windows Easy Transfer key on the destination computer, and then click Next.

3. The remote computer attempts to establish a connection with the old computer. When a connection is established, select the folders and files to transfer to your new computer and click Next.

At this point, the Windows Easy Transfer application begins reading and transferring your files from the external media. This could take some time. It is advisable not to use either computer during this process.

USING AN EXTERNAL HARD DISK OR USB FLASH DRIVE

1. If you selected External Hard Disk Or USB Flash Drive, select the files you want to save for transfer after the wizard has attempted to estimate the size of your files. Select the check boxes next to the items you want to keep or transfer and click Next.

2. Because the files are being saved to external media, it is a good idea to enter a password for the Easy Transfer file so that no one else can access the data after you have exported it. Enter and confirm your Windows Easy Transfer password and click Next.

3. On the next page, save the migration file to an external drive. Ensure that you have connected the external drive and that it has enough space to store your migration file, browse to that drive, and click Save.

When you save the migration file, all the selected information is transferred to this location as a .mig file.

Figure 2-8 shows the process of saving the migration file from the old computer to external media. Based on the amount of data being migrated, an external hard drive is likely to be a better choice than flash media.

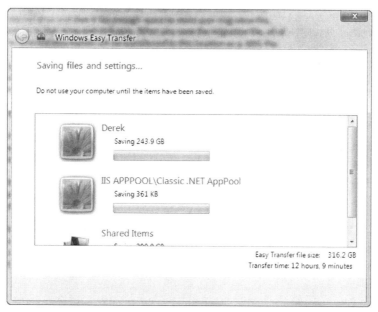

FIGURE 2-8 Saving migration data to external disk

4. After the file has been saved, the external disk can be connected to your new computer. On the new computer, select the option to transfer files through an external hard drive and then choose this computer as your new computer.

5. Windows asks you whether the files for the migration have already been saved to an external disk. Connect the disk and select Yes to continue. If you select No, the wizard returns to the previous page.

At this point, the Windows Easy Transfer application begins reading and transferring your files from the external media. This could take some time. It is advisable not to use either computer during this process.

Using the User State Migration Tool

Another way to get information from one computer to another is by using the User State Migration Tool (USMT). This tool is useful for large migrations such as moving many computers during an upgrade. The files captured by the USMT can be deployed to new Windows-based computers to ensure that no information is lost when performing an upgrade deployment across an organization. This tool is available for download from the Microsoft Download Center as part of the Windows Automated Installation Toolkit; the URL is listed in the "Before you begin" section of this chapter. USMT supports the migration of the following types of information:

- Desktop items
- Application items

- User account information
- User files

The User State Migration Tool has the following requirements:

- It must run using administrator elevated privilege in Windows Vista.
- It must run using an administrator account in Windows XP.
- No applications should be open when running the ScanState.exe or LoadState.exe operations within USMT.

The USMT can accept the following operating systems as ScanState (source) computers:

- Windows 2000 Professional with Service Pack 4
- Windows XP Home with Service Pack 2
- Windows XP Professional with Service Pack 2
- Windows XP Professional x64 edition with Service Pack 2
- Windows Vista 32-bit and 64-bit editions

NOTE **COPYING USMT TO MULTIPLE COMPUTERS**

When the Windows Automated Installation Toolkit is installed on one machine, you can copy the USMT files to other computers in your organization.

The USMT runs from the command line, using a utility named ScanState.exe to copy the items from the source computer to a network share or external disk. After the computer has been upgraded or a new computer has been configured, the LoadState.exe utility is run on the destination computer to migrate the information from the network share to the new computer. For example, Joe runs ScanState.exe to move the user information from Kevin's computer to the network so that Kevin's computer can be upgraded to Windows 8. Joe then runs LoadState.exe to import the data from that share.

ScanState has many options, as shown in Table 2-1. Some options can be used together and some cannot; but, in many cases, the same options will be used repeatedly.

IMPORTANT **KEEP TRACK OF THE OPTIONS CHOSEN**

When using the User State Migration Tool to transfer data to a new computer, keep track of the options used during the ScanState portion of the migration. These options tell the utility which data to migrate and specify options for the migration itself. Many of the options used with ScanState can also be used with LoadState to ensure that the data is imported in the same way and that the same options are used when the data is copied on the new computer. For example, specifying the options for ScanState individually and attempting to use the /auto option with LoadState might cause problems with the migration. Using the same options for both operations will produce better results.

To use the User State Migration Tool, complete the following steps:

1. Open an administrative command prompt on the computer from which the information will be migrated.

2. Navigate to C:\Program Files\Windows AIK\Tools\USMT or to whichever folder contains the files you have copied from the USMT folder.

3. On the source computer, execute ScanState.exe with the appropriate options specified to collect information from your computer for later use. The ScanState application supports the options shown in Table 2-1.

TABLE 2-1 ScanState options

Option	Description
StorePath	The path to where the migrated data will be stored.
/auto[:scriptdir]	Calls migapp.xml and migdocs.xml and sets logging level to 13 by using the scriptdir parameter to specify the location of the called .xml files.
/targetvista	Optimizes the ScanState application when the target computer will be running Windows Vista.
/genconfig:filename	Generates the config.xml file; when using /genconfig, StorePath cannot be used.
/o	Overwrites existing migration store.
/p:filename	Generates a space estimate file to help determine the disk space needed for the migration.
/localonly	Includes only files stored on local computer.
/efs:abort|skip|decryptcopy|hardlink	Controls the behavior of ScanState when it encounters Encrypting File System (EFS) files.
/encrypt:AES|AES_128|AES_192|AES_256|3DES|3DES_112	Encrypts the migration store by using the specified algorithm; 3DES selected by default. This option requires /key or /keyfile to be used.
/hardlink	Enables hard links for a non-compressed store. Should only be used in PC refresh scenarios.
/key:<string>	Specifies the encryption key.
/keyfile:filename	Specifies the path to and the name of a text file containing the encryption key.
/nocompress	Specifies that the migration store will not be compressed.
/l:filename	Specifies the location and file name of the log file.
/v:level	Enables verbose logging using the following levels: 0, 1, 4, 5, 8, 9, 12, and 13. Level 0 is default.
/progress:filename	Specifies the progress log file name and location.
/c	Configures ScanState to continue running even if there are non-fatal errors.
/r:TimesToRetry	Specifies the number of times to retry the ScanState operation; 3 tries is default.

Option	Description
/w:SecondsToWait	Specifies the number of seconds to wait between retry attempts; 1 second is default.
/all	Migrates all the users on the system.
/ui:[Domain\]Username	Migrates specified users. For local users, specify user name only. For domain users, specify domain name and user name, domain\user name.
/ue:[Domain\]UserName	Excludes specified users. For local users, specify user name only. For domain users, specify domain name and user name, domain\user name.
/uel:NumberOfDays|YYYY/MM/DD	Specifies that migration should exclude users who have not logged on within a specified time period. Number of days parameter can be 0 to exclude all users who are not currently logged on.
/i:Filename	Specifies location and name of .xml file that contains rules that define the settings and files to migrate.
/help or /?	Displays help at the command line.
/config:FileName	Specifies the config.xml file that USMT should use.
/offlineWinDir:WinDir	Specifies the path to the offline Windows directory that USMT should use to gather user state.
/offlineWinOld:WinDir	Specifies the path to the offline Windows old directory that USMT should use to gather user state.
/offline:FileName	Specifies the offline.xml file USMT should use to gather user state. An alternative to offlineWinDir or offlineWinOld.
/vsc	Enables volume shadow copy when file is in use.
/listfiles:filename	Specifies the location and name of a file that will list all the files gathered for migration.

> **MORE INFO** **SCANSTATE.EXE SYNTAX**
>
> You can find more information about the ScanState.exe syntax at *http://technet.microsoft.com/en-us/library/dd560781(v=WS.10).aspx*.

After you have the source information written to the StorePath, you can upgrade the existing system by installing Windows 8 or introducing a new Windows 8–based computer (using a side-by-side scenario). Following the initial setup of the new Windows 8–based computer, you can use LoadState.exe to retrieve information from the StorePath and bring migrated user information to the new computer.

This process requires an administrative command prompt to execute from the new computer. LoadState.exe supports many of the same parameters as ScanState. Table 2-2 lists the parameters that are different from the ScanState parameters.

TABLE 2-2 LoadState options

Option	Description
/lac[:Password]	Creates disabled local accounts if they do not already exist on the destination computer. The password parameter is the password used for these accounts.
/lae	Enables local accounts created by /lac. The /lac option is required.
/mu:[OldDomain\]OldUserName: [NewDomain\]NewUserName	Specifies a new user name. For local users, specify the user name only. Wildcards are not allowed.
/md:OldDomain:NewDomain	Specifies a new domain for the users. The oldDomain can use wild-cards (* or ?).
/decrypt:AES|AES_128|AES_192| AES_256|3DES|3DES_112	Specifies that the migration store is encrypted and must be decrypted to be used. The /key or /keyfile option must be specified.
/sf	Restores shell folder redirection.

All the options for both the scan and load operations might seem a bit overwhelming given the volume of things you can configure, but after you have determined what will work in your environment, the commands can be stored in a batch file and reused.

> **MORE INFO** **LOADSTATE.EXE SYNTAX**
>
> You can find more information about the LoadState.exe syntax at *http://technet.microsoft .com/en-us/library/cc766226(v=WS.10).aspx*.

Migrating user data

Consider an example in which you have a shared computer that the marketing department uses for interns who need to access the Internet. The computer is not connected to the domain, but it has a network connection. This summer, Bob, Mary, and John are the interns using the computer. Because of a policy to replace computers every three years, this computer is due for an upgrade to the new company standard computer. To migrate the user data between computers, the command looks like this:

```
ScanState c:\migstore /i:miguser.xml /r:5 /w:5
```

This ScanState command migrates all the user data for these users and the administrator to the local C:\migstore folder so all the users and their data are easily moved to the new system. If errors occur, five retries will be used, and the application will wait five seconds between attempts. After the information has been collected from the original computer, you can run Loadstate.exe to complete the migration process.

In many cases, a computer will have more than one user profile because several people have logged on to the system. In the previous example, ScanState found three user accounts; ScanState and the data for them was copied to the StorePath. The /i:miguser.xml option specifies that user data should be migrated, and by default, all the user profiles are included in this process.

The migration file can be stored on a network share as long as the user account running the User State Migration Tool has access to the share.

The process of bringing the migrated data to the new computer is as simple as changing from using the ScanState.exe command to using the LoadState.exe command. In many cases, the same options can also be used for the import. Both the ScanState.exe and LoadState.exe utilities contain an auto switch that uses predefined options to migrate data between computers.

Windows 8 uses a new tool for system deployment called the Assessment and Deployment Kit (ADK) for Windows 8, which contains the x86 and x64 versions of the User State Migration Toolkit. The Windows Assessment and Deployment Kit for Windows 8 can be used on previous versions of Windows, including Windows 7, Windows Vista, Windows Server 2008, and Windows Server 2008 R2.

You will still use LoadState.exe to complete a USMT migration; the tool looks much like it did in Windows 7. When the latest version of the USMT is installed on Windows 8 and the .mig file from the previous portion of this lesson has become available, you can begin LoadState.exe.

To start LoadState.exe, open an administrative command prompt on the target computer and navigate to the folder on which the USMT is located. By default, this is C:\Program Files (x86)\Windows Kits\Assessment and Deployment Kit\User State Migration Tool.

Choose amd64 or x86, depending on the architecture used in the migration. Like in other scenarios, information from a 64-bit Windows-based source computer must be migrated to a 64-bit target computer. Attempting to mix architectures will result in errors, causing the migration to fail before it starts.

Using LoadState.exe is fairly straightforward; however, it is important to be aware of the following restrictions:

- If the user account is not created as part of the data migration, the data will be migrated and accessible to those users with permissions, but no user account will be tied to that data. When attempting to create user accounts to rectify the issue, Windows will point out that the user account already exists.

■ Large user profiles will cause slower migrations, and not everything you might think is contained in a profile will be transferred. When performing user state migrations, files and folders can be contained within expected folders that are skipped during the process. For example, a Pics folder within My Photos might not be migrated, depending on the options used when performing the migration.

These aren't reasons to avoid the tools, but they are items that you should think about before going through migrations of data. Nothing is worse than finding out after the fact that things are missing.

Earlier in this chapter, data for five user accounts was migrated out of a Windows 7–based computer to be stored for later import into a Windows 8–based computer. The command for bringing this into Windows 8 by using LoadState looks like this:

```
Loadstate.exe c:\<storefolder>\ /i:miguser.xml /c /lac
```

This command creates the users found in the migration file as local users because of the /lac switch. In addition, /c allows LoadState to skip over non-fatal errors and continue without interruption.

Using /i:miguser.xml enables only the user data to be migrated into the Windows 8 environment. Because ScanState.exe and LoadState.exe have many of the same switches and options, keeping the options similar for each migration tends to make the process a bit smoother. Another thing to understand about LoadState is that the /lac switch allows the creation of user profiles, but it does not create actual user accounts for logon.

Lessons learned during a test migration

When creating a test user called Bob on a Windows 8–based client machine, who also happened to be a test user on the Windows 7–based machine used for migration, it was noticed that if Bob was around before pulling in the migrated data with LoadState, the user information appeared as expected on Bob's desktop.

After the migration completed, adding a user with the same user name as one used in the migration did not work. Windows indicated that this user name was already used. Doing this makes sense in some cases. If you are moving one user to a new computer and need to ensure that his or her account and all its information arrive, creating the account ahead of time can be helpful, especially for local users.

For domain accounts, the migration behaves a bit differently. Because user account information is accessed during the logon process, the logon can be tied to an existing set of user information, allowing access to the account data. For example, Bob works for Contoso and has a user object in the Contoso domain. He is getting a new Windows 8–based computer, and the IT department migrated his information. When looking at the C:\Users folder on the new computer, Bob has a user profile folder. When Bob logs on as Contoso\Bob, the Active Directory domain logs him on and attaches to the profile folder on the computer, providing access to the documents, settings, files, and other folders Contoso\Bob maintained in his profile that was migrated from his Windows 7–based computer. If the profile for a user, like Bob, already exists, the user's domain profile is stored using the <domain>.<user> nomenclature—in this case, contoso.bob, to ensure that it is separate from the bob local account folder.

> **IMPORTANT   MIGRATING LOCAL ACCOUNT DATA**
>
> When migrating local account data from one computer to another, ensure that the user account exists on the Windows 8–based target machine prior to migrating the user account data into that system. Failure to do so will likely render logon impossible. Because Active Directory accounts do not authenticate locally but can store data in profile folders, no staging of these accounts is required.

Note that the User State Migration Tool requires a top-level directory for the StorePath, such as C:\Store. This path is needed because compressed and uncompressed files can be within the same store. Using this path simplifies the migration process by allowing the migration tools to use both compressed and uncompressed files. More information about this configuration can be found at *http://blogs.technet.com/b/usmt/archive/2008/06/05 /why-scanstate-and-loadstate-require-a-top-level-directory-path-to-a-migration-store.aspx*.

When creating your store folder, remember the USMT folder that is created inside the path chosen during ScanState. Failure to include this folder when running LoadState, especially if you move the StorePath folder, will result in errors.

If you are logged on to the target computer as one of the user accounts being migrated from another computer, the settings might change for that account as they are imported. For example, if your user account is being migrated from another computer and you are logged on and performing the LoadState operation, you might notice that some settings, including desktop personalization items, change during the process.

In many cases, you are unlikely to work with local user accounts on the job because most organizations employ Active Directory domains to manage users and computers. Remember that when you are migrating user information, the user account must exist on the target computer for that data to be accessible. The easiest way to ensure that this happens is to log on to the target system as one of the users whom you are migrating while ScanState is running.

Remember that the User State Migration Tool exists to enable administrators or IT staff to ensure a smooth user experience during a computer change. When used carefully, the migration can be smooth for all parties involved.

Lesson summary

- Windows 7 has the most options in terms of upgradeability to Windows 8.
- Only certain components will be moved forward from both Windows Vista and Windows XP without additional tools.
- The User State Migration Tool requires administrative access to the command prompt; remember to run the console as an administrator to ensure that the tool functions as needed.
- When upgrading to Windows 8, consider all the items that already reside on your computer. You will need to allocate enough time for all the files on the system to be processed, which is why an upgrade can take longer than a fresh install.
- User accounts for local users and user accounts for domain users have similarities and differences. If your computer has a local user and a domain user with the same user name, the profile directories will be different, which can cause problems when attempting to access migrated data. If this occurs, log on to the new computer as one of the users who has data being migrated to ensure that this information remains accessible.
- You might need to create a local user account for users being migrated because the /lac switch creates the profile for the user but does not create an account that can log on to Windows.

Lesson review

Answer the following questions to test your knowledge of the information in this lesson. You can find the answers to these questions and explanations of why each answer choice is correct or incorrect in the "Answers" section at the end of this chapter.

1. Bob wants to upgrade his computer to Windows 8 from Windows 7 and is concerned that he will lose some or all of his information. He asks you for help in determining what he can expect. What information will remain intact when Bob performs this upgrade?

   A. All applications, Windows Settings, and User data will be preserved.

   B. Windows Settings and User Data will be preserved.

   C. User accounts and files will be preserved.

   D. User accounts will be preserved with no information.

2. One of your computers that is still running Windows XP needs a refresh, but instead of completely trashing the system and beginning again, you would like to see whether the system will support Windows 8. What should you find out before attempting an upgrade?

   A. Whether the hardware is compatible with Windows 8

   B. Whether the computer has a DVD drive to accept the Windows 8 media

C. Whether there are accurate backups of important information in case something goes wrong during the upgrade attempt

D. Whether the installed programs on the computer are Windows 8–compatible

3. A member of your staff, Alex, reports that there are problems migrating user and other data on to the new Windows 8–based PCs that were purchased for the accounting department. The outbound migration worked properly, and the files have been copied to external disks, but running LoadState produces errors when executing, stating that the store path is not found. What can you do to help Alex resolve this issue?

A. Help Alex run LoadState on a different PC.

B. Instruct Alex to review the log files to ensure that the application is looking for the store in the right place.

C. Inform the user that the data is lost and cannot be recovered.

D. Help Alex determine whether his user account has the correct permissions for the location of the store path.

4. During the completion of a user state migration from Windows 7 to Windows 8, a member of your team runs into a problem when working to import the information from the MigrationLibrary folder on the network. He has checked to ensure that the .mig file exists in the share, but continually encounters a return code of 27, stating that there are problems with the migration StorePath location. The command being used to migrate user information is the following:

```
Loadstate.exe \\servername\sharedfolder\ /i:miguser.xml /c
```

What might be the problem with the configuration of LoadState.exe?

A. The share is offline.

B. The switches for importing various .xml templates are missing.

C. The StorePath folder is missing files or folders that LoadState expects.

D. The name of the migration file is incorrect.

Lesson 3: Installing Windows 8 on startup VHD files

VHDs are files used by applications such as Virtual PC and Hyper-V to enable virtualized systems to function like their physical counterparts. Windows 8 enables a copy of the operating system to use a VHD to start. This process is much like creating a Windows To Go workspace in that the installation image must be placed on a VHD and then the media configured to start, but it is also like a standard configuration because, generally, VHD files are stored on a computer and used as the startup media for that system.

The idea of using a virtual hard disk on a workstation or laptop is interesting, and the performance and recoverability provided by doing this can be worth the extra work. Although they provide some benefits similar to those found with Windows To Go workspaces, startup

VHDs are more permanent than a version of Windows that travels like Windows To Go workspaces. Using VHDs to test new versions of Windows provides another way that your existing system can remain intact while allowing new functionality to be put through any testing needed to feel comfortable with the technology.

Windows 8 can be started from a VHD. The VHD in this case is a file that contains a functional copy of Windows and behaves like a physical hard disk. The computer is configured to start from either the physical hard disk or the VHD. During startup, you select which environment to load. Some of the benefits of using a VHD include the following:

- The ability to start multiple operating systems on the same hardware.
- Portability of the operating system contained within a VHD.
- Ease of creation and disposal. By using this environment, another operating system can be configured in a fairly short time. When you are finished with it, the files can be deleted to reclaim the disk space the virtual hard disk used.
- No damage to existing files. Using a VHD also keeps your original environment safe from any modifications made inside the new environment.

There are two ways to accomplish Windows 8 startup from a VHD file. The first option is to use a pre-created VHD file built using the Windows GUI, which you can attach to the operating system for use as a start device or during the installation process of Windows 8 using DiskPart. The second option is to create the VHD during the installation process by using DiskPart. This lesson describes both processes; they are similar and take about the same amount of time to perform.

After this lesson, you will be able to:

- Install Windows 8 into a VHD.
- Configure the VHD as a boot device.

Estimated lesson time: 55 minutes

Creating a VHD from an existing installation

As part of the following procedure, the DiskPart command-line utility will be used when the installation of Windows 8 gets underway to attach the virtual hard disk file to your computer to be detected by Windows. This allows the VHD to be used as a target for the Windows installation.

To create a virtual hard disk file from within your existing installation of Windows 8 by using the GUI, complete the following steps:

1. Tap or click the Desktop tile and then tap or click the File Explorer icon in the toolbar.
2. Press and hold or right-click Computer and then tap or click Manage.

3. Tap or click the Disk Management node in the navigation console. In the Actions pane, tap or click More Actions, and then tap or click Create VHD.

4. Type the following path and file name for the VHD: **C:\win8.vhd**.

5. Type a container size and select the unit (MB, GB, or TB). Select the VHD format and whether it will be expandable or fixed-size.

> *NOTE* **SELECTING THIN-PROVISIONED OR FIXED-SIZE VHDS**
>
> A fixed-size VHD file is limited to the size that is specified at creation. For example, creating a fixed-size VHD with 80 GB of space allocates the full amount of disk space at the time of creation, similar to a traditional hard disk that has a fixed size.
>
> Using thinly provisioned VHD files enables you to specify the same 80-GB maximum size, but the VHD file consumes only the actual storage space needed for the files it contains. For example, if the Windows 8 installation into an 80-GB, thinly provisioned VHD consumes only 10 GB of space after the initial installation, the size of the VHD file will be 10 GB. Windows, however, will report the full size of the disk, 80 GB, and the VHD will dynamically expand up to 80 GB to accommodate additional apps and data.

6. Tap or click OK.

   The new VHD appears in Disk Management as Not Initialized.

7. Close Computer Management and insert your Windows 8 media. Restart your computer and start from the Windows 8 media.

8. When the installation begins, tap or click Next, tap or click Install Now, enter the product key, accept the license terms, and select the installation type to perform: Upgrade or Custom.

   In this case, a custom installation would be appropriate because you are installing Windows 8 on a new VHD hard disk.

9. Press Shift+F10 to open a command prompt. Do not select a location to install Windows because your previously created VHD will not be listed in the available disks window.

10. At the command prompt, type **Diskpart** to enter the DiskPart tool. From within DiskPart, you need to discover some basic information about the disks available for use by the installer. You're looking for the following two things in particular:

    - The disk number you need to use
    - The drive letter the installer is using for that disk

11. Type **List Disk** at the DiskPart prompt and make a note of the ID numbers assigned to available disks in the system.

12. Type **select disk #** at the command line, where # is the number of the disk where your readied VHD is.

13. With the disk selected, type **List Volume** at the command line and press Enter.

This displays the volumes available and the drive letters associated with them. You will need the drive letter information to attach the VHD.

14. To identify the VHD you want to attach, type **select VDisk file=<path to VHD>** where *<path to VHD>* is the actual path to the VHD file, for example, C:\vhd \windows8.vhd.

15. With the VHD selected, type **attach VDisk** to attach the VHD.

16. Type **exit** and press Enter to exit DiskPart, then type **exit** and press Enter again to close the command prompt window.

17. Tap or click the refresh option on the disk selection window. You should now see your VHD file listed as an installation target, denoted by the size of the virtual disk specified at creation. Select this disk as an installation target, ignoring the warning that appears, saying that you cannot install Windows on this disk. Tap or click Next.

18. When the process completes, remove the installation media and restart your computer to the hard drive. When you do this, the Windows 8 boot menu displays your choices for any installations directly on the hard drive and any VHD installations you have available. Select the system you want to start and press Enter.

Creating the VHD during the installation by using DiskPart

This section discusses another installation to VHD. This time, the VHD file will be created as part of the installation process by using the DiskPart utility. This can save time during the process because the existing operating system does not need to be started to create the VHD file. To create a VHD file and install Windows 8, complete the following steps:

1. Insert the Windows 8 media and restart your computer.

2. At the first setup screen, press Shift+F10 to open a command prompt.

3. From the x:\sources directory, type **Diskpart** at the command line and press Enter to launch DiskPart.

4. Type **List Disk** at the DiskPart prompt and note the available disks in the system.

5. Type **select disk #** where # is the number of the disk.

6. With the disk selected, enter **List Volume** at the command line and press Enter.

This displays the volumes available and the drive letters associated with them. You will need this in the next step when creating a new VHD.

7. Type **select volume #**, where # is the number of the volume being selected, at the command line, and press Enter.

8. Type the following command:

```
Create VDisk file=x:\vhd\windows8.vhd maximum=<size in MB> type=<expandable |
fixed>
```

where $x:\backslash$ is the drive letter of the volume selected in the previous step and the vhd *type* is specified as expandable or fixed. The *maximum* value should be the maximum exposed size of the VHD in MB. If you choose a type of fixed for the VHD, you will need to specify the size=xx option rather than the maximum=xx option to designate the size of the disk file.

9. After the VHD file is created, locate the VHD and its information by typing **List Vdisk** at the DiskPart command line and pressing Enter.

10. Select the VHD by typing **Select vdisk file="<path to vhd>"** and pressing Enter. The path to the VHD is displayed by the List Vdisk command.

11. To attach the selected VHD so that Windows can use it as a target disk, type **attach vdisk** at the command line and press Enter.

12. Exit the DiskPart utility by typing **exit** on the command line.

13. Exit the command prompt by typing **exit** again and pressing Enter.

14. Now that the VHD is attached to the computer, select the language, keyboard, and time and currency settings and tap or click Next.

15. Tap or click Install Now.

16. Enter the product key for Windows 8 and tap or click Next.

17. Select I Accept on the End User License Agreement and tap or click Next.

18. On the Where Do You Want To Install Windows page of the Windows Setup Wizard, select the new disk as the installation location for Windows.

> *NOTE* **SELECTING THE RIGHT DISK**
>
> When you install Windows on a VHD, one way to determine which disk is the correct one is to look at the size of the displayed disk or partition. It should be roughly the size you specified when creating the file. Another way is to select that file and then look at the warning underneath the disk selection window. You see a message saying that Windows cannot install on the selected device; this warning can be safely ignored.

Starting the system from the VHD

Now that Windows 8 has been installed on a VHD, it is possible to start the system. In Windows 7, when performing the tasks to start a VHD, the editing of boot menus was left up to the user. Windows needed to be reminded that there were multiple installations from which to choose—some located on physical drives in traditional installations and others located inside VHD files. In Windows 8, this is handled as part of the installation to the VHD file. When the system completes its installation process, you are asked to choose an operating system, as shown in Figure 2-9. When this window appears, the default selection time is 30 seconds on the initial startup of the multi-boot environment, with the default startup option being the latest installation.

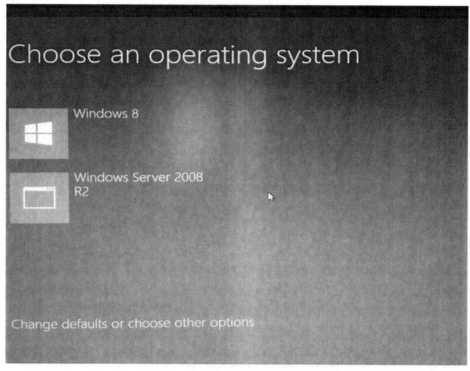

FIGURE 2-9 The Choose An Operating System window

After the initial startup to complete the process of readying devices in the new installation, the time that the boot menu is displayed defaults to 30 seconds, and the default operating system selection is the newest installation of Windows. The time limit to display the menu will disappear after you change your selection. If multiple VHD environments are available, the menu entries shown will display information about each VHD file so you can distinguish instances.

You can adjust the amount of time that the boot menu displays and the default choice of operating system by completing the following steps:

1. From the Choose An Operating System screen, select Change Defaults Or Choose Other Options.

2. To change the 30-second timer, select Change The Timer and select 5 minutes, 30 seconds, or 5 seconds.

3. Select Choose A Default Operating System to specify which operating system should be started by default.

4. Select Choose Other Options to perform the following tasks:

    ▪ Continue starting the default operating system.

    ▪ Use an operating system other than the default.

- Troubleshoot your computer.
- Turn off your computer.

If you select the option to troubleshoot your computer, the following options are available:

- **Refresh Your PC**   Reset windows without losing files.
- **Reset Your PC**   Remove all personal files and begin with a fresh copy of Windows.
- **Advanced Options**   These include:
    - System Restore: Restore your computer to an earlier time.
    - System Image Recovery: Use a specific image to recover Windows.
    - Automatic Repair: Fix issues that prevent Windows from starting up.
    - Command Prompt: Access advanced recovery tools such as DiskPart.
    - Startup Settings: Restart your computer to an options menu to enter Safe mode and access other traditional tools.

You can also change these settings in Windows 8 by using MSConfig. To change the boot menu settings, complete the following steps:

1. On the Start screen, type **msconfig**. When the application appears in the search results, tap or click it to start the program.
2. Tap or click the Boot tab in the system configuration window.
3. To adjust the default timer for the Operating System Selection menu, change the value in the timeout box from 30 seconds to any other value. Note that it is more flexible than the three options provided from the Windows 8 boot screen.
4. To change the default operating system, select an operating system not currently labeled Default OS in the top portion of the Boot tab, and then tap or click Set As Default.
5. Tap or click OK to save these changes.
6. Select Restart Now to restart the computer and apply the changes or select Exit Without Restart to save the changes and apply them at the next restart.

Removing VHD installations

If you later decide that you do not want to use the VHD installation to start Windows, you can just start the root version of Windows on the system and remove the VHD file from the hard disk. When doing this, you will need to clean up the boot menu to prevent confusion during future starts. The first time you restart your computer after removing a VHD, the Recovery screen appears, stating that your computer needs to be repaired. Start a different operating system by pressing F9; after the new system starts, you can clean up the boot menu to remove the entry for the VHD file that has been deleted.

To edit the boot menu, complete the following steps:

1. On the Start screen, type **msconfig** to search for the application. Tap or click to open it.

2. Select the Boot tab.

3. Select the installation you want to remove.

4. Tap or click Delete.

5. Tap or click Apply, and then tap or click OK to save the settings and exit MSConfig.

6. Restart your computer to commit the changes to the configuration.

When your computer restarts, the entry for the VHD files you deleted no longer appears in the boot menu.

Lesson summary

- Create a VHD to store data or operating systems.
- Configure Windows to start from a virtual hard disk (VHD).
- Manage virtual hard disk files with DiskPart.

Lesson review

Answer the following questions to test your knowledge of the information in this lesson. You can find the answers to these questions and explanations of why each answer choice is correct or incorrect in the "Answers" section at the end of this chapter.

1. Mike, a developer at your firm, has heard that some big changes are coming in Windows 8, and he would like to begin working on an application within his department. He intends to eventually create a desktop app, but first needs to become familiar with the new environment. Mike has asked you to help him get Windows 8 running on his workstation without disturbing any of his work files. What are your options for helping Mike?

   A. Provide Mike with a new workstation running Windows 8.

   B. Create a Windows To Go instance and let Mike carry it with him.

   C. Configure Windows 8 to boot from a VHD and install the VHD on Mike's workstation.

   D. Create a new partition on Mike's computer to install Windows 8.

2. Users in the development group complain that when they start their computers, they are taken right into Windows 7 and cannot see any options to start into the new VHDs that you created previously. What might be the cause of the problem? (Choose all that apply.)

   A. The start configuration has not been modified to enable the computer to use the VHD as a startup device.

   B. The VHD is not installed in the correct location.

   C. The file needed carries a .vmdk file extension, so the VHD will not work correctly.

   D. The timeout settings for the startup menu are set to zero to hide any options at startup and immediately select the default choice.

3. Seth, a trainer for your organization, uses several VHD files so his laptop can start different Windows environments for the training he is performing. When he returns to the office after the latest training session, he mentions that some of the VHD files no longer work. He has been trying to determine the cause of the problem all day and is looking for help removing the unusable VHD files to copy them back to his computer. How can you help Seth remove the VHD files with the least amount of administrative effort?

   A. Use DiskPart on the computer to detach and delete the unusable files.

   B. Delete the files in File Explorer.

   C. Copy new VHD files over the corrupted versions.

   D. Work with Seth to place the VHD files on a removable disk so they can be completely separated from the computer.

Practice exercises

In these practice exercises, you install Windows 8 on a new computer and build a new installation of the operating system.

Exercise 1: Install Windows 8

In this exercise, you install Windows 8 on a new computer (or into a new virtual machine). To complete this exercise, perform the following steps:

1. Insert the Windows 8 media.

2. Select language and keyboard settings for your region.

3. Tap or click Install Now.

4. Enter your product key.

5. Agree to the terms of the license agreement.

   Question: Which option should you select for type of installation when performing a fresh installation?

   Answer: Custom: Install Windows Only (advanced)

6. Choose the correct installation type.

7. Select the disk or partition on which you will install Windows.

8. Tap or click Next to complete the information-gathering portion of the installation.

   The installation begins. Several restarts can occur during this time.

9. Enter a name for your Windows 8–based computer.

10. Select a theme for your system.

11. Choose Express Settings or choose to customize the default settings for updates, file sharing, and other settings.

12. Begin using Windows 8.

Exercise 2: Configure Windows 8 to start from a VHD

In this exercise, you install Windows 8 into a VHD and start the system from this file. To complete this exercise, perform the following steps:

1. Insert the Windows 8 media.

2. Restart your computer and start from the Windows 8 media.

3. On the first setup screen, press Shift+F10.

4. Start DiskPart from the command prompt.

5. List the disks available in the system.

6. Select the internal hard disk of the computer.

7. List the volumes available on the selected hard disk.

8. Select the volume to use in creating the VHD.

> *NOTE* **IDENTIFYING THE VOLUME**
>
> **This will be the approximate size of the hard disk listed as installed on your computer.**

9. Using the Create VDisk command, create a new VHD file called **c:\VHDs\windows8.vhd**. Specify a fixed size or a maximum of 60 GB for the VHD.

10. Use the Select VDisk command to select the newly created VHD.

11. Attach the VHD.

12. Exit DiskPart and then exit the command prompt.

13. Install Windows 8 Release Preview, using the new VHD as the target disk.

 Quick check

- **How will you know whether your system is booting from the correct VHD after the installation completes?**

Quick check answer

- **The Windows boot menu displays a VHD icon next to the name of the operating system that is loaded on a VHD. If there are multiple installations on VHD files, the path to the VHD is included with the selection.**

Exercise 3: Set up a Windows To Go workspace

To complete this exercise, you need USB media with at least 32 GB of space. The device will be formatted during the process, so there should be no important data on the disk. To complete this exercise, perform the following steps:

1. Insert the USB drive to contain the Windows To Go workspace.

2. Select Windows To Go from the Control Panel.

3. Select the Windows To Go target media when it is detected by the wizard.

4. Insert the Windows 8 installation media and select Add Another Search Location to select the location of the source. Select the Windows 8 operating system the wizard found.

5. Tap or click Next.

6. Decide whether BitLocker should be enabled and tap or click Next or Skip as appropriate.

7. Wait for installation to complete.

8. Select the option to restart the computer using Windows To Go as soon as the wizard completes or not to restart the computer when the wizard completes, and tap or click Finish.

When these steps are completed, your Windows To Go installation process is finished, and you can begin using it on other hardware.

Suggested practice exercises

The following additional practices are designed to give you more opportunities to work on what you've learned and to help you successfully master the lessons presented in this chapter. Because Windows 8 functions efficiently on VHDs, creating a Windows installation on a VHD will provide skills to help you use the new operating system in your environment.

- **Exercise 1**   Install Windows 8 to a VHD, using DiskPart to create and configure the VHD, and using DISM to prepare Windows 8 on the VHD. Make sure the new environment can start up.

- **Exercise 2**   Upgrade from Windows XP to Windows 8, using a fresh installation of Windows 8 and user state migration. If you have access to an old computer that won't run Windows 7 and has a fair amount of user data on it, this might be a great way to test migrating from Windows XP to Windows 8.

Answers

This section contains the answers to the lesson review questions in this chapter.

Lesson 1

1. **Correct answer: B and C**

    A. **Incorrect:** Windows To Go cannot be run from a CD or DVD because these media types cannot be written to during processing.

    B. **Correct:** Windows To Go can be used from a removable hard drive and from other types of removable media.

    C. **Correct:** Windows To Go can be run from USB flash media of a large enough size; it can also be run from other types of USB removable media.

    D. **Incorrect:** Windows To Go cannot be run from a CD or DVD because these media types cannot be written to during processing.

2. **Correct answer: D**

    A. **Incorrect:** A Microsoft account can be used to log on in non-domain environments.

    B. **Incorrect:** User ID and password combinations can be used, but they are not the only credentials allowed.

    C. **Incorrect:** Domain-based credentials work only if the system is part of an Active Directory (or other) domain.

    D. **Correct:** All these methods can be used to authenticate on a Windows 8 system.

3. **Correct answers: A and D**

    A. **Correct:** Sleep and Hibernation features are disabled in Windows To Go.

    B. **Incorrect:** Device drivers must be downloaded each time Windows To Go uses new hardware for the first time.

    C. **Incorrect:** Windows To Go can install drivers for and use CD ROM/DVD ROM devices.

    D. **Correct:** Internal disks used by the computers hosting the Windows To Go environment will not be available for use.

Lesson 2

1. **Correct answer: A**

    A. **Correct:** Upgrading from Windows 7 to Windows 8 will preserve applications, Windows Settings, and User profiles and documents.

    B. **Incorrect:** Upgrading from Windows 7 to Windows 8 will preserve Windows settings and user data, but it also keeps applications.

C. **Incorrect:** User accounts and files will be preserved in addition to other information during the upgrade.

D. **Incorrect:** When migrating information from older operating systems to Windows 8, it is possible that only user accounts will be migrated: however, information stored within the profile is also migrated.

2. **Correct answer: A**

A. **Correct:** The hardware in your computer must be able to run Windows 8 before it will allow an upgrade.

B. **Incorrect:** The DVD drive is necessary only if the media is a DVD. Other media types can be used if there is no DVD.

C. **Incorrect:** Backups might rescue a system in the event of a problem but are not explicitly required for the upgrade to work.

D. **Incorrect:** If the hardware on a computer is not compatible with Windows 8, there is no reason to be concerned with application performance because an upgrade will not work as expected.

3. **Correct answer: B**

A. **Incorrect:** Although trying another PC might work, it is unlikely this computer will behave differently with no changes to the command string.

B. **Correct:** Log files for USMT are informative and can pinpoint issues locating the stored folder right away.

C. **Incorrect:** Having to tell a coworker that all his or her information is gone should always be a last resort. If there are issues with the utility, the information contained in the file is likely to be fine.

D. **Incorrect:** Because there may be other problems with the execution of LoadState, the user account permissions set should be examined first. This might point to problems with the files stored on the disk.

4. **Correct answer: C**

A. **Incorrect:** Because your team member browsed to the share to ensure the file was visible, this confirms that the share is online.

B. **Incorrect:** The command used includes the /i:miguser.xml template.

C. **Correct:** Because the LoadState application is expecting \\servername \sharedfolder to contain \USMT\file.mig without the \USMT folder, the operation will not succeed.

D. **Incorrect:** Migration files can have any name desired as long as they contain the .mig file extension.

Lesson 3

1. **Correct answer: C**

   A. **Incorrect:** Mike wants to use his existing hardware and not receive new gear for this project.

   B. **Incorrect:** Windows To Go would achieve a similar result, but because Mike uses his workstation only for coding, this option is unnecessary.

   C. **Correct:** If Mike wants to have a startup environment alongside the normal Windows 7 environment on his workstation, this achieves that goal.

   D. **Incorrect:** Configuring a new partition for Windows 8 on Mike's computer will allow dual booting, which will allow him to work with the new operating system, but creating another partition on disk that is in use could cause data loss.

2. **Correct answer: A**

   A. **Correct:** If the Boot.ini file is not updated with all startup volumes, the unlisted volumes will not start. Using the Boot Configuration Data Editor to modify these settings to add the Windows 8 VHD instance should get things moving again.

   B. **Incorrect:** The VHD presence has already been verified, but its presence does not ensure that it will start.

   C. **Incorrect:** VMDK files are used by a third-party hypervisor to store information for virtual machines.

   D. **Correct:** Modifying the default timeout value of 30 seconds would cause the computer to start the default operating system immediately.

3. **Correct answer A**

   A. **Correct:** Using DiskPart on the computer to detach and delete the unusable files will ensure that there are no problems deleting VHDs for being in use by the computer.

   B. **Incorrect:** Deleting these files likely needs to be done, but the files should be detached before being deleted to avoid problems if the files are in use.

   C. **Incorrect:** If the file is in use, Windows might not be able to copy a file over the original.

   D. **Incorrect:** Storing VHD files on external hardware might decrease their performance, depending on the speed of the drive. Seth should keep backup copies of the VHDs on removable media, however, to guard against losing information.

CHAPTER 3

Handling hardware and device drivers

Hardware and software are linked. Windows 8 is an operating system that unlocks the power of hardware; it's the hardware that people manipulate to do their work. This chapter discusses the components that enable hardware devices in Windows 8.

Some of the lessons in this chapter assume that, as an enterprise IT pro, you are already familiar with how to use Group Policy. This book does not go into detail about how to create Group Policy, but it does provide guidance on how administrators can use individual Group Policy settings to accomplish goals across the organization.

Lessons in this chapter:

Before you begin

To complete the practice exercises in this chapter, you will need:

- A USB device

Lesson 1: Managing drivers

Drivers are the software components that enable hardware to work in Microsoft Windows; device drivers enable communication between the operating system and hardware devices.

Remember these facts as you work with device drivers:

- Drivers are just software components.
- Not all drivers are created equal.
- Driver issues can be a support difficulty.
- Poorly written drivers can create system instability.

As an IT administrator in the enterprise, you will have to deal with installing hardware, updating driver software, and troubleshooting driver-related hardware issues.

After this lesson, you will be able to:

- Effectively use Device Manager to troubleshoot driver issues.
- Understand the purpose of the Driver Verifier utility and how to use it.
- Gather information from System Information to aid in troubleshooting.
- Update driver software to enable new features and close security holes.

Estimated lesson time: 60 minutes

Driver installation methods

Drivers can be added to a Windows system in a number of ways. The most common method is through the installation of Windows 8. During installation, drivers are installed for all the devices that are present.

- **Windows Update** In some cases, new drivers are installed or updated through regular Windows updates. As new drivers become available—particularly from Microsoft—they are delivered through the Windows Update process.

- **Hardware installation disc** Many devices ship with a hardware installation CD that includes all the drivers and software necessary to enable the device to operate. Just place the installation media into the CD-ROM drive of the computer and follow the installation instructions that came with the device.

    In some cases, device installation instructions require you to run the installation CD before you install the hardware so that the drivers are ready when the device is ultimately installed.

- **Internet download** As the age of the optical drive comes to an end, most companies also make driver and software downloads, which replace the antiquated CD, available on their websites. However, downloads are just new media for a new century. Otherwise, the installation process is the same as it is when using an installation disc.

- **Pre-staging drivers** In many organizations, administrators pre-stage drivers by installing all the drivers that someone might need before deploying a new computer. You learn more about pre-staging drivers in this chapter in the "Adding device drivers to the Driver Store" section.

Driver types

Two kinds of drivers are available: signed and unsigned. A signed driver carries with it a digital signature that verifies the publisher of the driver and ensures that the driver file has not undergone unauthorized modification, so it is less likely that someone has added malicious code to the driver file that could compromise the security of the system.

> **IMPORTANT DRIVER SIGNING IS NOT A CURE-ALL**
>
> Although driver signing improves the overall security of the system, it's important to remember that driver signing alone will not fix every security issue. It's still possible for bad code to be introduced in a driver before the signing process or for an unauthorized entity to attain access to driver signing. Either way, use caution, even with signed drivers.

An unsigned driver does not carry any guarantee that the company that issued it is legitimate, and there is no guarantee that the driver file has not been tampered with. Unsigned drivers are more likely to carry a driver file containing malware or be untrustworthy.

Remember that user-mode device drivers operate at a high level in the operating system with user rights. Kernel-mode drivers can create a major security issue.

You can use the Sigverif.exe utility to determine whether the files and drivers on a computer have been signed. To use Sigverif.exe, type **sigverif.exe** at a command prompt to open the Signature Verifier utility. Click Start to begin the scanning process. The utility displays the scanning progress, as shown in Figure 3-1.

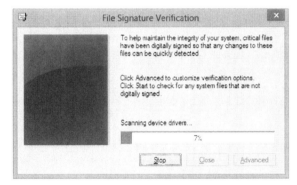

FIGURE 3-1 The File Signature Verification process

Using Device Manager

In Windows 8, Device Manager is the utility that manages driver software, which includes updating and configuring drivers. If you've used Device Manager in previous versions of Windows, you will already be familiar with Device Manager as it appears in Windows 8. If you're new to managing hardware and drivers in Windows, this section introduces you to Device Manager.

> **IMPORTANT** **WINDOWS 8 AND WINDOWS RT ARE MANAGED DIFFERENTLY**
>
> This chapter discusses managing a full Windows 8 installation on x86 hardware. Devices that use Windows RT are not managed by using the techniques described here. Instead, those devices are managed by using an upcoming version of Windows InTune or by using System Center 2012 Configuration Manager Service Pack 1. These services are expected to be available soon.

Opening Device Manager

You can open Device Manager in Windows 8 in a number of ways. The first method involves using the hotspot in the lower-left corner of the desktop. When you move your mouse pointer to that location or tap it, a small representation of the Start screen appears, as shown in Figure 3-2.

FIGURE 3-2 The hotspot in the lower-left corner of the desktop

On this miniature rendition of the Start screen, right-click or tap and hold to open the Power Users menu shown in Figure 3-3. The Device Manager tool appears on this menu.

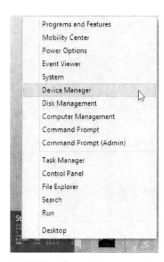

FIGURE 3-3 Power Users menu to access Device Manager

You can also open Device Manager by selecting the Settings charm from the Windows desktop and then selecting Control Panel. When Control Panel opens, start typing **Device Manager** in the Search box. Any items in Control Panel that match what you've typed will be displayed. In Figure 3-4, you can see that one of the first items that appears is Device Manager. To open it, click or tap Device Manager.

FIGURE 3-4 Opening Device Manager from Control Panel

A third way to open Device Manager is to open a command prompt and run the **devmgmt.msc** command. A fourth way is to open the Power Users menu, tap or click Run, type **devmgmt.msc**, and then tap or click OK.

When you have opened Device Manager, you can perform a number of device-related and driver-related tasks, including the following:

- Viewing the status of a device
- Finding the version of a particular driver
- Updating a driver
- Reinstalling a driver
- Rolling back a driver to a previous version
- Enabling or disabling a device

You learn about these actions in this chapter.

Viewing device and driver information

The Device Manager window (Figure 3-5) is organized in a tree view with the computer name at the top of the window and individual device categories nested beneath.

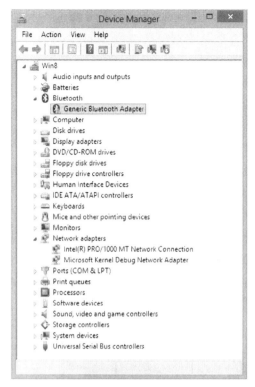

FIGURE 3-5 Device Manager in Windows 8

To view the details about a particular device, expand the appropriate hardware node and double-click or double-tap the device. This opens the Properties page for the device, like the one shown in Figure 3-6. There are several tabs; the tabs that you see depend on the particular device you open. The common tabs are as follows:

- General
- Advanced
- Driver
- Details
- Events

THE GENERAL TAB

The General tab provides you with a quick overview of the device, which includes the current status of the selected device. In Figure 3-6, you can see that this particular device is not functional because Windows automatically stopped the device due to too many errors.

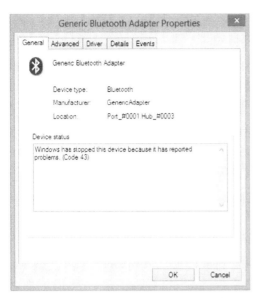

FIGURE 3-6 Properties for a failing Bluetooth device

THE ADVANCED TAB

Jumbo Packet in this configuration refers to the adopted standard Jumbo Frames technology. See this URL for more information: *http://www.ethernetalliance.org/wp-content/uploads /2011/10/EA-Ethernet-Jumbo-Frames-v0-1.pdf.*

If there are advanced configurable properties for the device, they appear on the Advanced tab, as shown in Figure 3-7. For the network adapter shown in this figure, there are advanced settings that control exactly how the device will behave on the network. In this case, Jumbo Packet is disabled. To enable it, select Enabled from the Value drop-down list. Available values change to whatever is appropriate for the selected property.

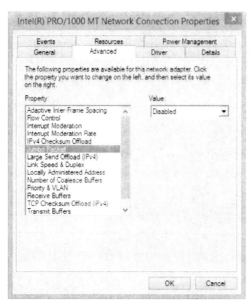

FIGURE 3-7 The Advanced tab in the Properties page for a network adapter

THE DRIVER TAB

The Driver tab includes all the items necessary to fully manage the driver software for the selected device. You learn more about this tab in the "Managing drivers" section later in this chapter.

THE DETAILS TAB

You find information about the hardware on the Details tab. Every hardware device has information associated with it. There can be just a little information or quite a lot of information.

THE EVENTS TAB

The Events tab provides you with a list of system events associated with the device. In Figure 3-8, three events associated with the Bluetooth adapter have taken place. By clicking the View All Events button in this window, the Event Viewer opens and displays the events in context with other system operations. Not every device has an Events tab.

FIGURE 3-8 The Events tab for the Bluetooth adapter

THE RESOURCES TAB

Early in the days of information technology (pre–Windows 95), technology professionals had to configure each component's resource settings manually to ensure that there were no resource conflicts and that all devices had the resources they needed to operate. In Figure 3-9, you can see the resources the hardware device is using.

FIGURE 3-9 Resources in use by the selected device

The resource types include Memory Range, I/O Range, and IRQ.

- Most devices require some memory. The Memory Range setting on the Resources tab identifies the memory location the hardware device is using.

- The I/O Range setting is reserved and helps the hardware device communicate with the system.

- The IRQ stetting is for the *Interrupt Request line (IRQ)*. A system has a predefined number of IRQs available. An IRQ provides a device that can interrupt system operations to service the needs of the configured hardware device.

If it is necessary to change a device's default configuration, clear the Use Automatic Settings check box and tap or click Change Setting; you can then provide new information for the device.

> **REAL WORLD** **THE DEFAULT DEVICE CONFIGURATION IS ALMOST ALWAYS FINE**
>
> Although there was a day when administrators manually modified all the settings you just learned about, those days are all but over. In almost every situation, devices are added to Windows with a default configuration that just works. Today's systems have evolved to a point that resource assignments are usually automatic. However, for troubleshooting purposes, you should have at least a basic understanding of these items in the event that you do find a system that is experiencing some kind of conflict requiring manual resolution.

Managing drivers

You can manage the power of some devices to reduce the amount of electricity they use. This can lower power bills and is especially useful for extending the battery life of a portable device. In Figure 3-10, note that there is an Allow The Computer To Turn Off This Device To Save Power check box. Clear the check box to prevent the system from turning off this device.

At times, the computer will go to sleep but can be awakened through various means such as opening a laptop lid or pressing the power button or a key on the keyboard. For devices that can wake up the computer to perform operations, the Allow This Device To Wake The Computer check box can also be selected.

FIGURE 3-10 Power management configuration for the network adapter

As mentioned previously, the Driver tab (Figure 3-11) contains a number of options for managing the drivers associated with a device. On this tab, you can get some details about the driver in use, including the name of the company that provided the driver, the date that the driver was last updated, the driver version, and the name of the company that digitally signed the driver.

Perhaps the most important details here are the driver provider and driver version data. When you're troubleshooting an issue related to hardware, you will want to ensure that you're using the latest drivers that are available for the device. This is generally considered the first troubleshooting step for hardware problems.

FIGURE 3-11 Driver information for the Bluetooth adapter

A number of options are available on the Driver tab, but this section focuses on just three. The Disable and Uninstall options are self-explanatory.

DRIVER DETAILS

Select Driver Details to display information about the driver associated with the currently selected device. Like the Driver tab, this informational page displays the driver version. It also shows you all the files that are associated with the driver. In Figure 3-12, you can see that the Bluetooth adapter has three files associated with it.

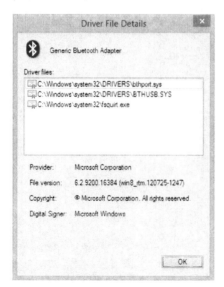

FIGURE 3-12 File information for the selected driver

UPDATE DRIVER

You learned that a first troubleshooting step is often ensuring that a device's driver files are the most current ones available. Here's how you update a driver:

1. On the Driver tab, tap or click Update Driver.

2. Decide how the driver should be updated and select one of the following options:

   - Search Automatically For Updated Driver Software   Selecting this option instructs Windows to search both your local computer and the Internet for new drivers.

   - Browse My Computer For Driver Software   If you've manually downloaded an updated driver for a hardware device, choose this option to direct Windows to the download location and install the updated driver software.

3. When you complete these steps, the new driver is installed, and the version number is updated.

> **REAL WORLD**   **DRIVER INSTALLATION PACKAGES**
>
> For some hardware, it might be necessary to use Driver Manager to install updated drivers. However, for many hardware devices, hardware vendors provide installation packages that make the driver update process a bit easier. This is especially true for graphics cards vendors such as Nvidia and BFG, who release new update packages on a regular basis. For these kinds of hardware, when you download the update package from the vendor and run the installation package, the drivers are also updated.

ROLL BACK DRIVER

As is the case with any software package, bad code or security flaws can occasionally be introduced in drivers that create system instability or that compromise system security. In these cases, you might find it necessary to revert to an earlier driver that worked.

This is the reason that the driver rollback feature exists in Device Manager on the Driver tab. If it is necessary to revert to a previous driver, Windows warns you (Figure 3-13) that you might experience problems, including reduced security and functionality. It's recommended that you roll back a driver only if you're experiencing a driver-related hardware issue.

FIGURE 3-13 Roll back a driver only if necessary

Displaying hidden devices

In some troubleshooting scenarios, you might want to display devices that the system has marked as hidden in the registry. By default, Device Manager does not display information for hidden devices.

To enable Device Manager to display devices that are marked as hidden:

1. Open Device Manager.

2. From the View menu, choose Show Hidden Devices.

In Figure 3-14, note that the Device Manager view now includes a number of additional nodes and devices that did not appear before. Although it might be difficult to see, the hidden devices are displayed in a dimmed font in the Device Manager view.

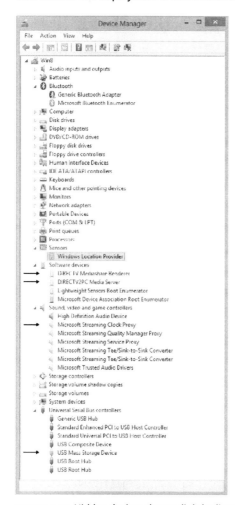

FIGURE 3-14 Hidden devices shown slightly dimmed

After you are able to view hidden devices, you can manage them as you would any other device. When you select a hidden device, you can see why the device is hidden. In Figure 3-15, note that the device is hidden from Device Manager because it's not currently connected to the computer. This is often the case for USB mass storage devices, which include portable thumb drives.

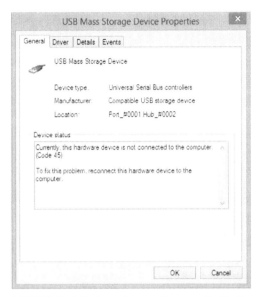

FIGURE 3-15 A device not currently connected to the computer

Using the System Information utility

The Device Manager utility provides you with a way to view and manipulate your hardware and the enabling software drivers. It's a read/write utility in that you can make changes to the system. However, that might be more than you need. Sometimes, you just need to view a lot of information all at once, even if you cannot make changes to the information. That's where the System Information utility is useful.

The System Information utility displays a plethora of information about your system that is read-only. You can't change any of the information. By using this utility, you can view details about hardware resources, system components, and the software environment.

To access the System Information utility, type **msinfo32** on the Start screen, and then tap or click the resulting entry.

Viewing conflicting or shared resources

With Device Manager, identifying resource conflicts or identifying devices that are sharing resources requires you to open details for every device. In the System Information utility, identifying these situations is as easy as selecting System Summary, Hardware Resources, and then Conflicts/Sharing. As you can see in Figure 3-16, the System Information utility makes it easier to see this information.

FIGURE 3-16 Viewing resource sharing and conflict information

Note that resource sharing and conflicts are not necessarily bad things. A number of years ago, administrators had to make sure that resource sharing never occurred, but modern systems use limited system resources much more efficiently by sharing these resources when it makes sense to do so.

System Information highlights

So much information is available in this utility that it's not possible to show everything in just a few pages. Take the time to review the System Information utility and get familiar with it. It contains a lot of information that you will find useful. Highlights of the utility are shown in Table 3-1.

TABLE 3-1 The System Information utility

Path	Description
Components, Network, Adapter	Displays a list of all the network adapters installed in the system along with all the configuration information related to each adapter, including IP address, DHCP lease information, adapter model, and MAC address
Components, Problem Devices	Displays a list of the devices that are currently experiencing some kind of problem and that need attention

Path	Description
Software Environment, Network Connections	Displays a list of network resources to which the local system is connected
Software Environment, Running Tasks	Displays a list of all running tasks along with the full path to the related executable, the process ID, software version, and size
Software Environment, Environment Variables	Displays a list of all the environment variables that have been created on the system

Discovering the Driver Verifier utility

Starting with Windows 2000, Windows has included a Driver Verifier utility intended for use by advanced users in troubleshooting particularly vexing driver-related issues. The Driver Verifier utility helps determine root cause for driver-related issues, including problems related to:

- Drivers that experience memory-based issues
- Poorly written drivers
- Drivers that cause the system to fail

> **IMPORTANT POTENTIAL PERFORMANCE ISSUES**
>
> The Driver Verifier utility can create system instability and performance issues. Use this tool with care and only after fully reviewing the documentation so that you are confident that you understand what is happening. The system is likely to fail more often while the Driver Verifier utility is collecting information and generating dump files that can be analyzed later.

Initializing a new Driver Verifier configuration requires you to restart your system for the configuration changes to take effect.

Table 3-2 lists the standard tests the Driver Verifier utility can perform.

TABLE 3-2 Standard tests

Test	Description
Special pool	When activated, selected driver memory is pulled from a special pool, which is monitored for memory overruns, memory underruns, and memory that is accessed after it is freed.
Pool tracking	A method for detecting memory leaks. Ensures that a driver returns all its memory after it is unloaded.
Force IRQL checking	Places a driver under pressure in an attempt to make the driver access paged memory at the wrong IRQL. (Interrupt Request Level is the priority of an interrupt request.)
I/O verification	Monitors the way a driver handles I/O to detect illegal or inconsistent use of I/O routines.

Test	Description
Deadlock detection	Detects whether the driver has the potential to cause a deadlock. A deadlock occurs when two or more threads conflict over a resource, thwarting execution.
DMA checking	Detects a driver's improper use of Direct Memory Access (DMA) buffers, adapters, and map registers.
Security checks	Enables Driver Verifier to look for common situations that can result in driver-based security vulnerabilities.
Force pending I/O requests	Ensures that pending I/O requests are handled.
Low resources simulation	Tests a driver's ability to cope with low-resource situations, which can create resource contention issues.
IRP logging	Monitors a driver's use of IRPs (I/O request packets).
Miscellaneous checks	Many common items create driver instability. This category catches these common items.
Invariant MDL checking for stack	Monitors how the driver handles invariant MDL buffers across the driver stack.
Invariant MDL checking for driver	Monitors how the driver handles invariant MDL buffers per driver.
Power framework delay fuzzing	Helps identify driver errors for drivers that use the system's power framework.
DDI compliance checking	Determines whether the driver interacts correctly with the Windows kernel.

You can use the Driver Verifier utility in one of two ways. If you want to use the tool from a command line, type **verifier** followed by a valid verifier command. If you want to use a GUI-based version of the tool, type **verifier** from a command line. In this section, you learn about the GUI-based tool.

1. At a command prompt, type **verifier** to open the Driver Verifier Manager (GUI-based tool), as shown in Figure 3-17.

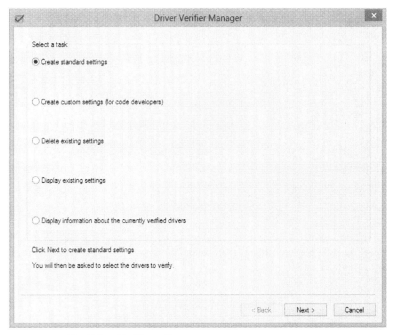

FIGURE 3-17 The Driver Verifier utility

The available tasks are:

- **Create Standard Settings** This task selects a standard set of options and then asks you to select the drivers that are to be verified.
- **Create Custom Settings** With this task, you choose the Driver Verifier tests that should be run against the drivers you choose.
- **Delete Existing Settings** This task deactivates any Driver Verifier settings that are in place. It's important to remember that Driver Verifier settings remain in place until you actively delete them.
- **Display Existing Settings** This task displays the settings that will be activated and the list of drivers that will be affected.
- **Display Information About The Currently Verified Drivers** This task displays information about the actions Driver Verifier is performing.

2. Select the Create Standard Settings option and tap or click Next. The Driver Verifier Manager displays the page, shown in Figure 3-18, on which you identify which drivers you want to verify.

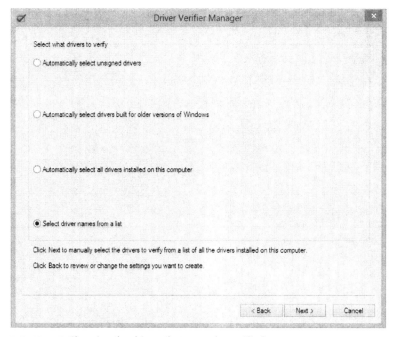

FIGURE 3-18 Choosing the drivers that are to be verified

3. Select the Select Driver Names From A List option and tap or click Next. Driver Verifier Manager displays the page shown in Figure 3-19.

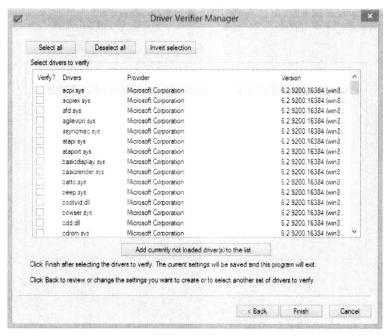

FIGURE 3-19 Selecting the drivers that are to be verified

4. Select the drivers you want to verify and then tap or click Finish.

5. You will probably have to restart your system. After the computer restarts, load the Driver Verifier GUI again. Choose Display Information About The Currently Verified Drivers and click Next. Driver Verifier Manager presents the current settings and verified drivers, including the status of every driver, as shown in Figure 3-20.

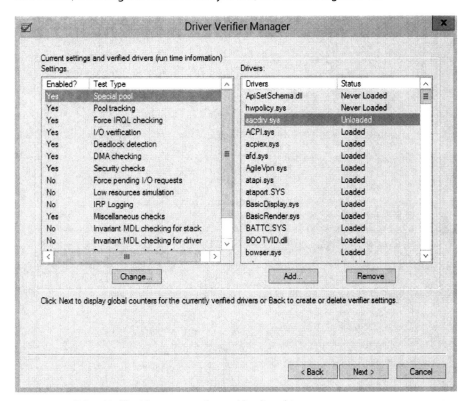

FIGURE 3-20 Driver Verifier Manager running and loading drivers

6. To view the global counter information for the verified drivers, click Next to see the global counter information, as shown in Figure 3-21.

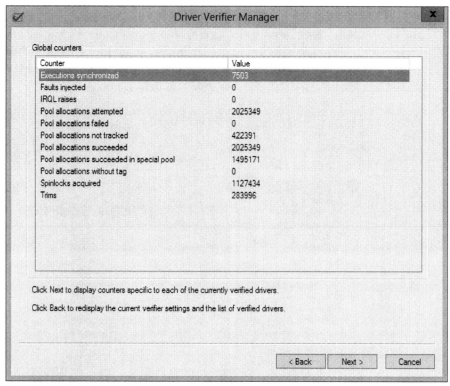

FIGURE 3-21 The Driver Verifier Manager global counters page

7. Click Next to move to the page, shown in Figure 3-22, on which you can select an individual driver to view its specific information. In Figure 3-22, the NDIS.SYS driver—which is linked to the networking component—is the selected driver, and its counter information is displayed.

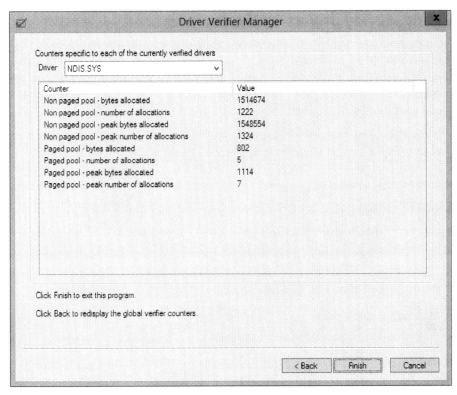

FIGURE 3-22 Driver Verifier Manager details for NDIS.SYS

8. Click Finish.

MORE INFO **DRIVER VERIFIER UTILITY FACTS**

To learn more about the Driver Verifier utility, review these resources, which go into great detail about how this utility operates and how to interpret the results:

- *http://support.microsoft.com/kb/244617*
- *http://msdn.microsoft.com/en-us/library/windows/hardware/ff545470(v=vs.85).aspx*

Make sure you understand that the driver utility only helps you track down a problem, not necessarily resolve it. Most driver issues identified by the driver utility must be rewritten to be fixed. Because you probably won't have the source code for the driver, you must work with the vendor to fix the driver, download a new driver, or use a different hardware device.

Adding device drivers to the driver store

In an enterprise environment, it can be important to preinstall drivers on a computer before deploying it in the organization. It's not uncommon for desktop administrators to make sure that all the drivers that a user would need are preloaded on the system. By doing so, when a user plugs in a supported device, the drivers are available and the device works for the user without any difficulty.

Windows includes a command-line tool called Pnputil.exe which you use to manage the driver store with a number of parameters, listed in Table 3-3.

TABLE 3-3 Pnputil.exe parameters

Parameter	Description
pnputil -a	Adds a driver package to the driver store.
pnputil -i	(Used with -a) If the driver matches any existing hardware devices on the system, the driver software will be installed.
pnputil -e	Shows you a list of third-party drivers currently loaded in the driver store.
pnputil -d	Deletes a package from the driver store.
pnputil -f	(Used with -d) Forces the deletion of a package from the driver store. The parameter is required when a driver you want to delete is associated with a device that is still connected to the system.

Sample commands:

- **pnputil -a c:\NewDriver.inf**   Loads the NewDriver.inf driver located in C drive into the driver store.

- **pnputil -d oem3.inf**   On the sample system used for this chapter, removes the driver associated with the VMware ThinPrint service.

- **pnputil -e**   Shows you a list of the third-party drivers currently loaded on the system (Figure 3-23).

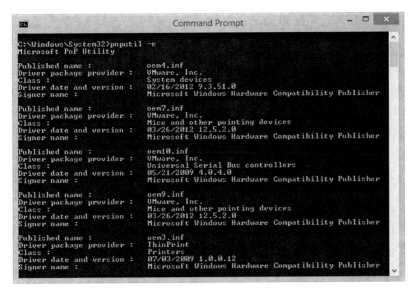

FIGURE 3-23 A list of the third-party drivers loaded on the system

Lesson summary

■ Drivers are the software glue that connects the operating system to the hardware devices.

■ The Device Manager tool is used to manage all aspects of driver software in Windows 8.

■ The Driver Verifier utility helps pinpoint potential driver issues that could be causing system instability.

■ By adding drivers to the Driver Store, you can help employees more easily add new devices to their computers.

■ You might have to roll back a driver to a previous version if a newer driver is unstable.

Lesson review

Answer the following questions to test your knowledge of the information in this lesson. You can find the answers to these questions and explanations of why each answer choice is correct or incorrect in the "Answers" section at the end of this chapter.

1. Which tool provides you with read-only access to a variety of system information elements?

   A. Device Manager

   B. Driver Verifier

C. System Information

D. Computer Management

2. How do you enable the viewing of hidden devices?

   A. In View, choose Hidden Devices in Driver Verifier.

   B. Open Device Manager, choose View, and then select Show Hidden Devices.

   C. Right-click a device category and choose Show Hidden Devices.

   D. Open System Information and navigate to the Hidden Devices node.

3. Which of these methods does not update drivers?

   A. Driver Verifier

   B. Windows Update

   C. Driver pre-staging

   D. Internet download

Lesson 2: Managing hardware devices

Drivers are the software that binds the operating system to the hardware connected to the system. Drivers bring you to the focus of this chapter, which is the hardware.

After this lesson, you will be able to:

- Enable and disable hardware devices by using Device Manager.
- Monitor the amount of power USB devices use.

Estimated lesson time: 20 minutes

Enabling and disabling hardware devices

Not all hardware has to be enabled all the time. In fact, as you work on troubleshooting hardware in your organization, you might find it necessary to disable a device if it is causing problems. Then, after you correct a problem, you must bring the device back into operation.

To disable and enable devices, open the Device Manager by using one of the methods discussed previously in this chapter. Open the Properties page for the device you want to enable or disable and navigate to the Driver tab. From there, click either the Disable button (if the device is presently enabled) or the Enable button (if the device is presently disabled).

In Figure 3-24, note that the Disable button is currently available.

FIGURE 3-24 Disabling devices that are causing problems

Monitoring USB devices

Most devices that employees in your organization attach to their computers are USB-based. Such devices include keyboards, mice, cameras, and thumb drives. USB is so popular because it's so easy to use. In many cases, all you have to do is plug in the device, and it just works. This is for two reasons. First, many common devices already have generic drivers loaded in Windows. When the device is plugged in, Windows already knows how to handle the hardware. Second, USB ports, in addition to enabling communication between the device and the computer, also provide power to the connected device. That's why you don't need to plug a thumb drive into a power source when you connect it to the computer.

Although some of the devices you use are connected directly to USB ports in the computer, others might be connected through a USB hub. There are two varieties of USB hubs:

- **Self-powered** A self-powered USB hub has a power supply that connects to an electrical outlet. These kinds of USB hubs provide their own power to connected devices.

- **Bus-powered** A bus-powered USB hub gets its power from the system's USB connectors and passes along that power to connected devices. The amount of available power in this scenario is more limited than it is with self-powered hubs.

USB devices can operate at multiple speeds, and each speed is based on a different USB standard. Different devices conform to different standards. Modern computers often include USB ports that operate at multiple speeds. For example, a single computer might include ports that operate at both USB 2.0 and USB 3.0 speeds. Here's a look at the different standards and the speeds at which each operates:

- **USB 1.0/USB 1.1**   Operates at a maximum speed of 12 megabits per second (Mbps)
- **USB 2.0**   Operates at a maximum speed of 480 Mbps
- **USB 3.0**   Operates at a maximum speed of 5 gigabits per second (Gbps)

Bandwidth is an important factor in USB troubleshooting, particularly when you're dealing with older USB 1.0 or USB 1.1 systems. If there isn't sufficient bandwidth to support the devices on a particular USB port, users can receive error messages such as "USB controller bandwidth exceeded." When this happens, devices might not operate correctly.

Many devices will report to Windows the amount of bandwidth they use on the Advanced tab of the device's Properties page in Device Manager. However, this is not true for all devices. This makes troubleshooting bandwidth issues a best-effort task rather than a scientific one. Fortunately, with the rise of USB 3.0 and a maximum bandwidth of 5 GHz, bandwidth issues are not as serious as they once were.

As mentioned previously, USB devices consume power from the USB bus. Therefore, it's important to watch the USB port's power budget to ensure that connected devices don't surpass the power limit on the port. When you use a bus-powered USB hub to connect many devices, the possibility of exceeding this limit becomes more likely.

To view the current power usage on a USB hub—even an internal one that just manages a computer's physical USB ports—open the Device Manager Properties page for a USB hub. On that page, select the Power tab to see a list of the devices connected to the hub and the power required to operate each device (Figure 3-25).

FIGURE 3-25 Hub showing a device consuming 200 mA of power

Lesson summary

- There are several versions of USB, each with its own speed limit.
- Device Manager is used to enable and disable devices.
- There are two kinds of USB hubs: bus-powered and self-powered.

Lesson review

Answer the following questions to test your knowledge of the information in this lesson. You can find the answers to these questions and explanations of why each answer choice is correct or incorrect in the "Answers" section at the end of this chapter.

1. How fast is USB 2.0?

   A. 400 Mbps

   B. 480 Mbps

   C. 12 Mbps

   D. 5 Gbps

2. Which is more important: bandwidth or power usage on USB?

   A. Bandwidth.

   B. Power.

   C. They are equally important.

   D. Neither is important.

Lesson 3: Managing enterprise hardware policies

Enterprises have stricter requirements with regard to hardware than do home computers. In the enterprise, the ramifications are far greater if information is stolen or if malware infects the organization.

After this lesson, you will be able to:

- Understand how you can prevent the installation of all removable devices.
- Describe which policies allow or prevent device installation on a granular basis.
- Describe the difference between device ID strings and device classes.
- Identify the ID string and class for a hardware device.

Estimated lesson time: 40 minutes

Managing enterprise hardware installation policies

Administrators can create organizational policies that define how devices are managed by using Group Policy. You can disable the installation of removable devices completely, or you can take a more surgical approach by allowing or preventing the installation of removable devices.

Before undertaking this effort, make sure you understand the two ways by which you can choose devices to allow or prevent such installations:

- **Device identification strings**   This is the most granular way to allow or prevent the installation of hardware devices. By using this method, you can identify specific devices to include in the policy.

- **Device setup classes**   By using device setup classes, you take a group-based approach to allow or prevent hardware devices from being installed. For example, you could prevent the installation of any device that's a scanner.

Identifying hardware strings and classes

To identify the hardware string and class for a hardware device:

1. Plug the device into a Windows-based computer.

2. Open Device Manager.

3. Open the Properties page for the newly installed device.

4. Navigate to the device's Details page.

    - Select the Hardware Ids property to view all the hardware IDs associated with the device (Figure 3-26).

    - Select the Compatible Ids property to view the device class for the new device (Figure 3-27).

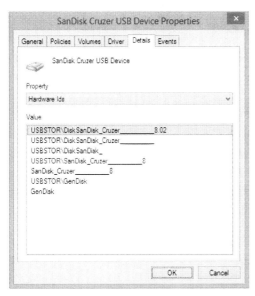

FIGURE 3-26 Hardware IDs for a USB thumb drive

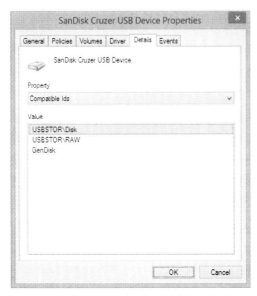

FIGURE 3-27 Compatible IDs for a USB thumb drive

Note that there are multiple options for both hardware ID and class ID. For the hardware ID, the options give you a way to be somewhat granular in how you handle devices. For example, you could choose to prevent or allow just SanDisk devices or prevent or allow just the specific device model.

To save a lot of trouble, copy and paste the hardware IDs rather than trying to type them and match the number of underscore characters. You will minimize errors this way.

Disabling installation of removable devices

High-security organizations do not generally allow the use of any removable devices on a system. To do so would enable an insider to just connect a USB thumb drive and steal corporate assets or other secrets. By using Group Policy, it's possible to disable the installation of removable devices completely. The Group Policy described in the following list will, when set, enable you to disable the installation of removable devices on as many computers in your organization as you like:

- **Policy name**   Prevent Installation Of Removable Devices.
- **Policy path**   Windows Settings, Administrative Templates, System, Device Installation, Device Installation Restrictions.
- **Policy description**   This policy setting enables you to prevent Windows from installing removable devices. A device is considered removable when its driver indicates that the device is removable. For example, a USB device is reported to be removable by the drivers for the USB hub to which the device is connected. This policy setting takes precedence over any other policy setting that allows Windows to install a device.
- **Enabled**   If you enable this policy setting, it prevents Windows from installing removable devices, and the drivers for existing removable devices cannot be updated. If you enable this policy setting on a remote desktop server, the policy setting affects redirection of removable devices from a remote desktop client to the remote desktop server.
- **Disabled or not configured**   If you disable or do not configure this policy setting, Windows can install and update device drivers for removable devices as allowed or prevented by other policy settings.

Managing installation of specific devices based on device ID or group

The ability to prevent the installation of removable devices is nice, but it is a heavy-handed approach to the problem. Other policies are available by which you can be a bit more granular in how you handle allowed and disallowed devices.

For these policies, you need to know the class of the device.

RESTRICTING DEVICE INSTALLATION BASED ON CLASS

The following Group Policy enables you to specify device classes that are not allowed to be installed in the organization:

- **Policy name**   Prevent installation of devices using drivers that match these devices' setup classes.

- **Policy path** Windows Settings, Administrative Templates, System, Device Installation, Device Installation Restrictions.

- **Policy description** This policy setting enables you to specify a list of device setup class globally unique identifiers (GUIDs) for device drivers that Windows is prevented from installing. This policy setting takes precedence over any other policy setting that allows Windows to install a device.

- **Enabled** If you enable this policy setting, Windows is prevented from installing or updating device drivers whose device setup class GUIDs appear in the list you create. If you enable this policy setting on a remote desktop server, the policy setting affects redirection of the specified devices from a remote desktop client to the remote desktop server.

- **Disabled or not configured** If you disable or do not configure this policy setting, Windows can install and update devices as allowed or prevented by other policy settings.

ALLOWING DEVICE INSTALLATION BASED ON CLASS

The following Group Policy enables you to specify device classes that are allowed to be installed in the organization. Use this policy only when you also configure the Prevent Installation Of Devices Not Described By Other Policy Settings policy setting. This policy overrides the hardware installation restrictions for any device classes you list.

- **Policy name** Prevent installation of devices using drivers that match these devices' setup classes.

- **Policy path** Windows Settings, Administrative Templates, System, Device Installation, Device Installation Restrictions.

- **Policy description** This policy setting enables you to specify a list of device setup class GUIDs for device drivers that Windows is allowed to install. Use this policy setting only when the Prevent Installation Of Devices Not Described By Other Policy Settings policy setting is enabled. Other policy settings that prevent device installation take precedence over this one.

- **Enabled** If you enable this policy setting, Windows is allowed to install or update device drivers whose device setup class GUIDs appear in the list you create unless another policy setting specifically prevents installation. (Examples are the Prevent Installation Of Devices That Match These Device IDs policy setting, the Prevent Installation Of Devices For These Device Classes policy setting, and the Prevent Installation Of Removable Devices policy setting). If you enable this policy setting on a remote desktop server, the policy setting affects redirection of the specified devices from a remote desktop client to the remote desktop server.

- **Disabled or not configured** If you disable or do not configure this policy setting, and no other policy setting describes the device, the Prevent Installation Of Devices Not Described By Other Policy Settings policy setting determines whether the device can be installed.

RESTRICTING DEVICE INSTALLATION BASED ON HARDWARE ID

The following Group Policy enables you to specify device IDs that are not allowed to be installed in the organization. You need to specify hardware IDs when enabling this policy.

- **Policy name**   Prevent installation of devices that use any of these device IDs.
- **Policy path**   Windows Settings, Administrative Templates, System, Device Installation, Device Installation Restrictions.
- **Policy description**   This policy setting enables you to specify a list of plug-and-play hardware IDs and compatible IDs for devices that Windows is prevented from installing. This policy setting takes precedence over any other policy setting that allows Windows to install a device.
- **Enabled**   If you enable this policy setting, Windows is prevented from installing a device whose hardware ID or compatible ID appears in the list you create. If you enable this policy setting on a remote desktop server, the policy setting affects redirection of the specified devices from a remote desktop client to the remote desktop server.
- **Disabled or not configured**   If you disable or do not configure this policy setting, devices can be installed and updated as allowed or prevented by other policy settings.

ALLOWING DEVICE INSTALLATION BASED ON HARDWARE ID

The following Group Policy enables you to specify device IDs that are allowed to be installed in the organization. You need to specify hardware IDs when enabling this policy.

- **Policy name**   Allow installation of devices that use any of these device IDs.
- **Policy path**   Windows Settings, Administrative Templates, System, Device Installation, Device Installation Restrictions.
- **Policy description**   This policy setting enables you to specify a list of plug-and-play hardware IDs and compatible IDs for devices that Windows is allowed to install. Use this policy setting only when the Prevent Installation Of Devices Not Described By Other Policy Settings policy setting is enabled. Other policy settings that prevent device installation take precedence over this one.
- **Enabled**   If you enable this policy setting, Windows is allowed to install or update any device whose plug-and-play hardware ID or compatible ID appears in the list you create unless another policy setting specifically prevents that installation. (Examples are the Prevent Installation Of Devices That Match Any Of These Device IDs policy setting, the Prevent Installation Of Devices For These Device Classes policy setting, and the Prevent Installation Of Removable Devices policy setting). If you enable this policy setting on a remote desktop server, the policy setting affects redirection of the specified devices from a remote desktop client to the remote desktop server.
- **Disabled or not configured**   If you disable or do not configure this policy setting, and no other policy setting describes the device, the Prevent Installation Of Devices Not Described By Other Policy Settings policy setting determines whether the device can be installed.

Creating an administrative override for device installation

As an administrator, it might be necessary to install a device that is generally restricted in the organization. To accomplish this goal, use the following policy settings:

- **Policy name** Allow administrators to override Device Installation Restriction policies.
- **Policy path** Windows Settings, Administrative Templates, System, Device Installation, Device Installation Restrictions.
- **Policy description** This policy setting enables you to determine whether members of the Administrators group can install and update the drivers for any device regardless of other policy settings.
- **Enabled** If you enable this policy setting, members of the Administrators group can use the Add Hardware Wizard or the Update Driver Wizard to install and update the drivers for any device. If you enable this policy setting on a remote desktop server, the policy setting affects redirection of the specified devices from a remote desktop client to the remote desktop server.
- **Disabled or not configured** If you disable or do not configure this policy setting, members of the Administrators group are subject to all policy settings that restrict device installation.

> *MORE INFO* **CONTROLLING DEVICE INSTALLATION BY USING GROUP POLICY**
>
> Microsoft has created a resource entitled *Step-By-Step Guide to Controlling Device Installation Using Group Policy*, which provides in-depth information about how to use the various Group Policy objects to control hardware installation in an organization better. It's an invaluable resource for any administrator who wants to implement granular controls over hardware devices; find it at *http://msdn.microsoft.com/en-us/library/bb530324.aspx*.

Lesson summary

- Hardware strings enable you to be as inclusive or as granular as you like when you must allow or prevent the installation of hardware devices.
- By using the Allow Administrators To Override Device Installation Restriction Policies policy, you can implement restrictive policies in the organization but still leave room for special cases.
- Device setup classes are used to take a device group–based approach to hardware management.
- When you enable the Prevent Installation Of Devices Not Described By Other Policy Settings policy, you should create policies that enable specific devices to override the restriction policies.
- Group Policy provides you with an easy way to create hardware installation policies across the organization.

Lesson review

Answer the following questions to test your knowledge of the information in this lesson. You can find the answers to these questions and explanations of why each answer choice is correct or incorrect in the "Answers" section at the end of this chapter.

1. Which hardware strings could be used to restrict the installation of a hardware device with ID USBSTOR\DiskSanDisk_Cruzer_____8.02? (Choose all that apply.)

   A. USBSTOR\DiskSanDisk_Cruzer_____8.02

   B. USBSTOR\DiskSanDisk_Cruzer_____

   C. USBSTOR\DiskSanDisk_

   D. USBSTOR\SanDisk_Cruzer_____8

2. Which method will encompass and restrict the greatest number of devices?

   A. Hardware ID

   B. Class ID

   C. Device Name

   D. Device SID

3. How do you allow an administrator to install hardware even when Group Policy forbids it?

   A. Enable the Allow Administrators To Override Device Installation Restriction Group Policy.

   B. Add the Administrators group to the No Hardware Restrictions group.

   C. Add users to the local Administrators group on their PCs.

   D. Enable Admin Mode in Device Manager.

Practice exercises

In these practice exercises, you navigate from the Windows 8 Start screen to find hardware IDs and create Group Policy to allow or prevent the installation of devices.

Exercise 1: Locate hardware ID for a USB thumb drive

In this exercise, you identify the specific hardware ID for a USB thumb drive. You probably have one of these devices lying around somewhere.

1. Open Device Manager.

2. Find your device.

3. Using the device properties, find the hardware ID.

Exercise 2: Create Group Policy to prevent the installation of hardware devices

In this exercise, you create Group Policy that prevents the installation of removable devices. To complete this exercise, your Windows 8 system must be joined to a Microsoft Windows Server domain.

1. Use the Group Policy Editor on the computer running Windows Server.

2. Configure the appropriate Group Policy and test it.

Suggested practice exercises

The following additional practices are designed to give you more opportunities to practice what you've learned and to help you successfully master the lessons presented in this chapter.

*   **Exercise 1**   Practice configuring and applying Group Policy to see how each policy works.

*   **Exercise 2**   Use Driver Verifier and learn to interpret its output.

*   **Exercise 3**   Add drivers to the Driver Store.

Answers

This section contains the answers to the lesson review questions in this chapter.

Lesson 1

1. **Correct answer: C**

   A. **Incorrect:** Device Manager is a read/write tool used to manage devices and drivers.

   B. **Incorrect:** Driver Verifier locates deep-rooted driver issues.

   C. **Correct:** System Info displays general information about hardware and software configured on a computer. Information displayed is read-only.

   D. **Incorrect:** Computer Management is a general-purpose tool used to manage the system.

2. **Correct answer: B**

   A. **Incorrect:** Driver Verifier checks the installation of device drivers; it does not display hidden devices.

   B. **Correct:** The Device Manager View menu can show or hide hidden devices.

   C. **Incorrect:** Selecting a device category will expand and collapse devices within that category, but doing so does not change the hidden status of a device.

   D. **Incorrect:** There is no Hidden Devices node in System Info.

3. **Correct answer: A**

   A. **Correct:** Driver Verifier locates driver issues.

   B. **Incorrect:** Drivers can be installed by using this method.

   C. **Incorrect:** Drivers can be installed by using this method.

   D. **Incorrect:** Drivers can be installed by using this method.

Lesson 2

1. **Correct answer: B**

   A. **Incorrect:** FireWire runs at 400 Mbps, which is slower than USB 2.0.

   B. **Correct:** USB 2.0 has bandwidth typically around 480 Mbps.

   C. **Incorrect:** USB 1.1 maintained speeds of around 12 Mbps.

   D. **Incorrect:** USB 3.0 is rated at around 5 Gbps.

2. **Correct answer: C**

   A. **Incorrect:** Bandwidth issues can cause problems ensuring that a USB device has enough power to function correctly.

   B. **Incorrect:** Improperly powered USB devices can affect bandwidth and performance of the device.

   C. **Correct** Power and bandwidth are equally important in determining USB device performance because underpowered devices will suffer bandwidth performance issues.

   D. **Incorrect:** USB has two components that are typically watched, bandwidth and power, and both are equally important in determining device performance.

Lesson 3

1. **Correct answers: A, B, C, and D**

   A. **Correct:** Installation of the specific device with version 8.02 will be prevented.

   B. **Correct:** No DiskSanDisk_Cruzer device can be installed, which includes the device in question.

   C. **Correct:** No SanDisk-based device can be installed.

   D. **Correct:** No DiskSanDisk_Cruzer version 8 device can be installed, which includes the device in question.

2. **Correct answer: B**

   A. **Incorrect:** The device ID would include only this specific device.

   B. **Correct:** The class ID for a set of devices would include any devices of the same class.

   C. **Incorrect:** The device name would include only devices with the same name, much like device ID covers only a specific device.

   D. **Incorrect:** Hardware devices are not assigned a SID; these are reserved for logical objects such as user accounts or computer accounts.

3. **Correct answer: A**

   A. **Correct:** Enable the Group Policy options to allow an override.

   B. **Incorrect:** There is no group called No Hardware Restrictions for use with this feature.

   C. **Incorrect:** Adding accounts to the local Administrators group will not specifically allow this action; Group Policy options must be configured so that domain administrators can override settings.

   D. **Incorrect:** The Device Manager snap-in does not have an admin mode specific to computer hardware; the MMC console has an author mode, but that is used to manage the console.

CHAPTER 4

Installing and configuring applications

Windows 8 introduces some new things for administrators and users alike to consider when using a new operating system, some of which focus on applications. This chapter discusses Windows 8 applications from installation to management and traditional applications with installation media.

Lessons in this chapter:

Before you begin

To complete the exercises in this chapter, you need a Microsoft account to download Windows Store apps covered in Lesson 2, "Managing Windows 8 native applications."

Lesson 1: Managing traditional desktop applications

Traditionally, computer software has been delivered in many ways: by floppy disks, CD/DVD packaged media, and, in recent years, by download from the publisher's or a third party's website. These applications are still important to businesses and individuals. This lesson discusses how to work with them in Windows 8.

> **After this lesson, you will be able to:**
> - Install and uninstall traditional media-based applications in Windows 8.
> - Configure compatibility mode and file associations.
> - Manage App-V applications.
>
> **Estimated lesson time: 60 minutes**

Using Windows Installer in Windows 8

Windows 8 includes version 5.0 of *Windows Installer*, the installation and configuration utility that enables corporate IT administrators to control how software is installed, uninstalled, and managed within a Windows environment. In addition to ensuring uniform installation of applications on computers, Windows Installer can ensure that applications are installed in a specific manner.

Windows Installer is used in many environments that run Active Directory directory service with Group Policy, which enables administrators to position user and computer objects within Active Directory to apply certain settings at computer startup or when a user signs in. Among these settings, application management is included through Windows Installer.

Windows Installer 5 brings a few enhancements to previous versions of the product, including:

- The ability to configure services on a computer.

- The MSIFastInstall property, which you can use to modify the options available during installation to reduce the amount of time needed to complete the process. The available options are listed in Table 4-1.

- The MSIInstallPerUser property, which you can use to install applications for the current user or for all users on a computer during installation, either within the graphical user interface or with the command line.

TABLE 4-1 MSIFastInstall options

Value	Definition
0	Default value
1	No restore point saved for the installation
2	Perform File Costing only, skip checking other costs of installation
4	Reduce progress message frequency during installation

Running Windows Installer packages and MSIExec

Many software vendors today include a Windows Installer package for their applications to make installation easier or at least more manageable for Windows administrators. There are multiple ways to install applications by using Windows Installer, including:

- Running an application's Setup.exe file many times. The Setup.exe file is a wrapper for a Windows Installer package that is extracted and run when the file is executed.

- Creating batch files to run Windows Installer packages. By running Msiexec.exe from a batch script, you can make the execution silent or scheduled.

- Double-tapping or double-clicking the Windows Installer package file. When an MSI package is double-clicked, it executes and behaves much like any other executable setup file.

- Using Group Policy to execute a published Windows Installer package. Use this method to publish or assign applications to user accounts at sign-in or to machines at startup. The installation process is generally visible to the individual signing in, but it is not interactive.

Often, Windows administrators want applications to run silently or be minimally visible while the installation completes. Using MSIExec at the command line can help accomplish these tasks. The options available for MSIExec include:

- Installation Options
  - **/package | /I** *<path to MSI package.msi>*   Specifies the install option and the path to the package to be configured
  - **/a** *<path to MSI package.msi>*   Specifies an administrative installation, creating a product installation on a network share
  - **/j (u|m)***<path to MSI Package.msi>*   Advertises the package for installation to m: All users or u: current user
  - **/t** *<path to transform file>*   Applies preconfigured settings to the MSI package at installation
  - **;g** *<language ID>*   Allows a specific language to be installed
  - **/uninstall | /x** *<path to MSI Package.msi | Product Code>*   Uninstalls the application
- Display Options
  - **/quiet**   Silent installation, no user interaction
  - **/passive**   Unattended mode, displays only a progress bar
  - **/q n|b|f**   Sets the user interface level; n: no user interface | b: basic user interface | f: full user interface
  - **/help**   Displays help information for Windows Installer
- Restart Options
  - **/norestart**   Specifies that Windows should not restart when installation completes
  - **/promprestart**   Displays a message following installation, prompting whomever is signed in to restart the computer
  - **/forcerestart**   Restarts the computer when the installation completes
- Logging Options   Allows specification of the logging level that should be used with the install
- Update Options
  - **/update** *<update package.msp>*   Applies the specified updates to applications
  - **/Uninstall** *<Patch code GUID>:<update package.msp>* **/package** *<path to MSI Package.msi | Product Code>*   Uninstalls the specified update from the specified product
- Repair Options   Specifies options to use in repairing Windows Installer installations

✓ **Quick check**

- Which Windows Installer option prevents the user from seeing an application installation taking place?

Quick check answer

- /quiet

Managing compatibility with Application Compatibility Toolkit and App-V

Some of the applications that existed before Windows 8 might experience general compatibility issues with the new operating system. Application Compatibility Toolkit (ACT) helps resolve these issues and provides a better working experience for these applications in Windows 8.

Testing for application compatibility

Microsoft has made several changes in Windows 8 that can affect the operation of applications and software that companies are using today. To help mitigate the problems with application compatibility, ACT has been updated to help test for compatibility issues that might appear for some applications.

Virtualizing incompatible applications

 When Windows 7 was released, Microsoft unveiled *App-V*, a technology that enables individual applications to be virtualized and used within different Windows environments. When an application is configured to run as an App-V application, the operating environment for that application is captured in a virtual machine. This allows all the settings and application configuration information to remain intact so the newly virtualized copy of the application can run on systems within which it might not have originally worked.

For example, suppose an organization uses an old reporting application as part of the financial reporting that it produces on a monthly basis. The application has not been updated for several years because things have been operating smoothly. Janet, the finance manager and primary report creator for the organization, gets a new computer that runs Windows 8, and is unable to access the reporting program she uses on a regular basis. Rather than deploy a previous version of Windows to accommodate the single application that does not function in Windows 8, App-V can virtualize the reporting program so that it can be used in Windows 8.

In addition to enabling earlier applications to function on newer computers, App-V can be used to configure an application and all its settings to run inside a virtual environment and require no installation on the client computers. This helps reduce the maintenance and overhead needed to use applications within an environment.

> **MORE INFO** **APPLICATION VIRTUALIZATION AND APP-V**
>
> To learn more about Application Virtualization and App-V, visit *http://www.microsoft.com /en-us/windows/enterprise/products-and-technologies/virtualization/app-v.aspx.*

Controlling program settings for traditional applications

When an application is installed on a Windows 8–based computer, some adjustments might need to be made in the way Windows interacts with the application. Although these adjustments do not affect the general operation of the application, modifying the interaction produces a seamless experience and makes the application more pleasing to use.

Modifying the compatibility settings for an application can help it operate better with Windows 8. There are two ways to modify compatibility settings for an application:

- Using the Program Compatibility troubleshooter
- Manually adjusting compatibility settings

Using the Program Compatibility troubleshooter

To run the Program Compatibility troubleshooter for an application, complete the following steps.

1. On the Start screen, search for Program Compatibility. Tap or click Settings.
2. Select Run Programs Made For Previous Versions Of Windows.
3. Tap or click Next to begin the troubleshooter.
4. If Windows detects no problems, enter the location of the program against which to run the troubleshooter and tap or click Next.
5. After the application has gone through the troubleshooter, select from the following options:
    - **Try Recommended Settings** This option applies known settings such as the service pack compatibility level for the application.

- **Troubleshoot The Application Based On Problems Noticed** This option presents symptoms that might indicate the cause of the problem and prompts you to select one.

6. If you select to troubleshoot the application, choose one of the following:

   - The Program Worked In Earlier Versions Of Windows But Won't Install Or Run Now.
   - The Program Opens But Doesn't Display Correctly.
   - The Program Requires Additional Permissions.
   - I Don't See My Problem Listed.

7. Depending on the option selected, the questions change to help you work toward a solution.

8. When a solution is ready to test, select Test Program.

9. If the application opens and displays or operates as expected, tap or click Finish.

Manually troubleshooting compatibility

To set the compatibility options for an application manually, complete the following steps:

1. Press and hold or right-click the application.

2. Tap or click Properties.

3. Tap or click the Compatibility tab.

4. To run the application in compatibility mode for a previous version of Windows, select Run This Program In Compatibility Mode For and choose the appropriate level:

   - Windows 95
   - Windows 98/Me
   - Windows XP (Service Pack 2)
   - Windows XP (Service Pack 3)
   - Windows Vista
   - Windows Vista (Service Pack 1)
   - Windows Vista (Service Pack 2)
   - Windows 7

5. To run the application with a different color profile, select Reduced Color Mode and choose a setting:

   - 8-bit (256 Color)
   - 16-bit (65536 Color)

6. To run the application with a minimal resolution, select Run In 640x480 Screen Resolution.

7. To run the application without high DPI scaling, select Disable Display Scaling On High DPI Settings.

8. To change the privilege level for this application, select Run This Program As An Administrator.

9. If the settings should be applied for anyone who signs in to this computer to use this application, select the Change Settings For All Users button.

   With this selection, the Properties dialog box opens for each user, and the options must be selected again.

10. Tap or click OK in the Compatibility For All Users dialog box if it is open.

11. Tap or click OK in the Properties dialog box for the application to save modifications to the compatibility settings.

Using the troubleshooter with an application: An example

Jennifer calls the help desk because her new computer will not run the screen capture application she was using on her previous computer. To assist Jennifer, the technician walks her through the troubleshooter for the application, first selecting the screen capture application within the troubleshooter and then selecting Troubleshoot Program in the Troubleshooting Options dialog box.

When the wizard asks what problem was noticed, the technician asks Jennifer to help choose the problem that is occurring. Because the application ran well on Windows 7, Jennifer selects "The program worked in earlier versions of Windows but won't install or run now" and taps Next. When the wizard prompts for the version of Windows in which the application worked correctly, Jennifer selects Windows 7 and taps Next. This places the program in compatibility mode for Windows 7. Jennifer selects the option to test the program.

After the program starts, the technician can tap or click Next to complete the troubleshooter. On the final screen of the troubleshooter, the technician can select from the following options:

■ **Yes, Save These Settings For This Program**   This option keeps the changed settings for subsequent launches.

■ **No, Try Again Using Different Settings**   This option reverses the changes and allows other settings to be selected.

■ **No, Report The Problem To Microsoft And Check Online For A Solution**   This option sends information about the problem to Microsoft for evaluation and troubleshooting and queries the Internet for possible solutions.

When the technician selects an option, the troubleshooter prepares a report of its findings and provides an opportunity for Jennifer or the technician to explore further options as needed. Either the technician or Jennifer can exit the troubleshooter by tapping or clicking Close.

Configuring default programs and file associations

Sometimes working with an application to access a file or type of document should happen just by double-clicking or double-tapping the file or document. When multiple programs can open the same file type—for example, WordPad and Microsoft Word—Windows can become confused about which application should be used to open a file by default. In addition, when other applications are installed that can open a particular type of file, the new programs can set themselves as the default application to use.

To change the default program used to open a file, complete the following steps:

1. On the Start screen, search for Default Programs.

2. Tap or click Default Programs.

3. Select a program from the list of programs on the left side of the screen.

4. Review the details for the selected program.

5. Select Set This Program As Default to configure this program as the default program for opening all file types and protocols it supports.

6. Tap or click OK to save these settings.

To change the file association for a file type, complete the following steps:

1. On the Start screen, search for File Associations.

2. Tap or click Settings.

3. Tap or click Change The File Type Associated With A File Extension.

4. On the Set Associations page, select a file extension to associate with an application.

5. Tap or click Change Program.

6. Select More Options to see other programs that can open the selected file type.

7. Tap or click the program that should be used for this file type from the list.

8. Tap or click Close.

 Quick check

■ **Why would you need to change an application's compatibility settings?**

Quick check answer

■ **If the application is not operating as expected under Windows 8, changing its compatibility settings to an earlier version of Windows might rectify the problem.**

Lesson summary

■ Traditional applications can be installed on computers running Windows 8 by using Windows Installer.

■ Configure virtualized applications to reduce application deployment time and meet additional compatibility requirements.

■ Set default programs and file associations to ensure that both applications and files open as expected.

Lesson review

Answer the following questions to test your knowledge of the information in this lesson. You can find the answers to these questions and explanations of why each answer choice is correct or incorrect in the "Answers" section at the end of this chapter.

1. Josef works in the office of the CFO for Tailspin Toys and is having trouble with an application that he uses every day. When he calls the help desk, he mentions that there is a brief flash on the screen when starting the application, but then it closes and does not function. What can be done to start and run the application for Josef with the least administrative effort?

   A. Restart Josef's computer.

   B. Reinstall the application, using original media.

   C. Repair the application by using MSIExec.

   D. Review the list of updates installed on Josef's computer and remove any that might be causing a problem.

2. Because the company has such a busy holiday season, Tailspin Toys wants to add several interns to its workforce while the interns are on holiday break. When these additional workers begin work, they will need access to the Tailspin Toys inventory application to perform their work. To facilitate the deployment of an inventory control application, which technology could be used to ensure the smallest footprint for the proprietary application?

   A. Configure the application to run in a browser.

   B. Outsource the application to run in the cloud.

   C. Use App-V to virtualize the application and enable it to remain in-house.

   D. Develop a new, Windows 8 native application to manage inventory control.

3. Frieda calls the help desk because she can no longer open PDF files. When she double-clicks a PDF document, she is prompted to locate a program for this type of file. What could be done to help ensure that Frieda can access PDF documents with the least amount of administrative effort?

   A. Reinstall the PDF reader on Frieda's computer.

   B. Troubleshoot compatibility of the PDF application.

   C. Require all the documents Frieda uses to be in Microsoft Works.

   D. Associate the file extension for PDF files with the PDF reader application on Frieda's computer.

Lesson 2: Managing Windows 8 native applications

Windows 8 native applications are applications built specifically to take advantage of the features and updates in Windows 8. They have a new appearance and are delivered in a different way than Windows applications have been in the past—by using an application store.

After this lesson, you will be able to:

- Control the installation of Windows 8 native apps within an environment.
- Sideload custom content or applications in Windows 8.
- Prevent access to the Windows Store and control application access.

Estimated lesson time: 55 minutes

Installing, updating, and uninstalling Windows 8 native applications

Windows 8 has introduced an entirely new way to access, purchase, and use applications on a Windows-based computer. These new applications built specifically for Windows 8 are available from Microsoft through the Windows Store. Rather than being contained on traditional media, these applications are delivered seamlessly by the Internet to improve their users' overall experience and usability.

Obtaining applications is straightforward. A number of applications are available across many price points and categories in the Windows Store. To access the store, complete the following steps:

1. From the Start screen, select the Windows Store app.
2. Browse the store for an app.
3. Tap or click the app you want to install.
4. Review the information about the app and tap or click Install to install it.

When the app is installed, a notification appears from the top-right corner of the screen to let you know that the app you selected has been successfully (or unsuccessfully) installed.

IMPORTANT **INSTALLATIONS ARE ALLOWED ON MULTIPLE DEVICES**

When an app is downloaded from the Windows Store, it can be used on up to five Windows 8 devices. This enables easy sharing across computers or other devices when apps are downloaded.

After an application has been installed from the store, the next time it is selected, the details screen for the app, similar to the one shown in Figure 4-1, indicates that you already own the app.

Never Late

FIGURE 4-1 An app already installed

When an app has been downloaded from the store, it appears on the Start screen along with other installed apps. Because apps are so much easier to access and install from the Windows Store than from traditional media, it is likely that applications will be tested more often than might have been the case with traditional software. If you no longer need an app on a computer, you can uninstall it as easily as it was installed. To uninstall a Windows 8 native app, complete the following steps:

1. From the Start screen, press and hold or right-click the app to be uninstalled.

2. From the options bar that appears, select Uninstall to remove the app.

Reinstalling apps that have been removed

When you purchase or install apps from the Windows Store, the apps are added to a section within the store app called Your Apps, which is tied to a Microsoft account. Any apps purchased or installed by the account can be used on other computers with access to this Microsoft account. In addition to the list of apps that have been downloaded, this view displays if the apps are installed.

Figure 4-2 shows the applications that have been downloaded but are not installed on this particular computer. To open Your Apps, open the Windows Store, and then press and hold or right-click any area without a tile.

In addition to apps available for installation from the store, any updates for apps that you have downloaded are displayed in the top-right corner of the store. Tapping or clicking the

Updates option displays apps that have available updates and allows them to be downloaded by tapping or clicking Install. Figure 4-3 shows apps with available updates.

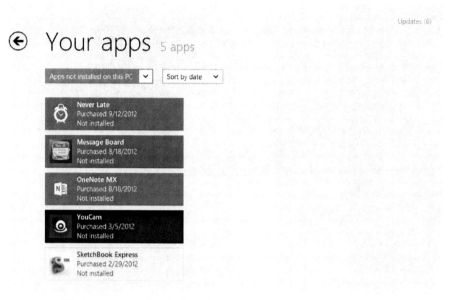

FIGURE 4-2 Windows apps not installed on this computer

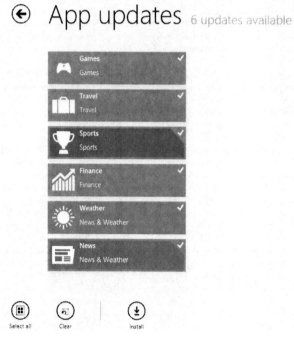

FIGURE 4-3 Updates available for apps

Acquiring desktop apps in the Windows Store

Some software manufacturers have chosen to publish their desktop applications in the Windows Store. These apps must be downloaded from the publisher's website rather than from the store, like a Windows 8 native app. Publishing in the Windows Store can increase visibility and customer awareness of these applications.

To install these apps, they must be downloaded from the publisher's website directly. When the download is completed, the application setup file can be executed from the Windows 8 desktop app and will then appear on the Start screen. When the application is opened, it will open inside the desktop app.

Disabling and controlling access to the Windows Store app

In some cases, organizations might want to keep their computers as close to a baseline configuration as possible, so the Windows Store application might need to be disabled. Managing the Windows Store app is handled by policy. It can be done either by Group Policy in a corporate or Active Directory environment or through local policy on an individual computer. To disable access to the Windows Store, complete the following steps:

1. Press the Windows logo key+R to open the Run box. (Alternatively, you can search for Run from the Start screen.)

2. Type **gpedit.msc** and press Enter or select OK.

3. In the Local Group Policy Editor, expand the navigation pane to the following location:

   User Configuration\Administrative Templates\Windows Components\Store.

4. Double-tap or double-click Turn Off The Store Application in the results pane.

5. Select Enabled to remove the Windows Store application from this computer.

6. Tap or click OK.

7. Close the Local Group Policy Editor.

8. Open the Run box by pressing Windows logo key+R or searching for Run from the Start screen.

9. Type **gpupdate / force** in the dialog box.

10. Press Enter or select OK.

> **IMPORTANT SEEING CHANGES TO POLICY SETTINGS**
> Changes to policy settings only take effect at computer startup, sign-in, or policy update. Running the gpupdate command with the /force switch avoids the need to wait until policy is refreshed or until the next sign-in to see the changes.

Managing access to hardware and installed applications

Technology changes constantly, and the applications and devices used with Windows 8–based devices are no exception. Hardware and applications might need to be replaced or removed because they are not needed. To manage devices connected to Windows 8, complete the following steps:

1. Select the Settings charm.

2. Select Change PC Settings at the bottom of the Settings pane.

3. Select Devices in the PC Settings navigational list on the left side of the screen.

The Devices section of Control Panel is shown in Figure 4-4.

FIGURE 4-4 Accessing devices in Windows 8

When Devices is selected, all the detected hardware devices are displayed. Selecting a device displays the Remove option for that device, which appears as a minus symbol in the top-right corner of the selected devices icon within Control Panel. To remove the selected device, just tap or click Remove when it is displayed.

In addition to removing existing devices, it is possible to add devices from Control Panel. Select Add A Device at the very top of the devices list. Windows searches for new devices to install and displays devices to be selected for installation. If you don't find necessary drivers, you can browse for the needed files.

To manage installed desktop applications, use Control Panel. To manage desktop applications, complete the following steps:

1. From the desktop, select the Settings charm.

2. Select Control Panel.

3. Tap or click Programs and Features.

4. Select the application to manage and choose Uninstall, Change, or Repair.

Controlling applications by using AppLocker

 First introduced in Windows 7, *AppLocker* is an application control feature that prevents unauthorized applications from being executed on Windows computers. In essence, through the use of AppLocker, an organization effectively whitelists authorized, secure applications and reduces the risk that an unauthorized application will introduce malware into the environment. As a Windows 8 administrator, it's not likely that you will be exposed to AppLocker on a regular basis. However, because the feature is a core security function that is in use in many organizations, a discussion of this topic is included in this section.

Understand that AppLocker is primarily a Group Policy management tool for Windows domains and has a complex interrelationship with Software Restriction Policies, so implementation of this feature requires a coordinated effort between desktop management and security teams in IT. If you'd like to learn more about AppLocker beyond what is included in this chapter, visit *http://technet.microsoft.com/en-us/library/hh831440.aspx*.

> **IMPORTANT USE CAUTION WHEN CONSIDERING AND IMPLEMENTING APPLOCKER**
>
> When implementing AppLocker policies to control access to certain apps, plan ahead to ensure that the policies and affected applications behave as expected.

You manage access to applications that are already installed by using AppLocker policies for an environment. AppLocker uses policies to enforce rules that allow or prevent applications from executing on computers in an environment. When creating a policy for AppLocker, consider:

- Rule definition
- Rule enforcement

Before configuring AppLocker to prevent the execution of applications, be sure that the policies are planned and tested in Audit-only mode to avoid any unnecessary disruption in the use of the applications.

Defining rules

AppLocker supports four types of rules in Windows 8:

- **Executable rules** These rules affect the execution of standard executable files. For example, if an organization wants to restrict access to an application, a rule to prevent access to Application.exe can be created.
- **Windows Installer rules** These rules enable administrators to control Windows Installer packages by specifying the publisher, path, or file hash for the package.
- **Script rules** These rules allow scripts to be restricted or executed.

- **Packaged app rules** These rules allow Windows 8 native applications to be restricted by AppLocker.

For example, an organization might want to configure AppLocker rules to prevent access to nonessential applications. This can benefit the organization by:

- Increasing productivity
- Reducing risk of malware
- Reducing maintenance

The organization can create rules for specific applications to ensure that these applications cannot be run either by specific groups of employees or by anyone. The control of applications is very granular based on properties that exist with the file. If an organization finds that an employee is constantly spending time using an instant messaging application that is not supported, the application can be restricted by using AppLocker.

When defining rules for Windows Installer and packaged apps, the installation process for apps can be controlled, preventing installation of these applications if necessary.

Enforcing rules

After rules for application management are created, they are not enforced by default. Because enabling rules in AppLocker can prevent software from running, rule enforcement is disabled. Each rule type described previously can be enabled independently of other rule types. Figure 4-5 shows the AppLocker Properties dialog box with Executable Rules configured and set to Enforce Rules.

FIGURE 4-5 Enabling AppLocker rules for audit or enforcement

After a rule type is configured, it has two modes:

- **Enforce rules**   This mode enforces any rules of the selected type.
- **Audit only**   This mode records the rule actions for computers and applications meeting rule conditions but does not enforce the rule.

When planning an AppLocker implementation, Audit mode gives administrators an idea of how a policy will control an application without affecting the use of the application.

To define a packaged app rule as part of an AppLocker policy, complete the following steps:

1. Open the Run box by searching for Run on the Start screen and tapping or clicking the result.

2. Type **gpedit.msc** and tap or click OK.

3. Expand the following path:

   ```
   Computer Configuration\Windows Settings\Security Settings\Application Control
   Policies\AppLocker
   ```

4. Press and hold or right-click Packaged App Rules.

5. Tap or click Create New Rule.

6. Review the Before You Begin information in the Create Packaged App Rules Wizard and tap or click Next to open the Permissions page, as shown in Figure 4-6.

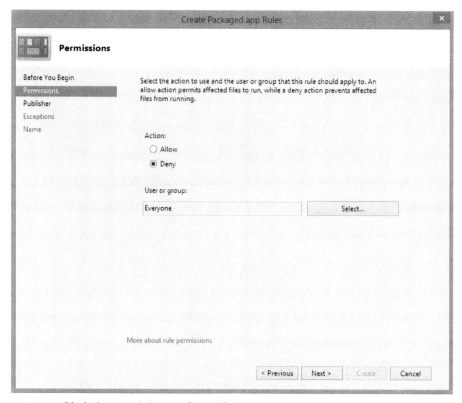

FIGURE 4-6 Displaying permissions configured for a packaged app in an AppLocker rule

7. Select an Action to be taken:
   - Allow   Permit the application to run.
   - Deny   Do not permit the application to run.

8. Select a user account or group to which to apply this rule. Everyone is selected by default.

9. Tap or click Next.

10. Specify the packaged app to use as a reference by choosing from the following:
    - Use An Installed Packaged App As A Reference   Select a native Windows 8 application installed on the computer.
    - Use A Packaged App Installer As A Reference   Specify the details about publisher, package name, and version to prevent installers that meet these criteria from running.

11. Tap or click Next.

12. Click Add to define exceptions for the rule.

13. Define any exceptions for apps that meet defined criteria but that should be allowed to run by selecting an existing application or defining information about an installer.

14. Tap or click OK to add the exception.

15. Tap or click Next to specify a name for the rule and a description (optional).

16. Tap or click Create to complete and save the rule.

After rules are defined to control certain applications, they must be enabled to allow enforcement. To configure the enforcement of packaged app rules in AppLocker, complete the following steps:

1. Open the Run box by searching for Run on the Start screen and tapping or clicking the result.

2. Type **gpedit.msc** and tap or click OK.

3. Expand the following path:

   ```
   Computer Configuration\Windows Settings\Security Settings\Application Control
   Policies
   ```

4. Select AppLocker.

5. In the results pane, tap or click the Configure Rule Enforcement link.

6. Select the Configured check box for the Packaged App Rules section.

7. Select Enforce Rules to enable enforcement.

8. Tap or click OK in the AppLocker Properties dialog box.

After AppLocker is configured, Group Policy must be refreshed to apply the new settings. This can be accomplished by restarting the computer or by running **gpupdate /force** from the Run box or command line.

Sideloading apps in Windows 8

Sideloading refers to a process for installing native Windows 8 applications that are not available in the Windows Store on devices within an organization. An example of this might be a line-of-business application the organization uses that was developed in-house.

To sideload applications on Windows 8–based computers, the computers must be domain joined or use a Windows sideloading product key on the computer. To configure Group Policy for domain-joined sideloading, complete the following steps:

1. Search for gpedit.msc on the Start screen.

2. Expand the following path in the left navigation pane:

   ```
   Computer Configuration\Administrative Templates\Windows Components\App Package
   Deployment
   ```

3. Double-tap or double-click the Allow All Trusted Apps To Install policy object, set the policy to Enabled, and then tap or click OK.

To activate a sideloading product key, type **slmgr /ipk** *<sideloading product key>* at an elevated command prompt and press Enter. For more information on sideloading applications, see *http://technet.microsoft.com/en-us/library/hh852635.aspx*.

Adding sideloaded apps to a user account

Individual app packages can be sideloaded for specific user accounts on a Windows 8–based computer. To add a line-of-business app for a user account, complete the following steps:

1. Launch Windows PowerShell as an administrator by searching for PowerShell on the Start screen and selecting Windows PowerShell. Press and hold or right-click and select Run As Administrator.

2. In the command line, type the following command, substituting *<path to . . .>* with the paths to your app packages:

   ```
   add-appxpackage <path to app package>.appx –DependencyPath <path to dependent file 1>.appx
   ```

3. Press Enter to execute the command.

There is no limit to the number of sideloaded apps that can be installed; however, use an image for deployment if there is a large number of apps to load or a large number of systems on which to load them.

Adding sideloaded apps to an image

Sideloaded apps can be added to an image either by using the *Deployment Image Servicing and Management (DISM) console*, which allows images to be created or modified offline, or by using Windows PowerShell cmdlets.

Using DISM, enter the following command:

```
DISM /Online /Add-ProvisionedAppxPackage /PackagePath:<path to package>.appx /SkipLicense
```

To use PowerShell, enter the following command:

```
Add-AppxProvisionedPackage -Online -FolderPath <Path to folder containing packages>
```

Inventorying and removing apps

After apps have been sideloaded, information can be gathered about these applications on either a per-user basis or for all users. The information includes application title and installation and the manifest information for sideloaded apps. In addition to the sideloaded apps, these commands can be used with apps installed from the Windows Store.

Using Windows PowerShell

To list applications for all users, enter the following:

```
Get-appxpackage -allusers
```

To list the details for a specific package and specific user account, enter the following:

```
Get-appxpackage -name <package name> -user domain\username
```

> *NOTE* **VIEWING APPS FOR OTHER ACCOUNTS**
>
> Viewing apps installed for accounts other than the currently installed user account requires an elevated session.

A *package manifest* is a file that contains product information and installation details about an app package.

To view package manifest information for an app, enter the following:

```
Get-appxpackagemanifest -package <full package name>
```

To remove an app from Windows 8, enter the following:

```
Remove-appxpackage <package>
```

To remove a provisioned app from an image, enter the following:

```
Remove-appxprovisionedpackage -online -packagename <Package Name>
```

Figure 4-7 shows the results of get-appxpackage in PowerShell for the Bing Maps App.

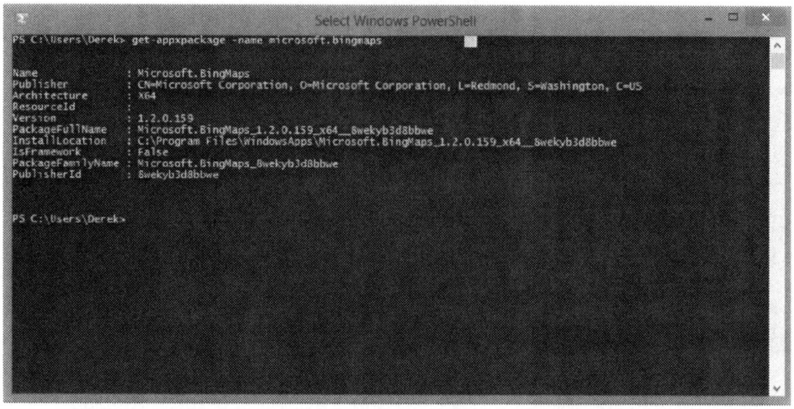

FIGURE 4-7 The app package details for the Bing Maps application

Using DISM at the command line

To list apps provisioned in an image, enter the following:

```
DISM.exe /Image::c:\provisionedimages /get-provisionedappxpackages
```

where *c:\provisionedimages* is the path to the location of the images.

To remove a provisioned app from an image, enter the following:

```
DISM.exe /Online /Remove-ProvisionedAppxPackage /Packagename:<package name>
```

The ability to manage applications developed specifically for an organization will encourage app development to meet specific business needs by using Windows 8.

Lesson summary

- Although the Windows Store makes apps easily available for Windows 8, organizations can restrict access to the store.
- Apps downloaded from the Windows Store can be shared across five devices.
- Sideloading custom-designed apps enables organizations to develop Windows 8 native line-of-business apps without publishing them in the Windows Store.
- Windows PowerShell can be used to manage both Windows Store–installed and sideloaded apps.

Lesson review

Answer the following questions to test your knowledge of the information in this lesson. You can find the answers to these questions and explanations of why each answer choice is correct or incorrect in the "Answers" section at the end of this chapter.

1. Craig, an employee in your organization's finance department, has discovered the Windows Store and installed the Finance application on his computer. Company policy states that all applications must be approved by a supervisor and the IT department; however, a new member of your team deployed the PC before the initial configuration could be tested. How can you prevent access to both the Finance app and the Windows Store?

    A. Uninstall the Finance app.

    B. Restrict Craig's Internet access.

    C. Create an AppLocker policy to restrict the Finance app from executing and disable the Windows Store app by using Group Policy.

    D. Make an exception for Craig.

2. Because of the volume of applications your organization uses on a daily basis, your supervisor asks you to compile a list of applications installed on select computers within the organization. She would like to see the findings by the end of the month and has provided a list of the computers to audit. How can you gather the requested information?

    A. Visit each listed workstation and take a manual inventory.

    B. Ask the employees using the selected computers to send a list of installed programs by email.

    C. Use PowerShell to collect inventory information for each computer.

    D. Access the Windows Store and review the applications that have been installed.

3. Lauren has been assigned a special project and given permission to access the Finance application until the project is completed. She mentions that when she browses for the Finance application, she cannot find it on her computer. How can you reinstall this application? (Each correct answer presents a complete solution. Choose three.)

    A. Visit the Windows Store and install the Finance app.

    B. Include an exception in AppLocker for the Finance app for all users.

    C. Include an exception in AppLocker for the Finance app for Lauren.

    D. Enable access to the Windows Store.

Practice exercises

The ability to manage applications from different sources, sideloaded applications, and Windows Store applications by using the same set of tools in Windows 8 provides organizations with a great deal of flexibility in the applications they can install and the way these applications are managed.

Exercise 1: Install line-of-business applications

Adding custom line-of-business applications to Windows 8 without needing to publish them provides additional flexibility to organizations. Complete this exercise to install a line-of-business application.

1. Copy the application package to a network share.
2. Open Windows PowerShell.
3. Using the add-appxpackage cmdlet, install the packages from the share.
4. Open the Start screen and locate the newly installed application.
5. Install the sideloading product key.
6. Test the sideloaded application to ensure that it behaves as designed.

Exercise 2: Prevent access to the Windows Store

In some cases, organizations might want to disable access to the Windows Store to prevent unnecessary applications from being installed or even requested.

1. Open the Local Group Policy Editor.
2. Locate the Windows Store policy settings in the navigation pane.
3. Enable the settings to prevent access to the Windows Store.
4. Refresh Group Policy.
5. Test the Windows Store app to ensure that it behaves as expected.

Suggested practice exercises

The following additional practice exercises are designed to give you more opportunities to practice what you've learned and to help you successfully master the lessons presented in this chapter.

- **Exercise 1** Configure AppLocker policy to prevent a computer from running games.
- **Exercise 2** Collect an inventory of installed Windows 8 native apps for all users on a computer.
- **Exercise 3** Configure an application to run in Windows 7 compatibility mode.

Answers

This section contains the answers to the lesson review questions in this chapter.

Lesson 1

1. **Correct answer: C**

   A. **Incorrect:** Problems starting applications with missing or corrupted files typically require action to be taken on their files; just restarting a computer will not fix these problems.

   B. **Incorrect:** The reinstallation from media might correct the issue, but using installation media does not accomplish the task with the least effort.

   C. **Correct:** Repairing an application often corrects problems with files that were corrupted or missing during the initial installation.

   D. **Incorrect:** Although managing updates is important, no single update can be easily identified to correct this problem.

2. **Correct answer: C**

   A. **Incorrect:** The application is not a web-based application.

   B. **Incorrect:** Migrating or upgrading the application to run in the cloud goes beyond addressing the stated problem.

   C. **Correct:** Virtualizing the application will enable it to run on the Windows 8–based computers with minimal investment.

   D. **Incorrect:** Because the application is mission critical, planning and testing are needed to ensure that the application will perform as expected when developed as a Windows 8 native app.

3. **Correct answer: D**

   A. **Incorrect:** Because the reason for the problem has not been determined, this might not solve the problem.

   B. **Incorrect:** The application starts without a problem but cannot directly access a file type. Adjusting compatibility is unlikely to correct this problem.

   C. **Incorrect:** This solution requires additional work and time commitment from everyone around Frieda; it does not correct the PDF issue.

   D. **Correct:** Resetting the file type association for PDF files on Frieda's computer will ensure that the PDF application is used to open the files.

Lesson 2

1. **Correct answer: C**

   A. **Incorrect:** Uninstalling the app would only prevent access to the application; it would not prevent access to the store.

   B. **Incorrect:** Craig might require access to the Internet to perform other parts of his job, so removing this access could affect other work.

   C. **Correct:** Using AppLocker to ensure that the Finance app does not run and removing access to the store by using Group Policy corrects both these issues with minimal steps.

   D. **Incorrect:** Changing organizational rules does not correct the issues at hand.

2. **Correct answer: C**

   A. **Incorrect:** Visiting each workstation would produce the information but requires more administrative effort than necessary to solve the problem.

   B. **Incorrect:** Although some employees might be able and willing to help, an automated solution can collect this information without interrupting anyone.

   C. **Correct:** Windows PowerShell can connect to each computer and collect the information needed. The results can be gathered into a .csv file for easy use and delivery to your supervisor.

   D. **Incorrect:** Because employees might have access to their own Microsoft accounts, this might not provide all the information required.

3. **Correct answers: A, C, and D**

   A. **Correct:** To install an application that has been removed, the Windows Store must reinstall the app.

   B. **Incorrect:** Lauren is working on this project, but other employees who are not working on the project do not need access to the Finance app.

   C. **Correct:** To allow Lauren to access the Finance app, set an exception in AppLocker.

   D. **Correct:** To reinstall the application, the store must be accessible.

CHAPTER 5

Managing Internet Explorer

For years, Internet Explorer has played a vital role in Windows. As new versions of Windows are released, new versions of Internet Explorer are often included, and Windows 8 is no exception. In Windows 8, Internet Explorer takes on a split personality thanks to the new operating system's dual operational modes. In this chapter, you learn how to manage Internet Explorer in the desktop environment.

Lessons in this chapter:

Before you begin

To get the most from this chapter, make sure you pay attention to which version of Internet Explorer is in use in the examples. Internet Explorer 10 in Windows 8 operates in one of two modes. The first mode, which operates from the desktop, is the traditional product to which you have become accustomed over the years. The second mode, which runs using the Windows 8 interface, carries with it some limitations that are discussed in this chapter.

Some of the material in this chapter assumes that, as an enterprise IT professional, you are already familiar with how to use Group Policy. This book does not go into detail on how to create and apply Group Policy but does provide guidance on how administrators can use individual Group Policy settings to accomplish goals across the organization. For more information about Group Policy settings in Internet Explorer 10, see *http://technet.microsoft .com/en-us/library/hh846775.aspx.*

Lesson 1: Configuring Internet Explorer 10

In Windows 8, a number of changes and improvements have been made to Internet Explorer 10. In addition, Internet Explorer is now a single product with two interfaces: one is optimized for touch and the other is the traditional Internet Explorer desktop application.

After this lesson, you will be able to:

- Describe the differences between the two Internet Explorer interfaces in Windows 8.
- Describe the limitations inherent in the touch-optimized interface.
- Configure Internet Explorer launch behavior.
- Identify the Group Policy settings that manage some of the Internet Explorer configuration options.

Estimated lesson time: 30 minutes

Managing two Internet Explorer experiences

Perhaps the biggest change in this newest version of Internet Explorer is that Internet Explorer 10, although a single product in Windows 8, actually operates in two variations, depending on the location from which you launch the web browser. One variation—Internet Explorer—is tailored for the Windows 8 touch-optimized interface (UI), whereas the other—Internet Explorer for the desktop—is an updated version of the familiar desktop application. Even though the two interfaces appear and feel very different from each other, they are the same application. In Figure 5-1, you see the Windows 8 touch-optimized variation of Internet Explorer 10, and in Figure 5-2, you see Internet Explorer 10 for the desktop.

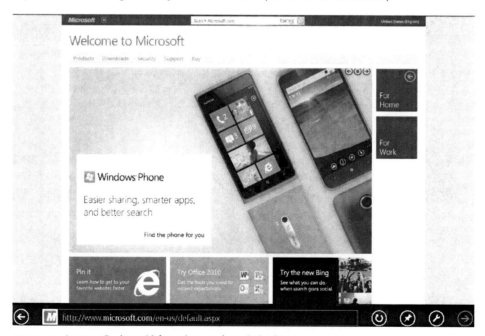

FIGURE 5-1 Internet Explorer 10 featuring touch optimization

FIGURE 5-2 Internet Explorer 10 as run from the desktop maintains a traditional appearance

> *IMPORTANT* **INTERNET EXPLORER VS. INTERNET EXPLORER FOR THE DESKTOP**
>
> Although Internet Explorer is a single application in Windows 8, its two operating modes and the differences between them can create confusion. Both versions have the same name, but they have different capabilities. For the purposes of this chapter:
>
> - Internet Explorer refers to the variation of Internet Explorer optimized for a touch interface.
> - Internet Explorer for the desktop refers to the traditional Internet Explorer variation.

Note that each operating variation renders the same baseline content. However, if that content requires add-ons, which are not supported by the touch-optimized version, major differences between the two interfaces begin to appear. In Figure 5-1, you can see Internet Explorer using the new Windows 8 touch-optimized UI, in which content is rendered above the address bar displayed along the bottom of the screen. In this mode, Internet Explorer is optimized for touch use, with larger, finger-friendly buttons.

In the traditional view, the address bar remains at the top of the window, and the screen maintains the controls you're used to. In this mode, Internet Explorer is more mouse-friendly or touchpad-friendly.

To run the touch-optimized variation of Internet Explorer 10, tap or click Internet Explorer on the Start screen (Figure 5-3). To run the desktop variation of Internet Explorer, tap or click the Internet Explorer icon in the taskbar on the desktop (Figure 5-4).

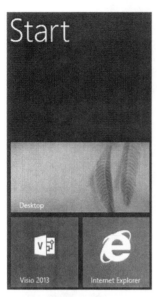

FIGURE 5-3 The touch-optimized version of Internet Explorer, available from the Start screen

FIGURE 5-4 The traditional desktop variation, opened from the taskbar

Configuring the startup Internet Explorer

In Windows 8, you can decide which variation of Internet Explorer should be used based on a few factors. By default, Internet Explorer decides how to open links:

- If you open a link from a Windows 8 native app, it opens in Internet Explorer.
- If you open a link from a desktop application, it opens in Internet Explorer for the desktop.

To force Internet Explorer to use one interface always, complete the following steps:

1. From Internet Explorer for the desktop, press Alt+X.
2. From the Internet Options page, choose the Programs tab.
3. In the Choose How You Open Your Links section of the Programs tab, tap or click the drop-down arrow, which displays the options shown in Figure 5-5.

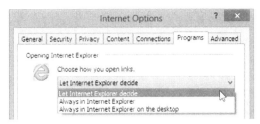

FIGURE 5-5 Choosing which Internet Explorer experience to use as the default

4. Decide which variation of Internet Explorer should be used to open links.

5. Tap or click OK until you're back at your webpage.

REAL WORLD **DON'T LEAVE INTERNET EXPLORER DEFAULTS IN PLACE**

If you're supporting Windows 8–based traditional desktops and laptops in an organization, don't leave the default—Let Internet Explorer Decide How To Open Links—in place. The constant switch between the two editions can be jarring and confusing. Choose one or the other for your users based on their work needs. If they require access to add-ons that extend the functionality of Internet Explorer, choose the desktop variation as the default. If not, choose the touch-optimized variation.

IMPORTANT **ADDITIONAL BROWSERS CHANGE THE EQUATION**

Many people add third-party web browsers such as Firefox, Chrome, and Opera to their systems. In Windows 8, if you install a third-party browser and set it as the default, the touch-optimized Internet Explorer is disabled. If you choose Internet Explorer while another browser is set as the default, only Internet Explorer for the desktop is available.

To reset Internet Explorer as the default browser:

1. From the desktop, select the Settings charm and then select Control Panel.

2. From Control Panel, choose Programs.

3. In Programs, choose Set Your Default Programs.

4. In Set Your Default Programs, choose Internet Explorer from the list of default programs.

5. Select Set This Program As Default, as shown in Figure 5-6.

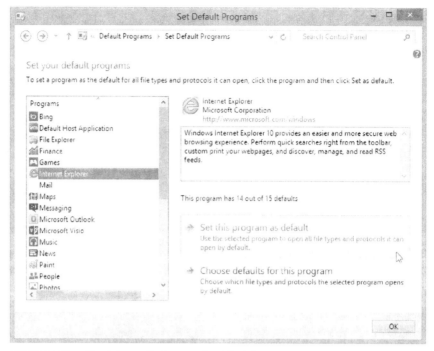

FIGURE 5-6 Resetting Internet Explorer as the default browser

Controlling Internet Explorer Start screen tile behavior

In Chapter 1, "Evaluating Windows 8," you learned that you can add web links to the
Windows 8 Start screen. By default, when you open those web links, they open in the touch-
optimized Internet Explorer. As discussed previously, you might want to provide your organization with a consistent web browsing experience by adopting one variation of Internet
Explorer. If this is the case, follow these steps so that Internet Explorer Start screen tiles open
in the desktop variation:

1. From Internet Explorer for the desktop, press Alt+X.

2. On the Internet Options page, choose the Programs tab.

3. In the Choose How You Open Your Links section of the Programs tab, select the Open
   Internet Explorer Tiles On The Desktop check box, as shown in Figure 5-7.

FIGURE 5-7 Instructing Internet Explorer to open Internet Explorer tiles in the desktop variant

4. Tap or click OK until you're back at your webpage.

You need to be aware of another option when using the touch-optimized Internet Explorer. If you are browsing the web with Internet Explorer but having trouble with content rendering, you can switch to Internet Explorer for the desktop.

To switch to Internet Explorer for the desktop, complete the following steps:

1. After the page is loaded into Internet Explorer, tap or click the wrench icon at the bottom of the window.

2. Choose View On The Desktop from the shortcut menu (Figure 5-8).

FIGURE 5-8 Open a page in the touch-optimized Internet Explorer in the desktop variant

Configuring Internet Explorer 10 (touch optimized)

The touch-optimized Internet Explorer 10 offers just a few configuration options. Whereas the desktop variation has a multitude of settings that can be tweaked, the touch-optimized edition is simple; however, as a result, some flexibility is lost.

Access the settings for Internet Explorer by opening Internet Explorer from the Start screen and then choosing the Settings charm. When the Settings sidebar appears, tap Internet Options to access Internet Explorer Settings, as shown in Figure 5-9.

FIGURE 5-9 Configuration options for touch-optimized Internet Explorer

Here's a look at these settings:

- **Delete Browsing History** You can delete your browsing history by selecting this setting.

- **Permissions** You can control whether your physical location is tracked. Because Windows 8 is an operating system intended to support a wide variety of devices, including tablets, the location questions in this section make sense. With a mobile device, location services become more important. However, for privacy reasons, you might want to disable sites' ability to ask for location. Move the slider to Off to disable tracking and reporting your physical location. If you've already authorized certain sites to track your location, you can clear these authorizations by tapping the Clear button.

- **Zoom**   You can modify the zoom factor for content rendered in Internet Explorer.
- **Flip Ahead**   You can make multipage-view websites easier to view. Many websites improve page views by breaking up articles into many parts and require you to flip through each part to read the full article. The Internet Explorer Flip Ahead feature is intended to make flipping through these articles faster. When Internet Explorer detects navigation links that indicate a multipart article, you can flip to the next page by swiping a finger rather than by tapping a link.
- **Encoding**   If webpages aren't displaying correctly, you might need to use a different encoding method, particularly if you are viewing foreign-language sites.

For the touch-optimized Internet Explorer, these are the settings that can be directly configured to modify the browsing experience.

Managing Internet Explorer settings by using Group Policy

The problems and solutions you've seen thus far have all focused on how to make changes at the desktop level. In an enterprise environment, performing work at the desktop level is inefficient because there are often dozens, hundreds, or thousands of computers to manage. For that reason, administrators often turn to the Group Policy feature, which provides centralized control over the entire Active Directory environment.

For Internet Explorer alone, more than 1,500 individual Group Policy settings can be manipulated to manage even the largest Windows environment. Further, with the release of Windows 8, Windows Server 2012, and Internet Explorer 10, there are dozens of new, changed, and deprecated Group Policy settings that an administrator can use to manage the new features in Internet Explorer 10. This book does not cover every Internet Explorer–focused Group Policy setting. However, it shows you how to accomplish some key tasks by using Group Policy. Figure 5-10 shows the Group Policy Management Console from Windows Server 2012, displaying nothing but Internet Explorer–focused Group Policy options.

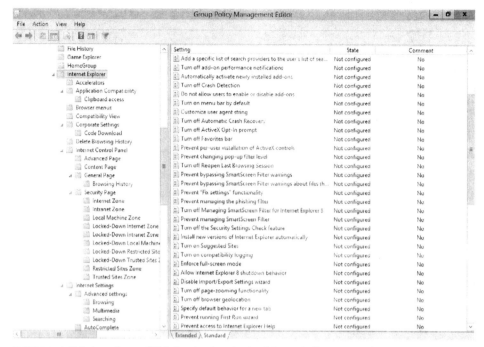

FIGURE 5-10 Windows Server 2012 showing hundreds of Group Policy settings for Internet Explorer

Managing link behavior by using Group Policy

In this lesson, you learned about the ways by which links can be configured to open in either Internet Explorer or Internet Explorer for the desktop. The settings you can configure to open individually in either Internet Explorer or Internet Explorer for the desktop can also be managed centrally through Group Policy. Note that these Group Policy settings work only with Internet Explorer 10 in Windows 8.

- **Policy name**   Set how links are opened in Internet Explorer.
- **Policy path**   Set the path to Windows Components in Internet Explorer Internet Settings.
- **Policy description**   Use this policy setting to choose how links are opened in Internet Explorer: Let Internet Explorer Decide, Always In Internet Explorer, or Always In Internet Explorer On The Desktop.
- **Enabled**   If you enable this policy setting, Internet Explorer enforces your choice. Users cannot change the setting.
- **Disabled or not configured**   If you disable or do not configure this policy setting, users can choose how links are opened in Internet Explorer.

Controlling Internet Explorer Start screen tile behavior by using Group Policy

You can also control the behavior of Internet Explorer Start screen tiles by using a new Group Policy setting.

- **Policy name** Open Internet Explorer tiles on the desktop.
- **Policy path** Set the path to Windows Components in Internet Explorer Internet Settings.
- **Policy description** Use this policy setting to configure Internet Explorer to open Internet Explorer tiles on the desktop.
- **Enabled** If you enable this policy setting, Internet Explorer opens tiles only on the desktop.
- **Disabled** If you disable this policy setting, Internet Explorer does not open tiles on the desktop.
- **Not configured** If you do not configure this policy, users can choose how Internet Explorer tiles are opened.

Lesson summary

- Internet Explorer 10 in Windows 8 is one program with a bifurcated interface; one interface is optimized for touch, whereas the other is a traditional desktop application.
- Touch-optimized Internet Explorer provides a clean, plug-in–free browsing experience.
- When a third-party web browser is configured as the default, the touch-optimized Internet Explorer interface is not available.
- Internet Explorer for desktop retains the configuration and extensibility options that are necessary for an enterprise environment.
- By default, Windows 8 launches the Internet Explorer variant based on the context in which you found the original link.
- You can configure Windows 8 always to launch the same Internet Explorer variant to provide a more consistent experience.

Lesson review

Answer the following questions to test your knowledge of the information in this lesson. You can find the answers to these questions and explanations of why each answer choice is correct or incorrect in the "Answers" section at the end of this chapter.

1. How do you disable location-based service requests in touch-optimized Internet Explorer?

   A. Open Internet Explorer from the Start screen, choose the Settings charm, and, in Internet Options, slide the Ask For Location indicator to Off.

   B. Disable Location Services in the Network and Sharing Center.

C. Open Internet Explorer for the desktop, choose Tools, and, in Internet Options, turn off location-based services.

D. Uninstall touch-optimized Internet Explorer 10.

2. What do you need to do to force all links to open in Internet Explorer for the desktop?

A. Open Internet Explorer from the Start screen, choose the Settings charm, select Internet Options, and choose Always In Internet Explorer.

B. Open Internet Explorer from the Start screen, choose the Settings charm, select Internet Options, and choose Always In Internet Explorer For Desktop.

C. In Internet Explorer for the desktop, open Internet Options and choose Always In Internet Explorer.

D. In Internet Explorer for the desktop, open Internet Options and choose Always In Internet Explorer For Desktop.

Lesson 2: Understanding and configuring browser security settings

Internet Explorer 10 includes a number of new security features and continues to support many of the security features that have been added to the product over time. In Windows 8, many new security features are enabled by default, and most security options are enabled to maximize system protection. Be sure to explore these options and understand how they work, even if they are mostly automatic and transparent.

After this lesson, you will be able to:

- Describe the security improvements made to Internet Explorer 10.
- Configure Protected Mode and Enhanced Protected Mode on a per-zone basis.
- Add trusted sites to Internet Explorer.
- Use Group Policy to deploy security configuration options.

Estimated lesson time: 30 minutes

Managing new Internet Explorer 10 security settings

Internet Explorer 10 includes a number of new security features designed to make the browsing experience more secure for Windows 8 users. Because web browsing is a common vector by which malware is introduced into an organization, new security features can help these organizations remain more secure. Three new security features are included in Internet Explorer 10.

Understanding enhanced memory protection

Through the use of creative attacks, attackers have discovered commonalities and patterns in system memory that make it possible to exploit them easily. Over time, Internet Explorer has added features to protect against this kind of activity. Two major memory-protection features have been added to Internet Explorer 10.

- **High Entropy Address Space Layout Randomization (HEASLR)** Technically, this feature is part of Windows 8, but Internet Explorer 10 uses it fully for security gains. This feature employs the 64-bit nature of processes to increase the entropy of physical RAM on a computer. The result: attackers cannot easily predict the locations at which specific code elements will reside, making it more difficult to determine a pattern.

- **ForceASLR** Not all Internet Explorer modules and add-ons were compiled using the option that allows the module or add-on code to be randomized in memory for maximum protection against predictive attacks. Forced Address Space Layout Randomization (ASLR) is a new feature in Windows 8 that Internet Explorer 10 uses to instruct the system to randomize the memory location of all modules and add-ons.

Understanding the HTML5 sandbox attribute

Inline Frames (IFrames) are a method by which HTML pages can be embedded inside other HTML pages. IFrames are often used to embed advertising content into webpages. The content in an IFrame doesn't have to come from the site that someone is browsing. In fact, it's common for the content in an IFrame to be sourced from a different site. IFrames have been used to distribute code that redirects unsuspecting people to malicious websites.

Internet Explorer 10 can help protect users against a number of IFrame-related exploits but only when web designers specifically include code that enables this new feature. When this feature, called the *HTML5 sandbox attribute*, is enabled, new security restrictions are put into place for IFrames that contain untrusted content. Among other restrictions, the HTML5 sandbox attribute has the following primary restrictions:

- When content is in this sandbox, it cannot open new browser windows.
- Links inside the sandboxed content cannot open in new windows.
- Sandboxed content cannot submit form data.

In other words, information inside the sandbox cannot be manipulated in the same way as information outside. The sandbox is intended to be a restricted area.

As an administrator, you don't control implementation of this feature directly. Rather, it works only when web developers include special code in their websites that turns this feature on.

Using Enhanced Protected Mode

Internet Explorer Protected Mode was originally introduced in Internet Explorer 7 and implements a policy based on the principle of least privilege. Under this principle, an application such as Internet Explorer is allowed access only to system elements and locations that are necessary for the application to complete its task. This limits the ability to exploit Internet Explorer to perform malicious activity on a host.

Internet Explorer 10 in Windows 8 adds restrictions to protect host systems further. These additional restrictions include:

- **64-bit processes** For systems that support running 64-bit processes, Internet Explorer 10 uses 64-bit processes for many operations. 64-bit processes carry much larger memory address spaces. The huge memory space provided by 64-bit address spaces makes it more difficult for attacks against process memory to be successful. Touch-optimized Internet Explorer automatically runs in 64-bit mode on 64-bit computers to take advantage of this enhancement. One reason that this variation of Internet Explorer can easily run in a 64-bit process is this variation's inability to run add-ons in Internet Explorer. With older versions of Internet Explorer, general guidance recommended the use of the 32-bit edition, even on 64-bit machines, due to add-on compatibility issues.

- **Reduced execution context** When you run a program on your computer, that program runs in the context of your user account and has access to all the same things that you do, including your personal files. With Enhanced Protected Mode, Internet Explorer must request your permission before it can access files from locations that contain your personal information.

The Enhanced Protected Mode in Internet Explorer 10 is not enabled by default, as shown in Figure 5-11, in which there is no check box next to Enable Enhanced Protected Mode. To enable this option, complete the following steps:

1. Open Internet Explorer on the desktop, and then press Alt+T. Choose Internet Options from the menu or open it from Control Panel.

2. Select the Advanced tab.

3. From the Advanced tab, scroll down until you see Enable Enhanced Protected Mode.

4. Select the check box next to that option and click or tap OK.

   You must restart Internet Explorer for Enhanced Protected Mode to take effect.

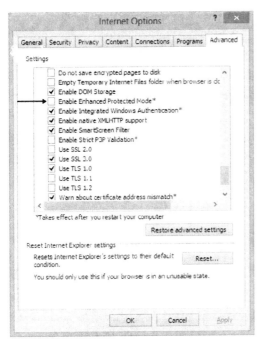

FIGURE 5-11 Enabling Enhanced Protected Mode

MORE INFO **ENHANCED PROTECTED MODE**

Enhanced Protected Mode helps you protect your users from themselves. The reality is that many malware infections brought into an organization through web browsing habits are successful because people are not careful about what they're doing.

To learn more about how Enhanced Protected Mode goes to new lengths to help protect users, review these resources:

- Understanding Enhanced Protected Mode at *http://blogs.msdn.com/b/ieinternals /archive/2012/03/23/understanding-ie10-enhanced-protected-mode-network -security-addons-cookies-metro-desktop.aspx*
- Enhanced Protected Mode at *http://blogs.msdn.com/b/ie/archive/2012/03/14 /enhanced-protected-mode.aspx*

Understanding Protected Mode (non-enhanced)

To provide continuous protection while you're using the web, Internet Explorer provides Protected Mode. Internet Explorer 10 includes a number of updates to Protected Mode; Enhanced Protected Mode was discussed in "Using Enhanced Protected Mode" earlier in this chapter.

In many organizations, employees continue to sign in to local computers using accounts that have far more privileges than are necessary to accomplish their work. Specifically, a great number of people have administrator access to their local desktop computers, although their rights are generally more restricted at the domain level. Because programs launched with the user's sign-in have the same rights as the user account itself, this can create a significant attack vector by which malware can be introduced onto the computer.

This is when Protected Mode becomes useful. Rather than running under the context of the user's full set of privileges, Internet Explorer operates with a very limited set of privileges. As a result, if someone browses to a website that attempts to deploy malicious code, the attack attempt would be limited to just a few areas of the system, none of them critical. Such malicious code would not have sufficient rights to perform software installations, access personal files, or perform other damaging operations.

Protected Mode operates based on the concept of integrity levels. Windows 8 is composed of securable objects, which include files, folders, and registry keys. Every securable object in Windows 8 has its own integrity level. The list of available integrity levels is shown in Table 5-1.

TABLE 5-1 Integrity levels

Integrity Level	Rights
High	An administrative integrity level. Processes with this integrity level can install files to the Program Files folder and write to restricted areas of the system registry.
Medium	A user integrity level. Processes with this integrity level can interact with user areas of the registry (HKEY_CURRENT_USER) and the user's documents folder.
Low	An untrusted integrity level. Processes with this integrity level can write to low-integrity locations only, including Temporary Internet Files\Low and low-integrity registry areas (HKEY_CURRENT_USER\Software\LowRegistry key).

When Internet Explorer is running with Protected Mode enabled, it is operating at a low integrity level, limiting it to the low-integrity areas of the system. This prevents an errant Internet Explorer process from accessing sensitive areas of the system and restricts the damage it can do.

Windows 8 and Internet Explorer 10 introduce *AppContainer*, a new process-isolation mechanism that takes the Protected Mode feature found in earlier versions of Internet Explorer to the next level by blocking even more areas of the system from both read and write activities initiated by Internet Explorer, including a user's personal files and certain network locations. All Windows 8 native apps use AppContainer to help protect the system.

Because Protected Mode restricts access to so many parts of the system, it follows that there would be significant compatibility issues with some websites, and users would face a multitude of user account control (UAC) elevation requests during which the operating system requests user permission to perform a potentially dangerous administrative function. However, this is not the case. When a user browses to a location that contains code requesting access to an area of the system protected by Protected Mode, by virtue of the Protected Mode Compatibility Layer the request is silently redirected to a safe, supported location.

Disabling Protected Mode

Although Protected Mode remains an important tool in the security arsenal, it does have the potential to disrupt productivity. Therefore, it's possible for you to disable this security feature on a zone-by-zone basis. For example, you might want to keep Protected Mode enabled for Internet sites but disable it for intranet-based sites so that users can run older intranet applications that might have compatibility issues with newer browsers. In addition, as a troubleshooting step when a user is having difficulty with a particular website, you might find it necessary to disable Protected Mode.

To disable Protected Mode for a zone, complete the following steps:

1. From Internet Explorer for the desktop, open Tools and select Internet Options. If the Tools menu isn't visible, press Alt+T on the keyboard.

2. Select the Security tab.

3. Choose the zone for which you'd like to disable Protected Mode (Figure 5-12).

4. Clear the check box next to Enable Protected Mode.

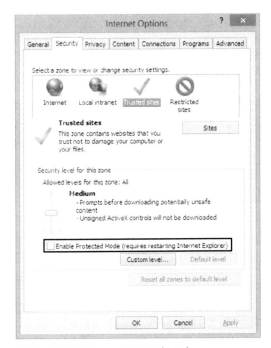

FIGURE 5-12 Disabling Protected Mode

5. Click OK until you're back at a browser window.

6. Restart Internet Explorer.

Adding trusted sites to Internet Explorer

Although Internet Explorer 10 contains a number of features intended to protect users from Internet-based threats delivered through the web, these protections can sometimes get in the way of productivity. In these cases, administrators can just add a website to the Internet Explorer list of trusted sites. By doing so, you enable the user to access the trusted site without interference from many of the Internet Explorer security measures.

To add a site to the Trusted Sites list, complete the following steps:

1. Open Internet Explorer from the desktop.
2. In Tools, select Internet Options and choose the Security tab.
3. On the Security tab, choose the Trusted Sites zone, and then click Sites (see Figure 5-12).
4. In the Trusted Sites dialog box, as shown in Figure 5-13, make sure that the address of the website you want to add is the one that appears in the Add This Website To The Zone box.

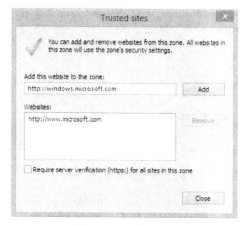

FIGURE 5-13 Adding a specified site to the list of trusted sites

5. If the site is using HTTP rather than HTTPS, clear the Require Server Verification (https:) For All Sites In This Zone check box.
6. Click the Add button next to the website URL and then click OK to return to the Internet Explorer page.

Managing Internet Explorer security settings by using Group Policy

A number of Group Policy items have to do with Internet Explorer security. Group Policy makes it easier to manage Internet Explorer settings across the organization.

Enabling Enhanced Protected Mode by using Group Policy

Rather than manually configuring Internet Explorer on each individual computer to use Enhanced Protected Mode, you can configure the following Group Policy settings:

- **Policy name**   Turn on Enhanced Protected Mode.
- **Policy path**   Windows Components, Internet Explorer, Internet Control Panel, Advanced Page.
- **Policy description**   Enhanced Protected Mode provides additional protection against malicious websites by using 64-bit processes on 64-bit versions of Windows. For computers running Windows 8, Enhanced Protected Mode also limits the locations Internet Explorer can read from in the registry and the file system.
- **Enabled**   If you enable this policy setting, Enhanced Protected Mode is turned on. Any zone that has Protected Mode enabled will use Enhanced Protected Mode. Users cannot disable Enhanced Protected Mode.
- **Disabled**   If you disable this policy setting, Enhanced Protected Mode is turned off. Any zone that has Protected Mode enabled will use the version of Protected Mode introduced in Internet Explorer 7 for Windows Vista.
- **Not Configured**   If you do not configure this policy, users can turn on or turn off Enhanced Protected Mode on the Advanced tab of the Internet Options dialog box.

Password display

For years, security professionals have asked users to be wary of people watching them as they type their passwords. In Windows 8, a new feature places a little eyeball in password fields. When this eyeball is clicked, the plaintext password is displayed, which might be considered a major security issue. The following Group Policy disables this feature.

- **Policy name**   Do not display the Reveal Password button.
- **Policy path**   The path is Windows Components, Internet Explorer, Security Features.
- **Policy Description**   This policy setting enables you to hide the Reveal Password button when Internet Explorer prompts users for a password. The Reveal Password button is displayed during password entry. When the user clicks the button, the current password value is visible until the mouse button is released (or until the tap ends).
- **Enabled**   If you enable this policy setting, the Reveal Password button will be hidden for all password fields. Users and developers will not be able to depend on the Reveal Password button being displayed in any web form or web application.
- **Disabled Or Not Configured**   If you disable or do not configure this policy setting, the Reveal Password button can be shown by the application as a user types a password. The Reveal Password button is visible by default.
- **Notes**   In Windows 8, if the Do Not Display The Reveal Password Button policy setting located in Computer Configuration\Administrative Templates\Windows Components \Credential User Interface is enabled for the system, it will override this policy setting.

Lesson summary

- Internet Explorer 10 includes a new security feature, Enhanced Protected Mode, which reduces the ability of a malicious website to gain access to unauthorized areas of a system.

- With support for a new HTML5 sandbox attribute, Internet Explorer 10 is well protected from being compromised by IFrame-based security attacks.

- Enhanced memory protection through High Entropy Address Space Layout Randomization for forced ASLR makes it more difficult for attackers to predict memory locations through which to launch an attack.

- Adding sites to the Trusted Sites list allows intentional access to these sites without interference from many of the Internet Explorer security features.

- Group Policy items can manage many of the Internet Explorer security features.

Lesson review

Answer the following questions to test your knowledge of the information in this lesson. You can find the answers to these questions and explanations of why each answer choice is correct or incorrect in the "Answers" section at the end of this chapter.

1. How does High Entropy Address Space Layout Randomization improve system security and prevent malware infections?

   A. It lays out memory space in an easily recognizable pattern so that antimalware tools know what to look for.

   B. It randomizes memory address spaces to prevent malware from predicting where certain code will reside.

   C. It prevents code from being loaded in certain areas of memory.

   D. It reduces the amount of memory available to potentially malicious programs so all their code can't fit in memory.

2. Which areas of the system are available to Internet Explorer when Protected Mode is enabled?

   A. All areas of the system are available.

   B. Only areas that contain program files and restricted registry keys are available.

   C. The user's documents folder is available.

   D. Areas identified as low integrity are available.

3. Which new Windows 8 feature further limits the ability of Internet Explorer to access sensitive areas of the system?

   A. Enhanced Protected Mode

   B. Protected Mode

   C. Enhanced Memory Protected

   D. Secure Boot

Lesson 3: Managing Internet Explorer add-ons

Add-ons are programs that extend the capability of Internet Explorer to handle other activities. For example, one of the most popular add-ons in use in Internet Explorer enables playing Flash-based media files from sites such as YouTube. Although many websites are switching to HTML5 to support multimedia, add-ons such as the Flash player remain critical for a seamless end-user browsing experience.

After this lesson, you will be able to:

■ Describe the positive and negative outcomes that arise from add-ons.

■ Manage ActiveX controls to balance security and usability.

■ Describe the various kinds of add-ons Internet Explorer supports.

■ Enable and disable add-ons.

■ Use Group Policy to manage Internet Explorer add-ons.

Estimated lesson time: 30 minutes

Understanding add-ons

Internet Explorer supports add-ons that provide a wide array of services. For example:

■ You can run an add-on that provides audio and video support for a unique protocol.

■ Businesses can use ActiveX-based add-ons to extend the capability of their web applications.

■ Users might unwittingly run an ActiveX add-on that installs malware on their PC.

Add-ons can be useful, but they can also create challenges. In Internet Explorer 10, your ability to use add-ons depends on which variation of Internet Explorer 10 you're using. One of the critical differences between the two variations of Internet Explorer 10 in Windows 8 is in how each supports add-ons. Add-ons have two important drawbacks:

■ They are not touch-friendly.

■ They have been one of the most common vectors by which attackers have managed to infect Windows systems with malware.

Therefore, the use of add-ons is not supported in the touch-optimized variation of Internet Explorer 10, although the desktop variation continues to provide full support. Because the touch-optimized UI in Internet Explorer 10 doesn't support add-ons, you might have a very different browsing experience as you move between the two variations of the product, and you might not be able to do everything in the touch-optimized UI to which you've become accustomed in the desktop UI.

Managing ActiveX controls

For those using the traditional Internet Explorer 10 for the desktop, ActiveX controls remain the most common type of add-on that users will experience. In modern versions of Internet Explorer, the user is protected from malicious ActiveX controls through a combination of administrator-defined parameters and warnings that appear when ActiveX content is about to be executed.

Controlling ActiveX opt-in

The most common interaction that you will have with ActiveX occurs when someone browses to a site on the Internet that requires an ActiveX add-on to be installed to enable some kind of functionality on the page. When this happens, an Active-X installation request like the one shown in Figure 5-14 appears at the bottom of the browsing window.

FIGURE 5-14 Request for user permission to install an ActiveX control

These kinds of ActiveX controls are not installed automatically. Instead, a user must deliberately click the Install button to proceed with the installation of the identified tool. When the user clicks Install, the Windows 8 User Account Control feature intercepts the installation request and requests permission for the installation to proceed. If the user allows the installation, the installation proceeds, and the ActiveX control is allowed to operate.

In the preceding example, the user was browsing to a site on the Internet, which is why she had to go through the multistep approval process to install the ActiveX control. The outcome is different if the user is browsing to a local site on the intranet or to a site on the Trusted Sites list. If browsing to a site that exists in one of those zones, the user is not prompted for the installation of the ActiveX control because controls in those zones are assumed to be trusted.

You can modify the behavior of Internet Explorer so that it requires permission before executing ActiveX controls. To change the configuration of a zone, complete the following steps:

1. Open Internet Explorer from the desktop.

2. In Tools, choose Internet Options and select the Security tab.

3. Choose the zone you'd like to modify and click the Custom Level button near the bottom of the window.

4. In the Security Settings window—which is like the windows shown in Figures 5-15 and 5-16—scroll down until you locate the ActiveX Controls And Plug-Ins section.

FIGURE 5-15 A list of ActiveX settings for the Internet zone

FIGURE 5-16 A list of ActiveX settings for the Local Intranet zone

5. Under Allow Previous Unused ActiveX Controls To Run Without Prompting, decide how you want to handle these items:

- Choose Enable to avoid the user having to intervene in the installation process.

- Choose Disable to require the user to approve the installation of all ActiveX controls from sites in this zone.

6. Click OK until you're back at the browsing window.

Managing ActiveX behavior

A number of other ActiveX configuration options are configured on a per-zone basis. Table 5-2 provides you with a look at the available settings that relate to ActiveX.

TABLE 5-2 ActiveX configuration behavior

Setting	Description	Internet	Intranet	Trusted
Allow Previously Unused ActiveX Controls To Run Without Prompt	If an ActiveX control already ran once, allow it to run again without prompting the user.	Disable	Enable	Enable
Automatic Prompting For ActiveX Controls	By default, a user is notified in the information bar that an ActiveX control is needed for an operation and is then provided with an opportunity to install it. Enabling this option bypasses the information bar and asks the user directly if the control should be installed.	Disable	Enable	Disable

Setting	Description	Internet	Intranet	Trusted
Download Signed ActiveX Controls	Allows the user to download ActiveX controls that have a valid signature. These are generally considered safer than unsigned controls.	Prompt User	Prompt User	Prompt User
Download Unsigned ActiveX Controls	Allows the user to download ActiveX controls that have not been signed. These are generally considered high-risk controls.	Disable	Disable	Disable
Initialize And Script ActiveX Controls Not Marked As Safe For Scripting	This setting is rarely used except when troubleshooting.	Disable	Disable	Disable
Only Allow Approved Domains To Use ActiveX Without Prompting	This policy setting controls whether the user is prompted to allow ActiveX controls to run on websites other than the website that installed the ActiveX control.	Enable	Disable	Disable
Run ActiveX Controls And Plugins	This setting is the master switch for ActiveX controls. When enabled, other ActiveX settings control behavior. When disabled, no ActiveX activity can take place.	Enable	Enable	Enable
Script ActiveX Controls Marked As Safe For Scripting	This setting is rarely used except when troubleshooting.	Enable	Enable	Enable

 Quick check

  ▪ **For sites in the Internet zone, if an ActiveX control already ran once, can it run again without prompting the user?**

  Quick check answer

  ▪ **No**

Managing other add-ons

ActiveX is just one method by which Internet Explorer for the desktop can be extended. A number of other add-ons are available in the Internet Explorer add-on area, including:

  ▪ **Toolbars and extensions**   These are add-ons that generally add visible elements to the Internet Explorer interface, including add-ons such as the Bing toolbar and weather information.

    ▪ ActiveX control   You've already learned about ActiveX controls and how to install new ones. An ActiveX control is a method by which developers enable Internet Explorer to handle new content types such as Flash video.

    ▪ Browser helper object   Browser helper objects are a second method developers use to enable new content-type handling in Internet Explorer. For example, if you install the Adobe Reader product, a new browser helper object is created that enables PDF files to be displayed in Internet Explorer by using Adobe Reader.

- Browser extension   A browser extension imbues Internet Explorer with new capabilities. For example, ieSpell (*http://www.iespell.com/*) is a spell-checker extension for Internet Explorer.

- **Search providers**   Although Bing is the default search engine in Internet Explorer 10, some users prefer to use a different search engine as their default or want to have the option to use a different search engine on demand. These preferences are satisfied through the installation of additional search providers in Internet Explorer, which appear as add-ons.

- **Accelerators**   An accelerator is an add-on that enables you to perform a specific function more quickly than would otherwise be possible. In Figure 5-17, you can see the Translate With Bing add-on in action. To use an accelerator, you just right-click or tap and hold somewhere on the page. When the shortcut menu appears, choose the desired accelerator action.

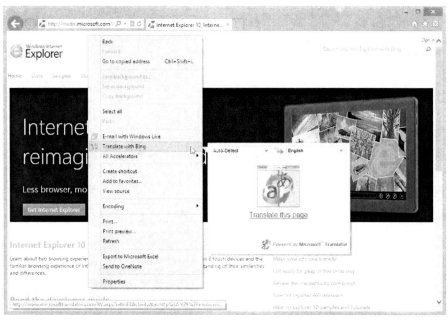

FIGURE 5-17 An accelerator streamlining the process of translating webpages

- **Tracking Protection**   Although tracking protection is displayed along with add-ons, it's really not an add-on. Rather, this is a security feature included in Internet Explorer that enables users to subscribe to protection lists, which include content that, if encountered, Internet Explorer blocks.

These kinds of additions can open Internet Explorer users to new vulnerabilities if the add-on is malicious or poorly written. In addition, having too many or using poorly developed add-ons can result in a degraded browsing experience for users. By understanding how to manage add-ons in Internet Explorer, administrators have at their disposal a method by which to troubleshoot security and performance issues related to web browsing.

Enabling or disabling add-ons

To enable or disable add-ons for Internet Explorer, complete the following steps:

1. Open the Manage Add-Ons window, shown in Figure 5-18.

FIGURE 5-18 The Manage Add-Ons window

2. If you can start Internet Explorer, choose Tools and select Manage Add-Ons.

   If Internet Explorer won't start, open Control Panel and choose Internet Options. On the Programs tab, click the Manage Add-Ons button.

3. From the Manage Add-Ons window, select the add-on you'd like to manage.

   If the add-on is disabled, click the Enable button to enable the add-on. If the add-on is enabled, click the Disable button to disable the add-on.

4. Restart Internet Explorer for your changes to take effect.

Starting Internet Explorer without add-ons

From testing, security, and troubleshooting standpoints, you can start Internet Explorer for the desktop without loading any add-on modules. In fact, this is often the first step administrators take when attempting to resolve browsing issues for a user.

To start Internet Explorer with all add-ons disabled, complete the following steps:

1. Start a command prompt.

2. At the command line, type **C:\Program Files\Internet Explorer\iexplore -extoff**.

   This opens an Internet Explorer for desktop window like the one you see in Figure 5-19. Note the multiple indications that add-ons are currently disabled. If you want to manage add-ons, just click the Manage Add-Ons button in the information bar.

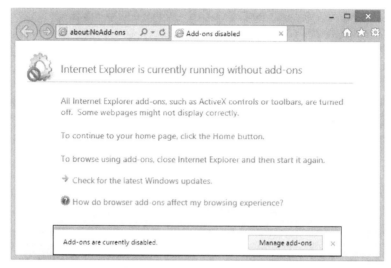

FIGURE 5-19 Internet Explorer running with no add-ons enabled

Managing Internet Explorer add-ons by using Group Policy

A number of Group Policy items can help you manage Internet Explorer add-ons throughout an organization. A few such Group Policy objects that complement previous topics in this chapter are described in the following sections.

Running ActiveX and Enhanced Protected Mode

By using Group Policy, you can also manage how ActiveX controls operate when Protected Mode is enabled.

- **Policy Name**   Do not allow ActiveX controls to run in Protected Mode when Enhanced Protected Mode is enabled.

- **Policy Path**   The path is Windows Components, Internet Explorer, Internet Control Panel, Advanced Page.

- **Policy Description**   This policy setting prevents ActiveX controls from running in Protected Mode when Enhanced Protected Mode is enabled. When a user has an ActiveX control installed that is not compatible with Enhanced Protected Mode and a website attempts to load the control, Internet Explorer notifies the user and offers the option to run the website in regular Protected Mode. This policy setting disables this notification and forces all websites to run in Enhanced Protected Mode. Enhanced Protected Mode provides additional protection against malicious websites by using 64-bit processes on 64-bit versions of Windows. For computers running Windows 8, Enhanced Protected Mode also limits the locations Internet Explorer can read from in the registry and the file system.

- **Enabled**   When Enhanced Protected Mode is enabled, and a user encounters a website that attempts to load an ActiveX control that is not compatible with Enhanced Protected Mode, Internet Explorer notifies the user and offers the option to disable Enhanced Protected Mode for that particular website. If you enable this policy setting, Internet Explorer will not allow the user to disable Enhanced Protected Mode. All Protected Mode websites will run in Enhanced Protected Mode.

- **Disabled Or Not Configured**   If you disable or do not configure this policy setting, Internet Explorer notifies users and provides an option to run websites with incompatible ActiveX controls in regular Protected Mode. This is the default behavior.

Preventing the installation of add-ons

By using the following Group Policy settings, you can prevent the installation of add-ons unless those add-ons are included as part of another Group Policy, called the Add-On List.

- **Policy Name**   Deny all add-ons unless specifically allowed in the Add-On List.

- **Policy Path** The path is Windows Components, Internet Explorer, Security Features, Add-on Management.

- **Policy Description**   This policy setting enables you to ensure that any Internet Explorer add-ons not listed in the Add-On List policy setting are denied. Add-ons in this case are controls such as ActiveX controls, toolbars, and browser helper objects (BHOs), which are specifically written to extend or enhance the functionality of the browser or webpages. By default, the Add-On List policy setting (described next) defines a list of add-ons to be allowed or denied through Group Policy. However, users can still use the Add-On Manager within Internet Explorer to manage add-ons not listed in the Add-On List policy setting. This policy setting effectively removes this option from users; all add-ons are assumed to be denied unless they are specifically allowed through the Add-On List policy setting.

- **Enabled**   If you enable this policy setting, Internet Explorer allows only add-ons that are specifically listed (and allowed) through the Add-On List policy setting.

- **Disabled Or Not Configured**   If you disable or do not configure this policy setting, users can use Add-On Manager to allow or deny any add-ons that are not included in the Add-On List policy setting.

If an add-on is listed in the Add-On List policy setting, the user cannot change its state by using Add-On Manager (unless its value has been set to allow user management; see the "Specify Approved Add-Ons" section, which follows, for more details).

Specify approved add-ons

Although you might establish a Group Policy that disallows the installation of add-ons, you can still enable the installation of specific policies by enabling and configuring the following policy, as shown in Figure 5-20:

- **Policy Name**   Add-On List.
- **Policy Path**   The path is Windows Components, Internet Explorer, Security Features, Add-on Management.
- **Policy Description**   This policy setting enables you to manage a list of add-ons to be allowed or denied by Internet Explorer. Add-ons in this case are controls such as ActiveX controls, toolbars, and BHOs that are specifically written to extend or enhance the functionality of the browser or webpages. This list can be used with the Deny All Add-Ons Unless Specifically Allowed In The Add-On List policy setting, which defines whether add-ons not listed here are assumed to be denied.
- **Enabled**   If you enable this policy setting, you can enter a list of add-ons to be allowed or denied by Internet Explorer. For each entry you add to the list, enter the following information:
  - Name of the value   The CLSID (class identifier) for the add-on you want to add to the list. The CLSID should be in brackets, for example, {000000000-0000-0000-0000-0000000000000}. The CLSID for an add-on can be obtained by reading the OBJECT tag from a webpage on which the add-on is referenced.
  - Value   A number indicating whether Internet Explorer should deny or allow the add-on to be loaded. To specify that an add-on should be denied, enter a 0 (zero) in this field. To specify that an add-on should be allowed, enter a 1 (one) in this field. To specify that an add-on should be allowed and to permit the user to manage the add-on by using Add-On Manager, enter a 2 (two) in this field.
- **Disabled**   If you disable this policy setting, the list is deleted. The Deny All Add-Ons Unless Specifically Allowed In The Add-On List policy setting will still determine whether add-ons not in this list are assumed to be denied.

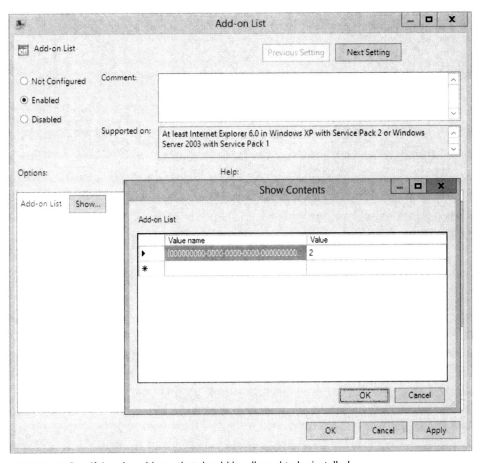

FIGURE 5-20 Specifying the add-ons that should be allowed to be installed

Lesson summary

- Add-ons are a method by which the capabilities of Internet Explorer can be extended to meet new needs.
- There are several kinds of add-ons, including toolbars and extensions, search providers, accelerators, and tracking protection.
- Because add-ons can be unfriendly for touch and are considered a security weakness, they are not supported by touch-optimized Internet Explorer.
- If they become a security risk or create system instability, add-ons can be disabled.
- During troubleshooting, an administrator can launch Internet Explorer with all add-ons disabled.

- A variety of ActiveX configuration options are available in Internet Explorer, each configured on a per-zone basis.
- Group Policy can be used in an enterprise environment to deploy add-on policies easily to all managed clients.

Lesson review

Answer the following questions to test your knowledge of the information in this lesson. You can find the answers to these questions and explanations of why each answer choice is correct or incorrect in the "Answers" section at the end of this chapter.

1. Which kind of add-on enables you to perform a specific function more quickly than would otherwise be possible?

   A. Accelerator

   B. Toolbar

   C. BHO

   D. Search provider

2. How do you start Internet Explorer in "no add-ons" mode?

   A. Right-click the Internet Explorer icon..

   B. From a command prompt, type **C:\Program Files\Internet Explorer\iexplore -noext**.

   C. From a command prompt, type **C:\Program Files\Internet Explorer\iexplore -extoff**.

   D. Open Internet Explorer from Control Panel.

Practice exercises

In these practice exercises, you practice different techniques for managing the Windows 8 Start screen and reinforce how to manage the new Windows 8 Start screen.

Exercise 1: Configure ActiveX (Internet zone)

In this exercise, you configure ActiveX settings so that an ActiveX control that's run once can run again without prompting the user.

1. Open Internet Settings.

2. For the Internet zone, configure ActiveX to meet the requirements of this exercise.

Exercise 2: Disable the Map With Bing accelerator

In this exercise, you synchronize two devices. To access the PC settings area, which provides you with access to the selections you need to enable or disable synchronizing settings between Windows 8 devices, complete the following steps:

1. Open Internet Options.

2. Open Manage Add-Ons and disable the accelerator.

Suggested practice exercises

The following additional practices are designed to give you more opportunities to practice what you've learned and to help you successfully master the lessons presented in this chapter.

■ **Exercise 1**   Configure Internet Explorer to open links by using just Internet Explorer for the desktop.

■ **Exercise 2**   Create a Group Policy that configures Internet Explorer to open links using just Internet Explorer for the desktop.

■ **Exercise 3**   Enable Enhanced Protected Mode in Internet Explorer.

Answers

This section contains the answers to the lesson review questions in this chapter.

Lesson 1

1. **Correct answer: A**

   A. **Correct:** Location services are managed from the touch-optimized variant.

   B. **Incorrect:** Location services are managed from touch-optimized Internet Explorer, not from Internet Explorer for the desktop.

   C. **Incorrect:** Internet Options in Internet Explorer for the desktop cannot be used to manage Location services.

   D. **Incorrect:** Touch-optimized Internet Explorer cannot be uninstalled from Windows 8.

2. **Correct answer: D**

   A. **Incorrect:** The Always In Internet Explorer setting is administered from Internet Explorer for the desktop.

   B. **Incorrect:** The Always In Internet Explorer For Desktop is administered from Internet Explorer for the desktop, not from touch-optimized Internet Explorer.

   C. **Incorrect:** "Internet Explorer" in this context refers to touch-optimized Internet Explorer.

   D. **Correct:** The Always In Internet Explorer For Desktop setting is administered from Internet Explorer for the desktop.

Lesson 2

1. **Correct answer: B**

   A. **Incorrect:** An easy-to-guess pattern enables attackers to exploit the system more easily.

   B. **Correct:** Randomizing memory locations for software code makes it more difficult for attackers to achieve their goals.

   C. **Incorrect:** Code is randomized in memory, not blocked.

   D. **Incorrect:** RAM is not artificially limited.

2. **Correct answer: D**

   A. **Incorrect:** Protected Mode significantly limits access to sensitive areas of the system.

   B. **Incorrect:** Protected Mode significantly limits access to sensitive areas of the system.

    C. **Incorrect:** Protected Mode significantly limits access to a user's personal files.

    D. **Correct:** Only low-impact areas are accessible, and even fewer areas are accessible when Enhanced Protected Mode is enabled.

3. **Correct answer: A**

    A. **Correct:** Enhanced Protected Mode picks up where Protected Mode leaves off and provides additional security.

    B. **Incorrect:** Protected Mode is not new to Windows 8.

    C. **Incorrect:** Enhanced Memory Protection is a technique by which code is randomized in memory to thwart attackers.

    D. **Incorrect:** Secure Boot is a feature intended to provide additional security to the system while it starts up.

Lesson 3

1. **Correct answer: A**

    A. **Correct:** An accelerator is an add-on that streamlines the overall user experience.

    B. **Incorrect:** A toolbar is a GUI add-on that adds functionality.

    C. **Incorrect:** A BHO enables Internet Explorer to handle new content types.

    D. **Incorrect:** A search provider is an additional search engine that can be added to Internet Explorer.

2. **Correct answer: C**

    A. **Incorrect:** Right-clicking the Internet Explorer icon is not a correct method.

    B. **Incorrect:** -noext is not a valid switch.

    C. **Correct:** The -extoff switch opens Internet Explorer with no add-ons.

    D. **Incorrect:** Internet Explorer cannot be opened from Control Panel.

CHAPTER 6

Using Hyper-V

Virtualization is no longer a technology reserved for the data center and server administrators. Windows 8 brings a new standard to the client operating system by including a very capable virtualization engine called Hyper-V. Windows 8 enables users to run virtual machines on a system with ease and incredible capabilities. In fact, the Hyper-V technology included with Windows 8 is the same engine as on Windows Server 2012. This feature is available only on Windows 8 Pro and is added as a Windows feature.

For many Windows users, this technology might pose a significant learning curve. Specifically, the concept of virtualized hardware resources for virtual machines is different from that of a physical computer. However, there are many use cases for Hyper-V with Windows 8 that you should consider; they are explained in this chapter.

Lessons in this chapter:

Before you begin

This chapter is targeted for Windows 8 users or administrators who have little to no experience with virtual machines. If virtualization is new to you, this chapter will be an important part of rounding out your understanding. Windows 8 introduces a powerful virtualization engine, and the high-level details in this chapter, supplemented by the practical exercises and use cases, will ensure that this important feature is not overlooked.

Lesson 1: Learning about Hyper-V for Windows 8

With Windows 8, a number of changes truly raise the bar for what you can expect from a client operating system. In this lesson, you learn about Hyper-V for Windows 8, a powerful virtualization engine. You might recognize Hyper-V as a server-side technology that has been used for running a virtual machine (VM). This same technology is now available on the client operating system.

To understand Hyper-V fully, first you should know a little about its history. Microsoft has long had a virtualization offering to run virtual machines, with products such as Microsoft Virtual PC and Microsoft Virtual Server. A *virtual machine* is a fully encapsulated instance of an operating system that can be run on a computer running Hyper-V. These are known as *Type 2 hypervisors*, by which the virtual machines run on top of the Windows operating system on which Virtual PC or Virtual Server has been installed. When Windows Server 2008 was released, the virtualization engine was materially changed and became a Type 1 hypervisor. As a Type 1 hypervisor, the virtual machines run directly on the hardware of the computer. Hyper-V can now exist in three key ways: as a role on a Windows Server system (Windows Server 2012 and Windows Server 2008), as its own operating system (Hyper-V Server 2012, Hyper-V Server 2008 R2), and in Windows 8.

After this lesson, you will be able to:

- Describe what a virtual machine is for Windows 8 and how it can be useful.
- Understand the system requirements for Hyper-V on Windows 8.
- Add the Hyper-V feature to a Windows 8 system.

Estimated lesson time: 60 minutes

Introducing Hyper-V for Windows 8

If you are new to virtualization, Windows 8 is the perfect platform to familiarize you with virtualization. For a number of reasons, it is a great technology that will enable you to do more with your computing environment. Further, there is an incredible virtualization community on social sites such as blogs, Twitter, and podcasts and at major events around the globe.

A virtual machine might at first seem difficult to explain. To compound this, a number of definitions in use in the technology space seem to vary based on which virtualization engine is in use. For Windows 8, a virtual machine running in Hyper-V is a contained instance of an operating system with direct access to physical hardware.

Hyper-V virtual machines run within the same computer on which Windows 8 is installed. Today, the hardware used for desktops, notebooks, and other mainstream computing devices are quite capable systems, and the processors have other virtualization technologies built in.

In terms of the operating system being an "instance," this just means that the computer running Windows 8 runs it with its own name, TCP/IP address, installed applications, and other aspects. The virtual machine has all these same, specific attributes and can be transported easily because it is contained in files, which is discussed in Lesson 3, "Configuring virtual machine networking and storage," later in this chapter.

Hyper-V Manager provides the console in which you perform virtual machine tasks, and, as shown in Figure 6-1, the Actions bar on the right is where many tasks and configuration settings are applied. It is important to note that multiple objects are in play. Both the individual virtual machines are a collection of objects, and the Windows 8 system with the Hyper-V feature is an object. Each type of object can have individual settings applied.

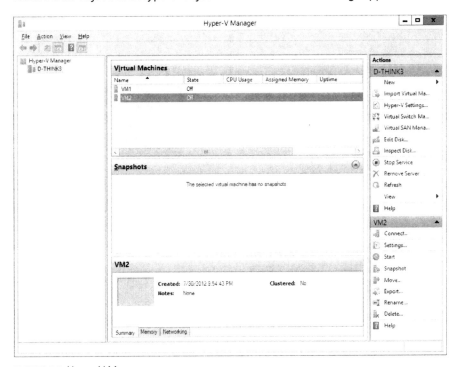

FIGURE 6-1 Hyper-V Manager

When to use Hyper-V

Not every Windows 8–based computer should have Hyper-V enabled. In fact, enabling it should be a selective process. Users who most often encounter the typical situations that warrant virtual-machine usage include developers, system administrators, and other power users who need access to many systems. Avoid putting Hyper-V on a computer running Windows 8 unless you have a specific need.

This poses the question of when Hyper-V should be enabled and for what specific uses. There are no clear-cut rules because every computing environment is different. However, a few popular cases should help you see when Hyper-V might be a good option on a client computer system.

Test environments for system administrators

If you are a system administrator, you might want to enable Hyper-V on your computer to provide test environments for client or server operating systems. In fact, on Windows 8 with the Hyper-V feature enabled, you can run a Windows Server 2012 virtual machine! This virtual machine can join the domain, have applications installed, and receive Windows updates (and set additional configuration options) without interfering with Windows 8. This use for critical applications can keep the Windows 8 environment clean, yet enable you to provide adequate and representative test environments for server applications.

Application compatibility situations

There are a number of situations when an application might not work on a newer operating system. This can be due to an application being built for x86 environments, needing a specific obsolete browser, or reproducing client computing environments in which the operating systems are mixed. With Hyper-V on Windows 8, virtual machines can be added to accommodate all these situations.

Test environments for desktop support technicians

Client computing professionals might want to have a virtual machine available to test configuration elements such as automated application deployments, granular permissions, environment scripting, and more. Having a Hyper-V virtual machine on the Windows 8–based computer can enable you, as the desktop support technician, to provide this test environment without compromising your primary workspace.

Environments for application developers

Application developers have an incredible opportunity with virtualization on the client. This can even be an opportunity to reduce unfavorable situations such as server sprawl in the data center. If you can run your critical virtual machines locally for testing and code development, that might also reduce the burden on the virtualized server infrastructure. Consider offering Windows 8 virtualization on the client to help reduce the development infrastructure requirement in the data center.

Data management and licensing

In all situations in which Hyper-V is deployed, data protection needs to be considered. Specifically, if any of the virtual machines are being used in any sort of production capacity (or code is kept there), additional steps need to be taken to ensure that the work is not lost and all data is kept in the correct locations. This primarily means backups or code revision control.

Enabling Hyper-V

The Hyper-V hypervisor is included with Windows 8 but must be enabled. This means it is a feature and can be added easily with Windows. Before you enable this feature, make sure you have the right configuration. The first configuration point is related to which Windows 8 edition you have; only Windows 8 Pro supports Hyper-V. Next, an x64 processor and a supported virtualization technology on the processor are required. The mainstream virtualization technology that will run Hyper-V on processors shipping around the release of Windows 8 is Second Level Address Translation (SLAT). Last, the computer running Windows 8 might need a virtualization technology enabled in the BIOS.

In addition to the SLAT virtualization technology for the processor described previously, Windows 8 needs at least 4 GB of memory for Hyper-V. Depending on which virtual machines will be used, more memory might be required.

No drive space in addition to the Windows 8 base amount is required; however, each virtual machine will consume drive space and reduce available disk resources as it grows.

To enable Hyper-V on Windows 8, complete the following steps:

1. Press the Windows logo key on your keyboard and then select Settings to open the Windows Features dialog box, as shown in Figure 6-2.

FIGURE 6-2 Adding the Hyper-V feature to a new computer running Windows 8

2. The Hyper-V feature is not turned on with a default installation of Windows 8. To turn on this or any other feature, select the check box next to the feature and click OK.

3. Restart your computer.

   The restart is required after a feature is added to the Windows 8–based computer.

4. Open Hyper-V Manager, and then add in the computer name of the server running Windows 8 with the Hyper-V feature enabled. The console will populate with the virtual machines on that host (which should be empty by default).

> **NOTE WINDOWS 8 AS A SERVER**
>
> When Hyper-V is enabled, the Hyper-V Manager tool is installed on the computer running Windows 8. To avoid confusion, refer to the Windows 8–based computer as a server. Even though it is a client operating system, in terms of the virtual machines it is providing, it functions as a server. This is evident within Hyper-V Manager because the first step in enabling Hyper-V is adding a server to the console.

What you need to know to succeed

Getting started with Hyper-V is easy, but a number of points should be addressed ahead of time. In addition to how and when Hyper-V will be used, you will also need a thorough understanding of a number of critical elements of the virtualization technology as a whole so you will be successful.

Hyper-V operating systems

A broad offering of the Windows family of operating systems is supported with Hyper-V. Windows Server families include Microsoft Windows Server 2003, Windows Server 2008, and Windows Server 2012. Client operating system families include Microsoft Windows XP, Windows Vista, Windows 7, and Windows 8.

Linux operating systems are also supported in the CentOS 6, Red Hat Enterprise Linux 6, and SUSE Linux Enterprise Server 11 families.

> **MORE INFO SUPPORTED OPERATING SYSTEMS**
>
> **A full breakdown of the supported operating systems can be found on TechNet at *http:// technet.microsoft.com/library/hh831531.aspx*.**

Guest enlightenment

With the broad set of operating systems offered for Hyper-V, it is important to understand a critical aspect of how these operating systems work on Hyper-V. *Guest enlightenment* is a generic term that refers to a virtual machine's ability to work correctly in the hypervisor. In layperson's terms, this means drivers. For most Windows family situations, this is built in, but a number of scenarios require interaction to optimize the virtual machine in the Hyper-V environment.

For Hyper-V on Windows 8, adding a Windows 8 Hyper-V virtual machine is a nonissue. Integration services are built in (see Figure 6-3). Adding a Windows 7 virtual machine, however, requires an update of the guest enlightenment drivers: Integration Services.

After a virtual machine is running, a virtualized disk can be inserted to update Integration Services by pressing Ctrl+I while viewing the virtual machine's console.

The Integration Services guest enlightenment kit provides drivers and critical Windows services on the virtual machine that can address critical topics such as *quiescence* (the act of quieting a virtual machine), time synchronization, shutdown events, and other critical virtual machine events.

> **NOTE INTEROPERABILITY**
>
> **Linux and Hyper-V will get along just fine.**

Integration Services took a major step forward recently when the Hyper-V drivers (components of Integration Services) were put into the main Linux kernel branch. This means that as the main Linux kernel is deployed across multiple additional distributions, Hyper-V will work right out of the box.

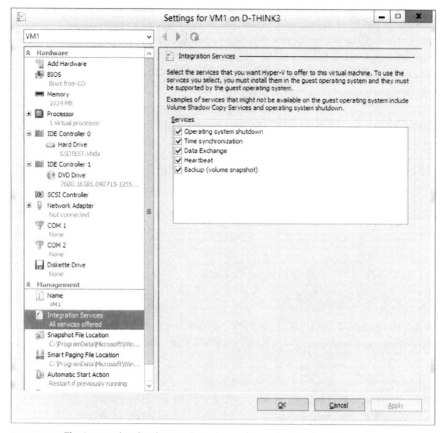

FIGURE 6-3 The Integration Services options shown for each virtual machine

> **IMPORTANT KEY DIFFERENCES**
>
> It is important to note the difference between "an operating system that works" and a supported Hyper-V operating system. To learn more about this difference, read "Ubuntu 12.04 under Hyper-V on Windows 8" by Ben Armstrong on his Virtual PC Guy Blog at *http://blogs.msdn.com/b/virtual_pc_guy/archive/2012/05/02/ubuntu-12-04-under-hyper-v-on-windows-8.aspx.*

Windows PowerShell extension

Windows 8 has Windows PowerShell 3.0 built in, and Hyper-V has a PowerShell extension. This makes automation easy and is an excellent opportunity to learn new ways to perform Windows administrative tasks. The latest commands for Windows PowerShell can be found on TechNet and other online communities such as blogs and PowerShell podcasts.

Virtualized media

Although mentioned previously for Integration Services, virtualized media is an important step in using Hyper-V virtualization. Specifically, it is how guest virtual machines can be installed on the Hyper-V server system. Although many of the Hyper-V technologies are new to Windows 8, virtualized media is something you have been using all along. Consider the CD-ROM or DVD-ROM ISO file used to install Windows. That is a form of virtualized media, and this file is downloaded and then written to an optical disk. This same ISO file is used in the first step to deploy a Hyper-V virtual machine. The ISO format is the most frequently used virtualized media for installing virtual machines.

If you will have a number of Hyper-V servers—which are computers running Windows 8 with the Hyper-V feature enabled—you should designate a predefined repository for all virtual media. In this manner, all virtual machines being built will use the same media without causing unnecessary bloat on client systems with a potentially confusing array of files. This repository can be a network drive letter or a Universal Naming Convention (UNC) path that the Hyper-V server can access. Non-virtualized media can also be used, such as a local CD/DVD drive for source media. The CD/DVD drive settings are shown in Figure 6-4.

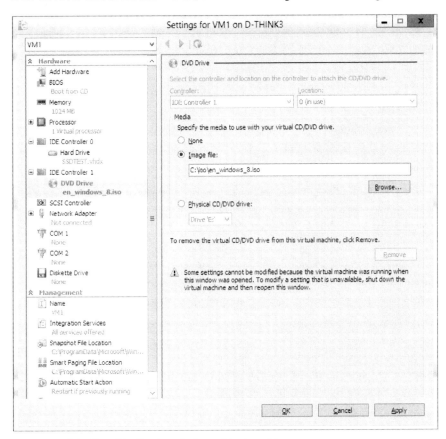

FIGURE 6-4 Selecting virtualized media for a virtual machine

If automated deployment technologies are already in place, you can also use these on Hyper-V. This can include technologies such as PXE (Preboot eXecution Environment) boot and Windows Deployment Services.

 Quick check

- How can you install an operating system in a virtual machine?

Quick check answer

- Start by determining what type of operating system needs to be created, and then obtain the installation image. That usually exists in the form of a CD-ROM or DVD-ROM disc, but can also be an ISO image file. Either of these can be used to install a virtual machine.

Windows Server 2012 Hyper-V technology and Windows 8

Hyper-V on Windows 8 is the same technology as the Hyper-V engine on Windows Server 2012. Therefore, a number of important features become available. Virtual machines can easily be moved from Hyper-V on Windows Server 2012 to Windows 8. Virtual machines can then be portable, which might work well in the "one user to one virtual machine" situation for certain development and test situations.

Lesson summary

- The Hyper-V virtualization engine is included at no additional cost in Windows 8 Pro.
- Virtual machines are managed in the Hyper-V Administrator console, which is available on the computer after Hyper-V is added.
- The Windows 8–based computer running Hyper-V can have virtual machines fully separated for many reasons, including accessing x86 operating systems, different Windows versions, or permissions configuration.
- Although Windows 8 Pro provides Hyper-V at no additional cost, virtual machines running in Windows 8 are not provided with licensing in most situations.
- Virtual machines are installed by having virtualized media such as a CD/DVD ISO file made available to the Windows 8–based computer with Hyper-V enabled.
- Virtual machines running on Hyper-V need guest enlightenment to operate correctly. The Hyper-V enlightenment driver is Integration Services and is built into Windows 8 (as a guest virtual machine) and Windows Server 2012. Earlier editions of Windows have guest enlightenment installed by default but might need updating when running on Windows 8 with the Hyper-V feature enabled.

Lesson review

Answer the following questions to test your knowledge of the information in this lesson. You can find the answers to these questions and explanations of why each answer choice is correct or incorrect in the "Answers" section at the end of this chapter.

1. The virtualization engine provided by Hyper-V in Windows 8 is which type of hypervisor?

   A. Type A hypervisor

   B. Type B hypervisor

   C. Type 1 hypervisor

   D. Type 2 hypervisor

2. Windows 8 offers Hyper-V as which component of the operating system?

   A. A Windows role

   B. A Windows feature

   C. A PowerShell module

   D. A Windows service

3. Windows 8 with the Hyper-V feature enabled is capable of running which of the following operating systems as a virtual machine? (Each correct answer presents a complete solution. Choose three.)

   A. Windows 8

   B. Windows Server 2012

   C. Windows NT

   D. Red Hat Enterprise Linux 6

4. What does Windows 8 require to run Hyper-V?

   A. At least two processors capable of running SLAT

   B. 8 GB of RAM or more

   C. Windows 8 Pro

   D. 127 GB of hard drive space for virtual machines

Lesson 2: Creating and using Hyper-V virtual machines

Creating a virtual machine is not difficult; in fact, it is quite easy. The difficulty will be in dissecting how the specific steps of the virtual machine–creation process are performed. This is especially critical as specific requirements arise. That's the case with many wizard-driven tools: the process is easy, but explaining the options or addressing a nonstandard configuration is difficult.

There are many options and limitations in the process. Although Hyper-V is a very capable virtualization engine, in most situations the virtual machine configuration cannot exceed the capacity of the Windows 8 system with Hyper-V enabled. Choosing specific options such as where the virtual machine will reside are also critical decisions.

> **After this lesson, you will be able to:**
>
> - Create a new virtual machine by using the Hyper-V New Virtual Machine Wizard.
> - Specify additional options aside from the default configuration.
> - Provision a virtual machine with virtual media for operating system installation.
>
> **Estimated lesson time: 60 minutes**

Planning your virtual machines

Each situation in which you might create a virtual machine is different. Therefore, the decision to create a virtual machine must be based on the needs of the particular situation and the policies of your organization. Because of the many variables, there is no best practice for how many or what types of virtual machines should be created. For example, a desktop support technician might maintain a virtual mausoleum of operating systems for large environments where multiple Windows versions are used. This repository can expand quickly when x86 and x64 variants are considered.

A Hyper-V virtual machine has a virtualized hardware inventory of all the components, like a standard Windows 8–based computer: disk, memory, network, and processing. The virtual machine creation process defines how these virtual elements will be configured for the virtual machine.

When you create the virtual machine, you are asked to provide several crucial pieces of information: the name of the machine, where the files will be stored, the amount of memory assigned to it, and the network connection options. Think each of these through before you start creating any virtual machines so that you have a consistent and useful plan in place. This will make troubleshooting easier.

Establishing names and locations

The virtual machine name and location are very important; the name of the virtual machine should match the computer name assigned to it. Consider creating a nomenclature that makes sense in your organization. For example, if computer accounts have a predictable naming pattern, follow it when deploying Hyper-V virtual machines. It might also be worth establishing a naming policy by which you designate a name that identifies it as a virtual machine name, assuming the computer name is the same. This can be something as simple as adding a "-V" to the name or some other addition that makes sense in your organization.

If non-Windows systems are used extensively, consider using fully qualified domain names (FQDNs) for these hosts.

For the location of the virtual machine files, the C drive is used by default in a designated path for Hyper-V in the C:\ProgramData\Microsoft\Windows\Hyper-V folder. If other drive letters or hard drives are added, they can be used as fixed local disk resources. This includes an iSCSI target that can be provisioned as a drive letter and formatted in Windows. Network resources can also be used with SMB 3.0, the Windows 8 and Windows Server file-based network protocol.

Understanding memory availability

Always consider the free space involved. Many Hyper-V administrators avoid placing virtual machines of any quantity or size on the C drive of the Windows 8–based computer with the Hyper-V feature enabled because of the risk of the drive filling to capacity and causing issues with both the virtual machines and the computer running Windows 8.

The memory options are important, and the shared resources should be considered. Depending on the amount of memory installed on the computer running Windows 8, there might be a maximum amount of memory that a virtual machine can use. The Hyper-V feature can be enabled only on computers running Windows 8 with 4 GB of memory or more, and there is a reserved amount for Windows 8. For the 4 GB minimum, 1,882 MB of memory is made available to Hyper-V for virtual machines. All virtual machines that are simultaneously turned on will work from that pool of memory, and virtual machines that are turned off will not consume memory.

 When you configure the storage for a new virtual hard disk, the default format with Hyper-V on Windows 8 is VHDX. *VHDX* is a virtual disk format used in Hyper-V that expands on the popular VHD format used by earlier versions of Hyper-V. The VHDX file format supports virtual disk files up to 64 terabytes (TB) in size, a substantial improvement over the VHD maximum of 2 TB.

The size for the VHDX file is set to 127 GB by default, which is fine for most Windows operating systems. You should consider your environment to determine if that is too large or too small as a maximum. One key technology to assist in this decision is thin provisioning, which will have the virtual disk consume the space used within the virtual machine. Thin provisioning won't provision the entire 127 GB at once, yet it could grow to that size or larger with snapshots, so keep this in mind in the provisioning process.

For new computers running Windows 8, there is usually a large amount of storage available for systems running traditional rotational storage. However, if the computer running Windows 8 is running an SSD, the total available space can be comparatively limited. Keep this in mind when provisioning virtual machines on Windows 8 systems.

Planning installation options

Use these tips for Hyper-V virtual machines to make the virtualized media management easy to use and to avoid duplicated instances of (potentially) large files such as CD/DVD ISO files:

- Have one designated location for virtual media. This can be local (such as C:\ISO) or on a network resource. If multiple Windows 8–based computers will have the Hyper-V feature enabled, it might be worthwhile to provision a dedicated storage resource for the virtual media for a workgroup to share.

- Use a simple name for the files, such as Windows8.iso.

- Keep only the files you need.

- Don't mix distributions of operating systems, such as a TechNet license distribution and possibly the company enterprise licensing media (and licensing).

The physical CD/DVD drive and network and virtual floppy disk resources can be used. For most situations, the virtualized media on a CD/DVD ISO file will be the most popular installation type.

Creating a new virtual machine

To create a new virtual machine, complete the following steps:

1. Press and hold or right-click the Hyper-V Server in Hyper-V Manager to launch the Hyper-V settings.

   The wizard opens and displays the Before You Begin page, shown in Figure 6-5.

FIGURE 6-5 The New Virtual Machine Wizard starting the virtual machine creation process

2. To create a virtual machine with a custom configuration, tap or click Next to open the Specify Name And Location page, shown in Figure 6-6.

FIGURE 6-6 The virtual machine name and location selected in the wizard

3. Type the name of the virtual machine; remember that it should match the computer name assigned to it.

4. Select the Store The Virtual Machine In A Different Location check box to specify a location path. When this check box is selected, the Location text box becomes available, as shown in Figure 6-7. Type the path to identify the designated folder for the virtual machine files, and then tap or click Next.

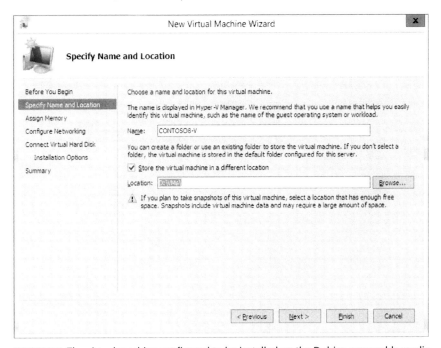

FIGURE 6-7 The virtual machine configured to be installed on the D drive, removable media

5. Type the amount of memory you are allocating to the virtual machine on the Assign Memory page, as shown in Figure 6-8. The Windows 8–based computer memory will be used directly to provide the memory for the virtual machine.

FIGURE 6-8 The virtual machine configured with 1 GB of memory

6. To conserve memory, you can select the Use Dynamic Memory For This Virtual Machine check box.

Dynamic memory provides a base amount of memory that Windows needs at startup and then increases as needed. This is known as startup memory and might not be as much as the defined amount of memory in the New Virtual Machine Wizard.

> **MORE INFO**   **DYNAMIC MEMORY FOR HYPER-V**
>
> This memory management technique is efficient for virtual machines to avoid unnecessary allocation. You can find more information about Hyper-V dynamic memory at *http://technet.microsoft.com/en-us/library/hh831766.aspx.*

7. Tap or click Next to open the Configure Networking page, as shown in Figure 6-9. In addition to Not Connected, there are three types of networking options for Hyper-V virtual machines in Windows 8. Select one of these options:

- **External** Virtual machines on an external virtual switch can communicate directly with the same network as the computer running Windows 8 with the Hyper-V feature enabled. Additional networks such as VLANs can also be used.

- **Internal** Virtual machines on an internal virtual switch can communicate with one another and with the computer running Windows 8 with the Hyper-V feature enabled. Communication with the external network is not provided by the Hyper-V networking in this configuration.

- **Private** A private virtual switch enables virtual machines to communicate with one another but not with the computer running Windows 8 with the Hyper-V feature enabled or the external network.

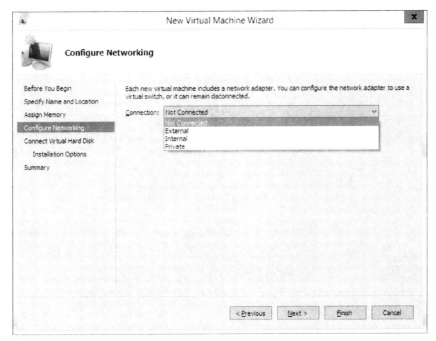

FIGURE 6-9 The virtual machine networking configuration determining where the virtual machine will reside

8. Tap or click Next to open the Connect Virtual Hard Disk page, as shown in Figure 6-10.

    You can create a new disk, use an existing VHD or VHDX disk, or attach a disk later. (Adding a disk later might be a good choice when selecting advanced tasks, such as specific sizing and disabling thin provisioning, are needed. These steps are explained more in Lesson 3.)

With a maximum VHD size of 64 TB, you give the virtual machine more resources than that of the computer running Windows 8 with the Hyper-V feature enabled. This is due to the thin-provisioning benefit of Hyper-V virtual disk files.

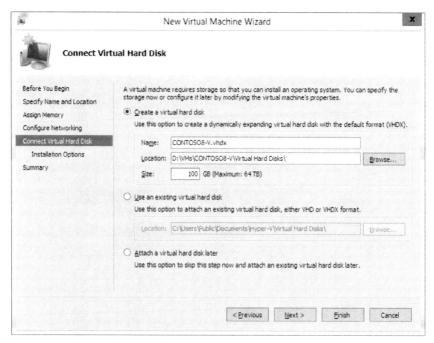

FIGURE 6-10 The virtual machine files and locations set

When you create a new disk, by default, the wizard uses the virtual machine name and location you set in step 4 to determine the name and location of the virtual machine's virtual disk files and the default format, VHDX. The wizard will provision one virtual disk; additional disks can be added later.

9. Make your selections and tap or click Next.

The wizard opens the Installation Options page, as shown in Figure 6-11, which presents the final configuration step. You can choose to install an operating system later or to install and start now from a CD/DVD, a floppy disk, or a network location.

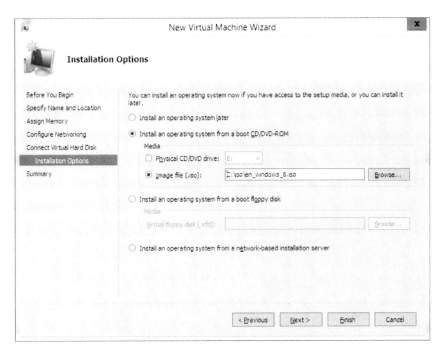

FIGURE 6-11 Virtual media set in the last actionable task of the wizard

10. Make your selections and tap or click Next.

The wizard displays a summary (see Figure 6-12) of the configuration for the virtual machine you are creating. This is the last step of the virtual machine–creation process for a Hyper-V virtual machine.

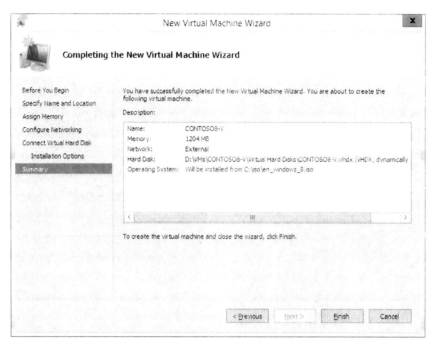

FIGURE 6-12 The New Virtual Machine Wizard providing a summary of the configuration

11. Click Finish.

The wizard will complete processing and create the virtual machine on the computer running Windows 8 with the Hyper-V feature enabled.

Using a Hyper-V virtual machine

After a virtual machine is created and running, you can install an operating system as long as valid physical or virtual media are provided to the virtual machine. When the virtual machine starts, it goes through a boot sequence much like that of a physical PC. The virtual machine attempts to start from a CD or DVD or a network boot (if configured) and then from the virtual disk drive (VHD or VHDX).

Many virtual machines are installed directly from CD/DVD ISO files, and with Hyper-V, this is a straightforward experience. Because of the broad list of supported operating systems for Hyper-V, a computer running Windows 8 with the Hyper-V feature enabled can easily have Windows Server 2012, Windows 7, Linux VMs, and more running directly as virtual machines on a capable computer.

> **NOTE** **MAKE GOOD USE OF THE OPERATING SYSTEM SUPPORT**
>
> This can be a great test environment for critical updates, application compatibility on newer (or older) operating systems, and consolidating multiple computers at a desk for power users.

When you turn on a virtual machine, a number of checks are performed. These include ensuring that enough memory is available on the computer running Windows 8 with the Hyper-V feature enabled for the virtual machine, that the VHDX or VHD files can be locked appropriately by the hypervisor, that any networking components (such as a virtual switch) are available and have enough virtual ports, and, last, that the user issuing the start request has adequate permissions to start a Hyper-V virtual machine on that computer.

When you make a virtual machine connection, you are accessing the virtual console. The *virtual console* is an important concept. Because the virtual machine has a virtual hardware inventory, a virtual monitor or console is connected to it in the Virtual Machine Connection view. This view of the console allows the operating system to be installed on the virtual machine and enables you to view the virtual machine if any problems (such as an error message on the console) occur later in the life of the virtual machine.

The process for installing an operating system in the virtual machine is similar to installing Windows (or other operating systems) on a physical PC:

1. Press and hold or right-click a virtual machine on the Start screen to turn it on.

   A series of checks is performed in the background.

2. When the virtual machine has started, open the Virtual Machine Connection window shown in Figure 6-13 to view the virtual console of the virtual machine.

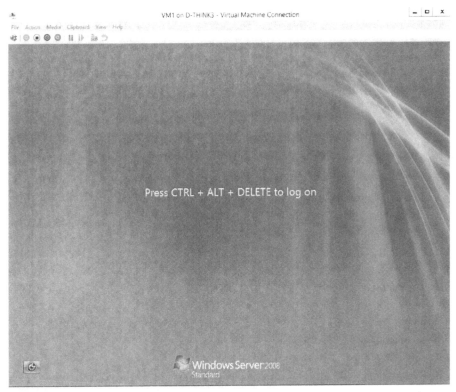

FIGURE 6-13 Viewing the Virtual Machine Connection screen on the virtual machine console

Several critical tasks are available on the Virtual Machine Connection screen:

- With the virtual media options, you can change the current mapping to the local media or disconnect it altogether.

- One of the more helpful options is the ability to send a Ctrl+Alt+Delete keyboard sequence to sign in interactively on the console.

- The Power Off option is different from the Shut Down option. The Power Off task effectively removes the power to the virtual machine. The Shut Down option uses Integration Services to send a proper shutdown command to the virtual machine, and the Windows system shuts down.

- Virtual machine snapshots can be taken from the Virtual Machine Connection screen. This is a handy technique to mark progress on a virtual machine right where you need it.

 A *virtual machine snapshot* is a point-in-time view of that virtual machine, which can be reverted to that point in time if something changes on the virtual machine. *Snapshots* are a great way to mark progress when testing certain situations, but they can quickly be forgotten and just consume endless amounts of drive space. Further, a snapshot by itself is not a backup, so if critical data elements are in play, ensure that none are at risk on Windows 8 virtual machines versus data directly on the Windows 8 file system running Hyper-V.

When you are finished with the virtual machine, just shut it down as you would shut down any other computer or use the action tools in the Hyper-V Manager console.

State-changing tasks

The following state-changing tasks are available for Hyper-V virtual machines on the Virtual Machine Connection screen:

- **Turn Off**   Virtual power-off of the virtual machine.
- **Shut Down**   Sends a shutdown command to Windows, executed through Integration Services, and is a clean shutdown in most situations.
- **Reset**   A hard restart of the VM; for example, if it has stopped responding.
- **Pause**   A way to suspend the VM's running state. The memory allocated on the computer running Windows 8 with the Hyper-V feature enabled will not be released. Conversely, this makes the resume task very quick on the VM.

Migrating a virtual machine to another storage resource

Another powerful feature with Hyper-V on Windows 8 is the ability to migrate a VM to a different storage resource, either while it is running or if it is turned off. The Live Migration technology can place the virtual machine's VHDX and VHD files and other configuration components on a different storage system.

For example, to get started with Hyper-V, you might put all the virtual machines on the C drive in the default path. You have limited drive space because you are using an SSD. The Move VM Wizard is a migration tool in Hyper-V that you can use to migrate the VMs from the C drive to a new drive that you add to the computer, such as a USB removable storage device.

The Move VM Wizard picks up a VM and moves it partially or entirely to different resources on your Windows 8–based computer. It is important to note that Hyper-V virtual machines don't exist only on disk. They also have components in the Windows registry and in .xml files and other components. You should use the Move VM Wizard rather than try to add a VM manually to the Hyper-V Manager by virtual disk files alone.

To move your virtual machine storage to another location, complete the following steps:

1. Press and hold or right-click a virtual machine and select Move to launch the Move VM Wizard.

2. On the Choose Move Type page, shown in Figure 6-14, select Move The Virtual Machine's Storage and tap or click Next.

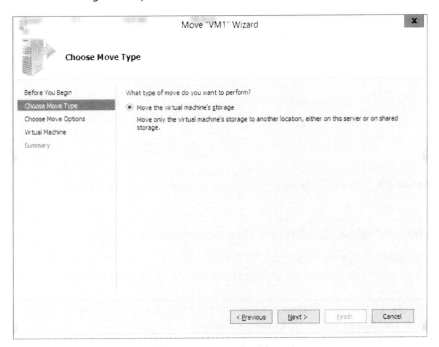

FIGURE 6-14 Moving virtual machine storage as a flexible option

3. On the Choose Options For Moving Storage page, shown in Figure 6-15, select one of the options: to move storage to a single location, to move specific items to specific locations, or to move only the virtual hard disks. Tap or click Next.

Virtual machines can be split to multiple locations if multiple VHDX or VHD files are in use.

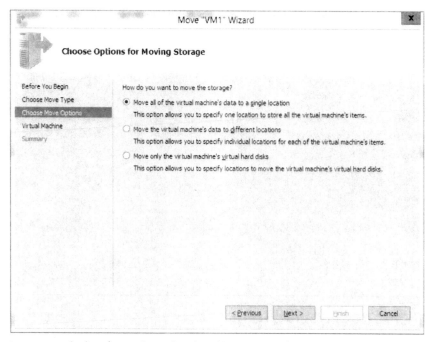

FIGURE 6-15 Options for moving a virtual machine or parts of a virtual machine

---

PLANNING **VIRTUALIZATION IS ALL ABOUT CHANGING YOUR MIND**

Virtualization with Hyper-V is a flexible and agile platform. Virtual machines can be moved and reconfigured quickly. There are no tedious tasks involved to make new virtual machines or to reconfigure existing virtual machines for more virtual hardware. The easy-to-use, wizard-driven interface makes quick work of this feature-rich virtualization platform, available in a client-computer environment.

Lesson summary

- Creating a Hyper-V virtual machine is easy and is performed by using the New Virtual Machine Wizard.
- The two most critical decision points are virtual machine name and location.
- It is recommended to give the virtual machine in Hyper-V Manager the same name as the operating system's computer name or fully qualified domain name.

- Virtual media can be set during the New Virtual Machine Wizard to install an operating system.
- The memory assigned to a virtual machine is deducted from the inventory of memory on the computer running Windows 8 with the Hyper-V feature enabled.
- A virtual machine snapshot can be used to mark progress on a virtual machine and revert quickly to a specified point in time.
- The Virtual Machine Connection screen gives a view of the console of the virtual machine.
- The Ctrl+Alt+Delete key sequence can be sent through the Virtual Machine Connection screen to log on to the VM.
- Virtual machines can be provisioned with VHDX files up to 64 terabytes.
- By using the Move VM Wizard, a virtual machine can be moved to new storage resources when it is running.

Lesson review

Answer the following questions to test your knowledge of the information in this lesson. You can find the answers to these questions and explanations of why each answer choice is correct or incorrect in the "Answers" section at the end of this chapter.

1. How big can Hyper-V VHD and VHDX files be? (Choose all that apply.)
   A. 16 TB and 32 TB, respectively
   B. 2 TB and 16 TB, respectively
   C. 4 TB and 32 TB, respectively
   D. 2 TB and 64 TB, respectively

2. Which of the following is not a valid start option for Hyper-V to install an operating system? (Choose all that apply.)
   A. Starting from a CD/DVD ISO file
   B. Starting from a network interface
   C. Using the CD/DVD drive on the Windows 8–based computer with the Hyper-V feature enabled
   D. Using a CD/DVD ISO file hosted on a web server over HTTP
   E. Starting from a virtual floppy drive

3. Where are Hyper-V VMs placed by default?
   A. C:\VMs
   B. C:\Users\Public\Documents\Hyper-V
   C. C:\ProgramData\Microsoft\Windows\Hyper-V
   D. D:\VMs

Lesson 3: Configuring virtual machine networking and storage

Now that you know the process of provisioning a virtual machine, you can learn the more complicated aspects of a Hyper-V virtual machine. If you have ever interacted with a server virtualization technology, including Hyper-V for Windows Server 2008 R2 or Windows Server 2012, you know that the networking and storage decisions are critical because the number of virtual machines greatly influences the performance and provisioning aspects of networking and storage.

Luckily, using Hyper-V on Windows 8 won't require as much capacity planning, shared storage consideration, or large-scale networking consolidation technologies as in the past for most situations. Why only most situations and not all situations? This is because Hyper-V for Windows 8 has the same virtualization engine as Hyper-V for Windows Server 2012, and there are key networking and storage technologies for both.

For networking, the fundamental concept for Hyper-V is the virtual switch, which exists in three modes for Hyper-V: external, internal, and private. For storage, Windows 8 also supports the Virtual Fibre Channel storage area network (SAN). This is quite a lot of technology for the typical Windows 8 system.

> **After this lesson, you will be able to:**
> - Add storage and networking components to a Hyper-V virtual machine.
> - Describe the three networking types for the Hyper-V virtual switch.
> - Identify storage options for Hyper-V virtual machines.
>
> **Estimated lesson time: 60 minutes**

Introducing storage and networking for Hyper-V

The key concept for both storage and networking for Hyper-V is that, in both situations, the virtualized devices are communicating on behalf of the Windows 8 connectivity technologies. Both the Hyper-V virtual switch and Virtual Fibre Channel technologies have an underlying address scheme.

Networking technologies

In the case of the networking technologies associated with Hyper-V, as with physical network interfaces, a MAC address is used. A *MAC address* is the hardware address of a network interface. Hyper-V virtual machine MAC addresses have a range that starts with the first three sections of this format: 00-15-5D-xx-xx-xx. In this example, the xx-xx-xx placeholders are the unique elements of the MAC address for the specific network interface. Physical interfaces have a MAC address format; for example, 00-05-B5-xx-xx-xx is for the network interface manufacturer Broadcom. Every brand of network interface has its own format of MAC address, and Hyper-V virtual machines are easy to find because they adhere to this format in default configurations. Figure 6-16 shows the Hyper-V Virtual Switch Manager, located in the Action menu of Hyper-V Manager. Virtual machines that are on the Hyper-V virtual switch will have MAC addresses in the defined range.

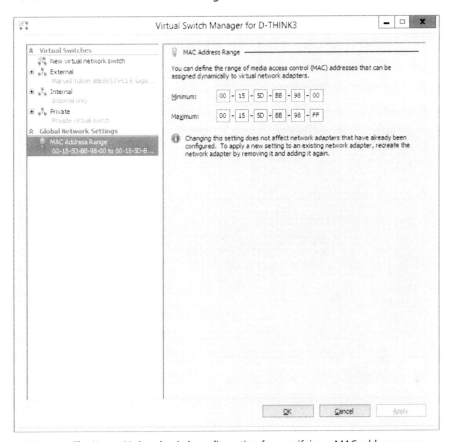

FIGURE 6-16 The Hyper-V virtual switch configuration for specifying a MAC address range

---

NOTE **TRACKING DOWN A VIRTUAL MACHINE CAN BE DIFFICULT**

Be sure you know the MAC addresses for Hyper-V virtual machines (00-15-5D-xx-xx-xx) because this will help you quickly identify a system on the network that needs to be located. It will help to know whether the address you are looking for is a virtual machine.

Storage

Storage functions in much the same way. The Virtual Fibre Channel host bus adapter (HBA) interface technology for Hyper-V uses an implementation of N_Port ID Virtualization (NPIV) for storage networking. For Fibre Channel networks, this means that individual World Wide Names (WWNs) of virtualized Fibre Channel interfaces can be presented on the storage network. For most Windows 8 systems, having Fibre Channel interfaces is more storage I/O than is needed, but it is a great option for the technology to be available in the hypervisor (Figure 6-17).

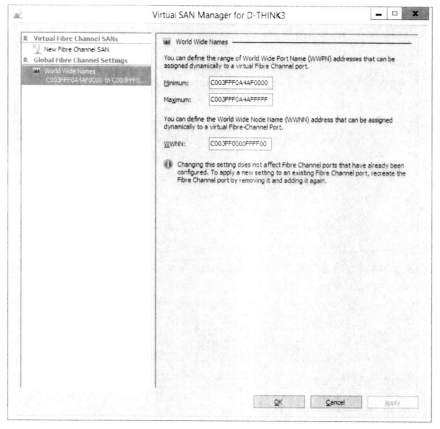

FIGURE 6-17 The virtual storage options in Hyper-V enabling NPIV virtualization of Fibre Channel interfaces

Hyper-V virtual switch

As mentioned previously, the Hyper-V virtual switch can operate three modes: external, internal, and private. Each of these switch modes has different characteristics that need to be considered before placing VMs on them.

By far, the external virtual switch type is the most commonly used option. External mode places a virtual machine (with its 00-15-5D-xx-xx-xx MAC address) on the same Ethernet network as the computer running Windows 8 with the Hyper-V feature enabled. When this happens, the virtual machine can communicate with other network systems and externally with the Internet if routed correctly. The TCP/IP address will also be the same as physical systems in this configuration. Other networking protocols can also be used. The external mode operates much like an uplink function on a physical switch.

The external virtual switch type has granular configuration options, which can be important if technologies such as virtual local area networks (VLANs) are used in your environment. If a VLAN configuration is necessary, the Hyper-V virtual switch can deliver multiple external virtual switches on multiple VLANs—much like the Hyper-V configuration found frequently in Windows Server 2012 virtualized infrastructures. The external virtual switch can use dedicated interfaces or can share traffic with the computer running Windows 8 with the Hyper-V feature enabled, as shown in Figure 6-18.

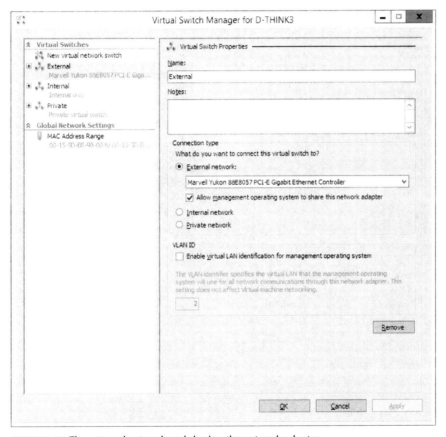

FIGURE 6-18 The external network and sharing the network adapter

The internal virtual switch type (Figure 6-19) enables virtual machines to interact with the computer running Windows 8 with the Hyper-V feature enabled and with one another but does not allow communication with the physical network. This is good when you need to move files between the virtual machines and the Windows 8–based computer; however, you might not want to allow the virtual machines to communicate externally. Network placement situations with earlier operating systems without critical updates and service packs might not be desirable. With the internal virtual switch, their presence is off the physical network.

If the virtual machines on the internal switch type need to interact with resources on the network or Internet when the external type is not an option, it might be possible to have software on the Windows 8–based computer with the Hyper-V feature enabled run a router or proxy service. In this manner, outbound traffic to the network would be sent directly from the computer running Windows 8 and not from the virtual machines (as is the case with the external virtual switch type). Traffic on the internal switch type does not travel on an actual network interface; it is provided by the Hyper-V engine itself. This situation might arise when there are restrictions on the physical network of what type of systems can be connected; also, the virtual machines might not meet the requirements for the network (security, updates, operating system type, and so on).

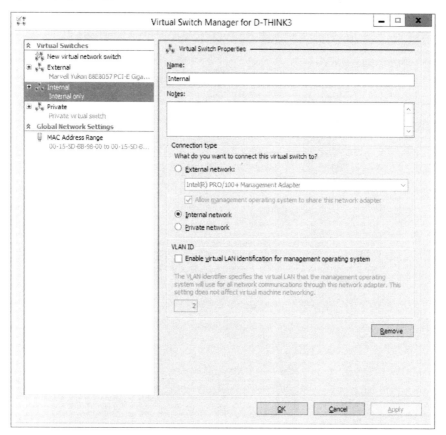

FIGURE 6-19 Internal type limiting traffic for virtual machines to the computer running Windows 8 with the Hyper-V feature enabled and the virtual machines

The last type option for the Hyper-V virtual switch is the private type (see Figure 6-20), which keeps traffic contained to the virtual machines on the computer running Windows 8 with the Hyper-V feature enabled. Although the Windows 8–based computer provides the virtual switch for the virtual machines, it is not connected to it. In this situation, the only way to interact with the virtual machines is to use the Virtual Machine Connection screen to access the virtual console. The private type is useful for specific and isolated testing situations when minimal networking is required.

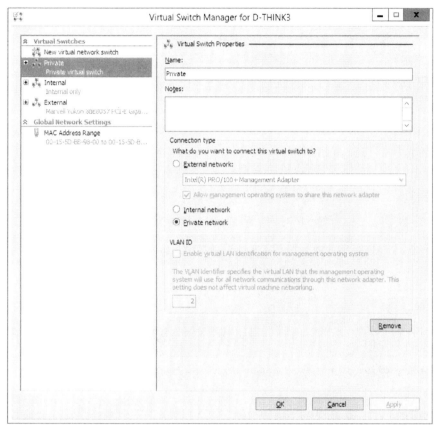

FIGURE 6-20 Private type limiting VM network traffic to VMs on the computer running Windows 8 with the Hyper-V feature enabled

Assigning a virtual switch to a virtual machine

After a virtual switch type is selected, it functions as an object that can be assigned to one or more virtual machines. Further, each virtual machine has a virtual hardware inventory in which each network adapter can be assigned a virtual switch. Virtual machines can have multiple network adapters and exist on multiple virtual switches. A number of additional features, such as bandwidth management, MAC address assignment (if an address other than the 00-15-5D-xx-xx-xx format is required), and VLAN identification, can be set as properties of the virtual machine. The virtual switch selection can be done as part of the virtual machine creation process or afterward as a task of editing the settings, as shown in Figure 6-21. The virtual switches are a configuration item and property of the host, to which VMs can be assigned.

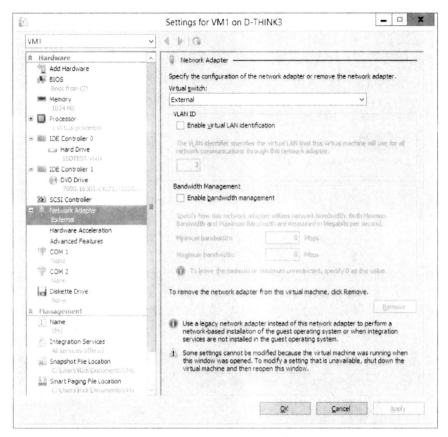

FIGURE 6-21 Enabling virtual machine settings assignment of a virtual switch to the network adapter

Assigning storage to a virtual machine

A virtual machine can be assigned storage in a number of ways. The Virtual Fibre Channel feature of Hyper-V provides virtual machines with access to a storage network directly, such as to run a storage management tool. In most situations, a Hyper-V virtual machine running on Windows 8 uses the VHDX or VHD virtual disk format. The VHDX file is the Hyper-V virtualization format that encapsulates a hard drive for a virtual machine. Virtual machines can also access a *pass-through disk*, which is a physical hard drive on the computer running Windows 8 with the Hyper-V feature enabled that a virtual machine uses exclusively. The pass-through configuration is not very transportable or scalable, so in most situations, VHDX and VHD virtual disk files are recommended.

Each Hyper-V virtual machine can have virtualized I/O controllers to provide storage resources (Figure 6-22), including IDE and SCSI controllers. Both these controllers can provide virtual disks in the VHDX or VHD format, and the virtual IDE controller can provide a virtual-ized optical drive for CD/DVD ISO files. Like the physical IDE and SCSI controllers in comput-ers, these virtualized controllers have addresses. For example, the IDE controllers can provide a virtual machine with individual VHDX or VHD files on IDE Controller 0 and IDE Controller 1 and, within that, on address 0 or 1. This is much like a physical controller in many PCs. The Hyper-V virtual SCSI controller can address positions from SCSI ID 0 up to 63 and assign devices to virtual machines. Individual Hyper-V virtual machines can have both virtual IDE and SCSI controllers and can have multiple controllers. The virtual switches are a configura-tion item and property of the host, to which virtual machines can be assigned.

> **REAL WORLD** **UNDERSTAND THIS ABILITY BUT DON'T WORRY TOO MUCH ABOUT IT**
>
> Most Windows administrators don't need to change the IDE or SCSI addressing, but you can adjust this property of the individual virtual machine if needed. Changing this can affect the start order of the virtual machine, so proceed carefully if you add VHDX or VHD files to a virtual machine.

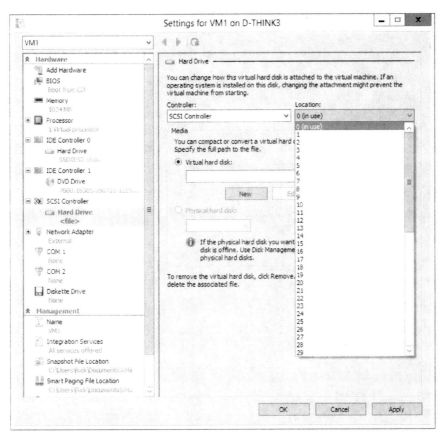

FIGURE 6-22 Virtual IDE and SCSI for each virtual machine

Windows 8 storage considerations for Hyper-V

The VHDX and VHD files associated with a VM have to reside on a disk resource that the Windows 8–based computer with the Hyper-V feature enabled can access. This can be fixed local disk resources (SATA, USB, Thunderbolt, and so on), a network resource with the new SMB 3.0 support from Windows Server 2012, or Windows Server 8 as a block storage resource. The block storage resource can be an iSCSI target formatted as an NTFS file system and assigned directly to the computer running Windows 8 with the Hyper-V feature enabled. A Fibre Channel logical unit number (LUN) can also be deployed to a computer running Windows 8 and formatted. This is different from the Virtual Fibre Channel technology that can place a virtual machine on the storage network in that the LUN would be assigned to the Windows 8–based computer with the Hyper-V feature enabled and then formatted as NTFS. After the iSCSI or Fibre Channel LUNs are formatted, virtual machines can reside on these storage resources.

> *NOTE* **WINDOWS 8 STORAGE SHOULD BE SIMPLE**
>
> Although Windows 8 with the Hyper-V feature enabled has the same rich storage options as Hyper-V on Windows Server 2012, virtual machines running on local storage and removable media are a popular choice for most Windows 8 users. If SAN storage infrastructures are deployed, consider using the free Hyper-V hypervisor, Hyper-V Server 2012. This is much like a core installation of Windows Server with the Hyper-V role, but it is free.

Lesson summary

- Hyper-V network switches can be configured as internal, external, or private.
- By default, Hyper-V uses a MAC address format of 00-15-5D-xx-xx-xx.
- The computer running Windows 8 with the Hyper-V feature enabled can share its network interface with VMs.
- Hyper-V can place virtual machines on VLANs on a physical switch infrastructure with the external virtual switch type.
- The Virtual Fibre Channel SAN technology enables Windows 8 to present a virtual machine on the storage network.
- Multiple virtual network controllers can be assigned to a virtual machine.
- A virtual machine can reside on multiple virtual switches.
- Hyper-V can use both VHDX and VHD files for virtual disks.
- Each virtual machine can have virtual IDE and SCSI controllers to access storage resources.

Lesson review

Answer the following questions to test your knowledge of the information in this lesson. You can find the answers to these questions and explanations of why each answer choice is correct or incorrect in the "Answers" section at the end of this chapter.

1. A virtual machine can have which types of disk controllers? (Choose all that apply.)

   A. Virtual IDE

   B. Virtual SATA

   C. Virtual SCSI

   D. Physical SCSI

2. Hyper-V virtual machines that are configured to have a network controller on a virtual switch configured as an internal type can do all but which of the following on the network?

   A. Connect to Windows Update directly.

   B. Communicate with one or more virtual machines on the same virtual switch.

   C. Communicate with the computer running Windows 8 with the Hyper-V feature enabled.

   D. Connect to the network through a proxy on the computer running Windows 8 with the Hyper-V feature enabled.

3. The Virtual Fibre Channel features for Hyper-V enable virtual machines to do which of the following?

   A. Function like a Fibre Channel switch

   B. Have an interface on the storage network

   C. Read VMDK disk files

   D. Fully control a Fibre Chanel interface from the computer running Windows 8 with the Hyper-V role enabled

Practice exercises

In these practice exercises, you apply what you have learned in this chapter.

Exercise 1: Create a virtual machine

In this exercise, you create a virtual machine in Hyper-V Manager. To complete this exercise, perform the following steps:

1. Ensure that the Hyper-V feature is enabled on the Windows 8–based computer. This might require using settings to add the Hyper-V feature.

2. Open Hyper-V Manager.

3. Right-click the computer name, select New Virtual Machine, and click Finish.

4. Ensure that the virtual machine is now listed in Hyper-V Manager as New Virtual Machine.

Exercise 2: Customize a virtual machine

In this exercise, you customize a newly created virtual machine. To complete this exercise, perform the following steps:

1. Right-click the newly created virtual machine created in Exercise 1 and select Settings.

2. Select the memory value in the hardware section. Note the default assignment (512 MB). Change it to 256 MB.

3. Select the IDE Controller 1 device in the virtual machine.

4. Click the DVD Drive assigned to the virtual machine.

5. Assign the DVD drive either a CD-ROM ISO file or the physical CD/DVD drive of the computer running Windows 8 an operating system installation image.

6. Click the name of the virtual machine in the Management section of the settings.

7. Change the name to VM-2 from New Virtual Machine.

Suggested practice exercises

The following additional exercises are designed to give you more opportunities to practice what you've learned and to help you successfully master the lessons presented in this chapter. Virtualization involves a learning curve for many IT professionals. Developing skills in this area helps many areas of your Windows usage.

- **Exercise 1**   Install an operating system on a virtual machine.
- **Exercise 2**   Create a virtual network for Hyper-V virtual machines.
- **Exercise 3**   Create a virtual machine with a custom configuration, such as needing multiple VHD or VHDX files and multiple network interfaces.

Answers

This section contains answers to the lesson review questions in this chapter.

Lesson 1

1. **Correct answer: C**

   A. **Incorrect:** Although a number of hypervisors are available, there is no Type A hypervisor.

   B. **Incorrect:** Although a number of hypervisors are available, there is no Type B hypervisor.

   C. **Correct:** Windows 8 Pro can enable Hyper-V, which is a Type 1 hypervisor that enables virtual machines to access the hardware directly.

   D. **Incorrect:** Type 2 hypervisors can be installed on Windows 8, but they do not include Hyper-V.

2. **Correct answer: B**

   A. **Incorrect:** Windows Server 2012 and Windows Server 2008 R2 support adding Hyper-V as a role, but Windows 8 does not.

   B. **Correct:** Hyper-V is a feature of Windows 8 Pro and must be explicitly enabled to add the hypervisor capability.

   C. **Incorrect:** Windows 8 Pro and Hyper-V have a PowerShell module, but Hyper-V does not exist within it.

   D. **Incorrect:** Hyper-V runs on the hardware directly and therefore not as a Windows service of the computer running Windows 8.

3. **Correct answers: A, B, and D**

   A. **Correct:** Windows 8 supports running Hyper-V as a virtual machine.

   B. **Correct:** Windows Server 2012 is a supported operating system that can run in Hyper-V as a virtual machine.

   C. **Incorrect:** Windows NT and other earlier operating systems are not supported as virtual machines to run in Hyper-V.

   D. **Correct:** Hyper-V is not just for Windows; selected Linux distributions such as Red Hat Enterprise Linux 6 are supported operating systems that can run as a virtual machine in Hyper-V.

4. **Correct answer: C**

   A. **Incorrect:** Only one SLAT-capable processor is supported to run Hyper-V.

   B. **Incorrect:** 4 GB of RAM or more is required to run Hyper-V on Windows 8.

C. **Correct:** Windows 8 Pro is a requirement to run Hyper-V.

D. **Incorrect:** There is no fixed hard drive space requirement to add the Hyper-V feature; however, virtual machines require hard drive space.

Lesson 2

1. **Correct answers: B and D**

   A. **Incorrect:** VHD files cannot be 16 TB, but VHDX files can be 32 TB (or more).

   B. **Correct:** A VHD file can be 2 TB, and a VHDX file can be 16 TB; in this case, the VHD file is at the maximum size limit, but the VHDX file is not.

   C. **Incorrect:** A VHD file cannot be 4 TB, but a VHDX file can be 32 TB (or more).

   D. **Correct:** In this example, both VHD and VHDX files can exist at their respective maximum sizes, 2 TB and 64 TB.

2. **Correct answers: A, B, C, and E**

   A. **Correct:** The CD/DVD ISO file can be used as virtual media for a virtual machine to install an operating system.

   B. **Correct:** The virtual network adapter of the virtual machine can start with network-based utilities to install an operating system.

   C. **Correct:** The physical drive for a CD or DVD disc on the computer running Windows 8 with the Hyper-V feature enabled can be used to install a virtual machine.

   D. **Incorrect:** HTTP locations cannot be used to access virtual media files on a Hyper-V virtual machine to install an operating system.

   E. **Correct:** A virtual floppy drive image can be configured on a virtual machine for operating system installation.

3. **Correct answer: C**

   A. **Incorrect:** A Windows 8 user can place virtual machines in C:\VMs, but that is not the default location.

   B. **Incorrect:** Although this path has Hyper-V contents, it is not where the virtual machines are stored by default.

   C. **Correct:** This is where the virtual machine configuration, virtual disk, and snapshot information is kept for Hyper-V virtual machines by default.

   D. **Incorrect:** A Windows 8 user can place virtual machines in D:\VMs, but that is not the default location.

Lesson 3

1. **Correct answers: A and C**

   A. **Correct:** The virtual IDE type is available for Hyper-V virtual machines.

   B. **Incorrect:** There is no virtual SATA type, even though the disks running Hyper-V might be of the SATA type.

   C. **Correct:** The virtual SCSI type is available for Hyper-V virtual machines.

   D. **Incorrect:** Physical SCSI is not available for Hyper-V virtual machines, even though the virtual machine might reside on a physical SCSI controller from the computer running Windows 8.

2. **Correct answer: A**

   A. **Correct:** Windows Update would have to be accessed through a proxy server or a different virtual switch type (external) to provide the virtual machine access to the Internet.

   B. **Incorrect:** The internal type allows communication to the other virtual machines on the same internal switch.

   C. **Incorrect:** The computer running Windows 8 can communicate on the internal switch.

   D. **Incorrect:** If a proxy is in place, the virtual machines on the internal switch type can access an external network such as the Internet.

3. **Correct answer: B**

   A. **Incorrect:** If a virtual machine has a virtual Fibre Channel interface, it can be on a Fibre Channel network, but that is different from the Ethernet technologies in that there is no virtual Fibre Channel switch.

   B. **Correct:** The virtual Fibre Channel technology with Hyper-V allows virtual machines to access a Fibre Channel network directly with their own addressing by using N_Port ID Virtualization.

   C. **Incorrect:** The VMDK disk technology is for a different virtualization engine, and Hyper-V cannot use Virtual Fibre Channel to access those disk types.

   D. **Incorrect:** The computer running Windows 8 with the Hyper-V feature enabled still has its own Fibre Channel interfaces and addressing.

CHAPTER 7

Administering Windows networking

J ohn Burdette Gage was the twenty-first employee of Sun Microsystems. During his time at Sun, he was credited with creating the phrase "the network is the computer." Today, those words ring true more than ever as the information technology world undergoes a paradigm shift that will see both consumers and organizations using an increasing number of cloud-based services and relying increasingly on the network to achieve goals. As a result, never before has the networking component in Windows played a more crucial role than it does today. In this chapter, you learn how to manage the Windows 8 networking options.

Lessons in this chapter:

Before you begin

To complete the practice exercises in this chapter, you should be familiar with basic networking concepts. In addition, you need:

- A wired Ethernet connection
- A wireless networking adapter

Lesson 1: Configuring networking

The ability to communicate on a network and on the Internet is an essential element of today's modern computing environment, particularly as companies continue to move closer to cloud-based services. For a Windows 8–based computer to be a full participant in the wider Internet community, you need to ensure that the computer's networking feature is properly configured.

After this lesson, you will be able to:

■ Describe in detail the new features that are available in Windows 8.

■ Configure a network adapter for automatic IP configuration.

■ Manually populate the IP settings for a network adapter.

■ Change a wireless network to be configured as a metered connection.

■ Add a secondary DNS suffix to a network adapter.

Estimated lesson time: 60 minutes

What's new in networking in Windows 8

Windows 8 includes a number of new features and enhancements designed to streamline and improve the networking capabilities of the product. This section covers the following:

■ Enhancements in Server Message Block (SMB) version 3

■ Viewing networking in Windows 8

■ Controlling metered connections

Enhancements in SMB 3

As a desktop administrator, *Server Message Block (SMB)* version 3 might not be at the top of your Windows 8 to-learn list. However, as you examine the details of this protocol, you will find a lot of useful information.

SMB is a file-sharing protocol and the method by which computers running Windows communicate with one another. With the release of Windows 8 and Windows Server 2012, organizations can begin to use SMB 3, which provides a number of benefits over earlier versions, including:

■ **New security features** SMB 3 includes new encryption capabilities to ensure that data is not intercepted while in transit between servers and workstations. In addition, SMB 3 uses new signing algorithms to protect data further in transit.

■ **New performance capabilities** SMB 3 includes a number of performance enhancements.

■ **New availability features** SMB 3 has the potential to make systems more highly available than was possible with earlier versions of the protocol due to new capabilities that include SMB Transparent Failover, which enables a system to fail over quietly to a different storage path, and SMB Multichannel, which enables a system to communicate with storage by using multiple discrete channels.

■ **New management features** SMB now includes its own full set of Windows PowerShell cmdlets, enabling administrators to script storage-based tasks. SMB 3 adds new performance counters, enabling administrators to watch storage traffic more closely. In addition, SMB 3 writes more events to the Windows event log, making it easier for administrators to take troubleshooting steps when problems arise.

You don't need to do anything to enable SMB 3. When your Windows 8–based computer communicates with other systems on the network, the latest possible version of SMB is automatically negotiated between the two systems. Table 7-1 shows you which SMB version will be used.

TABLE 7-1 SMB versions between different versions of Windows

Client/Server OS	Windows 8, Windows Server 2012	Windows 7, Windows Server 2008 R2	Windows Vista, Windows Server 2008	Previous versions of Windows
Windows 8 and Windows Server 2012	SMB 3.0	SMB 2.1	SMB 2.0	SMB 1.0
Windows 7 and Windows Server 2008 R2	SMB 2.1	SMB 2.1	SMB 2.0	SMB 1.0
Windows Vista and Windows Server 2008	SMB 2.0	SMB 2.0	SMB 2.0	SMB 1.0
Previous versions of Windows	SMB 1.0	SMB 1.0	SMB 1.0	SMB 1.0

With each release of a new version of SMB, desktop administrators have had to troubleshoot issues related to communications between versions. By knowing where to start troubleshooting communications problems, you're better able to craft solutions.

REAL WORLD **THE IMPORTANCE OF SMB 3**

Although learning about SMB 3 might seem like an esoteric exercise except when you need to troubleshoot connections to servers, don't dismiss this as an unimportant technology. Your Windows Server 2012 administrator counterparts are looking at ways SMB 3 can supplant competing protocols and drastically simplify the IT landscape.

Viewing network connections

With a new interface comes a new way to interact with many parts of the operating system. The Windows 8 interface includes a new way to interact with some networking settings. However, Windows 8 also retains the earlier Network and Sharing Center. For Windows 7 administrators who are making their way to Windows 8, this will provide some comfort while learning the new Windows 8 methods for managing networks and network devices.

To view connected networks in Windows 8, from the desktop, open the Settings charm and then tap or click Network. You will receive network information similar to that shown in Figure 7-1. The computer shown in this figure is connected to a wired network, and three Wi-Fi networks are available. Note that you can enable or disable Airplane mode from this screen. Airplane mode shuts down the computer's networking features so that the device can be used while in flight and adhere to U.S. Federal Aviation Administration requirements.

FIGURE 7-1 Windows 8, seeing one wired and three wireless connections

Controlling metered connections

 Metered connections to the Internet are becoming ubiquitous, particularly as the use of mobile devices increases. *Metered connections* are connections to the Internet that are based on usage. Most people have their home Internet connection provided for a flat monthly fee. Cellular communications companies also provide Internet services, but most of them have stopped providing unlimited data connections and now provide a monthly data transfer allotment after which the user is charged. Moreover, as people roam the world and leave the confines of their local cellular service provider, providers are beginning to charge roaming fees that can quickly add up to large monthly bills.

As companies provide workers with mobile devices, such as Windows 8–based tablets or laptops, the potential for large communications charges increases significantly. To help users keep costs under control, Windows 8, by default, blocks downloads of apps over what could be expensive metered connections. Apps will not be downloaded and installed until the device is connected to an unmetered network. However, you can change this behavior. To do so, complete the following steps:

1. From the desktop, open the Settings charm.

2. Scroll to the bottom of the Settings taskbar and tap or click Change PC Settings.

3. On the PC Settings page, choose the Devices option.

4. At the bottom of the list of devices in the work area is the Download Over Metered Connections option shown in Figure 7-2. Move the slider to the right to allow Windows 8 to download files over metered connections.

Download over metered connections

To help prevent extra charges, keep this off so device software (drivers, info, and apps) for new devices won't download while you're on metered internet connections.

Off

FIGURE 7-2 Configuring Windows 8 to allow or prevent downloads over metered connections

In the "Managing a wireless network" section of this chapter, you learn how to tag a particular network connection as metered so that this feature works properly.

Installing a network adapter

In the past, a network adapter was an optional component for a computer, but this is no longer the case. Almost 100 percent of the PCs, laptops, and tablet devices that are sold today come with some form of network connectivity. Desktop PCs have a wired Ethernet port; laptops often have both a wired Ethernet port and wireless ability; tablet devices come with either Wi-Fi or cellular 3G or 4G service.

Even so, you might need to install an additional network adapter in one of your Windows 8 systems. For example, if you have a desktop PC that needs wireless capability, you need to add a wireless network adapter to the PC.

The exact steps depend on the kind of network adapter you're adding to the device. If you're adding an internal network adapter, you must physically open the PC and install the network adapter. However, it's much more common today for wireless connectivity to be added by using USB-based wireless networking adapters.

In general, the steps to install a network adapter are as follows:

1. Insert the CD that accompanied the network adapter into the computer.

2. Run the setup program the CD contains.

   This installs the software drivers that are necessary for the new network adapter to operate. In some cases, the network adapter manufacturer also includes other network management tools that you can use to manage the adapter, but the important part of this step is to make sure that the drivers are installed.

3. After the drivers finish installing, connect the new network adapter. This might mean installing a card inside a PC, but more often it means plugging the network adapter into an available USB port on the computer.

   Because you've already installed the drivers, Windows 8 will recognize the new hardware device and make it available for your use.

Every network adapter is different, but most follow the same installation process. Don't make assumptions. If you install a new network adapter, read the instructions first. Doing so can save you hours of troubleshooting later.

After you've successfully installed your new network adapter, you can configure it for use on your network.

Managing network settings

Although Windows 8 includes new ways to handle some networking tasks, many of the traditional methods for managing networks remain available to administrators. As a Windows 8 administrator, you need to know both new and traditional methods for managing networks so that you can move comfortably between tablet-based and traditional Windows systems and have available to you all the configuration options you're used to seeing.

Using the Network and Sharing Center

The Network and Sharing Center has been the main location for managing networks in Windows for quite some time, and this tool remains available in Windows 8. You can access this tool in a number of ways.

USING THE TASKBAR

At the lower-right corner of the desktop, tap and hold or right-click the network icon and choose Open Network And Sharing Center (Figure 7-3).

FIGURE 7-3 Opening Network And Sharing Center from the desktop

USING CONTROL PANEL

To access Control Panel, either tap and hold or right-click the lower-left corner of the desktop. This opens a shortcut menu that provides access to a number of system utilities, including Control Panel. Select Control Panel. Under Network And Internet, choose View Network Status And Tasks, as shown in Figure 7-4; this opens the Network and Sharing Center.

FIGURE 7-4 Using Control Panel to access the Network and Sharing Center

USING THE START SCREEN

You can also use the new Windows 8 interface to access the Network and Sharing Center. There are two ways to accomplish the goal. First, on the Start screen, type **Control Panel**. As you type, Windows searches for the options that match what you are typing (Figure 7-5).

FIGURE 7-5 Looking for Control Panel on the Start screen

Alternatively, from the Start screen, start typing **Network** and, in the Search bar, select Settings. Scroll through the list and then tap or click Network And Sharing Center, as shown in Figure 7-6.

FIGURE 7-6 Finding settings related to the network by using the Start screen

When Network And Sharing Center is open, it provides you with a number of options by which to make granular changes to how Windows 8 operates on the network. Initially, it shows you the basic network information for your computer. In Figure 7-7, you can see a computer that is connected to an Ethernet (wired) network and joined to a homegroup. You can see that the wired network connection is configured as Private Network. In addition, you can tell that this connection is allowed to access the Internet.

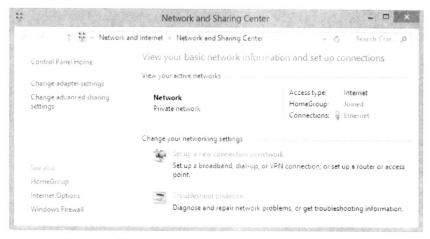

FIGURE 7-7 Network and Sharing Center

On the left side of the Network And Sharing Center window, two options are presented:

- **Change Adapter Settings**   Select this option to manipulate the networking hardware directly. You can change adapter settings and common network settings such as IP address.

- **Change Advanced Sharing Settings**   Select this option to modify the way Windows interacts with other computers on the network.

In addition to the links at the left, you can see further information in the Network And Sharing Center window. From a connectivity standpoint, the most important information is in the View Your Active Networks section of the window.

Managing network profiles

In the View Your Active Networks section, shown in Figure 7-7, you can see that the current network is listed as Private Network. In Windows 8, you can choose from three network profiles:

- **Domain**   A network connection type of Domain indicates that the computer is joined to the company's Active Directory domain. The Domain network type is automatically detected.

- **Private**   A private network is one that you control or trust. For example, if your company does not have an Active Directory domain but has many computers, the network connections would most likely be configured as Private.

- **Public**   A public network connection is one that is used in a public place. For example, if you're visiting a coffee shop or other location with free Wi-Fi, you would configure the connection as Public.

The type of network you select matters. Windows 8 enables you to create firewall rules that depend on the type of network to which you're connected. For example, public networks are generally considered hostile environments from a security perspective. For a public network you might have a much more restrictive set of firewall policies than you would for a domain network or a private network.

In addition, the network profile you select has a direct impact on how various assets are shared on the network. For each network location, you can control what is shared by clicking the Change Advanced Sharing Settings link at the left side of the window. When you select this link, the Advanced Sharing Settings dialog box opens. This dialog box displays the details for the current profile. Figure 7-8 shows the default details for the Private network type.

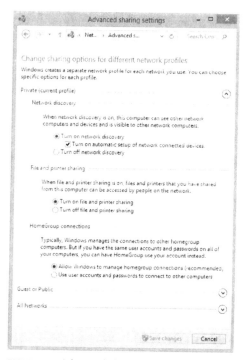

FIGURE 7-8 Advanced Sharing Settings for the Private network profile

There are three primary areas of information in the Advanced Sharing Settings window:

- **Network Discovery** When Network Discovery is enabled, the Windows 8–based computer can find other devices on the network and is itself visible on the network. This feature plays a prominent role in sharing resources such as documents and printers. When this feature is disabled—which is often the case for security reasons—the Windows 8–based computer doesn't seek out and display network resources and doesn't advertise itself on the network. However, even when Network Discovery is disabled, the Windows 8–based computer can use resources shared by other computers or servers on the network, but the administrator or person using the computer needs to know the network path to access those resources.

- **File And Printer Sharing**   When File And Printer Sharing is enabled, the Windows 8–based computer can share its resources on the network. This feature accompanies Network Discovery. Network Discovery makes shared resources visible on the network, whereas File And Printer Sharing is the mechanism by which those resources are shared. You learn much more about sharing in Chapter 10, "Sharing resources."

- **HomeGroup Connections**   In non-domain environments, Windows 8 provides HomeGroup functionality, which streamlines the process of sharing resources on smaller or home networks. HomeGroup connections are not available for public networks.

Configuring IP settings

As an administrator of desktop computers in an environment with multiple computers, you probably won't have to configure a production desktop computer's IP settings manually very often. Most organizations use a Dynamic Host Configuration Protocol (DHCP) server. A DHCP server automatically configures all the network settings that are necessary for a computer to operate on the network and connect to the Internet.

However, in some cases, you might need to configure a computer's IP settings manually to troubleshoot network problems.

> **REAL WORLD   USE DHCP WHENEVER POSSIBLE**
>
> Unfortunately, many organizations do not use DHCP servers and instead rely on their desktop and network administrators to track, assign, and configure IP addresses manually on all the machines in the organization. This occurs even in organizations that have hundreds of devices.
>
> In many cases, these networks have eschewed some modern tools because of inexperience with or fear of DHCP or an automated technology. The alternative, however, is massively inefficient and extremely error prone.
>
> Even as a desktop administrator, you can recommend improvements and automation in your environment. With so many IT departments being asked to do more with less, it's up to every IT staff member to find ways to streamline common tasks. If you work in an organization that doesn't use DHCP, research the pros and cons of the technology in the desktop environment and don't be afraid to take a recommendation up the chain of command.

DHCP isn't the only automated method by which a computer can obtain an IP address. When no DHCP server is available, but a Windows 8–based computer is configured to obtain an address by using DHCP, that computer will fail over to a mechanism known as Automatic Private IP Addressing (APIPA).

When a DHCP server is unavailable, APIPA automatically assigns an IP address in the range of 169.254.0.1 to 169.254.255.254 to Windows 8 clients. The default network subnet mask of 255.255.255.0 is used for all APIPA addresses, and all the Windows computers using APIPA reside on the same subnet and are visible to one another on the network. In Windows 8, all network adapters have APIPA enabled, although this feature can be disabled on a per-network adapter basis. In general, APIPA is rarely disabled because most organizations rarely have major DHCP problems.

Now that you understand that Windows 8–based computers can automatically receive IP addresses by two methods, you need to understand how you can modify a computer's IP configuration manually if that becomes necessary. To configure a computer's IP settings manually, complete the following steps:

1. Open Network And Sharing Center.

2. Tap or click Change Adapter Settings.

3. When the list of network adapters appears, press and hold or right-click the appropriate adapter and, from the shortcut menu, choose Properties (Figure 7-9).

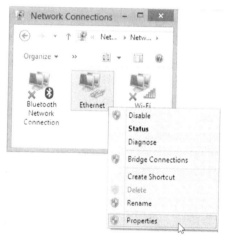

FIGURE 7-9 Opening the Properties page for the Ethernet adapter

4. Under This Connection Uses The Following Items, choose Internet Protocol Version 4 (TCP/IPv4).

5. Click the Properties button to open a dialog box like the one shown in Figure 7-10.

   This system is currently configured to obtain an IP address from a DHCP server.

6. Provide appropriate configuration settings and tap or click OK.

FIGURE 7-10 The default Windows 8 IP settings

As you can see in Figure 7-10, a number of items can be configured for each network adapter. In this example, the network adapter is configured to Obtain An IP Address Automatically and to Obtain DNS Server Address Automatically. In short, the adapter is using DHCP. To configure the adapter to use manually assigned IP settings, choose Use The Following IP Address and Use The Following DNS Server Addresses.

After you do so, provide these values:

- **IP Address**   This is the IP address you want to assign to this Windows 8–based computer.

- **Subnet Mask**   The subnet mask helps Windows determine which resources are local to the computer and which are remote. When you attempt to access a resource that is identified as remote from the Windows 8–based computer, Windows automatically passes the traffic to the default gateway.

- **Default Gateway**   The default gateway is the doorway into and out of the local network. When Windows 8 attempts to access resources that are identified as local, the network traffic can safely ignore the default gateway. However, when Windows attempts to access remote resources, that network traffic passes through the default gateway and is routed around the network and possibly even the Internet until the desired remote resource is located.

- **Preferred DNS Server** When you browse to *www.microsoft.com*, your computer doesn't have any idea what www.microsoft.com means. Behind the scenes, Windows is looking up www.microsoft.com on a Domain Name Server (DNS) system. DNS is a phonebook for the network. Without DNS, you would have to remember the IP address for every resource you want to use.

- **Alternate DNS Server** Because DNS is so important to the proper functioning of a network, most organizations have more than one DNS server. The alternate DNS server is used when Windows is unable to use the preferred DNS server.

The IP addresses with which you're working in this section are also referred to as IPv4 addresses; when someone talks about setting an IP address, she is generally referring to an IPv4 address. These addresses are expressed in *dotted quad notation*; they look like this: 192.168.0.1. There are four numbers (quad), and they're separated by periods (dotted). Subnet masks provide a way for a huge network to be broken down into smaller, more manageable pieces. These smaller pieces are called subnets, which is where the term "subnet mask" originates. The default gateway is the IP address for a local router, which is a hardware device that connects separate subnets and networks and enables them to communicate with one another. The settings for a manually configured network adapter on Windows 8 might look similar to the settings shown in Figure 7-11.

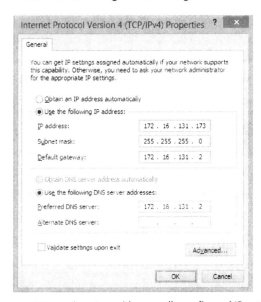

FIGURE 7-11 A system with manually configured IP settings

A number of IP addresses are reserved for special use. In addition, the Internet Engineering Task Force (IETF) has set aside four IP address ranges. Addresses in these ranges cannot be used on the Internet but can be used on internal networks. When they are used on internal networks, specialized network devices at the network edge translate these private IP addresses into ones that are usable on the Internet.

Here are the four reserved private IP address ranges:

- 10.0.0.0 through 10.255.255.255
- 169.254.0.0 through 169.254.255.255 (APIPA, as previously discussed)
- 172.16.0.0 through 172.31.255.255
- 192.168.0.0 through 192.168.255.255

Whereas normal IP addresses are unique around the world, the addresses in the private IP address ranges can be used in any organization because those addresses can't be used on the Internet. Because of this, and because the world is running out of IP addresses (which you learn about later in this chapter), many organizations use these private IP address ranges, so make sure you understand them.

- **Network address** As organizations break up their networks, multiple network addresses are created. These cannot be used on individual computers. Check with your network administrator to learn about your company's network addresses.

- **Broadcast address** Every subnet has its own broadcast address that can't be used on computers.

Understanding the dual TCP/IP stack in Windows 8

A number of years ago, it was projected that the world would run out of IPv4 addresses because there were so few. IPv4 provides computers with a 32-bit network address. Therefore, there are just fewer than 4.3 billion possible IP addresses with IPv4. Even though that sounds like a large number, there is a lot of waste in the system and, in the early years of IPv4, there was a lot of inefficiency in how addresses were distributed. Because there was a perception that 4.3 billion was plenty of IP addresses, some organizations were given far more IP addresses than they needed.

Between the waste in the system and the rapid increase in the number of network-connected devices, 4.3 billion addresses are far from sufficient. In response, the IETF created a new version of the Internet Protocol. Today, that protocol is known as IPv6 and, although it's still in the process of worldwide deployment in many places, over time it's expected to supplant much of the use of IPv4.

Windows 8 includes full support for both IPv4 and IPv6, although at present you will rarely need to touch the IPv6 settings. That said, you should understand at least the basics of IPv6 because it's enabled by default on Windows 8, and at times some services will use it.

Whereas IPv4 provides 32-bit IP addresses, IPv6 provides 128-bit addresses, with each address represented in eight 16-bit blocks. For example, here's the IP address used by the networking adapter in the system used throughout this chapter: fe80:0:0:0:7860:1f99:c25a:c329. As you can see, it looks radically different from an IPv4 address. Further, the address as presented isn't what is actually displayed in the sample computer. Windows 8 displays the address as fe80::7860:1f99:c25a:c329. Note the double colon between the first and second parts of the address. This is the way IPv6 indicates that certain sections of the address are just zero. To make it easier to read, the zeroed sections are omitted and a double colon is put in their place.

In most organizations today, you won't need to work with the IPv6 settings manually, but the day is coming when IPv4 will be phased out, so make sure you at least understand how to change your IPv6 settings.

Here's how you change your IPv6 settings:

1. Open Network And Sharing Center and tap or click Change Adapter Settings.

2. When the list of network adapters appears, double-tap or right-click the appropriate adapter and, from the shortcut menu, choose Properties.

3. Under This Connection Uses The Following Items, choose Internet Protocol Version 6 (TCP/IPv6).

4. Click the Properties button to open a Properties dialog box similar to the one in Figure 7-12. This system is currently configured to obtain an IP address from a DHCP server.

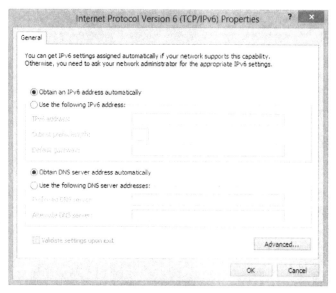

FIGURE 7-12 Windows 8 default IPv6 configuration

5. Provide appropriate configuration settings and tap or click OK.

> **REAL WORLD** **DON'T DISABLE IPV6**
>
> Even though you might not be using it yet and even though there is a lot of information that describes in detail how to disable IPv6, it's best if you just leave the IPv6 configuration on your Windows 8 systems. Even if your organization doesn't use IPv6, some underlying Windows Services do use specific IPv6 components, even when those services are used on an IPv4-only network.

Configuring name resolution

You've already learned how to add DNS server entries to a network adapter's configuration. There are additional name resolution options that you might want to consider using on your computers. Note that some of these name resolution options can be configured on a DHCP server so that you don't have to configure every computer manually.

To change advanced name resolution properties for a network adapter, complete the following steps:

1. Open Network And Sharing Center and tap or click Change Adapter Settings.

2. When the list of network adapters appears, press and hold or right-click the appropriate adapter and, from the shortcut menu, choose the Properties option.

3. Double-tap or double-click either Internet Protocol Version 4 (IPv4) or Internet Protocol Version 6 (IPv6), depending on which version of TCP/IP you want to configure.

4. When the Internet Protocol properties page appears, tap or click the Advanced button and choose the DNS tab, shown in Figure 7-13.

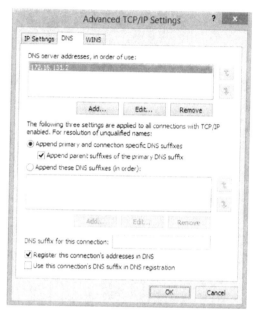

FIGURE 7-13 Configuring advanced DNS settings

5. Make the configuration changes with the following options, and then tap or click OK.

   ■ **DNS Server Addresses, In Order Of Use**   In Figure 7-13, note that this box contains a single entry. This computer has just one DNS server IP address configured. You can add a second DNS server address on the TCP/IP configuration page. However, you're not limited to just two DNS servers. By using this screen, you can add more DNS servers. The more DNS servers you have available, the less likely it is that the client will be left without a DNS server due to DNS failures. The order here is important; Windows 8 uses the DNS servers in the order that they are listed. Use the up and down arrows to change the order of the listed DNS servers.

   ■ **Append Primary And Connection Specific DNS Suffixes**   If you're using DNS, you're also using a domain name such as contoso.com as part of your computer naming convention. Suppose this computer is attempting to reach a computer named fileserver.contoso.com on the network. When this option is enabled, Windows will automatically append the .contoso.com name to the end of network names, thus creating a fully qualified domain name that DNS can use.

   ■ **Append Parent Suffixes Of The Primary DNS Suffix**   In larger organizations, DNS is broken down into smaller units. For example, Contoso might have sales.contoso.com and marketing.contoso.com. In that case, this computer name would be win8.sales.contoso.com. When you select the check box next to this option, Windows searches all the way up the name resolution hierarchy looking for resources that match what you're looking for. As a result, if you attempt to access a resource named fileserver and you don't put the .contoso.com on the end, Windows will look for resources named fileserver.sales.contoso.com and fileserver.contoso.com.

- **Append These DNS Suffixes (In Order)**   If you have other names you want Windows to search for resources, you can add those here. Windows searches these resources in the order in which they appear on the list. Use the up and down arrows to change the order of the DNS suffixes.

- **DNS Suffix For This Connection**   Use this box to override any DNS suffix that has already been assigned to this computer.

- **Register This Connection's Addresses In DNS**   This option uses a technology called Dynamic DNS, which allows the desktop computer to update its own DNS record on your organization's DNS servers. If the computer's IP address changes, the computer will update DNS proactively so that an administrator doesn't have to remember to do it.

- **Use This Connection's DNS Suffix In DNS Registration**   By selecting this check box, you instruct Windows to update the DNS zone for the parent connection.

Adding a second default gateway

Because companies rely heavily on technology to meet basic business needs, making sure that technology remains available is increasingly important. As a result, companies deploy backup systems and secondary systems intended to pick up the load if one fails. Earlier in this lesson, you configured your network adapter to have just one default gateway. That one gateway represents a single point of failure in the network. To combat this, some companies deploy networks that have multiple gateways. To use the additional gateways, you need to configure advanced TCP/IP settings in Windows 8:

1. Open Network And Sharing Center and tap or click Change Adapter Settings.

2. When the list of network adapters appears, tap and hold or right-click the appropriate adapter and, from the shortcut menu, choose Properties.

3. Double-tap or double-click either Internet Protocol Version 4 (IPv4) or Internet Protocol Version 6 (IPv6), depending on which version of TCP/IP you want to configure.

4. When the Internet Protocol Properties dialog box appears, tap or click Advanced to open the Settings tab shown in Figure 7-14.

FIGURE 7-14 Changed advanced TCP/IP and gateway settings

5. From the following options, make the configuration changes, and then tap or click OK.

   ■ **IP Addresses** Add IP addresses to the computer running Windows 8. Assigning multiple IP addresses to a single network adapter is a relatively common task in Windows Server, but in Windows 8 on a desktop, it's rare. If you want to add an IP address, tap or click the Add button. To change an already assigned IP address, tap or click the Edit button. To remove an assigned IP address, tap or click the Remove button.

   ■ **Default Gateways** To add another default gateway to your Windows 8–based computer, tap or click the Add button. To edit an entry, tap or click the Edit button. To remove an assigned gateway, tap or click the Remove button.

Connecting to a wireless network

To connect to a wireless network, complete the following steps:

1. From the desktop, open the Settings charm and tap or click the Network icon. This opens the screen shown in Figure 7-15.

FIGURE 7-15 Multiple available wireless networks

NOTE ALTERNATIVE WAYS TO OPEN THE NETWORKS TASKBAR

You can open the Networks taskbar in several ways so that you can join a wireless network.

2. If the Desktop is already open, tap or click the Network icon in the system tray at the lower-right corner of the screen next to the clock to open the Networks taskbar.

3. From Network And Sharing Center, open Change Adapter Settings, press and hold or right-click a wireless adapter, and choose Connect/Disconnect.

4. From Control Panel, open Network And Internet and Connect To A Network.

   Windows 8 scans the local area for wireless networks that are within range. Next to each wireless network's name is a signal strength indicator. Hover the mouse pointer over a network name to reveal security details for the selected network. In Figure 7-15, this is an 802.11n (wireless-N) network that is secured using WPA2-PSK.

5. To connect to one of the wireless networks, tap or click its name.

   When you do so, that network's entry on the list of networks expands, and you see a Connect button and a check box marked Connect Automatically.

6. Select Connect Automatically to instruct Windows 8 to connect to this network each time it sees it. If you do not select this option, you must reconnect manually to the network each time you want to use it.

7. Tap or click Connect.

8. When promoted, enter the password for the network and tap or click Next.

9. Windows asks whether you want to use this network adapter to share resources on your home or work network (Figure 7-16). If you're in a public place with a wireless network, choose No. Otherwise, choose whichever option suits your needs.

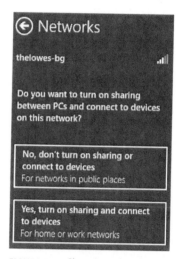

FIGURE 7-16 Choosing whether to share resources on this network

10. When you've successfully connected to a wireless network, go back to the Network settings for Windows 8 and tap or click your wireless connection. Press and hold or right-click the connection to display a screen like the one shown in Figure 7-17.

FIGURE 7-17 Available new wireless networking management options

You can see that Windows is keeping track of approximately how much data is flowing through the wireless adapter. Because this adapter was enabled only four minutes ago, only 2.01 MB of data has been transmitted.

11. If you want to reset this counter, tap or click the Reset link.

You can also disconnect from this wireless network by tapping or clicking Disconnect.

Managing a wireless network

You can manage the wireless network by using the options presented in the shortcut menu that you opened in the previous procedure and that was shown in Figure 7-17:

- **Hide Estimated Data Usage**   Hides the statistics that you see about estimated usage.
- **Set As Metered Connection**   Instructs Windows to use the data connectivity of this device sparingly. Earlier in this chapter, you learned about the new ability in Windows 8 to prevent downloads over metered connections.
- **Forget This Network**   Disconnect from this network and forget it. This erases the network from Windows memory. If you want to reconnect to this network later, you need to go through the connection process again.
- **Turn Sharing On Or Off**   Enable or disable the sharing option on this connection.
- **View Connection Properties**   Opens a traditional Windows dialog box with additional configuration options for this network (Figure 7-18).

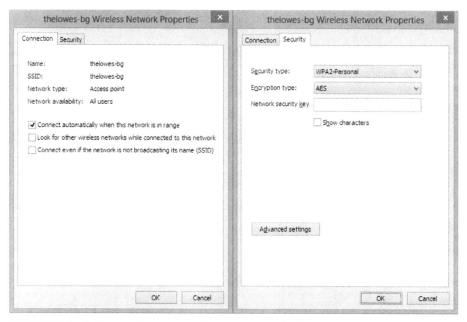

FIGURE 7-18 Available new wireless networking management options

There are two tabs on the properties page for this network, and each has a number of options that you can configure or view.

CONNECTION PROPERTIES

The Connection Properties page provides you with general information about the configuration of the network adapter:

- **Name**   This field displays the name of the network as Windows has it stored.

- **SSID**   The service set identification (SSID) is the identifier that the wireless access point broadcasts when it advertises itself as available for connections.

- **Network Type**   Most often, you will connect to an access point–type network. In this configuration, your computer is connected to a wireless access point, which acts as the doorway to the network. Sometimes, you might participate in an ad hoc network, which provides direct, computer-to-computer wireless communication without an access point present.

- **Network Availability**   This network is available to all users of this Windows 8–based computer.

- **Connect Automatically When This Network Is In Range**   When selected, if the Windows 8 device enters the range of this network, the device will automatically connect to the network.

- **Look For Other Wireless Networks While Connected To This Network**   When selected, Windows 8 continues to look for other wireless networks, even if the current one is usable.

- **Connect Even If The Network Is Not Broadcasting Its Name (SSID)**   For security reasons, some wireless network operators hide their SSID. Windows 8 can still connect to these networks as long as the SSID is already known.

SECURITY PROPERTIES

The Security Properties page provides options for securing the wireless network by using one of a number of options:

- **Security Type**   Choose from a number of security options.

  - No security   This is a wireless network that has no security built in. It is considered dangerous computing to use a wireless network that has no security.

  - WPA2-Personal   Wi-Fi Protected Access version 2 for personal use. This security option uses a pre-shared key—a password—to enable access to the network.

  - WPA-Personal   Wi-Fi Protected Access version 1 for personal use. This version is not nearly as attack resistant as WPA2.

  - WPA2-Enterprise   Wi-Fi Protected Access version 2 for enterprise use. Enterprise-grade WPA and WPA2 use Secure Socket Layer (SSL) certificates to secure communication between clients and the wireless network. WPA2 Enterprise is the most secure wireless option currently available.

  - WPA-Enterprise   Wi-Fi Protected Access version 2 for enterprise use.

  - 802.1X   An authentication method that is used in some enterprises.

- **Encryption Type** There are different kinds of encryption that can be used to secure wireless communication.

- **Network Security Key** If you've selected a Personal option, this is the password for the network.

- **Show Characters** Display the actual Network Security Key instead of dots.

> *MORE INFO* **LEARN MORE ABOUT WINDOWS 8 WIRELESS SECURITY FEATURES**
>
> Windows 8 includes updates to the encryption methods and other security items that make wireless networking safer in the new operating system. However, some of the functionality is beyond the scope of this book. To learn more about these enterprise-grade features, follow TechNet and study some of the security improvements in Windows Server 2012.

Lesson summary

- Windows 8 includes a new capability that saves money by preventing downloads over expensive metered wireless connections.

- Windows includes three network profiles—Domain, Private, and Public—which enable administrators to apply different policies for different networking scenarios.

- A number of restricted IP address ranges cannot be used on the Internet but can be used internally. These are considered private IP address ranges.

- When a DHCP server is unavailable, a Windows 8–based computer will be assigned an IP address from the APIPA range.

- Windows 8 includes full support for both IPv4 and IPv6.

- You can add networking settings—additional DNS servers and additional gateways—to help keep your Windows 8–based computer working even when there are network problems.

Lesson review

Answer the following questions to test your knowledge of the information in this lesson. You can find the answers to these questions and explanations of why each answer choice is correct or incorrect in the "Answers" section at the end of this chapter.

1. A computer on your network has an IP address of 169.254.0.2, and the user is complaining that he's unable to access network resources. Which one of these statements is NOT true?

   A. The DHCP server might be down.

   B. A network cable might be unplugged.

C.   The DHCP server might have assigned the computer an address from the wrong pool of addresses.

D.   The user might have mistyped the Wi-Fi password.

2.   Which network profile is automatically assigned when a computer is a part of Active Directory?

A.   Private

B.   Public

C.   APIPA

D.   Domain

3.   How do you configure a Wi-Fi connection for metering in Windows 8?

A.   From the Networks taskbar, tap and hold or right-click the network and choose Set As Metered Connection.

B.   Open Network And Sharing Center and select Set As Metered Connection.

C.   From the command prompt, execute ipconfig /setasmetered:true.

D.   From the IP settings page, select the This Connection Is Metered check box.

Lesson 2: Troubleshooting networking

The downside of technology is that it doesn't always work the way it's supposed to, particularly as pieces are put together and the environment becomes increasingly complex. Regardless of the technology solution you deploy, you will eventually have to troubleshoot it as problems arise. This lesson is relatively short; you've already learned a few troubleshooting tips in Lesson 1 of this chapter. In this lesson, you add a few more tools to your network troubleshooting arsenal.

> **After this lesson, you will be able to:**
>
> ▪ Describe some new Windows 8 features that aid in troubleshooting.
>
> **Estimated lesson time: 30 minutes**

Updating the Task Manager view for networking

Task Manager is one of the first places to which administrators generally turn when it becomes necessary to review what's happening on the network. Is the system consuming an inordinate amount of network resources? If so, what process is responsible for that consumption?

In Windows 8, Task Manager has been completely overhauled and now provides information in a much friendlier way than in previous versions of Windows. To start Task Manager, from the desktop, either press and hold or right-click any blank area of the taskbar at the bottom of the screen. When the shortcut menu appears, choose Task Manager.

In Figure 7-19, you can see that opening the Performance tab in Task Manager and selecting Ethernet displays network traffic flowing both into and out of the local system.

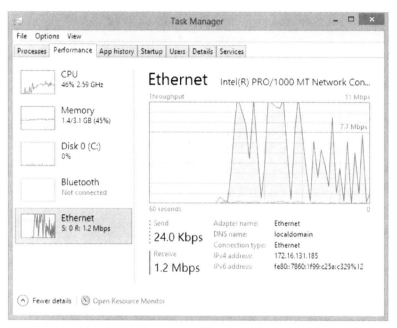

FIGURE 7-19 A detailed look at network traffic statistics in Task Manager

However, the Performance tab's network graph doesn't give you much detail about which processes are consuming that bandwidth. The Processes tab gives you this information. In Figure 7-20, note that every process in Windows 8 includes detailed information regarding the resources that process is using, including the amount of bandwidth in use. On the sample system, you can see that the Internet Explorer process is responsible for the current bandwidth load.

Name	Status	23% CPU	42% Memory	2% Disk	0% Network
Apps (4)					
▷ Internet Explorer (3)		7.1%	201.2 MB	0.8 MB/s	7.9 Mbps
▷ Microsoft Word (32 bit) (2)		0%	29.9 MB	0 MB/s	0 Mbps

FIGURE 7-20 Internet Explorer using 7.9 Mbps of network bandwidth

Viewing Windows 8 network settings

You've learned how to configure basic Windows 8 network settings, but how can you view the results of your work? You can use a couple of methods to view your network settings. Viewing the various network settings is one of the first troubleshooting steps you take when things go awry.

Viewing network settings by using Network and Sharing Center

To view your IP settings by using Network and Sharing Center, complete the following steps:

1. Open Network And Sharing Center.

2. Click the Change Adapter Settings link.

3. When the list of network adapters appears, right-click the appropriate adapter and, from the shortcut menu, choose Status.

   This opens a screen like the one shown at the left side of Figure 7-21.

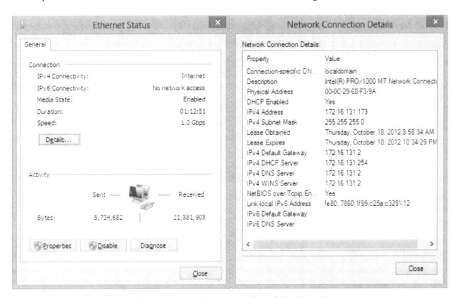

FIGURE 7-21 Viewing network settings in the Network and Sharing Center

When the Status page is open for the selected network adapter, click the Details button to get the granular details about the network connection. These details are shown on the right side of Figure 7-21. Notice that both the IPv4 and IPv6 configuration items are displayed. The IPv6 Default Gateway and IPv6 DNS Server settings are empty because the network on which this Windows 8–based computer resides does not use IPv6.

Here's what the information on the Status page means:

- **IPv4 Connectivity** You can see in Figure 7-21 that this computer has Internet access. If the computer were on the network but did not have Internet access, this entry would read Local. If the network adapter were not connected to a network, it would read No Network Access.

- **IPv6 Connectivity**   This acts the same as the IPv4 Connectivity entry.
- **Media State**   When the network adapter is operating and connected to a network, Media State reads Enabled.
- **Duration**   The duration is a timer that indicates how long the network connection has been active. Whenever the network resets for any reason, this timer starts over.
- **Speed**   This status reading displays the speed of the network to which this network adapter is connected. For a wired network, this is generally 10 Mbps, 100 Mbps, or 1 Gbps.
- **Activity**   The activity graph at the bottom of the window displays the amount of traffic that has been sent and received by the selected network adapter.

Viewing network settings by using the command prompt

You don't have to use the Network and Sharing Center to view the configuration information for your Windows 8–based computer. Windows has always supported the ability to view network settings from the command prompt, and this capability has been retained in Windows 8.

To view network settings from the command prompt, complete the following steps:

1. Open a command prompt by clicking the command prompt icon on the desktop's taskbar or by running the command prompt app from the Start screen. You don't need to use an administrative command prompt to view network settings.

2. At the command line, type **ipconfig /all** and press Enter.

   This command provides you with information such as the information you see in Figure 7-22.

The command results in a plethora of information about the various network adapters that are installed on the computer running Windows 8. In earlier screen shots, you saw both the Bluetooth and Ethernet adapters shown in the graphical interface. Here, you can see some additional adapters that you did not see before:

- **isatap.localdomain**   This is a software-based network adapter that is used behind the scenes to aid in a transition from IPv4 to IPv6. In normal operations, you will almost never need to worry about this adapter.
- **Teredo Tunneling Pseudo-Interface**   Teredo is an IPv4/IPv6 network address translation service that is also designed to help systems exist seamlessly on IPv4 and IPv6 networks. In normal operations, you should almost never have to touch this adapter's configuration.

FIGURE 7-22 Using the command prompt to view network settings

---

NOTE **OBTAIN A SIMPLER SET OF INFORMATION FROM THE COMMAND PROMPT**

The output that you saw in Figure 7-22 was a complete set of information that included all pertinent information about the network adapter configuration. If you'd like a simpler display that includes a little less information, run the ipconfig command without the /all parameter.

Viewing wireless network details

Previously, you learned how to view network information for a wired Ethernet connection. To view the status for a Wi-Fi adapter, complete the following steps:

1. Open Network And Sharing Center.

2. In the View Your Active Networks section of the window, tap or click the name of the wireless network to which you're connected.

You see a screen like the one in Figure 7-23.

FIGURE 7-23 Status of the Wi-Fi connection

In this status dialog box, note that you are now shown the SSID of the network to which you're connected and the current speed of the network. Unlike a wired network, your wireless network speed will fluctuate as conditions change. This is normal and expected. You're also shown a Signal Quality indicator that can be useful in troubleshooting.

Using the network troubleshooters

Windows 8 includes a set of built-in tools that are intended to help you determine the cause of problems that might arise with Windows 8 networking components. To access these tools, complete the following steps:

1. Open Network And Sharing Center.

2. Tap or click the Troubleshoot Problems link.

   This opens a list of troubleshooting tools (Figure 7-24).

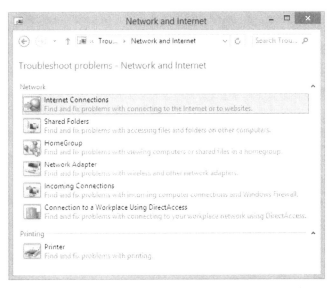

FIGURE 7-24 A list of the troubleshooting tools available in Windows 8

There are six network troubleshooters at your disposal:

- **Internet Connections** This tool assists you in locating problems that are preventing the computer from connecting to the Internet or to specific websites. When you run this troubleshooter, you're asked to provide the address of a specific website. In Figure 7-25, you can see the results. In this example, the user reported that he was unable to browse to *http://www.contosobank.com*. In this case, Windows 8 is working fine, but there is a problem at the remote site hosting contosobank.com.

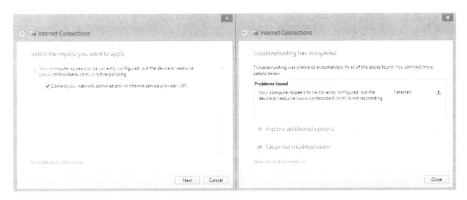

FIGURE 7-25 Troubleshooter finding the problem

- **Shared Folders** If you are sharing folders and experiencing problems, use this troubleshooter to help determine the cause.
- **HomeGroup** HomeGroup is a consumer feature that enables easy sharing of resources on a home network.

- **Network Adapter**   Network adapters can sometimes be the cause of problems. Use this troubleshooter to enable Windows to identify common problems with network adapters.

- **Incoming Connections**   A very common source of perceived networking problems is Windows Firewall. This troubleshooter can help you determine whether this is applicable to your situation.

- **Connection To A Workplace Using DirectAccess**   DirectAccess is a remote-connection tool that can replace traditional VPNs. If you are experiencing a problem with this service, use this tool.

Using command-line tools

Not every troubleshooting tool has a graphical user interface. Sometimes, command-line tools are better options. In this section, you explore two such command-line tools.

Using ipconfig

After you've been supporting desktops for a while, you will find that the IPconfig tool is indispensable. You already saw the results of ipconfig /all, but the ipconfig command also has some more substantial troubleshooting capabilities. For some of the troubleshooting elements, you need to run ipconfig in a command prompt with elevated (administrator) privileges.

The following table describes some troubleshooting scenarios that can be corrected by using ipconfig.

TABLE 7-2 Ipconfig troubleshooting capabilities

Problem	Possible cause	Possible solution
A user indicates that he is no longer able to access a website that was working earlier.	The Windows 8 DNS cache might have become corrupted or stale.	ipconfig /flushdns
A computer is using an out-of-date, DHCP-provided IP address.	Release and renew the computer's DHCP lease.	ipconfig /release followed by ipconfig /renew
A computer is using an out-of-date, DHCP-provided IPv6 address.	Release and renew the computer's DHCPv6 lease.	ipconfig /release6 followed by ipconfig /renew6

Using netstat

The netstat command can be used to troubleshoot individual network connections and to get a very granular look at the traffic on the network. Netstat is useful when you are attempting to verify whether a computer has a specific open connection. Figure 7-26 shows the results of using the netstat command.

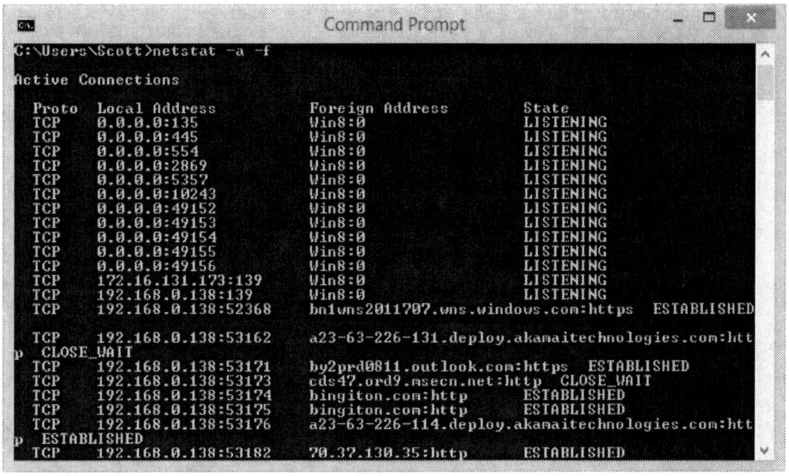

FIGURE 7-26 Results of the netstat command

MORE INFO **LEARN HOW TO USE NETSTAT**

A complete guide to netstat is beyond the scope of this book. However, if you'd like some additional guidance on how to use this powerful troubleshooting command, the article "Netstat Tips And Tricks For Windows Server Admins," available at *http://www.techrepublic .com/blog/datacenter/netstat-tips-and-tricks-for-windows-server-admins/3371*, is a very good resource. Although it's targeted at Windows Server administrators, the information is also pertinent to desktop administrators.

Lesson summary

- The first troubleshooting step is just viewing the state of a network connection to see whether everything looks correct. Windows 8 provides administrators with detailed statistics about each connection.
- Windows 8 Task Manager is completely overhauled and provides administrators with a detailed breakdown of how much network capacity is being consumed by each app.
- The ipconfig command-line tool is useful for both viewing the status of a network connection and resolving specific networking issues.
- Windows 8 ships with a number of built-in troubleshooters that can help administrators identify and resolve networking problems more quickly than previously possible.

Lesson review

Answer the following questions to test your knowledge of the information in this lesson. You can find the answers to these questions and explanations of why each answer choice is correct or incorrect in the "Answers" section at the end of this chapter.

1. Which ipconfig parameter is used to clear the DNS cache?

    A. releasedns

    B. flushdns

    C. renewdns

    D. flush

2. What information is NOT available when you are viewing the statistics of a network connection?

    A. The speed of the network

    B. The length of time the network connection has been active

    C. The network profile the network connection is using

    D. Whether the network adapter can access the Internet

Practice exercises

In these exercises, you practice what you learned about different techniques for managing and troubleshooting Windows 8 networking.

Exercise 1: Disable Network Discovery on the Private network profile

In this exercise, you disable the ability for the computer running Windows 8 to locate other resources on the network automatically. This also makes the Windows 8–based computer effectively invisible on the network and can improve security.

1. Open Network And Sharing Center.

2. Change the configuration for the Private network profile.

3. Disable network discovery on that profile.

Exercise 2: Manually configure IP settings for one of your network adapters

In this exercise, you manually configure Windows 8 network settings rather than allowing DHCP to assign them automatically.

1. Open the properties for a network adapter.

2. Provide the necessary settings for your network.

Exercise 3: Use the netstat command

The netstat command is a powerful troubleshooting tool. Practice using this tool on your Windows 8–based computer.

1. Open a command prompt.

2. Use the command's help screen (netstat /?) to learn about the various parameters.

Suggested practice exercises

The following additional practices are designed to give you more opportunities to practice what you've learned and to help you successfully master the lessons presented in this chapter.

- **Exercise 1** Add a USB wireless adapter to your computer and connect it to a wireless network.
- **Exercise 2** Manually assign the IP settings for one of your network adapters.
- **Exercise 3** Experiment with the various troubleshooters to learn how they function.

Answers

This section contains the answers to the lesson review questions in this chapter.

Lesson 1

1. **Correct answer: C**

    A. **Incorrect:** The symptoms indicate that the DHCP server could be down.

    B. **Incorrect:** The symptoms indicate that a network cable could be unplugged.

    C. **Correct:** If the DHCP server had assigned the IP address, it would not start with a 169 prefix.

    D. **Incorrect:** Computer Management is a general-purpose tool used to manage the system.

2. **Correct answer: D**

    A. **Incorrect:** The Private profile is not used on a domain-joined computer.

    B. **Incorrect:** The Public profile is used in areas with, for example, unsecured Wi-Fi.

    C. **Incorrect:** APIPA is a range of IP addresses used when a DHCP server is unavailable.

    D. **Correct:** The Domain profile is automatically assigned when a computer is part of an Active Directory domain.

3. **Correct answer: A**

    A. **Correct:** From the Networks taskbar, tapping or right-clicking the network and choosing Set As Metered Connection is the correct process.

    B. **Incorrect:** Opening Network And Sharing Center and selecting Set As Metered Connection is a process that does not exist.

    C. **Incorrect:** Ipconfig does not have a setasmetered parameter.

    D. **Incorrect:** Selecting the This Connection Is Metered check box from the IP settings page is a process that does not exist.

Lesson 2

1. **Correct answer: B**

    A. **Incorrect:** Releasedns is not a valid parameter.

    B. **Correct:** The flushdns parameter clears the DNS cache.

    C. **Incorrect:** Renewdns is not a valid parameter.

    D. **Incorrect:** Flush is not a valid parameter.

2. **Correct answer: C**

   A. **Incorrect:** The network speed is visible.

   B. **Incorrect:** The connection time length is visible.

   C. **Correct:** The network profile is not visible.

   D. **Incorrect:** The Internet connectivity status is visible.

CHAPTER 8

Configuring security

Security becomes a more important consideration every day. With the changes in technology to combat exploits and enhance security comes the struggle to keep up with new exploits. Administrators must stay up to date on security within their organizations and keep all the Windows 8–based computers in their environments as secure as possible while ensuring that Windows remains easy to use and enables people within the organization to do their work. All the security in the world does little good if an organization cannot achieve its business goals.

This chapter focuses on security and configuring these settings in Windows 8.

Lessons in this chapter:

Before you begin

This chapter requires the ability to test both inbound and outbound configurations for firewalls and other elements. There are no specific hardware requirements for the exercises in this chapter.

Lesson 1: Managing Windows Firewall and exceptions

Windows 8 includes a firewall to help ensure that only necessary traffic is allowed into and out of a computer. This lesson discusses the configuration of the firewall in Windows 8, including inbound rules, outbound rules, profiles, and other configuration settings.

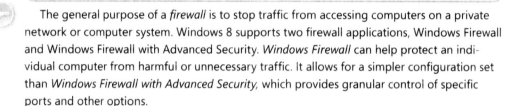

The general purpose of a *firewall* is to stop traffic from accessing computers on a private network or computer system. Windows 8 supports two firewall applications, Windows Firewall and Windows Firewall with Advanced Security. *Windows Firewall* can help protect an individual computer from harmful or unnecessary traffic. It allows for a simpler configuration set than *Windows Firewall with Advanced Security,* which provides granular control of specific ports and other options.

With the introduction of Windows Firewall with Advanced Security in Windows Vista, Microsoft offered the ability to configure granular rules about which traffic to allow into or out of a computer system. For example, Windows 8 allows IP version 6 Internet Control Message Protocol (ICMP) echo requests to come in by default. If certain computers should not respond to these requests, the rule allowing the responses can be disabled, and any further responses will fail.

Choosing Windows Firewall

Standard configuration options with Windows Firewall include:

■ **Allow An App Or Feature Through Windows Firewall**   This option enables administrators to configure the firewall based on applications that need specific access.

■ **Change Notification Settings/Turn Windows Firewall On Or Off**   Both of these items allow changes to the firewall configuration, including:

  ■ Enabling/Disabling Windows Firewall   Turns the firewall on or off

  ■ Block All Incoming Connections, Including Those In The List Of Allowed Apps   Blocks all incoming traffic to the computer

  ■ Notify Me When Windows Firewall Blocks A New App   Displays a balloon notification when a new app is blocked

■ **Restore Defaults**   This option returns Windows Firewall to its original configuration.

■ **Advanced Settings**   This option opens Windows Firewall with Advanced Security.

■ **Troubleshoot My Network**   This option launches the network troubleshooter.

Figure 8-1 displays Windows Firewall in its original configuration.

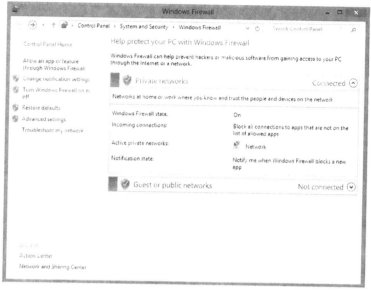

FIGURE 8-1 Windows Firewall

In addition to the configurable options of the standard firewall, the initial window displays the status of the firewall for each configured network type.

Windows Firewall can block or allow access to applications installed on Windows 8. For example, Tailspin Toys has a written policy covering the use of chat applications on company computer systems. Because the organization has internal instant messaging (IM) to provide an additional way for employees to communicate, public chat clients are not allowed, and Windows Firewall blocks them. However, with the evolution of social media and Internet marketing to help grow the business of Tailspin Toys, this policy has been reviewed, and some applications are being allowed for some individuals. By configuring Windows Firewall, you can control which applications are allowed to access the network and the Internet. The system administrator can designate applications to use in the Tailspin Toys social media marketing campaign while still preventing the use of public IM clients on the network.

Configuring Windows Firewall to allow specific apps

To configure Windows Firewall to allow an application through, complete the following steps:

1. Search for Firewall on the Start screen and select Settings.
2. Tap or click Windows Firewall in the list of results.
3. Tap or click Allow An App Or Feature Through Windows Firewall.
4. Tap or click Change Settings to grant the elevated permissions necessary to change firewall settings.

5. To allow an app already known by Windows Firewall, scroll through the Allowed Apps And Features list and select the check box next to the name of the app.

6. Select Private to allow the app when connected to private networks or select Public to allow it when connected to public networks.

7. Tap or click Allow Another App to browse for an application that is not listed.

8. Tap or click OK to save the new settings.

After configuring a rule to allow the application through the firewall, open the application to ensure that it can access necessary resources. If the app does not function as needed, select the firewall rule associated with it again.

Removing an app from a Windows Firewall configuration

You can remove an app that you have previously granted access through the firewall. This works only with apps you have added to the list; it does not work with Windows 8 apps or services. To remove the previously allowed application, complete the following steps:

1. Locate Windows Firewall by searching for Firewall on the Start screen and selecting Settings.

2. Tap or click Windows Firewall in the list of results.

3. Select Allow An App Or Feature Through Windows Firewall.

4. Locate the application you want to remove from the Allowed Apps And Features List.

5. Select the application, and then tap or click Remove. In the confirmation dialog box, tap or click Yes.

Choosing Windows Firewall with Advanced Security

Sometimes, just allowing applications or features to pass through Windows Firewall is not granular enough for the type of control needed. Specific ports might need to be configured as allowed, or a specific set of ports might need to be blocked to ensure the security of the computer. These types of configurations are best accomplished by configuring Windows Firewall with Advanced Security, which can be accessed from the Windows Firewall application by tapping or clicking the Advanced Settings link.

Figure 8-2 shows Windows Firewall with Advanced Security before any changes have been made to the configuration.

> **SECURITY ALERT** **CONTROLLING ADVANCED SETTINGS**
>
> You can control ports and other advanced settings individually only by using the advanced feature set.

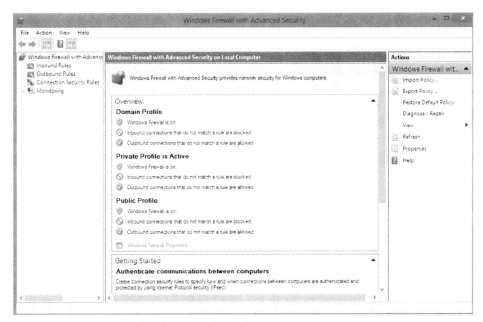

FIGURE 8-2 Windows Firewall with Advanced Security

Viewing the initial configuration

The initial settings displayed for Windows Firewall with Advanced Security are similar to those for Windows Firewall in Windows 8. The Overview pane, shown in Figure 8-2, displays each network profile along with information about how it is configured. The domain profile is also displayed in the advanced firewall overview.

Modifying a firewall profile

In Windows Firewall with Advanced Security, a *profile* is the network type to which the settings apply. Profiles enable the firewall to behave differently, depending on the type of network to which the computer connects. For example, a laptop computer that connects to the contoso.com domain when a user is at work might connect to the wireless network at the local coffee shop on the weekend. Windows might need to block more items on this local network and be more secure than on the contoso.com network. The profiles available for Windows Firewall with Advanced Security enable you to configure these settings.

The profiles available in Windows Firewall with Advanced Security are:

- **Domain Profile** Specifies firewall behavior when the computer is connected to a domain

- **Private Profile** Specifies firewall behavior when the computer is connected to a private network location (for example, a home network)

- **Public Profile**   Specifies firewall behavior when the computer is connected to an unsecured or public network

To modify the profile settings, from the Overview pane (see Figure 8-2), select the Properties link in the Actions pane to open the profiles configuration dialog box shown in Figure 8-3. Each profile has a tab in the dialog box, and each tab contains the settings for the profile.

FIGURE 8-3 Windows Firewall properties

For each firewall profile, you can configure the following settings:

- **Firewall State**   Determines whether the firewall is on or off.
- **Inbound Connections**   Determines how the profile handles inbound connections. The following options are available:
    - Block (Default)   Blocks inbound connections that have not been allowed
    - Block All   Blocks all inbound connections, including those that have been allowed
    - Allow   Does not block inbound connections
- **Outbound Connections**   Determines how the profile handles outbound connections. The following options are available:
    - Block   Does not allow outbound connections
    - Allow (Default)   Allows outbound connections
- **Protected Network Connections**   Identifies the network connections within the computer that are protected by the selected firewall profile. Select Customize to add or remove network connections from a firewall profile.

- **Settings** Identifies items that control the overall behavior of the firewall for a profile. Select Customize to modify the following items:

  - Display A Notification   Determines whether the firewall will display notifications for this profile.

  - Allow Unicast Response   Determines whether the firewall will allow a unicast response to broadcast traffic. A *unicast response* is a reply directed at the computer broadcasting items rather than broadcasting the response to all hosts on the network.

  - Allow Rule Merging   These settings must be configured by using Group Policy, but they allow local rules and Group Policy distributed rules to be used together.

- **Logging** Determines the level of logging for traffic the firewall sees by using this profile. Tap or click Customize to configure the following options:

  - Name   The path and file name of the log file.

  - Size Limit (KB)   The size of the log file.

  - Log Dropped Packets   Determines whether packets the firewall discards will be logged; No is the default.

  - Log Successful Connections   Determines whether packets passed through the firewall will be logged; No is the default.

Configuring IPsec settings

In addition to the profiles, there is a tab for IPsec Settings in the Properties dialog box, as shown in Figure 8-3. *Internet Protocol Security (IPsec)* ensures that communication between two points on a network is secured. For example, some point-to-point virtual private network (VPN) connections use IPsec to secure the tunnels created between locations. These settings w.ll most likely be configured through Group Policies on enterprise networks; for most smaller organizations, you will not need to adjust these settings.

The IPsec Settings tab is shown in Figure 8-4.

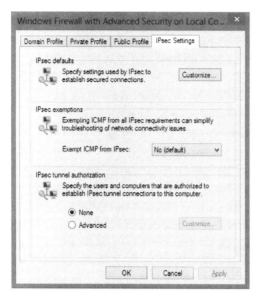

FIGURE 8-4 Configuring IPsec Settings in Windows Firewall with Advanced Security

This dialog box allows configuration of the following settings:

- **IPsec Defaults**   Connection settings used when active security rules exist
- **IPsec Exemptions**   Allows ICMP traffic to be exempt from IPsec security
- **IPsec Tunnel Authorization**   Specifies user accounts and computers that are authorized to establish tunneled connections

If you want to change IPsec Defaults, tap or click Customize. You can change the following settings:

- **Key Exchange (Main Mode)**   Defines the algorithm used to exchange keys during connection configuration. Selecting Advanced allows the selection of security algorithms and the configuration of the key lifetimes in minutes or by number of sessions.

- **Data Protection (Quick Mode)**   The default Quick Mode uses built-in encryption algorithms to secure IPsec connections. Selecting Advanced and then tapping or clicking Customize opens another dialog box, in which you can select both the amount of data integrity and the encryption that is applied to network packets and add or select other encryption algorithms for network devices.

- **Authentication Method**   Determines the authentication type IPsec and Windows Firewall support. Options include:
  - Default
  - Computer and user (Kerberos 5)
  - Computer (Kerberos 5)
  - User (Kerberos 5)
  - Advanced

Configuring inbound rules

Windows Firewall with Advanced Security enables you to control inbound and outbound traffic separately. *Inbound traffic* is any traffic that accesses a computer. For example, a computer configured with an inbound rule to allow echo responses for ICMP traffic would respond to a ping.

When inbound rules are selected, all the previously configured rules are listed. Enabled rules have a green icon next to the rule name, and disabled rules have a dimmed icon next to the rule name.

Apps that are installed with Windows 8 and access the Internet have preconfigured rules in Windows Firewall. An example is the rule for Mail, Calendar, and People. These applications are Windows 8–native apps and install with the operating system. The inbound firewall rule for these applications is shown in Figure 8-5.

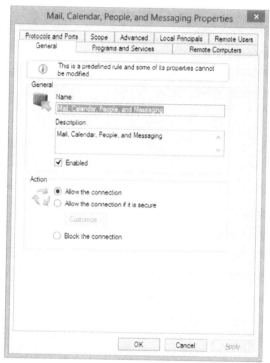

FIGURE 8-5 Examining existing firewall rules

There might be certain configurations in which modifying existing rules is necessary, which you can do by opening the Properties page for the rule and editing the settings. Some settings within predefined rules cannot be edited.

Allowing the secure connection

One of the actions that can be specified when creating a new inbound rule is Allow The Connection If It Is Secure (see Figure 8-5). This option is useful when an incoming connection needs to be authenticated before it can be allowed.

When this option is selected in the New Inbound Rule Wizard, tap or click Customize to expose additional options for authenticated users and an exceptions list when the rule will be skipped if the connection is attempted by specific user accounts.

The options available here are:

- **Allow The Connection If It Is Authenticated And Integrity-Protected** This option allows the connection to succeed only if the initiating party is authenticated and the connection is secured by IPsec. This type of connection is available for Windows Vista and later Microsoft operating systems.

- **Require The Connection To Be Encrypted** This connection type forces the connection to be encrypted to ensure privacy of information.

- **Allow The Connection To Use Null Encapsulation** This option allows an authenticated connection, but integrity is not required.

- **Override Block Rules** This option allows the rule to be overridden for services that must remain available.

To configure new inbound rules, complete the following steps:

1. Locate Windows Firewall by searching for Firewall on the Start screen and selecting Settings.

2. Tap or click Windows Firewall in the list of results.

3. Select Advanced Settings in the navigation pane.

4. Select Inbound Rules from the navigation pane.

5. In the Actions pane, select New Rule.

6. On the first page of the New Inbound Rule Wizard, select the type of rule to create:

   - **Program** A rule that controls access and connections for a program

   - **Port** A rule that controls access to a specific port

   - **Predefined** A rule that controls connections for a Windows Experience

   - **Custom** A rule with custom options

7. After selecting the rule type, tap or click Next to continue.

   Depending on the type of rule selected, the next page asks for information about the item to be tracked by the rule. For example, selecting a port rule type asks port-related questions.

8. Select the type of port to configure the rule against, TCP or UDP.

9. Select the scope of the rule, All Local Ports or Specific Local Ports.

10. Enter the specific port number to be monitored by the rule.

11. Tap or click Next to continue.

12. Select an action for the rule to take:

   - **Allow The Connection**   Connections on the monitored ports are allowed, secured or not.
   - **Allow The Connection If It Is Secure**   Secure connections to the monitored ports are allowed.
   - **Block The Connection**   Connections to the monitored ports will be blocked.

13. Tap or click Next to continue.

14. Select the firewall profiles to which this rule should belong from the following:

   - **Domain**   Applies when the computer is connected to a corporate domain
   - **Private**   Applies when the computer is connected to a private network
   - **Public**   Applies when the computer is connected to a public network

15. Tap or click Next to continue.

16. Enter a name and description for the rule.

17. Tap or click Finish to save and enable the new rule.

> *NOTE* **SELECTING PROFILES FOR FIREWALL RULES**
>
> Profiles are not mutually exclusive, and a rule can be applied by more than one profile.

Configuring outbound rules

Outbound rules prevent certain applications or local ports from sending data out of the computer. For example, if a computer in an environment should not be allowed to access the Internet, outbound access on port 80 (and other ports) could be disabled to ensure that this computer does not connect to the Internet. Just as a number of inbound rules are preconfigured for certain applications, there are outbound rules for these items.

Outbound rules are also configured by using a wizard. For example, many organizations employ email servers that communicate with the Internet. The client computers are configured to send email to the mail server and not beyond that point. However, many client computers have not been configured to disallow port 25 outbound to ensure that no SMTP traffic can be sent from the client computers directly. If malware were to infect a client computer and try to send email to itself by using an included SMTP server, the message could be easily propagated using port 25. If this port is disallowed by a firewall rule, the client computer is less likely to infect other computers.

> *SECURITY ALERT* **PORTS**
>
> Although SMTP traffic can travel on ports other than port 25, this is the most common port. If you are configuring rules to block SMTP, research which other SMTP ports on your network to include.

To configure an outbound rule to disallow traffic to go out through port 25, complete the following steps:

1. Locate Windows Firewall by searching for Firewall on the Start screen and selecting Settings.
2. Tap or click Windows Firewall in the list of results.
3. Select Advanced Settings from the navigation pane.
4. Select Outbound Rules in the navigation pane.
5. Select New Rule in the Actions pane.
6. Select Port as the type of rule and tap or click Next to continue.
7. Select TCP as the port type and specific remote ports.
8. Enter **25** for the remote port number and tap or click Next to continue.
9. Select Block The Connection as the action for the rule and tap or click Next to continue.
10. Select Domain, Private, and Public as the profiles to which this rule will be applied and tap or click Next to continue.
11. Enter a name for the rule (NO SMTP Outbound, for example) and a description.
12. Tap or click Finish to save and activate the rule.

> **IMPORTANT CREATE GOOD RULE DESCRIPTIONS**
>
> Using a description for all the rules created in the Windows Firewall is a good habit to develop. It will help others determine the rule's function without needing to comb through the entire rule. More important, a good description can also aid in determining how a rule operates when troubleshooting becomes necessary later.

After adding an outbound rule such as the one blocking SMTP, it is a good idea to test the rule. In this case, using a Telnet client to access port 25 on a remote system should be denied by the outbound rule preventing SMTP.

After a rule has been created, either inbound or outbound, you can make additional changes by selecting the rule and choosing properties from the rule Actions pane within the Windows Firewall with Advanced Security console.

 Quick check

- True or False? Configuring an application to be allowed through Windows Firewall modifies the necessary ports for that application.

Quick check answer

- True. When an application is allowed through the firewall, the ports needed by that application are opened. This works for applications that use known firewall ports.

Configuring connection security rules

In addition to standard inbound and outbound rules governing applications or ports, Windows Firewall with Advanced Security can also apply rules governing connections. These can be useful if certain activities need to be blocked when a computer is running on a wireless connection versus an available LAN cable.

Unlike inbound and outbound rules, no connection security rules are configured by default.

Windows Firewall with Advanced Security supports the following connection security rule types:

- **Isolation**   This rule type restricts connections based on authentication criteria.
- **Authentication exemption**   This rule type allows connections from certain computers to be exempted from authentication.
- **Server to server**   This rule type authenticates connections between specified computers.
- **Tunnel**   This rule type authenticates connections between two computers.
- **Custom**   This rule type is completely customizable and has no predefined items.

Connection security rules can help ensure that computers that come into an organization meet compliance and antimalware requirements. For example, when an organization has a large remote sales force of employees who are on the road more than they are in the office, this configuration can help ensure that these computers are clean of any malware before they can authenticate to the domain when they are being used in the office.

To configure a health check rule, complete the following steps:

1. Locate Windows Firewall by searching for Firewall on the Start screen and selecting Settings.
2. Tap or click Windows Firewall in the list of results.
3. Select Advanced Settings in the navigation pane.
4. Select Connection Security Rules in the navigation pane.
5. Select New Rule from the Connection Security Rules in the Actions pane.
6. Select Isolation as the rule type and tap or click Next to continue.
7. Select the appropriate authentication timing for the rule from the following options:
   - Request Authentication For Inbound And Outbound Connections   Authenticate when possible but do not require authentication.
   - Require Authentication For Inbound Connections And Request Authentication For Outbound Connections   Inbound connections must be authenticated. Outbound connections will authenticate when possible, but this is not required.
   - Require Authentication For Inbound And Outbound Connections   Both connection types require authentication. If it is not available, the connection will fail.

8. Tap or click Next to continue.

9. Specify an authentication method for the rule from the following options:

    ▪ **Default**   Use the options configured in IPsec settings.

    ▪ **Computer And User (Kerberos v5)**   Communications are restricted to connections from domain-joined users and computers. This allows specific user and computer accounts to be authorized to make inbound and outbound connections.

    ▪ **Computer (Kerberos v5)**   Communications are restricted to domain-joined computers.

    ▪ **Advanced**   Customizable authentication types allow specified first and second authentication settings.

10. Tap or click Next to continue.

11. Specify the firewall profiles to which the rule should be assigned (Domain, Private, or Public) and tap or click Next to continue.

12. Enter a name and description for the connection security rule and tap or click Finish to save and enable the rule.

Monitoring rules configured in Windows Firewall

All rules enabled for use in Windows Firewall appear under the monitoring section within Windows Firewall with Advanced Security. These are the active rules for the computer. In the other areas available, where rules are configured, all rules—whether enabled or disabled—are listed.

 Additional options for monitoring include *security associations*, shared security information between two computers. This information protects the information being shared during the connection.

Lesson summary

▪ Configure inbound, outbound, and connection security rules in Windows Firewall with Advanced Security.

▪ Manage firewall profiles to apply rules based on the type of network to which the computer is connected.

▪ Configure isolation to prevent a computer from connecting to a domain environment before it has met security requirements.

▪ Use monitoring to manage enabled firewall rules and current security associations between computers.

Lesson review

Answer the following questions to test your knowledge of the information in this lesson. You can find the answers to these questions and explanations of why each answer choice is correct or incorrect in the "Answers" section at the end of this chapter.

1. After receiving several calls reporting that a line-of-business application is not operating correctly, the help desk staff attempts to ping the computer on which the application is running. When the ping attempts come back as failed, one of the technicians connects to the computer by using Remote Desktop and finds that the computer is online and running as needed. What might be causing the initial ping tests to fail? (Choose all that apply.)

   A. The ping requests are timing out before they reach the computer.

   B. An inbound firewall rule on the remote computer is preventing ICMP traffic.

   C. An outbound rule on the remote computer is preventing ICMP replies.

   D. An outbound rule on the local computer is preventing ICMP traffic.

2. Because of recent problems with malware, Contoso wants to prevent outbound traffic for SMTP from being sent by client computers. Even though SMTP is required for email leaving the organization, sending SMTP traffic from a client workstation could be an indication of a malware installation. How can workstations be configured to prevent this type of traffic?

   A. Uninstall all email software from the client.

   B. Configure an inbound firewall rule to block traffic on SMTP-related ports.

   C. Configure an outbound firewall rule to block traffic on SMTP-related ports.

   D. Configure Windows Firewall to block traffic from the client email application.

Lesson 2: Configuring network discovery and wireless security

Using network discovery is typically how a computer accesses the Internet, other local computers, printers, homegroups, and any other resources outside its local ports. An IT administrator who understands how discovery works can use this to ensure that a computer is secure while still allowing that resource to access other devices. In addition, managing wireless security is becoming extremely important as technology advances and more devices gain the ability to communicate over wireless networks.

Creating network discovery profiles

Network discovery is the method a computer running Windows 8 uses to locate available networks and devices connected to those networks.

SECURITY ALERT   BE AWARE OF POTENTIAL SECURITY RISKS WITH NETWORK DISCOVERY

The technology used to allow network discovery has the potential for misuse and should be carefully considered before the technology is used.

When network discovery is turned on, which it is by default if the Express Settings option was chosen during initial configuration, your computer can connect to other devices, and other devices can connect to your computer. Because networks can have very different characteristics and usages, Windows offers two profiles for network types regarding network discovery. These profiles are found in the Network and Sharing Center. At the desktop, open the Settings charm, and then tap or click Control Panel. Tap or click Network And Sharing Center, and then tap or click Change Advanced Sharing Settings. The available network profiles are:

■ **Private** Settings in this profile are applied when connected to a secured network. Options available for this profile include:

  ■ Turn On Network Discovery   Selecting this option allows the local computer to see networked computers and devices and be seen by other computers or devices on the network.

  ■ Turn On Automatic Setup Of Network Connected Devices   Selecting this option queries networked devices to configure them automatically on the computer.

  ■ Turn Off Network Discovery   Selecting this option prevents the computer from seeing or being seen by other computers or devices on the network.

  ■ Turn On File And Printer Sharing   Selecting this option enables the ability to share files and printers or other devices.

  ■ Turn Off File And Printer Sharing   Selecting this option disables the ability to share files and printers or other devices.

- **Allow Windows To Manage HomeGroup Connections (Recommended)**   Selecting this option automates the configuration of homegroups on private non-domain networks.

- **Use User Accounts And Passwords To Connect To Other Computers**   Selecting this option requires user names and passwords to be provided when connecting to shared resources on other computers.

- **Guest or Public**   Settings in this profile are applied when connected to an open network. The options available for this profile include the following from the preceding list:

  - Turn On Network Discovery

  - Turn Off Network Discovery

  - Turn On File And Printer Sharing

  - Turn Off File And Printer Sharing

The third option contained in network profiles is for all networks. Settings configured here are used regardless of public or private network type. Settings available include:

- **Public Folder Sharing**   When this setting is enabled, other computers can access files and folders in the public profile folders of the computer.

- **Media Streaming**   When this setting is enabled, other people or computers on the network can access photos, music, and video on the local computer. Tap or click Choose Media Streaming Options. The Media Streaming Options dialog box, as shown in Figure 8-6, enables you to configure additional settings for sharing your media on the network. These options include:

  - Show Devices On   Select whether media devices should be visible on the local network or on all networks.

  - Allow All   Select this option to configure settings so that all computers and devices on this network can access streaming media.

  - Block All   Select this option to disable access to shared media by any devices or computers.

  - Customize   Select the Customize link to allow media to be streamed based on ratings. You can also indicate whether unrated content should be included.

FIGURE 8-6 Configuring options for media streaming on a network

- **File Sharing Connections**   These settings determine the encryption level used for sharing files. By default, 128-bit encryption is used; however, some devices require different encryption levels. Options include:

    - Use 128-Bit Encryption To Help Protect File Sharing Connections.

    - Enable File Sharing For Devices That Use 40- Or 56-Bit Encryption.

- **Password Protected Sharing**   This setting requires incoming connections to have a user name and password on the local computer to access files. Password-protected sharing can be managed by using the following options:

    - Turn On Password-Protected Sharing

    - Turn Off Password-Protected Sharing

To configure a computer to allow only content rated four stars or higher and to exclude unrated content, complete the following steps:

1. Open the Network and Sharing Center by searching for Network Sharing on the Start screen and tapping or clicking Network And Sharing Center in the results pane.

2. Select Change Advanced Sharing Settings in the navigation pane.

3. Expand the All Networks section on the Profiles page.

4. Select the Choose Media Streaming Options link.

5. Select Choose Default Settings on the Default Media Streaming Settings page, shown in Figure 8-7.

FIGURE 8-7 Configuring default options for media sharing

6. For Star Ratings, make sure that Only is selected, and then select Rated 4 Stars Or Higher in the drop-down box.

7. Clear the Include Unrated Files check box.

8. Tap or click OK.

In addition to sharing based on content ratings, permissions can be assigned to content types within a homegroup. After modifying the default sharing settings, complete the following steps:

1. On the Media Streaming Options page (Figure 8-6), tap or click Choose Homegroup And Sharing Options.

2. On the HomeGroup page, tap or click Choose What You Want To Share, And View The Homegroup Password.

3. Select either Shared or Not Shared, as shown in Figure 8-8, for the following media types and devices:

- Pictures
- Videos
- Music
- Documents
- Printers and Devices

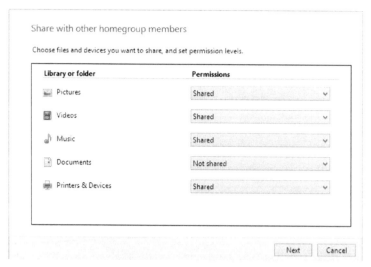

FIGURE 8-8 Sharing individual media types and devices with a homegroup

4. After these permissions have been configured, tap or click Next to continue.

5. On the next page, write down or print the homegroup password so that other computers can join your homegroup and access your shared resources.

Even though homegroups are password protected and only devices and computers with that information can join them, information is still shared across multiple computers and has the potential to be shared outside the homegroup, especially when documents and other files are involved.

When network discovery settings are used or allowed, Windows makes changes to the firewall rules to ensure that the selected services operate as needed. If the settings are disabled, Windows will close the ports in the firewall by disabling rules to allow these items to be used. Working with these features can increase the security risk on a given computer because connections to other networks, computers, or devices are allowed. Before enabling any settings involving sharing, carefully consider security and how the computer might be used.

Managing wireless security

Wireless networks are everywhere, and nearly every device is capable of wireless connection. This makes it easy to connect anywhere. With this always-on availability for numerous devices come security considerations about joining a computer to a particular network.

Designing a secure wireless infrastructure is an increasingly important responsibility for administrators, and understanding the options available and the factors to take into account when deciding on the right security for a particular environment is critical.

Understanding types of wireless security

Because the technology surrounding wireless connection changes constantly, and the previous security models are always under scrutiny, wireless equipment manufacturers are working to develop the next great way to keep information secure. The currently available security options for wireless networking are:

- **Wired Equivalent Privacy (WEP)**   This standard was developed for the original 802.11 wireless infrastructure. It allows the computer connecting to the wireless network to supply a password of a defined encryption level (from 40-bit to 256-bit) when connecting. The communication between devices on the network is scrambled to be unreadable by humans.

- **Wi-Fi Protected Access (WPA)**   This wireless standard was developed to address the weaknesses of WEP by providing better encryption and authentication capabilities than WEP could offer. The encryption for WPA is provided through the Temporal Key Integrity Protocol (TKIP) or Advanced Encryption Standard (AES) to boost the security of wireless networking. Similar to WEP, WPA uses passphrases to initiate the connection, but at predetermined intervals, making the passphrase more difficult to guess for those attempting to gain unauthorized access.

- **Wi-Fi Protected Access v2 (WPA2)**   This wireless standard was developed to replace or advance WPA by moving away from TKIP security models due to known flaws in these security encryption configurations that could allow unauthorized access.

- **Extensible Authentication Protocol (EAP)**   This wireless standard (and its many variants) uses a centralized authentication server to authorize access to the wireless network.

Administrators need to consider several things when preparing a wireless networking infrastructure. Security and encryption methods are near the top of the list, but the types of devices that will be connected using wireless technology must also be considered. If the devices that connect within an organization do not support the newer standards, considerations must be made for these devices, or the devices will not be able to connect.

For example, the CEO at Contoso loves her smart phone and finds it very easy to use. The phone is about four years old and does not support the latest wireless security technology. When the IT department is working on plans for a wireless network, this is something that must be considered. Many times, suggesting an upgrade and pointing out the benefits of upgrading might be effective, but existing hardware has to be considered to avoid problems in the future.

Wireless networking risks

Configuring wireless solutions to allow both employees and nonemployees to connect wirelessly to the Internet is a good idea generally; however, even the most secured wireless networks face risks associated with each type of wireless security configuration, such as:

- **No security** Providing no security for a wireless network creates a great deal of risk because any computer attempting to connect to that network will be allowed without being prompted for additional information.

- **Easily discoverable passphrases** WEP and, in some cases, WPA, have been very easily cracked using various methods to gain access to the pre-shared key or even the passphrase.

- **Denial of service** As with any networking technology, wireless networks can be susceptible to denial-of-service attacks caused by repeatedly bombarding an access point with information. This does not allow access to the keys necessarily but can render the network unusable by those connected to it.

- **Malicious associations** These attacks appear as access points available for connection. When someone connects to the access point, she might really be connecting to a laptop used by a malicious entity to attempt to gain access to legitimate networks.

- **MAC spoofing** This type of attack occurs when an attacker attempts to present a legitimate MAC address for his computer when trying to gain access to a certain network.

The list of threats presented here is not exhaustive. It is meant to provide an idea of some of the attack types being used to gain access to wireless networks that you should consider when planning the deployment of a wireless infrastructure.

 Quick check

- **When connecting with WEP or WPA to a wireless network, what information is needed to complete the connection?**

Quick check answer

- **A passphrase or shared key information is needed to connect.**

Reducing security issues on a wireless network

In addition to choosing the correct security options for an environment, simple and practical actions can help keep the wireless network secured. These include:

- **Use long passwords** When choosing a password to associate with a wireless network, use a longer password than you might initially think necessary. Longer passphrases are more secure than shorter ones because they can be more difficult to guess. This should not be the only means of security, however.

- **Use at least WPA2 encryption**   Many wireless networks are left open, although this is now decreasing. On any wireless network, the encryption level should be set to at least WPA2. The stronger the encryption level, the safer the network can be.

- **Routinely change administrator passwords**   Creating a policy for the people within an organization to change their passwords every 90 days is a good start; the local computer administrator accounts should also have their passwords changed on a set schedule to enhance the security for these accounts.

- **Maintain a guest wireless network**   Creating a wireless network for nonemployee use helps increase security by providing access to the Internet rather than to a corporate network.

This list is intended to spark some critical thinking about security for wireless networks and about security in general.

In addition to anticipating possible threats to help keep the wireless networks deployed within an organization secure, IT needs to educate others within that organization about these risks because they can also occur on home networks. If a computer is compromised while on a home network, it can cause problems when connected to a corporate network.

Lesson summary

- Configuring network discovery settings for a computer can enhance security.
- Managing media-sharing default settings prevents certain types of content from sharing.
- Configure permissions for media access in a homegroup to keep data secure even when away from the corporate network.
- Consider all wireless security options when choosing a configuration for your environment.

Lesson review

Answer the following questions to test your knowledge of the information in this lesson. You can find the answers to these questions and explanations of why each answer choice is correct or incorrect in the "Answers" section at the end of this chapter.

1. An employee in your organization mentions that he cannot see other computers on the network. He is concerned that the computer is broken because he had been able to see devices and computers connected to the company wireless network last time he was in the office, just under one week before. What can be done to correct this problem?

    A. Enable the wireless adapter.

    B. Enable network discovery.

    C. Restart the computer.

    D. Ensure that the network is using the correct profile.

2. Carol has been experiencing problems when accessing shared media. A coworker has told her that he placed photos of his vacation on his computer and shared them for her to view. When she attempts to view the photos, no photos are available for viewing. However, she can see the photos folder. What could be causing this problem?

   A. The photos have not yet been shared.

   B. The content rating settings are not configured to allow the photos to be shared.

   C. Public folder sharing is disabled.

   D. Carol's computer is not connected to the same network.

Lesson 3: Using Secure Boot and SmartScreen Filter

Working with security on a modern computer begins at startup, and Windows 8 has incorporated the *Secure Boot* feature to enable firmware to validate certificates used by the operating system. Also included in Windows 8 is the Internet Explorer feature called *SmartScreen Filter*. This feature helps prevent phishing and browser-based malware attacks. This lesson covers how to configure both Secure Boot and SmartScreen Filter.

After this lesson, you will be able to:
- Configure Internet Explorer SmartScreen Filter.
- Understand the configuration of Secure Boot in Windows 8 and configure it to meet the needs of an organization.

Estimated lesson time: 45 minutes

Ensuring that Windows has been signed using Secure Boot

Windows 8 supports the Unified Extensible Firmware Interface (UEFI) as a replacement to basic input/output system (BIOS). UEFI behaves much more like an operating system that lives in nonvolatile RAM than a firmware-loading boot environment. This enables the application to be programmable and to support several features. There are many more features included in UEFI than in BIOS, but one feature stands out from the rest. This feature is Secure Boot.

Secure Boot requires an operating system to be signed by the manufacturer to start. In the case of Windows 8, Microsoft or one of its original equipment manufacturer (OEM) partners would sign the build to ensure that it hasn't been modified and install it on a computer by using UEFI with Secure Boot enabled.

UEFI does more than just allow a computer to boot; it supports diagnostics, rootkit detection, and other features that follow the evolution of BIOS. All of this helps keep the pre-operating system environment secure to ensure that there is less chance of malware infections and other undesirable software execution before the operating system starts. If UEFI detects an operating system loader that is not signed by the publisher, it prevents the operating system loader from running. Because the process requires signing, malware applications are unable to redirect the boot loader to start another application.

Secure Boot is not required for the computer to start and can be disabled in UEFI settings; however, OEMs can customize these features and restrict certain things. From the Microsoft point of view, this setting is configurable by the customer to provide the best experience for her use.

Some IT professionals prefer to build their own computers. These computers can still take advantage of Secure Boot, but some additional configuration at the UEFI/BIOS level will be required to begin the process of configuring Secure Boot. All Windows RT devices require the use of Secure Boot. Newer desktop and laptop PCs are likely to support UEFI options and features such as Secure Boot, but an older PC might not be able to take advantage of this feature.

MORE INFO **UEFI**

For more information about UEFI, Secure Boot, and Windows 8, visit the following URLs:

- *http://blogs.msdn.com/b/b8/archive/2011/09/22/protecting-the-pre-os-environment -with-uefi.aspx*

- *http://blogs.msdn.com/b/b8/archive/2012/05/22/designing-for-pcs-that-boot-faster -than-ever-before.aspx*

Staying safe by using SmartScreen Filter

The SmartScreen Filter feature has been included in Internet Explorer for some time to help protect Internet sessions from phishing attacks and malware. Internet Explorer SmartScreen Filter uses the following methods to keep Internet sessions safe:

- **Background real-time analysis** Browsing the Internet can take someone seemingly anywhere, providing endless information about any topic. As the Internet browsing continues, SmartScreen Filter checks the information it receives and determines the intent of code presented on webpages. If the code is suspicious or deemed potentially harmful, the filter will produce an alert, warning of potential issues. It is then up to the individual to decide whether to proceed.

- **Blocking known bad software downloads** When applications are downloaded from the Internet by using Internet Explorer, they are compared to a list of known malware sites and known malware applications to determine whether they are safe and should be allowed. If the application matches an entry on the list, the download is blocked and an alert is displayed about the blocked item. If the person downloading the application knows it is safe, he can download it anyway.

- **Phishing and malware checking** Another feature of SmartScreen Filter protects those using Internet Explorer from phishing attacks. In addition to analyzing general content as previously mentioned, the sites visited are compared to known malware and phishing sites to determine whether they are safe to use. If a match is detected, a warning is displayed to help a user browsing the Internet decide whether to visit that website.

In Windows 8, SmartScreen Filter helps Windows keep computers safe from unrecognized applications.

To configure SmartScreen Filter, complete the following steps:

1. Search for SmartScreen on the Start screen.

2. Select Settings and tap or click Change SmartScreen Settings from the results pane.

3. Select Change Windows SmartScreen Settings from the navigation pane in the Windows Action Center.

4. The available settings for Windows SmartScreen are:

   ■ Get Administrator Approval Before Running An Unrecognized App From The Internet (Recommended)   This option allows Windows to prompt for elevated security credentials before allowing apps it doesn't know to be safe to execute.

   ■ Warn Before Running An Unrecognized App, But Don't Require Administrator Approval   This option displays a warning about the potentially unsafe application but does not require elevated or administrative credentials to proceed.

   ■ Don't Do Anything (Turn Off Windows SmartScreen)   This option disables SmartScreen and allows applications to run regardless of their type or configuration. Windows does not check to ensure that they are safe.

5. Tap or click OK to save the selected settings.

Using SmartScreen Filter can improve security on a computer by making people aware of potentially bad software before they execute it. Short of preventing a download entirely, using SmartScreen Filter on Windows 8 devices forces a user to pay attention, at some level, when running applications.

Lesson summary

■ UEFI and Secure Boot ensure that even the operating system is verified before starting it.

■ Using UEFI enables a computer to be checked for malware before Windows starts, lessening issues with malware and rootkits.

■ SmartScreen Filter helps ensure the integrity of apps by warning about unrecognized apps when they attempt to execute.

■ SmartScreen Filter helps keep browsing safe from phishing and other malware.

Lesson review

Answer the following questions to test your knowledge of the information in this lesson. You can find the answers to these questions and explanations of why each answer choice is correct or incorrect in the "Answers" section at the end of this chapter.

1. Caroline is a web designer for Tailspin Toys and has been working on her new Windows 8–based computer for a few days. She has heard about a testing app that speeds up the time it takes to test a website for cross-platform use and downloads the application immediately. Windows prompts for administrative credentials upon execution of the application, and Caroline isn't sure why this is happening; she calls the help desk to report the issue. What could be the cause of this issue?

   A. Internet Explorer is filtering the content.

   B. Windows SmartScreen is enabled and requires administrative privileges to proceed.

   C. Windows Firewall wants to block the application.

   D. Universal account control (UAC) is set too high.

2. Since upgrading to Windows 8 for the IT department, much praise has been offered, comparing subtle differences in how a new laptop performs to how an old laptop performs. To test a feature, one of the support technicians was working to modify his new laptop to run a different operating system. He was unable to start the operating system successfully. What caused this problem?

   A. The operating system is unsupported on the new hardware.

   B. Windows 8 is preventing the installation because UAC is turned on.

   C. Secure Boot is enabled, and the operating system image is not signed.

   D. The installation files for the other operating system are corrupted.

Practice exercises

With the focus on security in this chapter, configuring both inbound and outbound rule types ensures that you consider these options when needed in an environment. The addition of exceptions allows appropriate decisions and changes to be made when certain traffic needs to be allowed through the firewall.

Exercise 1: Configure inbound firewall rules for programs

1. Open Windows Firewall with Advanced Security.

2. Select Inbound Rules in the navigation pane.

3. Select New Rule from the Inbound Rules section of the Actions pane.

4. Select Program Type for the type of rule to create and tap or click Next.

5. Browse to the path of the specified program for which to create the rule and tap or click Next.

6. Select the action for the rule and tap or click Next.

7. Choose the firewall profiles to which this rule will apply and tap or click Next.

8. Type a name for the rule created, enter a detailed description of the rule for later reference, and tap or click Finish to create and enable the rule.

Exercise 2: Configure outbound firewall rules for ports

1. Open Windows Firewall with Advanced Security.

2. Select Outbound Rules in the navigation pane.

3. Select New Rule from the Outbound Rules section of the Actions pane.

4. Select Port Type for the type of rule to create and tap or click Next.

5. Select the port type (TCP or UDP), enter the port number to use in creating the rule, and then tap or click Next.

6. Select the action for the rule and tap or click Next.

7. Choose the firewall profiles to which this rule will apply and tap or click Next.

8. Type a name for the rule created, enter a detailed description of the rule for later reference, and tap or click Finish to create and enable the rule.

Exercise 3: Configure firewall exceptions

1. Open Windows Firewall with Advanced Security.

2. Select Outbound Rules in the navigation pane.

3. Locate and select the rule created in Exercise 2, "Configure outbound firewall rules for ports," and tap or click Properties in the Rule Settings section of the Actions pane.

4. Click the Local Principals tab and select the Skip This Rule For Connections From These Users check box.

5. Tap or click Add to specify user accounts that should be exempt from this rule.

6. Tap or click the Remote Computers tab and select the Skip This Rule For Connections To These Computers check box.

7. Tap or click Add to specify computers that will be exempt from this rule.

8. Tap or click OK in the rule's Properties dialog box to save the settings.

Suggested practice exercises

The following additional practice exercises are designed to give you more opportunities to practice what you've learned and to help you successfully master the lessons presented in this chapter.

- **Exercise 1** Configure IPsec options within Windows Firewall with Advanced Security.
- **Exercise 2** Configure network discovery to allow the local computer to be visible on the network.
- **Exercise 3** Configure the local computer to be isolated from connection to a corporate domain.

Answers

This section contains the answers to the lesson review questions in this chapter.

Lesson 1

1. **Correct answers: B, C, and D**

    A. **Incorrect:** The remote computer has been located in DNS; however, the traffic cannot be returned.

    B. **Correct:** If an inbound firewall rule prevents ICMP traffic on the remote computer, the ping attempts will fail.

    C. **Correct:** If an outbound firewall rule prevents ICMP replies, the sender will not receive a response for any ping attempts she sent.

    D. **Correct:** If the local computer is unable to send out ICMP traffic, no pings will be allowed to any other host.

2. **Correct answer: C**

    A. **Incorrect:** Uninstalling email client software would prevent the use of email on this computer.

    B. **Incorrect:** An inbound rule would prevent any SMTP servers from sending this traffic to the computer but would not prevent the computer from sending SMTP traffic to other hosts.

    C. **Correct:** An outbound rule would prevent the computer from sending any SMTP-based traffic.

    D. **Incorrect:** Blocking email applications on the computer would also prevent the correct use of email on the computer.

Lesson 2

1. **Correct answer: B**

    A. **Incorrect:** Although connecting to a disabled network adapter will fail, the fact that the connection had worked previously makes this option unlikely.

    B. **Correct:** With network discovery disabled on the computer, no other devices will be visible, and other resources will remain unavailable.

    C. **Incorrect:** Restarting the computer will not change the network discovery settings.

    D. **Incorrect:** Incorrect profiles can prevent certain settings from functioning, depending on the network type being used; however, the existing network is a private network that allows more settings by default than other network types.

2. **Correct answer: B**

    A. **Incorrect:** The owner of the photos confirmed that they have been shared.

    B. **Correct:** When shared content is incorrectly rated, additional settings can prevent the files from being shared.

    C. **Incorrect:** Other content on the computer is visible through the network.

    D. **Incorrect:** Because Carol can see other folders on the computer, she is able to connect to it through the network.

Lesson 3

1. **Correct answer: B**

    A. **Incorrect:** Internet Explorer filtering does not directly prevent downloaded applications from starting.

    B. **Correct:** Windows SmartScreen will require elevated privileges if it is using the recommended settings.

    C. **Incorrect:** Windows Firewall does not prompt for additional credentials when an application is blocked.

    D. **Incorrect:** UAC can cause prompting for application launch, but it cannot distinguish between recognized and unrecognized applications automatically.

2. **Correct answer: C**

    A. **Incorrect:** Although earlier operating systems can experience issues running on newer hardware, many newer computers support BIOS emulation to allow older operating systems to access necessary items and function with no problems.

    B. **Incorrect:** UAC is a Windows feature that requires the operating system to be running before it can affect application launches.

    C. **Correct:** Because Secure Boot requires an operating system image to be signed to execute, there might be images that do not load correctly without some modification to the settings for the boot environment.

    D. **Incorrect:** Although files on the media for an operating system can become corrupted, more than one corrupted copy of the media is unlikely, and a fresh download of the application would likely remedy the situation.

CHAPTER 9

Working with remote management tools

Managing Windows 8 client computers is likely to consume a large portion of any IT professional's time. There are two ways to ensure a good user experience: visit each workstation and perform any maintenance tasks or perform maintenance tasks remotely. This chapter looks at the remote tools available in Windows 8 and examines which tools to use for each task.

Focusing on remote management will help you understand the details of working with Windows 8 on remote systems. Many of the tasks you will perform can be done even when another user is connected to the system, and will cause little or no interruption for the user. Using these tools will reduce the amount of time needed to accomplish tasks by eliminating the travel to the desktop on which the problem is occurring.

> **NOTE** **USING REMOTE TOOLS VERSUS VISITING THE WORKSTATION**
>
> You will not always be able to use remote tools to accomplish every task. There are times when visiting the workstation is the best way to correct an issue.

Lessons in this chapter

Before you begin

Before you start the lessons in this chapter, make sure you have two computers running Windows 8. One will act as the management computer, and the other will act as the computer you are managing. These can be physical computers or virtual machines.

Lesson 1: Working with Remote Assistance

Remote assistance can be a challenge for both you and the user you are assisting. There are barriers to assistance, such as different dialects and accents when speaking on the phone and the speed of connection if you're troubleshooting a problem that requires online access. In many situations, especially in a corporate environment, these challenges lead the IT professional to visit the user's workstation and correct the problem by working directly with the user. However, the need to be on-site has decreased with changes in the technology.

 Windows 8 includes a tool called *Remote Assistance* that is designed to help you assist users without being physically at their workstations. This tool might be familiar if you have used it in earlier versions of the Windows operating system. This lesson examines Remote Assistance and provides you with the knowledge you need to use this tool effectively to help coworkers, clients, and even family members with computer issues.

After this lesson, you will be able to:

- Explain how to start a Remote Assistance session.
- Initiate connections to receive assistance.
- Receive connections to provide assistance.

Estimated lesson time: 45 minutes

Initiating Remote Assistance

Remote Assistance sessions must be initiated by the person requesting help. Although you might walk the user through the process over the phone, through instant messaging, or even email, the person requesting your help must take the steps to start a session.

The connection is established through an invitation. There are a few types of connections, all of which require an Internet or local area network connection. It is important to know and trust that the other person on the connection is who he or she says he or she is. When a connection is made, the person who is providing the assistance will have access to the desktop and data on the computer of the person receiving the assistance. Both users see the same screen while the connection is active.

To locate Remote Assistance, search for Remote Assistance on the Start screen and select Settings. Four options are returned:

- **Allow Remote Assistance Invitations To Be Sent From This Computer**   This option enables the computer to send out invitations for Remote Asistance.

- **Allow Remote Access To Your Computer**   This option enables you to initiate remote access to your computer for other users.

- **Select Users Who Can Use Remote Desktop**   This option allows certain user accounts permission to access this computer by using Remote Desktop.

- **Invite Someone To Connect To Your PC And Help You, Or Offer Help To Someone Else** This option enables you to create or respond to a Remote Assistance session.

To start Remote Assistance, choose Invite Someone To Connect To Your PC And Help You, Or Offer Help To Someone Else. This opens the Remote Assistance dialog box shown in Figure 9-1. You can select whether you would like to receive help or offer help.

> **NOTE REMOTE ASSISTANCE SETTINGS MIGHT BE CONTROLLED BY GROUP POLICY**
>
> In addition to being available to configure on a local computer, these settings can be controlled by using Group Policy. However, when Group Policy manages these settings, they might not be available for selection on the local computer if disabled by policy.

After an option for Remote Assistance is selected, Windows displays the desktop to introduce the Remote Assistance Wizard to configure the settings for a new session or a session being joined.

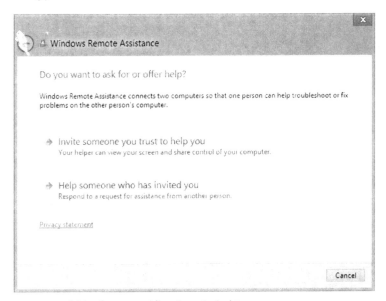

FIGURE 9-1 Asking for or providing Remote Assistance

To request assistance, complete the following steps:

1. Tap or click Invite Someone You Trust To Help You.
2. Choose the method of connection to use for the assistance session. The connection options are:
   - Save this invitation as a file.

   After saving the file, you can decide how to get the file to the person providing assistance. After you save the file, a password is generated for the session and displayed.

This password is required to access the remote session that is saved in the invitation file. You can share the required password over the telephone or in email, but remember to protect the password for the session.

- Use email to send an invitation.
- Use Easy Connect. This feature is the easiest way to connect, and you will use it most often.

3. Tap or click Next.

Easy Connect removes the need for the invitation file but still requires the exchange of a password for the connection to open. Easy Connect has some caveats: both computers must run the same operating system, Internet connectivity for both parties must be functioning normally, and the user's router must support the Easy Connect protocol.

After the connection is initiated, Remote Assistance prompts for acceptance. This operation times out after about one minute of inaction.

Providing remote assistance

When the session is accepted, you as the helper can see the screen of the person you are assisting in addition to a session control window by which you can pause screen sharing, chat, and configure settings. When the connection begins, it will be in view-only mode, allowing you to see, but not control, the user's screen. To control the screen, choose Request Control at the top of the Windows Remote Assistance window. The person you are helping is prompted to give you permission to control the screen.

When the user grants you permission, you can control the screen and manipulate the system to help solve any problems. The user can see that you are connected and sharing control of the computer (see Figure 9-2). The user can pause or stop the screen-sharing session at any time, removing your access to that system.

While the screen is being controlled remotely, all actions are visible to the other party, and you can walk him or her through the process of correcting the issue.

If you cannot use the phone or instant messenger to communicate while working in a shared session, Remote Assistance provides a chat that exists within the session. This enables quick communication during the session.

While in a Remote Assistance Chat session, the default is to create a log of all session activities, which appears at the top of the chat window. It is a good idea to leave this option enabled in case a similar problem occurs in the future. That way, you can refer to the process that solved the problem.

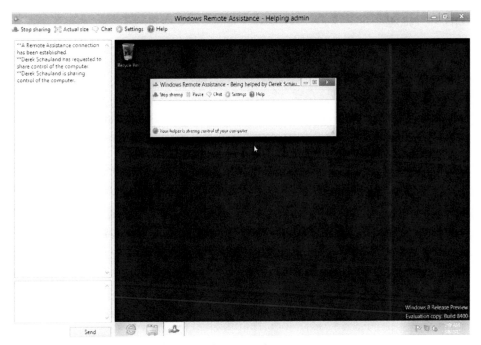

FIGURE 9-2 Using Chat during a Remote Assistance session

Overall, Remote Assistance is an excellent tool for direct interaction to solve a problem without being physically present at the user's location. Depending on the nature of the problem and the instruction required to start a session, using Remote Assistance can save significant time in the troubleshooting process. Because it works over the network or across the Internet by using an invitation file and password and is encrypted from end to end, it can be used safely across the enterprise.

Lesson summary

- All Remote Assistance sessions must be initiated by the person requesting assistance.
- Remote Assistance provides secure, hands-on support across both local area networks and the Internet.
- Remote Assistance sessions can be terminated by the person requesting assistance at any time.
- All Remote Assistance sessions begin in view-only mode; control of a screen must be granted after the connection is established.

Lesson review

Answer the following questions to test your knowledge of the information in this lesson. You can find the answers to these questions and explanations of why each is correct or incorrect in the "Answers" section at the end of this chapter.

1. Melanie, a new employee with your company, is having trouble finding applications necessary to do her work on her Windows 8–based computer. She can access her email but has trouble finding the Start screen with the mouse. How can you walk Melanie through these steps to help her understand Windows 8 better?

   A. Initiate a Remote Assistance session with Melanie.

   B. Connect to the computer as Melanie and start her applications.

   C. Initiate a phone call with Melanie to walk her through the process of starting Remote Assistance and emailing a session request to you. After the session is enabled, work with Melanie to address her computer issues.

   D. Explain to Melanie that the Windows key on the keyboard will also access the Start screen.

2. You constantly receive calls from a particular coworker who works in an out-of-state location, complaining that Windows 8 is too different from previous versions of Windows and that the application he needs to perform his work is not installed on his computer. He mentions he found the Remote Assistance application when searching the Start screen and asks whether he can initiate a session to get help locating and running the applications he needs. What do you need to get from this coworker to help him? (Choose all that apply.)

   A. An invitation to connect to a Remote Assistance session

   B. A password to unlock the session

   C. A shipping box containing his computer for troubleshooting

   D. The coworker's Windows username and password

Lesson 2: Configuring and using Remote Desktop

Remote Desktop is a tool for administration and support of remote users. It is used primarily on computers to which no user is signed in, and most often used to access other sessions on a workstation computer without physically accessing the computer. When managing an environment with more than a few computers, it is sometimes hard to imagine how you might access each computer if support is needed without visiting the computer and logging on interactively. Being able to apply an update or check the status of your backup jobs without leaving your desk is certainly appealing when you aren't physically near the computer you need to access.

Remote Desktop Services is the replacement technology for Terminal Services. This is not a new technology in Windows 8, but it can be a great time saver for accessing remote systems.

Using Remote Desktop Services to enable connections to computers across an environment can reduce travel time for IT professionals and provide access to resources on any computer. It helps IT professionals or other individuals access remote sessions of desktop environments, applications, and other tools running on a remote computer. In many cases, Remote Desktop will be used to work with or troubleshoot server computers, but workstations can also be controlled by using Remote Desktop.

> **After this lesson, you will be able to:**
>
> - Configure Remote Desktop sessions.
> - Use Remote Desktop to connect to other computers within your organization.
>
> **Estimated lesson time: 50 minutes**

Configuring Remote Desktop

Before you can use Remote Desktop on a system, it has to be enabled, and the users who will have access to this method of connection must be selected.

When would you use Remote Desktop? Consider the following scenario. Your company hired three new help desk staff members to help with a project over the summer. The project involves about 15 workstations running Windows 8 at three locations throughout the region.

Your boss asks you to make sure the help desk staff can access these computers remotely to save on travel expenses. Allowing access to Remote Desktop on the workstations is a viable option, but allowing only the administrator account or the domain administrator group to have this access does not solve the problem unless you also provide that set of credentials to the help desk staff. In this situation, adding user accounts or groups to Remote Desktop access could be worth your time.

> **Quick check**
>
> - What is the fastest way to ensure that multiple people have access to several workstations running Windows 8?
>
> **Quick check answer**
>
> - Create a group in the domain, add the users to this group, and then allow the group access to the Remote Desktop application of the affected systems.

SECURITY ALERT **GIVING COMPLETE CONTROL OF A COMPUTER**

Remote Desktop connections can allow complete control of a computer. When choosing user accounts to allow Remote Desktop connections, be mindful of security and the role of the user and computer.

To enable Remote Desktop access on a computer, complete the following steps:

1. Select the desktop from the Start screen.

2. Select the Settings charm.

3. Choose Control Panel.

4. In Control Panel, select System And Security. Under System, select Allow Remote Access.

5. Select Allow Remote Connections To This Computer, as shown in Figure 9-3.

NOTE   SIMILAR ITEMS MIGHT APPEAR IN SEARCH RESULTS

Alternatively, you can access Allow Remote Access by searching for Remote Assistance on the Start screen.

FIGURE 9-3 Enable Remote Desktop

6. If you need to connect to this system from versions of Windows earlier than Windows Vista, clear the check box for Allow Connections Only From Computers Running Remote Desktop With Network Level Authentication (Recommended). If you will be using Windows Vista and later versions, make sure the check box is selected.

7. Tap or click Select Users.

8. Type the user names of any people or groups that will need Remote Desktop access to this computer and tap or click OK.

9. Tap or click OK in the System Properties dialog box to save these changes. Remote Desktop is now enabled.

Opening the Remote Desktop application

There are a few ways to access the Remote Desktop application in Windows 8:

- Search for Remote Desktop on the Start screen.
- Pin it to your taskbar in the Desktop application or Start screen after the first run or from the Start screen. You can then access it at any time from the taskbar or Start screen.
- Run Mstsc.exe, the executable name for Remote Desktop, by typing **mstsc** on the Start screen. MSTSC is the acronym for Microsoft Terminal Services Client.

When you start Remote Desktop, you must identify the computer to which you want to connect by providing the computer name, as shown in Figure 9-4.

FIGURE 9-4 Starting Remote Desktop Connection

You can change the way Remote Desktop behaves for each connection and save the connection to a particular server for later use. To view these options, tap or click the Show Options arrow at the bottom of the Remote Desktop Connection window. The configurable options are, in order of tabbed appearance:

- General
- Display
- Local Resources
- Programs
- Experience
- Advanced

General

On the General tab, shown in Figure 9-5, you can modify sign-in and connection settings.

FIGURE 9-5 The General tab

The following two sections provide the options you can set:

- **Logon Settings** You can enter the name of the remote computer and the user name of an account allowed access to the computer through Remote Desktop.

- **Connection Settings** When you have configured the options you want for the remote computer, you can save the configuration as an RDP file and use these options the next time you connect without reconfiguring them.

Display

On the Display tab, shown in Figure 9-6, you can modify settings for display color and size.

FIGURE 9-6 Remote Desktop Display options

The available options are:

- **Display Configuration**   You can set the size of the screen, from small to large, when you connect, with large being full-screen. You can also set this connection to use all the monitors connected to your system by selecting the Use All My Monitors For The Remote Session check box.

- **Colors**   You can specify the color settings for the session, similar to the way you can for the local desktop.

- **Display The Connection Bar When I Use The Full Screen**   When you select this check box, a tab displays the name of the machine to which you are connected at the top of the screen when you are connected in full-screen mode. The tab can be pinned to be visible always, or it can be set to autohide to appear only when you move the mouse over it.

Local Resources

On the Local Resources tab, shown in Figure 9-7, you can modify settings for the local experience during a remote connection.

FIGURE 9-7 Remote Desktop Local Resources options

The Local Resources tab has three sections:

- **Remote Audio**   Tap or click the Settings button to reveal options for both audio playback and recording. For audio playback, you can play the audio on this computer (locally), play the audio on the remote computer, or not play the audio. For audio recording, you can record audio from this computer (your local computer) or not record audio.

  When you have configured these settings, tap or click OK to save them and return to the Local Resources tab of the Remote Desktop options dialog box to configure additional options.

- **Keyboard**   Select a choice from the list to define how the remote session handles Windows key combinations. For example, if you press Windows logo key+R, the Run dialog box opens on your computer. This can be redirected into the Remote Desktop session to work on the remote computer, meaning that all Windows logo key+key combinations take place on the computer selected in this section. The options for keyboard settings are:

  - On This Computer   All Windows logo key+key combinations operate only on the local computer.

  - On The Remote Computer   All Windows logo key+key combinations operate only on the remote computer.

  - Only When Using Full Screen Mode   When the remote desktop session is running in full-screen mode, Windows logo key+key combinations are directed to the remote computer; otherwise, they function on the local computer.

- **Local Devices And Resources** The last section of the Local Resources tab identifies the local devices you will share in your remote session. You can select either the Printers check box, the Clipboard check box, or both, as appropriate. Tap or click More if you have additional devices to share. The available device types include:

  - Smart cards
  - Ports
  - Drives
  - Other plug-and-play devices

  After you have selected the devices, tap or click OK to save these settings and return to the Local Resources tab of the Remote Desktop Connection dialog box.

Programs

The Programs tab, shown in Figure 9-8, gives you the option of starting a specific program when a remote session is initiated. Select the Start The Following Program On Connection check box, and then provide the path and file name of the application you want to start.

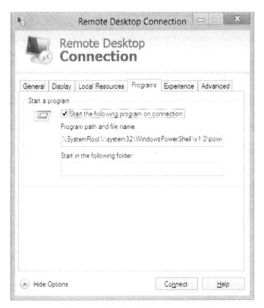

FIGURE 9-8 Remote Desktop Programs options

PLANNING   CONFIGURING MULTIPLE SESSIONS

You can configure multiple Remote Desktop sessions to the same computer and save different settings for each session. In some sessions, it might be useful to have a specific application, such as Windows PowerShell or the Exchange Management Console, launch when the connection is initiated. Creating and saving these settings can save you time later.

Experience

The Experience tab, shown in Figure 9-9, displays performance settings you can use to help improve the experience during the remote session. These settings can improve performance over slow connections.

FIGURE 9-9 Remote Desktop Experience options

Detect Connection Quality Automatically is a connection optimization option that disables or enables the following items if the connection is too degraded to use them:

- Desktop background
- Font smoothing
- Desktop composition
- Show window contents while dragging
- Menu and window animation
- Visual style

The other options specify bandwidths from which you can choose to ensure that your remote desktop session performs appropriately. For example, if a remote site has a connection speed of less than 2 Mbps, selecting Low-Speed Broadband might be appropriate for those sessions. However, items at the corporate office or items with high-speed links might not need any configuration.

Typically, this setting works well when connection speed is detected because many sessions are over high-speed links.

The remaining two options on the Experience tab are as follows:

- **Persistent Bitmap Caching** This setting stores images on the local computer to improve performance while in the Remote Desktop session.

- **Reconnect If Connection Is Dropped** This setting causes the remote session to be retried up to 20 times if the link becomes degraded and the connection to the session is dropped.

Advanced

The Advanced tab, shown in Figure 9-10, addresses the need for server authentication and permission to configure settings remotely. Your company security policies will determine which settings you should use.

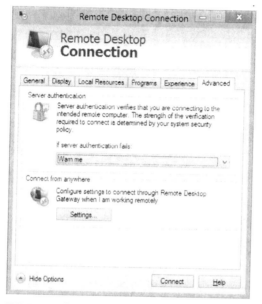

FIGURE 9-10 Remote Desktop Advanced options

The following sections are on the Advanced tab:

- **Server Authentication** Indicate the required authentication verification for the remote session when verifying that the remote computer is the correct computer for the remote connection. The default setting sends you, the helper, a warning if authentication fails. Other options are Connect And Don't Warn Me and Do Not Connect.

- **Connect From Anywhere** Select this option if you will be connecting to remote sessions when you are also remote. This option ensures that your remote connections are initiated through a Remote Desktop (RD) Gateway server, available in Windows Server 2008 R2 and later. An *RD Gateway server* is a perimeter server that effectively hosts the connections to other machines within your environment. In the RD Gateway Server Settings dialog box, you can configure the following settings:

- **Connection Settings** These settings determine if you want incoming sessions to locate the RD Gateway or if you will be specifying the server name and sign-in information. You can also select not to use an RD Gateway server. The default is to locate the server automatically. If you do not use an RD Gateway server, you do not need to change this setting.

- **Logon Settings** Select these settings to identify which settings are to be collected and passed through to the sessions on remote computers.

After these settings are configured, tap or click OK to return to the Remote Desktop settings dialog box.

 Quick check

- **To establish a Remote Desktop session in the most secure way, which setting should be selected when server authentication fails?**

Quick check answer

- **The Do Not Connect setting is most secure because it provides the most security for Remote Desktop connections.**

Usually, the default settings will work for quick access to a resource, but there are scenarios in which you might want to change the options to suit the task you need to perform in the session. When you have configured the options for a session, it is always a good idea to save the settings to a file so they are not lost.

When you have finished configuring the options, enter the name of the system (or the IP address) on the General tab and tap or click the Connect button to begin your session.

Lesson summary

- Configure options for Remote Desktop Connection to allow specific user accounts to connect to a computer by using Remote Desktop.
- Establish connections by using network-level authentication.

Lesson review

Answer the following questions to test your knowledge of the information in this lesson. You can find the answers to these questions and explanations of why each is correct or incorrect in the "Answers" section at the end of this chapter.

1. Mae, a receptionist at your company, is having trouble accessing an application used to view multiple schedules concurrently. She calls to tell you that the application is broken and that she cannot connect. How can you verify the status of the application, which you know runs on a server named Scheduling-01, and take the necessary action to correct the problem?

A. Restart the server.

B. Drive to the location of Scheduling-01 and sign in directly at the computer.

C. Use a Remote Desktop session to connect and troubleshoot the issue.

D. Use a Windows PowerShell script to retrieve the processes running on the Schedule-01 server.

2. Your email server has been a bit slow in recent weeks, and you need to understand why. You will be filling in for one of the Exchange administrators at your company, but you are not sure where the Exchange tools are located on the server. You want to gain quick access in case you need them. How can you configure access to the Exchange server so that the Exchange Management Console starts automatically when you sign in?

A. Place a shortcut to the management console in the startup folder for your sign-in to the server.

B. Add a shortcut to the desktop and double-click it to start the console after signing in.

C. Configure the Exchange Management Console to start when the remote desktop session has launched, using the Programs tab of Remote Desktop options.

D. Pin the Exchange Management Console application to the taskbar after signing in to the server.

Lesson 3: Configuring, managing, and troubleshooting connections

This lesson discusses optimizing the connections that are necessary for accessing the Internet and various tools. Windows 8 can detect many of the device drivers available on the market, ensuring that many connections will be available as soon as the computer starts. However, connections can be lost. How can you diagnose and fix a lost connection? This lesson addresses that question. It also covers connecting to virtual private network (VPN) connections and managing available connection types.

The initial connection for most computers running Windows 8 will likely be a broadband connection. With access to the Internet spreading and connection speed increasing every day, many new computers do not come with dial-up modems unless the modems are ordered specifically. Because the drivers for most network cards and even wireless cards on the market today are included in Windows 8, these connections are there when you need them. However, what happens when they aren't?

Troubleshooting network problems

Microsoft has built solid troubleshooting utilities over the years, and the general tools built into Windows 8 have made the client experience of repairing network connections straightforward for most users. However, issues outside the computer, including problems with switching or other hardware, remain problems for the IT staff to troubleshoot.

To view information about current connections, navigate to the Network and Sharing Center and complete the following steps:

1. Open Control Panel by choosing the Settings charm while in the Desktop application.

2. Select Network And Internet.

3. Select Network And Sharing Center.

   Here you will see the current connections in use, the type of each connection, and what type of network it is accessing. The networks available are:

   ■ **Home Or Work Network**   This network type is password-protected and can be more secure than an open or a public network.

   ■ **Public Network**   This type of network is typically found in public places such as hotel rooms or coffee shops; access data over this network type at your own risk.

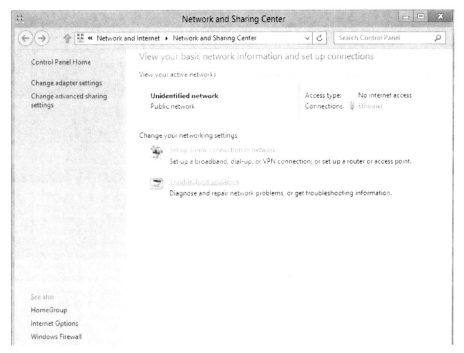

FIGURE 9-11 Network And Sharing Center

The sharing of devices and connections in Windows was improved in Windows 7, and these items have persisted in Windows 8 to provide easier access to resources and other network-specific items. Two of the features that stand out are:

- **Manage Default Printers** When using a mobile computer, you can make devices on one network, such as a printer or a shared drive, visible when your computer connects to that network. These devices become unavailable when that connection is broken or the computer is moved to another network.

- **HomeGroups** Computers connected to the same Home network can share resources by connecting to a homegroup. The group has a password that each member must enter to join. When joined to the group, shared resources are managed within the homegroup while a user is on that network.

For example, Joe has a new laptop that is running Windows 8 that he uses both at work and at home. While he is at work, he is connected to a corporate network, contoso.local, on which he can see the printers he can use. When Joe leaves work and connects to his wireless home network, the printers that were available at the office are no longer available. In fact, they are not even visible to Joe. This is how Manage Default Printers works: when a service or device is associated with a specific network, it will not be visible when disconnected from that network.

Homegroups work in a similar way but require the network type to be a home network. When Joe connects to his home network, Windows 8 detects that a homegroup is available for him to access. The files and printers on the home network are available to him because he is a member of the group.

Creating a location-aware device requires a portable computer or tablet. To configure these options, complete the following steps:

1. Open Devices And Printers by searching for it on the Start screen or by selecting Settings and then Devices And Printers.

2. Select any printer that is installed on the computer.

3. Select Manage Default Printers.

4. Select Change My Default Printer When I Change Networks.

5. In the Select Network list, choose a network.

6. In the Select Printer list, choose a printer that's available when it is on the selected network.

7. Tap or click Add.

8. Repeat steps 5 through 7 for additional networks and printers to set as default.

9. Tap or click OK in the Manage Default Printers dialog box when finished.

To create a homegroup, complete the following steps:

1. On the Start screen, select the Settings charm.

2. Select Change PC Settings.

3. On the PC Settings screen, select HomeGroup in the navigation pane on the left side of the screen. Change the sharing setting for any type of content you want to share from Off to On. The following content types are available to share:

    ■ Documents

    ■ Music

    ■ Pictures

    ■ Videos

    ■ Printers And Devices

    ■ Media Devices

When the sharing settings have been configured, decide who is allowed to join your homegroup. To allow someone into a group, give him or her the password displayed under Membership on the HomeGroup screen. Anyone who joins this homegroup will have access to all items enabled for sharing.

You can belong to only one homegroup. If you want to join another homegroup, you must leave the group you are currently using. Once you have done this, you can join another group by completing the following steps:

1. Search for HomeGroup on the Start screen.

2. Select Settings.

3. Select HomeGroup and tap or click Join Now.

4. Type the password for the homegroup and tap or click OK.

If no other homegroups exist when you leave a group, you see the option to create one instead of the option to join one.

Using Troubleshooter

If your network is down and there are problems with switches or routers, seeing information from a stack of workstations won't be helpful. However, if your workstation (or someone else's) goes offline intermittently, the Network and Sharing Center has a Troubleshooter option that might provide insight into which connections are offline. Troubleshooter is a good starting point for diagnosing and repairing connections when there are problems with connections in Windows 8.

In many cases, it's unlikely that you will take a lot of time to work with Troubleshooter. However, some of the steps it can perform, such as releasing and renewing IP addresses or reconfiguring the entire IP stack (which you might do by using netsh), might be faster, especially when a coworker is using the computer and you are coaching him or her over the phone.

> *NOTE* **TROUBLESHOOTING A KNOWN CONNECTION**
>
> If you are trying to work with someone to troubleshoot a specific Internet issue on a known connection, you can tap and hold or right-click the connection icon in the system tray and select Troubleshoot Problems to open Troubleshooter.

To start Troubleshooter, open the Network and Sharing Center and tap or click Troubleshoot Problems. Choose the area in which you are experiencing an issue from the following list:

- Internet Connections
- Shared Folders
- HomeGroup
- Network Adapter
- Incoming Connections
- Printer

When you select an option (for example, Internet Connections), the Welcome screen for the Troubleshooter opens. Tap or click Next to begin troubleshooting the problem. Figure 9-12 shows the Internet Connections Troubleshooter.

You can select either general connection troubleshooting for when the Internet itself is not working or specific webpage connections when the Internet works but access to a particular website is not working. Select the option most applicable to your problem and tap or click Next.

FIGURE 9-12 Troubleshoot Internet connection problems

Windows 8 then searches some general settings from your Internet Options settings to diagnose problems with DNS and Network Interface Card configurations and attempts to correct any issues it finds. In many cases, the Windows troubleshooting tools can diagnose and correct problems without manual intervention.

When Windows 8 finds an issue by using one of the troubleshooting tools, it will display a message noting the problem found to help diagnose the issue. However, sometimes Windows will need help from you during the troubleshooting process. For example, the Internet Connections Troubleshooter may find that the cause of the problem is possibly the modem or router. Windows 8 cannot fix issues with these devices, so the Troubleshooter will ask you to take steps with the other device to see whether you can correct the problem. After you have checked the other devices, tap or click the next step in the Troubleshooter to initiate the diagnosis again and see whether you have corrected the problem.

If you are certain that other computers can connect through your modem and you want the Troubleshooter to skip this step and proceed, tap or click Skip This Step And Continue. Windows 8 will try to correct the problem. The Troubleshooter will come back to this step if it cannot work around the problem; it will tell you that it was unable to fix your problem and will indicate a possible reason. In this case, additional options are available, and they might include:

- Remote Assistance
- Online support
- System recovery

Connecting to VPNs in Windows 8

Today, people can work from just about anywhere as long as they have a computer and an Internet connection. Many companies configure VPNs to enable employees in remote locations to connect securely from their local computer to the office network. When employees do this, the resources they would use while in the office are available.

To locate the options for and establish a VPN connection, complete the following steps:

1. On the Start screen, search for VPN and select Settings.
2. Select Connect To A Network Or Set Up A Virtual Private Network Connection.
3. Type the address of the VPN to which you want to connect in the Create A VPN Connection dialog box.
4. Type a Destination Name (for example, **Work VPN**).
5. If your company requires the use of a smart card, select the Use A Smart Card check box.
6. Select Remember My Credentials to allow the user name and password to be saved for this connection.
7. If other people need to share your connection to the VPN, select Allow Other People To Share This Connection.

> **SECURITY ALERT** **BE MINDFUL OF YOUR SECURITY POLICIES**
>
> Allowing others to share this computer's VPN connection can pose a security risk within your organization. Carefully consider this option before it is enabled to ensure that everyone involved understands how this option works.

8. Tap or click Create to add the connection.

When you click Create, the connection will be added to your computer, but it will not be active. To connect to the VPN, you need to access it in the Network Connections application in Control Panel and choose Connect/Disconnect.

Remember that various types of VPNs are available, and you need to know which type of VPN your company has so that it can be configured properly. To access the properties of a VPN connection, complete the following steps:

1. Press and hold or right-click the VPN Connection adapter in the Network Connections window.
2. Select Properties.

The Properties dialog box displayed for VPN connections contains options for VPNs to be configured for the selected connection. The VPN Connection Properties dialog box is displayed in Figure 9-13.

General

On the General tab, as shown in Figure 9-13, you provide the initial information for the VPN connection.

FIGURE 9-13 The General tab

The options on this tab are:

- **Host Name Or IP Address Of Destination**   This box contains the address you need to use to establish the tunnel.
- **First Connect**   If you select the Dial Another Connection First check box, the VPN dials the phone number you provide before connecting to the VPN.

Options

On the Options tab, as shown in Figure 9-14, you can save your credentials for future use and add some Point-to-Point Protocol (PPP) settings.

FIGURE 9-14 The Options tab

The Options tab gives you the following choices:

- **Remember My Credentials**   Instructs the VPN configuration to cache credentials.
- **Idle Time Before Hanging Up**   Establishes how long the VPN can wait for activity before disconnecting.
- **PPP Settings**   If you select this button, a dialog box gives you the following options:
    - **Enable LCP Extensions**   Select the Link Control Protocol (LCP) extensions to allow performance parameters to be negotiated during the connection process.
    - **Enable Software Compression**   Select this check box to allow Windows to reduce the size of IP packets to improve performance and throughput.
    - **Negotiate Multilink For Single-Link Connections**   Select this check box to separate high-priority and low-priority channels when using a single-link connection.

Security

On the Security tab, as shown in Figure 9-15, you define the VPN type. These settings require knowledge of your organization's VPN configuration.

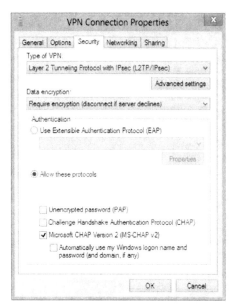

FIGURE 9-15 The Security tab

The options on this tab are:

- **Type Of VPN** Choose the type of VPN you will use from the list.
- **Advanced Settings** Tap or click this button to see additional settings for the type of VPN you have selected. This button is available only if your selected VPN type has additional settings.
  - For the Layer 2 Tunneling Protocol (L2TP) VPN type, you can select Use A Preshared Key For Authentication. You must specify a key file on both ends of the connection to prove that each computer knows the other. Your other choice is to select Use Certificate For Authentication. This option uses a certificate to prove that the server is the correct one for this connection and that the client is allowed to connect. The option to verify the server certificate provides a bit more security, because if it is turned on the client will not connect to servers it cannot verify.
  - For the Internet Key Exchange Version 2 (IKEv2) VPN type, you can select the Enable Mobility check box. You can also configure the amount of time the connection will try to reconnect.
- **Data Encryption** Select the appropriate encryption options for your organization.
- **Use Extensible Authentication Protocols (EAP)** If you choose this option, you can select from the list to specify how your computer will prove its identity to the server. Available choices include:
  - Microsoft: EAP-AKA (Encryption Enabled)
  - Microsoft: EAP-SIM (Encryption Enabled)

- Microsoft: EAP-TTLS (Encryption Enabled)
- Microsoft: Protected EAP (PEAP) (Encryption Enabled)
- Microsoft: Secured Password (EAP-MSCHAP v2) (Encryption Enabled)
- Microsoft: Smart Card Or Other Certificate (Encryption Enabled)

- **Allow These Protocols**   Select this option for authentication if your environment does not support the use of EAP protocols.
- **Unencrypted Password (PAP)**   This protocol sends the password in plaintext.
- **Challenge Handshake Authentication Protocol (CHAP)**   This protocol authenticates the connection by using a series of challenges and responses from the originator to determine a matching hash. If the hash provided by the originator is what the server expects, the connection succeeds. The password for validation of CHAP-based authentication is sent using plaintext.
- **Microsoft CHAP Version 2 (MS-CHAP v2)**   This protocol operates similarly to CHAP but requires an MD4 hash of the password to validate the authentication. This is more secure and does not send information in plaintext.
- **Automatically Use My Windows Logon Name And Password (And Domain If Any)**   This option specifies that the currently signed-in Windows user credentials should be passed for sign-in to the VPN connection when the Microsoft CHAP v2 protocol is used.

Networking

The Networking tab, shown in Figure 9-16, displays the network protocol configuration for the VPN connection. On this tab, you configure IP address settings and other network items related to the VPN.

FIGURE 9-16 The Networking tab

In environments in which VPN connections do not receive dynamically assigned IP addresses, it might be necessary to configure an address for this connection under the properties for Transmission Control Protocol (TCP)/IP (version 4 or 6, depending on your environment).

You can also configure File and Print Sharing for this connection on this tab, which allows other computers on the network to use resources shared on your computer.

Sharing

On the Sharing tab, shown in Figure 9-17, you indicate whether the connection is available through a shared Internet connection on this computer.

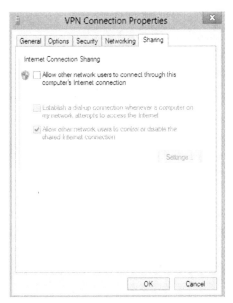

FIGURE 9-17 The Sharing tab

The choices on this tab are:

- **Allow Other Network Users To Connect Through The Computer's Internet Connection** If selected, the VPN connection is available to other computers within an environment. The next two choices are available only when this choice is selected.

> *NOTE* **USER CREDENTIALS FOR THIS OPTION**
>
> When this option is enabled, user names and passwords for the current user cannot be stored for use by others. If your user account is signed in and enables this setting, the dial-up options will function only when this account is signed in. Creating a new connection for all users and saving the sign-in credentials with that connection will ensure that the dial-up options work regardless of the signed-in user account.

- **Establish A Dial-Up Connection Whenever A Computer On My Network Attempts To Access The Internet** If selected, the VPN connection is attempted by dialing out to an ISP whenever a remote computer attempts to use the shared connection.
- **Allow Other Network Users To Control Or Disable The Shared Internet Connection** If selected, other users can have control over the shared connection resources. These users would be able to turn off the shared resources and prevent others from using them.

Lesson summary

- Configure default Print settings based on the established network connection.
- Use the Troubleshooter to determine and correct network problems.
- Configure and manage virtual private network connections.

Lesson review

Answer the following questions to test your knowledge of the information in this lesson. You can find the answers to these questions and explanations of why each is correct or incorrect in the "Answers" section at the end of this chapter.

1. You support several remote workers for your company. Until recently, they have only needed email access and a connection to a File Transfer Protocol (FTP) server for sharing files with others at Contoso. One of these employees has asked whether there is a way to access a reporting tool used internally. How can you provide access to this person on a test basis?

   A. Move the application to the cloud to allow all external users to access reports.

   B. Create a VPN between the corporate office and the user's computer.

   C. Ask for an email each time a report is needed and return the results for the user.

   D. Schedule the report to be delivered every day.

2. The VPN connection for Glen, a senior executive at Tailspin Toys, has stopped working. He is leaving for a business trip to Europe in a few days and hopes you can get the VPN working on his laptop before he leaves. The VPN connection was working recently, and Glen is also having trouble accessing the Internet. With this in mind, what should you attempt as a first step in helping Glen get back online?

   A. Ask him to restart the computer.

   B. Work with him to run the Network Adapters troubleshooter to check for general problems.

   C. Delete the VPN connection and re-create it to ensure that the settings are correct.

   D. Rebuild the laptop to restore the original settings used for that computer.

3. Your company is exploring the use of VPNs to provide greater access to the company's line-of-business applications and data. Using the built-in client to connect to an existing VPN device within your company seems the best option. Because of the nature of the information, each side of the connection must verify the other side. Which options make this possible for the Windows 8 VPN client on an IPsec connection? (Choose all that apply.)

   A. DES and 3DES connection authentication

   B. Pre-shared key authentication

   C. Certificate authentication

   D. Requiring smart cards for authentication

Lesson 4: Using other management tools remotely

In addition to using Remote Assistance to help users and Remote Desktop to connect to and manage other systems, Windows 8 offers other tools that might reduce the reliance on connecting to a session on a remote system. This lesson covers these tools and their usages. You will likely be familiar with some of the tools, but some are new. These tools include the following:

- Netsh
- WinRS
- Remote authentication
- Windows PowerShell
- Microsoft Management Console

This lesson also covers the management and configuration of these tools. Windows PowerShell is used to complete certain tasks in this lesson, but it is not limited to performing these tasks.

Netsh

Netsh has been around for several versions of Windows and is used to manage networking components on both local and remote computers. This command-line tool and scripting shell can help troubleshoot, correct, and automate working with network adapters and other components in Windows.

Netsh allows many parameters, listed in Table 9-1, to help with different components and scripts, both locally and remotely.

TABLE 9-1 Netsh command options

Netsh command	Details
Help or ?	Displays the help for Netsh
Add helper	Adds a Netsh helper DLL
Delete helper	Removes a Netsh helper DLL
Show helper	Lists the installed helper DLLs
Cmd	Starts a command-line session
Online	Sets Netsh to online mode
Offline	Sets Netsh to offline mode
Set mode	Changes the mode of Netsh to online or offline
Show mode	Displays the current mode of Netsh
Flush	Discards changes in offline mode
Commit	Saves changes in offline mode
Set machine	Selects the computer on which Netsh commands will run
Exec	Executes a script file with Netsh commands
Quit, bye, exit	Exits Netsh
Add alias	Creates an alias for an existing Netsh command
Delete alias	Removes an alias for an existing Netsh command
Show alias	Lists all existing Netsh aliases
Dump	Writes configuration to a text file
Popd	Script command that removes the current context from the Netsh stack
Pushd	Script command that pushes the active context onto the stack

Netsh can help you accomplish many things. Many real-world examples work with network interfaces. Netsh can be used to modify the IP address or reset the TCP/IP stack for an adapter if the GUI is not available.

For additional information on netsh, visit the following resources:

- *http://support.microsoft.com/kb/242468*
- *http://technet.microsoft.com/en-us/library/cc785383(v=WS.10).aspx*

 Quick check

- **When working in offline mode, how can changes be saved?**

Quick check answer

- **Using the Commit command will save or commit changes made in offline mode.**

Windows Remote Shell

Windows Remote Shell (WinRS) is designed to help you work on and troubleshoot problems on remote Windows systems from the command line. It enables execution of any shell-based commands that might work in the command shell (Cmd.exe) against remote computer systems. Using WinRS can speed up performance of routine tasks because it doesn't require visits to each machine.

Before using WinRS on computers in an environment, the computers must have Windows Remote Management (WinRM) configured to accept connections. The most straightforward way to accomplish this goal is as follows:

1. Open an elevated command prompt.
2. Type the command **WinRM quickconfig** and press Enter.
3. When the prompt appears asking if you'd like to accept the proposed changes, type **Y** and press Enter.
4. Await the return of a message indicating that the process was successful.

This command carries out the following actions:

- Starts the WinRM service and sets the service startup type to auto-start
- Configures a listener for the ports that send and receive WS-Management protocol messages using either HTTP or HTTPS on any IP address
- Defines firewall exceptions for the WinRM service and opens the ports for HTTP and HTTPS

After WinRM has been configured, you can move on to managing WinRS.

The available switches for WinRS are:

- **-r[emote]:endpoint**   Tells WinRS to connect to a remote system when *endpoint* is the computer name for the remote system.

- **-un[encrypted]** Determines whether the connection to the specified machine should be unencrypted.

- **-u[sername]:username** Specifies the user name credential used to connect to the remote system.

- **-p[assword]:password** Specifies the password for the credential needed to connect to the remote computer.

- **-d[irectory]:path** Specifies the starting directory for WinRS on the remote system.

- **-env[ironment]:string=value** Sets an environment variable on the remote system when the session begins. This switch supports multiple occurrences for multiple environment variables.

- **-noe[cho]** Disables *echo* or screen output. In some cases, answers to remote commands need not be displayed locally. Echo is turned on by default.

- **-nop[rofile]** Prevents the user profile from loading during the session. If the connecting user is not an administrator on the local computer, the -nop switch is required to prevent profiles from loading.

- **-comp[ression]** Enables compression. This option is turned off by default because older computers might not support the option.

- **-[use]ssl** Connects to a remote computer by using a Secure Sockets Layer (SSL) connection on the default WinRM port instead of HTTPS, which uses port 443.

- **-?** WinRS help.

WinRS is useful for performing command-line tasks on remote computers. Many administrators might already know these tasks and use them frequently on local machines. Using WinRS will keep the syntax the same for many commands so they can be executed easily on other systems. Many of the commands available from the command line can also be performed in Windows PowerShell, but in some cases, the syntax is different. WinRS can ease this learning curve.

The syntax for a WinRS command is as follows:

```
WinRS -r:Server02 cmd
```

Specify WinRS, and then use the -r switch with a computer name to point the connection to a remote system and issue the command to open a command prompt.

```
WinRM quickconfig
```

Using quickconfig will ready your system to accept connections on the remote management port.

Windows PowerShell

Windows PowerShell is a command shell and scripting language designed to help you achieve all you can from the Windows GUI at the command line. Windows PowerShell is not new in Windows 8, but it is becoming more prevalent within the management of the operating system. You can run cmdlets (pronounced command-lets) to view and manipulate Windows systems all the way down to Windows Management Instrumentation (WMI) configurations or run scripts to accomplish its management tasks in batches. Because Windows PowerShell is object-based, items that it returns can be treated and manipulated as objects for greater flexibility in how actions can be performed when managing systems.

What can Windows PowerShell do for administrators that the GUI cannot?

The GUI can accomplish many things, from modifying user information to adding mailboxes in Exchange. These tasks can also be accomplished from within Windows PowerShell. In many cases, for newer versions of Microsoft technologies, even the tasks performed in the GUI-based Management utility are actually running Windows PowerShell commands behind the scenes. In some cases, certain attributes of an object are not visible within the GUI, so they cannot be managed or accessed this way. However, Windows PowerShell can access additional attributes of these objects and populate them with data, providing administrators with greater access and control within their Windows environments.

> **MORE INFO** **DELVING INTO WINDOWS POWERSHELL**
>
> If you want to learn more about Windows PowerShell, there are several good sources for the IT professional, including:
>
> - *Windows PowerShell 2.0 Administrator's Pocket Consultant* by William R. Stanek (Microsoft Press, 2009).
> - *Windows PowerShell 2.0 Best Practices* by Ed Wilson (Microsoft Press, 2009).

Putting Windows PowerShell to work

The following example illustrates how Windows PowerShell can help you work with items on a certain system and determine which applications are running.

Fred works for Contoso as an IT help desk employee. He has noticed that many help desk calls center on applications just do not seem to start properly; they either present no error or information to the user or they produce a message stating that an instance of the application is already running on the computer. He wants to generate a list of running applications on the user's computer to see whether he can help the user close previously running applications before trying to start new instances of them.

The next time Fred receives a call about this problem, he opens an Administrator command prompt, types PowerShell.exe, and then runs the following Windows PowerShell commands to see which applications are running:

```
$computer "computername"
Get-Process -computername $computer
```

This brief use of Windows PowerShell displays all the processes running on the specified computer on Fred's computer screen. The *$computer* variable is set to the name of a computer that causes the get-process cmdlet to run on that computer.

After Fred has the list of processes, he can work with the person on the phone to close applications that might not be needed. The user might be able to do this, or, if an application is frozen and needs help closing, Fred can use Windows PowerShell to close the application.

```
$computer = computername
Get-process -computername $computer -process notepad.exe | kill
```

This command pipes (or passes) any instances of the Notepad.exe process to the kill alias, which runs the stop-process cmdlet, to stop the process.

> **IMPORTANT   DATA LOSS IS A POSSIBILITY**
>
> Forcing processes to close on a computer can cause data loss because it will not gracefully terminate the process.

Windows PowerShell is meant to be an intuitive experience, and it includes an intuitive (and now online) help system for the cmdlets that do the behind-the-scenes work. Comment-based help enables authors of cmdlets, functions, and scripts to include commented lines about how to interact with their code, which ensures that help is available whenever needed by just entering the following on the command line, and then tapping or clicking Enter:

```
Help <cmdlet|function|script>name
```

For example, the help get-process cmdlet displays the help for the get-process cmdlet. This provides not only information about the syntax of the cmdlet but also example cases about how the item works. This is how Windows PowerShell teaches its users as they go. Because this technique is comment help–based, administrators can ask the shell for help. It does not force them to do a lot of preparation to get started.

Windows 8 includes Windows PowerShell 3.0, which brings many updates to the code; one of those is online help. This enables Windows PowerShell to check in with servers at Microsoft to see whether updates are available to the help files for a cmdlet. When Help is called, it prompts you to use local help or online help when used online. The help within Windows PowerShell can provide more information about cmdlets as its help items are modified.

Microsoft Management Console

Management consoles have been part of Windows for a long time and remain useful in Windows 8. Many, if not all of the GUI-based management tools are actually run inside a management console, which shows how much they are used every day. In many cases, the existing management tools provide a good starting point or opportunity to work with the out-of-the-box tools such as Server Manager or Certificate Stores, but Microsoft Management Consoles (MMCs) can be created as custom toolkits for a wide variety of solutions to assist in your day-to-day work.

The management console is still a blank canvas for administrators. The functionality comes in at the snap-in level. (Snap-ins are components that can be added to the management console.) Adding snap-ins to a management console brings all the tools needed for performing tasks. The snap-ins available in the Windows 8 management console are as follows:

- **ActiveX Control**   Allows an ActiveX control to appear in the results view
- **Authorization Manager**   Enables configuration of role-based permissions for applications that support them
- **Certificates**   Enables management of installed certificates and certificate stores
- **Component Services**   The component services (Com +) management utility
- **Computer Management**   Enables system management for the connected computer
- **Device Manager**   Enables viewing and management of peripherals and other hardware connected to the computer
- **Disk Management**   Enables management of physical and logical disks within a computer
- **Event Viewer**   Manages Windows and other events on the local or a remote computer
- **Folder**   Enables organization of other snap-ins in folders within the tree view
- **Group Policy Object Editor**   Enables editing and review of local Group Policy objects on a computer
- **IP Security Monitor**   Enables you to monitor the status of IP security on a computer
- **IP Security Policy Management**   Enables you to define policies concerning IP security
- **Link to Web Address**   Displays the specified webpage in the results view
- **Local Users and Groups**   Enables management of users and groups on the local computer
- **Network Access Protection (NAP) Client Configuration**   Helps manage Network Access Point (NAP) client settings
- **Performance Monitor**   Provides information about the performance of the computer in terms of networking, hard disks, and RAM
- **Print Management**   Enables management of local and remote printers
- **Resultant Set of Policy**   Enables you to view the resultant set of policy for a user, to determine which policies apply to the specified account
- **Security Configuration and Analysis**   Provides security configuration and analysis of security templates
- **Security Templates**   Enables the creation and management of system security templates
- **Services**   Enables you to manage services on the local or a remote computer

- **Shared Folders** Displays information about current sessions and currently shared folders and open files on the connected computer

- **Task Scheduler** Enables the creation and management of scheduled tasks

- **Trusted Platform Module (TPM) Management** Enables you to manage and configure TPM security hardware if present on the computer

- **Windows Firewall with Advanced Security** Enables management of the local Windows firewall, including inbound and outbound rules

- **Windows Management Instrumentation (WMI) Control** Enables management of the WMI service

NOTE ADDITIONAL SNAP-INS

Other installed applications might also have MMC snap-ins. The preceding list includes the items that are included with Windows.

Adding snap-ins

Because you can plug tools into the console, it's the only place you need to go to for some tasks. For example, services, Windows Firewall, and Performance Monitor are snap-ins that provide insight into how a system performs when certain conditions are true. These tools can be added to a single console to provide the monitoring tools for local and remote systems.

To add snap-ins to a console, complete the following steps:

1. On the Start screen, type **mmc**.

2. Tap or click the search result.

3. Tap or click Yes when prompted to elevate the utility.

This opens a blank management console window. To add snap-ins, select the File menu and choose Add/Remove Snap-in. Figure 9-18 shows an empty management console.

The list of available snap-ins appears, as shown in Figure 9-19. You can tap or click the components needed and then tap or click the Add button, which moves an instance of the tool to the right pane in the window. If the snap-in you have selected allows connections to other computers, a dialog box appears asking which computer this instance of the snap-in should be used against. The selection dialog box for the services snap-in is shown in Figure 9-20.

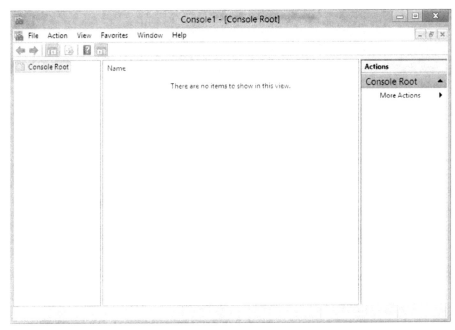

FIGURE 9-18 Microsoft Management Console without snap-ins

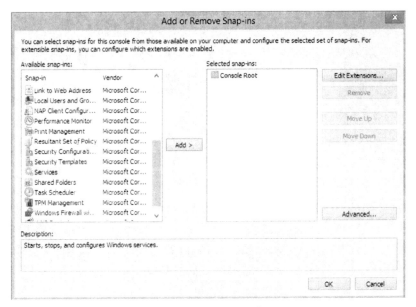

FIGURE 9-19 Adding snap-ins to a management console

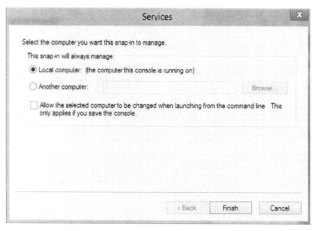

FIGURE 9-20 Choosing the computer to which an instance of a snap-in should connect

> **NOTE MULTIPLE INSTANCES**
>
> **Snap-ins can be added as multiple instances so that iterations for several computers can be configured within the same MMC.**

If necessary, some of the extensions of added snap-ins can be disabled (and selected ones can be enabled), but All Extensions For A Snap-in is the default configuration. This means that any items with which a snap-in can work are available when it is added. To modify these settings, tap or click the Edit Extensions button in the Add Or Remove Snap-Ins dialog box.

Snap-ins are added to the Console Root node by default. However, the parent snap-in can be modified by selecting the Allow Changing The Parent Snap-In check box in the Advanced Options dialog box to enable grouping similar snap-ins. For example, the Windows Firewall snap-in configured for the local computer might make a good parent snap-in for Windows Firewall snap-ins for other systems in an environment. This way, these configuration tools are grouped for ease of use.

When the snap-ins have been added to the console, tap or click OK in the Add Or Remove Snap-ins dialog box to add the tools to the MMC.

Using the MMC to manage resources

Selecting a snap-in listed under Console Root displays its available navigation options in the left pane of the console and the details of the item in the center pane. The right portion of the MMC lists available actions for the selected item. Figure 9-21 shows the Windows Firewall With Advanced Security snap-in displayed in an MMC.

The center details pane and the right Actions pane change as the selections on the left change. If a snap-in has only one level of tools, no nested levels of items are available to select.

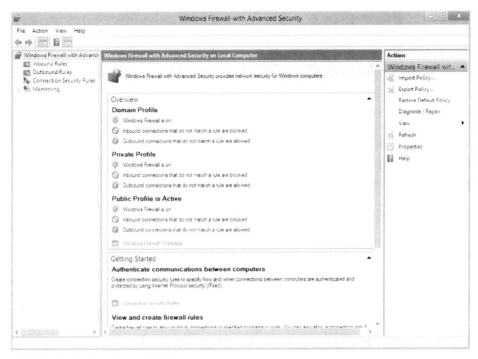

FIGURE 9-21 Windows Firewall MMC

The actions you take using a management console are performed on the computer that is configured when adding the snap-in. By default, this will be the local computer; however, remote computers can be specified instead.

MMCs are similar to a tool belt for administrators, but certain administrators or help desk professionals might not have permissions to change available options and settings. You can control permissions in the options for an MMC.

Table 9-2 lists the modes that are available when saving an MMC.

TABLE 9-2 Save modes available for MMCs

Console Mode	Description
Author mode	Allows full access to the MMC, including the addition and removal of snap-ins, creation of new windows, addition of taskpad views and tasks to the MMC, and view of the entire tree of items
User mode - full access	Prevents the addition, removal, and modification of snap-ins but allows full access to the tree of items
User mode - limited access, multiple windows	Prevents users from accessing areas of the tree that are not visible in snap-in console windows
User mode - limited access, single window	Opens the snap-in console in a single window and prevents access to other parts of the tree that are not available in that window

In addition to these settings, each console can be assigned a name; the default name is console1. This can be helpful when sharing multiple versions of an MMC with different users because you can set the name to be more descriptive about what the console allows.

In all the modes except author mode, the option to allow customization of views is available. Selecting this option enables users of this console to change the options that are visible within the saved management console. The console can be locked down by removing options from the view and saving it in a limited mode without the option to customize views.

Management consoles are useful tools not only in the day-to-day administration of Windows environments but also as powerful training tools that you can use to create a limited custom console for help desk employees or junior-level administrators. This helps them become familiar with the available tools without providing too much access to an environment.

Lesson summary

- Windows Remote Shell requires the configuration of the Remote Management service before it can operate successfully
- The WinRM quickconfig command is used to enable the ports used by WinRS and to create the necessary firewall exceptions used by the service.
- The MMC provides a common administrative framework for administrators and is used by many programs.
- Administrators can add snap-ins to the MMC and create what amounts to a custom administrative console for the environment.

Lesson review

Answer the following questions to test your knowledge of the information in this lesson. You can find the answers to these questions and explanations of why each is correct or incorrect in the "Answers" section at the end of this chapter.

1. The IT department has hired some summer interns to help with day-to-day help desk tasks and administration. Because these interns are all studying in the Management Information Systems program at a local college, they are given access to a custom set of tools to help them understand how these tools work in the real world. Which tool enables this controlled access?

   A. A custom PowerShell script

   B. Microsoft Management Console with specified snap-ins and a limited mode

   C. Netsh run from a shortcut that elevates the application to run as an administrator

   D. Remote Desktop sessions to each computer

2. Because Windows PowerShell aims to make administration not only easier but also more functional, it provides great control in almost every area of Windows. How can you get help with a bit of code that is not working correctly?

A. Press F1 in the Windows PowerShell console to open Help.

B. Type the question on the command line.

C. Type the help alias or get-help cmdlet for the troublesome command.

D. Download a PDF copy of the help files from the Microsoft website.

3. A computer in your environment is having trouble keeping an IP address on the network. The user on this computer reports that the Internet connection is intermittent at best, and email often gets disconnected. You want to reset the TCP/IP stack on this computer. Which tools can you use to perform this action?

A. iisreset

B. Windows PowerShell

C. Netsh

D. MMC containing the Windows Firewall snap-in

Practice exercises

These exercises help you practice configuring and connecting to computers by using Remote Desktop and other tools. Completing these exercises will improve your familiarity with the tools covered in this chapter.

Exercise 1: Configure a Remote Desktop session that launches PowerShell.exe and connect to a remote computer

In this exercise, you configure a connection to another computer. When connected, the session should start PowerShell.exe.

1. On the Start screen, locate and launch Remote Desktop Connection.

2. Type a server name to which to connect for this session; for example, NYDC1.

3. Ensure that the desktop experience has the correct resolution to fill your monitor.

4. On the Programs tab, launch a specified application.

5. Type the following path to the Windows PowerShell executable file:

   `c:\windows\system32\WindowsPowerShell\v1.0\powershell.exe.`

6. Save the session, noting that Windows PowerShell starts when it connects.

7. Connect to your saved Remote Desktop session.

8. PowerShell should open and load the default profile if one exists.

9. Return a list of processes and running services on the remote computer:

```
Get-process
Get-service | where-object {$_.status -eq "running"}
```

10. Close Windows PowerShell.

11. Disconnect from the remote session.

Exercise 2: Help another user initiate a Remote Assistance session

If you will assist others with Remote Assistance, it will help you to understand it from their perspective. In this exercise, you initiate a session in Remote Assistance.

1. On the Start screen, locate and launch Remote Assistance.

2. Select the best option for your environment to use in initiating a session.

3. If necessary, record the password for the session.

4. Provide the password for the Remote Assistance session to the person who will be providing help.

Take notes as you work through these steps so you can use them to explain the process to others. Be sure to use the preferred initiation method for your environment.

> **NOTE** **PRACTICE IN MULTIPLE ENVIRONMENTS**
>
> It is a good idea to complete this practice both within a lab environment, where you participate on both ends of the Remote Assistance session, and with others in your department to help them understand how to use the tool.

Exercise 3: Work with Windows PowerShell to obtain information about a remote system

Windows PowerShell is a powerful object-based tool aimed at providing an intuitive and easy-to-use command-line experience and scripting environment for automating administrative tasks. In this exercise, you find information about a group of computers as part of a routine maintenance check performed daily. For this practice, the test computer is your local workstation.

1. Open Windows PowerShell.

2. Enter the following on the command line:

```
get-winevent | select-object -first 25
```

This command returns the first 25 Windows events found in the event log. If Windows PowerShell is not opened as an administrator, the security log might display an Access Denied error. This will depend on the credentials of the logged-on user.

3. To run this command against a predefined list of computers, use the following syntax:

```
$computers = Get-content c:\computers.txt
Foreach $computer in $computers
{
$computer; Get-winevent -computername $computer |select-object -first 25
}
```

This returns the name of the computer and the first 25 events listed in available logs. The log can also be configured to get the first 25 events from a specific log file on each remote computer.

Suggested practice exercises

The following suggested practices are designed to give you more opportunities to practice what you've learned and to help you successfully master the lessons presented in this chapter.

- **Exercise 1** Configure Remote Desktop sessions to frequently accessed computers and create shortcuts for them on the desktop.
- **Exercise 2** Create a VPN connection to a remote network to enable remote access to internal resources.
- **Exercise 3** Assist a remote user by using Remote Assistance.

Answers

This section contains answers to the lesson review questions in this chapter.

Lesson 1

1. **Correct answer: C**

    A. **Incorrect:** As a support provider, you cannot initiate a Remote Assistance session. You can only participate in sessions you receive from others.

    B. **Incorrect:** Connecting to the computer would interrupt the interactive session, and Melanie would not be able to see what steps to take to solve this problem. Further, it is not likely that you would have Melanie's password. Connecting with her credentials would require you to reset the password first.

    C. **Correct:** A phone call or even a desk visit to help initiate the session would help by enabling you to walk Melanie through the problem and familiarize her with the Remote Assistance process for items with which she might need help in the future.

    D. **Incorrect:** Telling Melanie how to access Remote Assistance from the Start screen might be useful later but might not be enough to help her now because she is still learning about Windows 8.

2. **Correct answers: A and B**

    A. **Correct:** Although an invitation is needed, additional items are needed to connect to the computer.

    B. **Correct:** Along with an invitation or an Easy Connect configuration for providing Remote Assistance, the password will establish a connection.

    C. **Incorrect:** Although shipping the computer would work, the user would be affected severely due to loss of time with the computer. In addition, he would not be able to participate in the session and learn how to locate solutions within Windows 8.

    D. **Incorrect:** When you have received both the invitation and password, you can work with the employee to increase his comfort level with the Windows 8 environment.

Lesson 2

1. **Correct answer: C**

    A. **Incorrect:** Restarting the server should be a last resort in fixing any problem unless a restart is the only immediate solution that enables you to look for clues to the problem with minimal interruption to the users.

    B. **Incorrect:** Sometimes visiting remote locations is necessary, but in many cases, accessing a server on your network by physically using its keyboard to sign in is not required.

C. **Correct:** A remote desktop session enables you to see what might be going on with the affected server without driving there to troubleshoot the problem. If a restart is necessary after initial troubleshooting, you can accomplish this through the remote desktop session, too.

D. **Incorrect:** The running processes show you only the applications that are running on a computer. They do not necessarily provide additional tools to correct any problems.

2. **Correct answer: C**

A. **Incorrect:** The startup folder would open the tools for Exchange, but there might be situations when you do not want to see the tools at logon. For example, if you log on interactively, or if you add the management console to the startup folder, it will always start regardless of how you log on.

B. **Incorrect:** The shortcut would only allow you to start the tools; it would not start them for you in a remote session. Although this might be helpful in some situations, it is not a direct solution to the problem.

C. **Correct:** Configuring a Remote Desktop connection to the Exchange server(s) and specifying that the connection should launch the Exchange Management Console when logging on is the best way to enable the tools when this particular session is launched. A benefit of this approach is portability; the session configuration files can be stored on the network or a USB drive.

D. **Incorrect:** Adding the management console to the taskbar makes it easier to access after the first time you have logged on but will not run the application automatically at logon.

Lesson 3

1. **Correct answer: B**

A. **Incorrect:** Although many businesses might consider using the cloud in the future, moving critical application data there without a test run would be risky.

B. **Correct:** Creating a VPN between the office and remote users would be a relatively inexpensive method to provide the tools the users need to efficiently access this information.

C. **Incorrect:** Asking for an email might solve the problem in the short term and provide information in an absolute emergency, but it will add extra work for others in your office every time they get an email for reporting information.

D. **Incorrect:** Scheduling the report for daily delivery does not correct issues with the VPN connection.

2. **Correct answer: B**

   A. **Incorrect:** Restarting the computer may fix the problem, but the troubleshooting steps may include this at a later time. Restarting multiple times, unless absolutely needed, just adds time to the troubleshooting process.

   B. **Correct:** Because Glen reported problems accessing the Internet recently, running the Network Adapters troubleshooter with him is a great place to start for two reasons. First, it exposes Glen to tools he can use to gather information before contacting support. Second, it helps ensure that the Internet connection is not the cause of the problems with the VPN connection.

   C. **Incorrect:** Without first looking at the settings for the existing VPN connection, it is likely that if there is an issue with the connection, the same settings will be used when re-creating it. This would result in Glen experiencing the issue again.

   D. **Incorrect:** Spending additional time to rebuild a laptop completely takes more administrative effort than required to correct Glen's Internet problems.

3. **Correct answers: B, C, and D**

   A. **Incorrect:** DES and 3DES are encryption methods for the information being passed across the connection. They do not handle authentication of connections.

   B. **Correct:** Although pre-shared keys can verify both partners in a VPN connection, this is not the only method for this operation.

   C. **Correct:** Like pre-shared keys, certificates can authenticate partners in a tunnel, but this is not the only method for this operation.

   D. **Correct:** Smart card authentication can verify both parties to a connection by verifying the certificate contained on the card and the PIN entered to connect.

Lesson 4

1. **Correct answer: B**

   A. **Incorrect:** Although a Windows PowerShell script might be great for some tasks and one-off configuration changes, it is too advanced to use at this point.

   B. **Correct:** MMC is capable of containing many tools in the same console. This enables any user to focus on several tasks without leaving this tool.

   C. **Incorrect:** Netsh is built for a very specific type of problem and is mostly focused on network adapters and configurations. It is useful for those situations but not for all situations.

   D. **Incorrect:** Connecting to the desktop of each computer individually is time-consuming, especially to access a few tools for management.

2. **Correct answer: C**

   A. **Incorrect:** Because Windows PowerShell is a command-line tool, it doesn't support an F1 graphical help tool.

   B. **Incorrect:** Windows PowerShell is intuitive and uses natural language for commands, but just entering a question will generate an error, not the help sought by the user.

   C. **Correct:** The Windows PowerShell Get-Help cmdlet is the best way to access the help. Because help is comment-based in Windows PowerShell, it comes back in a quick, structured format for easy-to-use, learnable solutions.

   D. **Incorrect:** Help is not available as a PDF document.

3. **Correct answer: C**

   A. **Incorrect:** The iisreset tool only restarts the IIS Admin service.

   B. **Incorrect:** Windows PowerShell can run other commands, just like the command prompt, and access WMI information, but the Netsh command is more straightforward for this solution.

   C. **Correct:** Netsh provides a context-based command line for working with network configurations. Using Netsh can reset the TCP/IP stack very quickly.

   D. **Incorrect:** The Windows Firewall snap-in will not help you reset the TCP/IP stack.

CHAPTER 10

Sharing resources

From the earliest days of computing, it's been necessary to be able to share information between computers. After all, users are generally disinterested in creating the same documents and spreadsheets on multiple computers. As a result, the earliest business networks were implemented to facilitate sharing files, folders, and expensive devices—such as laser printers—between users and between departments. The ability to share created major efficiencies while helping companies save money.

Lessons in this chapter:

Before you begin

To complete the practice exercises in this chapter, you need to:

- Create a few test folders on your Windows 8–based computer that you can use to practice setting permissions.
- Have at least one installed printer that you can use to practice sharing printers and establishing printing permissions.

Lesson 1: Sharing files and folders

Windows 8 provides many of the same features as Windows Server 2012 for sharing files and folders, including granular sharing options, multiple permissions sets, and the ability to share both single files and complete folders. However, Windows 8, like previous versions of Windows, also includes the HomeGroup feature, which provides basic file-sharing and resource-sharing capabilities suitable for home and personal use.

After this lesson, you will be able to:

■ Enable file and folder sharing in Windows 8 by using two methods.

■ Share a folder with other users.

■ Limit access to files and folders on a Windows 8 system by using two methods.

■ Describe the differences between share and NTFS permissions.

■ Describe how NTFS permissions operate.

Estimated lesson time: 60 minutes

Configuring the Network and Sharing Center

The Network and Sharing Center has been the primary location for managing networks in Windows for quite some time and remains available in Windows 8. This tool includes some high-level options for how sharing options operate in Windows 8.

You can access the Network and Sharing Center from the taskbar, Control Panel, or the Start screen.

Using the taskbar

At the lower-right corner of the desktop, press and hold or right-click the network icon and choose Open Network And Sharing Center, as shown in Figure 10-1.

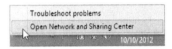

FIGURE 10-1 Opening Network And Sharing Center from the taskbar

Using Control Panel

To access Control Panel, either press and hold or right-click the lower-left corner of the desktop. This opens a shortcut menu that provides access to a number of system utilities, including Control Panel. From this shortcut menu, choose the Control Panel option. When Control Panel opens, choose the View Network Status And Tasks option, as shown in Figure 10-2. This opens the Network and Sharing Center.

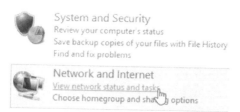

Adjust your computer's settings

System and Security
Review your computer's status
Save backup copies of your files with File History
Find and fix problems

Network and Internet
View network status and tasks
Choose homegroup and sharing options

FIGURE 10-2 Using Control Panel to access the Network and Sharing Center

Using the Start screen

You can also use the new Windows 8 interface to access the Network and Sharing Center. There are two ways to do so. First, with the Start screen open, start typing **Control Panel**. As you type, Windows narrows the results to match what you've typed. Figure 10-3 shows the results of this search.

FIGURE 10-3 Searching for Control Panel on the Start screen

Alternatively, from the Start screen, start typing **Network** and, in the Search bar, choose Settings to tell Windows that you're looking for settings rather than apps. Tap or click Network And Sharing Center (Figure 10-4).

FIGURE 10-4 Finding settings that are related to the network by using the Start screen

In the Network and Sharing Center, you have several options by which to make granular changes in how Windows 8 operates on the network.

Sharing files and folders

The ability to share files and folders remains one of the most basic reasons that organizations deploy networks in the workplace and why more people are deploying networks in their homes. In Windows 8, you must enable sharing on your network, go through the process of sharing resources, and then secure access to those resources by setting varying levels of permissions.

Enabling folder sharing using the Windows 8 interface

To enable file and folder sharing in Windows 8, complete the following steps:

1. Tap or move your mouse pointer to the upper-right or lower-right corner of the screen to access the charms.
2. Click the Settings charm to open the Settings menu.
3. Tap or click Network.
4. When the list of networks appears, press and hold or right-click the network with which you'd like to share resources.
5. When the shortcut menu appears, choose Turn Sharing On Or Off.
6. Tap or click Yes, Turn On Sharing And Connect To Devices, as shown in Figure 10-5.

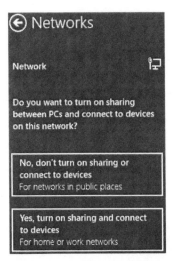

FIGURE 10-5 Enabling file sharing on a particular network

Enabling folder sharing using the traditional interface

Alternatively, you can enable file sharing in a more traditional way in Windows 8 by configuring the network profile settings for the network to which you're connected. To do so, complete the following steps:

1. Open the Network and Sharing Center.

2. Tap or click the Change Advanced Sharing Settings option to open a dialog box like the one shown in Figure 10-6.

3. To enable folder sharing, select the Turn On File And Printer Sharing option.

4. Tap or click Save Changes.

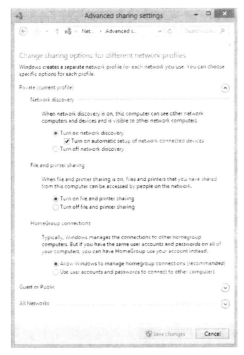

FIGURE 10-6 The Advanced Sharing Settings for the Private network profile

There are a number of additional options on this page.

For private networks, three settings are available:

- **Network Discovery**   When Network Discovery is enabled, the Windows 8–based computer can find other devices on the network and is itself visible on the network. This feature plays a prominent role in sharing resources such as documents and printers. When this feature is disabled—which is often the case for security reasons—the Windows 8–based computer doesn't seek out and display network resources and doesn't advertise itself on the network. However, even when Network Discovery is disabled, the Windows 8–based computer *can* use resources shared by other computers or servers on the network, but the administrator or person using the computer needs to know the network path to access those resources.

- **File And Printer Sharing**   When File and Printer Sharing is enabled, the Windows 8–based computer is allowed to share its resources on the network. This feature accompanies Network Discovery, which makes shared resources visible on the network; File and Printer Sharing is the mechanism by which those resources are shared.

- **HomeGroup Connections**   In non-domain environments, Windows 8 provides HomeGroup functionality, which streamlines the process of sharing resources on smaller or home networks.

For guest or public networks, the options are the same as for private networks, with one exception. If the selected network is a public network, the HomeGroup Connections option is not available.

In the All Networks section of the Advanced Sharing Settings dialog box (Figure 10-7), you find other settings that are pertinent to file and folder sharing:

- **Public Folder Sharing**   Anyone on the network can access the contents of folders marked as public that are shared from this computer.

- **Media Streaming**   When Media Streaming is enabled, other people and devices on the network can access pictures, movies, and music from this computer. In addition, this computer can find media on the network.

- **File Sharing Connections**   This setting requires an encrypted, 128-bit connection for file-sharing connections. Some earlier versions of Windows and some devices on the market do not support this level of encryption. If you are having trouble with a device, try to use the 40/56-bit option instead.

- **Password Protected Sharing**   This setting ensures that people accessing the resources on this computer—files, folders, and printers—actually have an account and password on this computer. If not, the user is denied access to the resource.

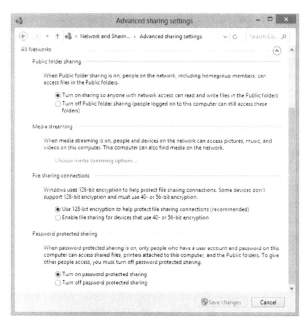

FIGURE 10-7 The Advanced Sharing Settings dialog box

Sharing a folder: simple method

Now that Windows 8 has been configured to enable file and folder sharing, you can share a folder on the network. To share a folder quickly, complete the following steps:

1. Open that folder's Properties page and tap or click the Sharing tab to open a window like the one shown in Figure 10-8.

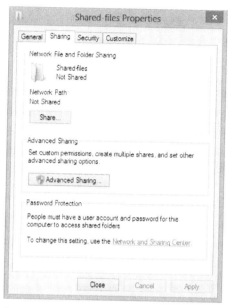

FIGURE 10-8 Enabling file sharing on a specific network

2. Tap or click Share to open the File Sharing window shown in Figure 10-9.

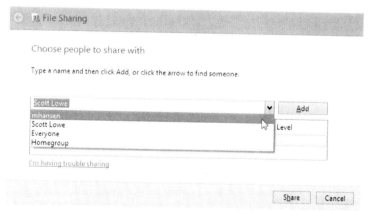

FIGURE 10-9 Enabling file sharing on particular networks

3. Tap or click the down arrow in the list box and find the user with whom you want to share the folder. Tap or click the Add button.

4. Choose the permission level you would like the user to have.

   Choose either Read or Read/Write. With Read permissions, the user can read the contents of the shared folder but can't make changes. With Read/Write permissions, the user can make changes to the contents of the folder. You can see the permission options in Figure 10-10.

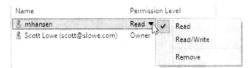

FIGURE 10-10 Choosing permission level for sharing with selected users

5. When you have added users and settings permissions, tap or click the Share button to proceed.

   You receive a notice like the one shown in Figure 10-11, telling you the folder is now shared, using the same name as the name of the folder. By using this method, you cannot change the name of the folder.

FIGURE 10-11 Notifying that a folder is now shared

6. If you want to notify the user that the folder is shared and available, tap or click the E-Mail link to send an email to specified users with the link to the folder.

Now, users with appropriate rights can access that folder by browsing the network or by going directly to the folder's universal naming convention (UNC) path name, which in this example is \\WIN8\Shared-files.

Sharing a folder: advanced method

By using the simple method, you can't control the name of the share; it will always assume the name of the folder you're sharing. Although you will want to do this in some instances, it won't always be the case. To account for this, Windows 8 also includes a more advanced method for sharing folders. Like the simple method, you access this from the Sharing tab on the Properties page for a folder (see Figure 10-8).

To share a folder by using the advanced method, complete the following steps:

1. On the Sharing tab, tap or click Advanced Sharing to open the dialog box shown in Figure 10-12.

FIGURE 10-12 The Advanced Sharing dialog box

In the Advanced Sharing dialog box, you have more options than were available with the simple method.

2. To share the folder, select the Share This Folder check box at the top of the dialog box.

3. Provide a share name in the text box.

By using the advanced sharing method, you can have a share name that is different from the name of the folder you're sharing.

4. In the Limit The Number Of Simultaneous Users To box, select the number of users who can access the share at the same time. The default number of simultaneous connections is 20, which is also the maximum number of connections that can be made to a Windows 8–based computer.

REAL WORLD THE 20-CONNECTION LIMIT

The 20-connection limit to a Windows 8–based computer is not a technical limitation, but rather a limitation based on the licensing terms of Windows 8. Windows 8 might work well in a very small environment, but as organizations scale to larger sizes, the 20-connection limit forces these organizations to consider Windows Server for file sharing needs rather than continuing to rely on Windows 8, which is a desktop operating system.

5. To change the permissions for the shared folder, select the Permissions button, which opens a dialog box like the one shown in Figure 10-13.

FIGURE 10-13 The Permissions For Any-name dialog box

6. Select the group or user for which you want to establish permissions. You have three options:

   ▪ **Full Control**   A user with full control for the shared folder can do anything, including changing the permissions.

   ▪ **Change**   The user can both read and modify the contents of files in the folder.

   ▪ **Read**   The user can view folder items but can't make changes.

   You can have multiple entries in the Group Or User Name box. For example, you might grant administrators full control for a folder but grant the sales team only view rights.

7. Make your selections and tap or click OK.

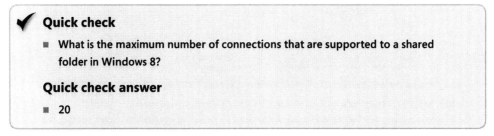

✔ **Quick check**

   ▪ **What is the maximum number of connections that are supported to a shared folder in Windows 8?**

Quick check answer

   ▪ **20**

Understanding NTFS permissions

In addition to the permissions that you can set when you share a folder, Windows includes a second, more comprehensive set of permissions. Called *NTFS permissions*, these can allow or deny permissions on a per-file or per-folder basis on the Windows 8–based computer.

If you're used to the NTFS file system permissions in earlier versions of Windows, you'll find that not too much has changed in Windows 8. NTFS permissions are still straightforward for the most part. In this section, you learn about how NTFS permissions operate.

It's important to understand that NTFS permissions are local permissions and are always in effect, regardless of how the server is accessed. Whereas the shared permissions you just learned about come into play only when resources are accessed over the network, NTFS permissions are enforced all the time, even when signing on to the machine directly from the console. It is through the use of NTFS permissions that organizations can secure their data without regard to access method.

NTFS has both basic and advanced sets of permissions. On desktops, it's rare that you will need advanced NTFS permissions; the basic permission set is almost always sufficient. You'll learn about the basic permission set first. Bear in mind that NTFS permissions can be applied to entire folders or to individual files. There are some minor differences between the permissions in each case. NTFS permissions are outlined in Table 10-1.

TABLE 10-1 NTFS permissions

Permission name	Description (folder)	Description (file)
Full control	The user has full permission to the folder and can add, change, move, and delete items. In addition, the user can add and remove permissions on the folder and on any subfolders.	The user has full rights to the file and can change, move, or delete it. The user can also add and remove permissions on the file.
Modify	The Modify permission is a conglomeration of the Read and Write permissions, which gives the user the ability to delete files inside a folder and to view the contents of subfolders.	The user can modify the contents of the selected file.
Read & execute	The user can read the contents of files in the folder or execute programs inside the folder but cannot make changes to the items in the folder.	The user can read the contents of the file or execute the program but cannot make changes to the file.
List folder contents	The user can view the contents of the selected folder but cannot read a file's contents or execute any of the files.	This permission is not applicable at the file level.
Read	The user can read the individual items inside a folder.	The user can read the contents of a file.
Write	The user can create files and folders but cannot modify existing items.	The user can create a file.

As you create groups for permissions reasons, understand that the permissions you assign are cumulative. Perhaps you grant a user permission to read and execute the contents of a folder, and you grant a group to which the user belongs the permission to write to a folder. The user will get all those permissions because NTFS permissions are cumulative.

Modifying file or folder permissions

To modify the NTFS permissions on a file or folder, complete the following steps:

1. Press and hold or right-click the folder and select Properties.

2. On the Properties page, choose the Security tab, as shown in Figure 10-14.

FIGURE 10-14 The current security settings for the selected folder

> **NOTE MULTIPLE USERS**
>
> You can see that a number of permissions are available for the selected user. Any per-missions you change will affect only the selected user or group. If you want to make changes to multiple users, either add the user to a group and then apply permissions to the group or individually apply permissions to individual users.

3. To make changes to the permissions for the selected user or group, tap or click the Edit button on the Properties page to display the Permissions dialog box shown in Figure 10-15.

FIGURE 10-15 Editing the permissions for a selected user

Here you can see that the permissions are broken down into Allow and Deny columns. You can allow a user a particular set of permissions or deny a user access to a particular file or folder by selecting the Allow or Deny check box for each permission.

> **NOTE CUMULATIVE PERMISSIONS**
>
> Cumulative permissions apply only when you're adding up permissions in the Allow column. When Deny permissions are involved, they *always override Allow permissions*. It's not considered a best practice to use Deny permissions very often. Doing so can create administrative nightmares that are difficult to solve. However, Deny can be useful when group Allow permissions have been applied to a folder, but you still want a user in that group to be denied access to the folder. Because the Deny permission overrides the Allow permission, the user is denied that particular permission.

4. Make your selections and tap or click OK.

Creating advanced security settings

NTFS permissions can get confusing because of the way they work. What you just saw was straightforward information—apply a permission, and it takes effect. However, as you investigate further, additional complexity becomes apparent.

This complexity is simplified through the use of advanced security settings. By viewing these settings, you gain insight into the real state of permissions for the selected file or folder. In the main section of the window, you see that each permission entry is individually delineated, showing you exactly which permissions are assigned to specific users and groups (called principals).

To view or change the advanced security settings for a file or folder, complete the following steps:

1. On the Properties page shown in Figure 10-14, tap or click the Advanced button to open the Advanced Security Settings window shown in Figure 10-16.

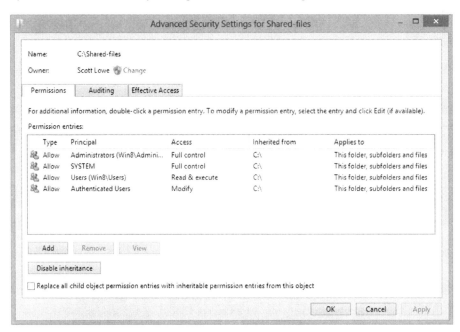

FIGURE 10-16 The current security settings for the selected folder

Each permission entry is individually listed, showing you exactly which permissions have been assigned to which users and groups, called *principals*. To the right, you can see the reason the principals are granted the permissions they carry. These permissions have been inherited from C:\. The folder you're working with in Figure 10-16 is C:\Shared-files. By default, folders in Windows 8 inherit the permissions of their parent folder. This avoids the need for an administrator to specify permissions for each folder in the system manually.

However, you might want to have permissions change on folders deeper in the hierarchy. Fortunately, that's not difficult, and the result is that the selected folder will have permissions that are both inherited from the parent folder and set directly. In Figure 10-17, you can see that the folder now has additional permissions, but these permissions were not inherited.

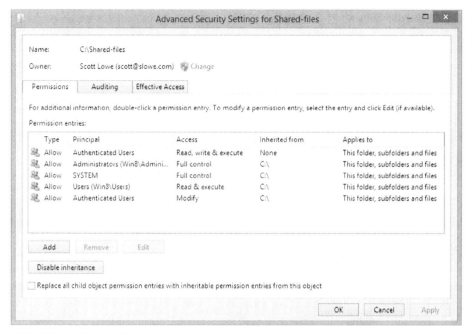

FIGURE 10-17 Advanced Security Settings window showing a directly granted level of permissions

To add a permission directly to the selected folder from the Advanced Security Settings, tap or click the Add button. This opens the Permission Entry window shown in Figure 10-18.

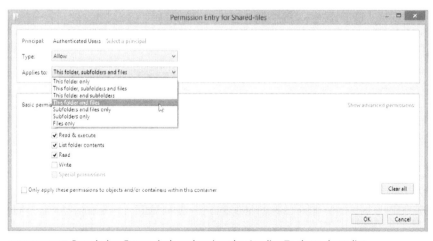

FIGURE 10-18 Permission Entry window showing the Applies To drop-down list

2. In the Permissions Entry dialog box, provide the Principal name.

This is the name of the user or group to which you want to apply new or additional permissions. In Figure 10-18, the administrator has already selected the group named

Authenticated Users. To specify a different user or group, tap or click Select A Principal and make a selection.

3. In the Type drop-down list, select either Allow or Deny as the permission type.

4. Make a selection from the Applies To drop-down list.

   By default, Windows applies your new permissions settings to the current folder and to all subfolders and files according to the default inheritance rules in Windows 8. You can override this behavior by choosing a different entry from the Applies To drop-down list. Table 10-2 lists the available options and the impact of your selection.

TABLE 10-2 Default permissions impact

Apply permissions to	Apply to current folder ONLY	Apply to subfolders in current folder	Apply to files in current folder	Apply to all subfolders	Apply to files in all subfolders
This folder only	X				
The folder, subfolders, and files	X	X	X	X	X
This folder and subfolders	X	X		X	
This folder and files	X		X		X
Subfolders and files only		X	X	X	X
Subfolders only		X		X	
Files only			X		X

Under Basic Permissions, you can choose different basic permissions for the selected principal.

5. If you'd like to see additional available permissions, tap or click Show Advanced Permissions.

   Table 10-3 describes the available advanced permissions.

TABLE 10-3 Advanced NTFS permissions

Folder permission name	Description (folder)	File permission name	Description (file)
Traverse Folder	Allows the user to browse to folders beneath the current one	Execute File	Allows the user to execute the file
List Folder	Allows the user to view file names and subfolder names	Read Data	Allows the user to read data from a file
Read Attributes	Allows the user to view the attributes of a file or folder (such as Read-Only, Hidden)		

Folder permission name	Description (folder)	File permission name	Description (file)
Read Extended Attributes	Allows the user to view the extended attributes of a file or folder; extended attributes may be assigned by an application		
Create Files	Allows the user to create files inside the folder	Write Data	Allows the user to write data to a file
Create Folders	Allows the user to create new folders within a folder	Append Data	Allows the user to add data to the end of a file but not to change the existing content
Write Attributes	Allows the user to change the attributes of a file or folder (such as Read-Only, Hidden)		
Write Extended Attributes	Allows the user to change the extended attributes of a file or folder; extended attributes may be assigned by an application		
Delete Subfolders and Files	Allows the user to delete subfolders and files; works even if the user has not been assigned the Delete permission		
Delete	Allows the user to delete a file or a folder		
Read Permissions	Allows the user to read the permissions for a file or folder		
Change Permissions	Allows the user to change the permissions on a file or folder		
Take Ownership	Allows the user to take ownership of a file or folder without regard to other permissions that might already be assigned		

6. Select the Only Apply These Permissions To Objects And/Or Containers Within This Container check box to limit the containers to which new permissions apply.

Table 10-4 lists the permissions impact when this check box is selected.

TABLE 10-4 Permissions impact when Only Apply These Permissions To Objects And/Or Containers Within This Container is selected

Apply permissions to	Apply to current folder ONLY	Apply to subfolders in current folder	Apply to files in current folder	Apply to all subfolders	Apply to files in all subfolders
This folder only	x				
The folder, subfolders, and files	x	x	x		
This folder and subfolders	x	x			
This folder and files	x		x		
Subfolders and files only		x	x		
Subfolders only		x			
Files only			x		

Identifying permissions

With this permission sleight of hand, you might wonder how you can discover who has permissions to what. As you move deeper into the folder hierarchy and as permission inheritance is blocked at different levels, it can become confusing. Further, when you must troubleshoot a user's access-related issue, you might need a little help. This is when the Effective Access tab on the Advanced Security Settings window becomes useful.

To use this tool, complete the following steps:

1. Navigate to the Effective Access tab, as shown in Figure 10-19, and select a user.

2. Tap or click the View Effective Access button to get a complete list of permissions that apply to the selected user or group.

    You can see every advanced permission and which factors might be limiting access. Note also that you can change ownership of the selected resource from this window, which you will see happen in the next section.

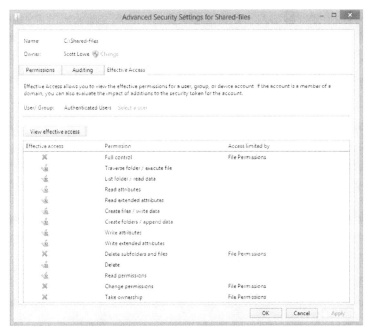

FIGURE 10-19 The Effective Access tab in the Advanced Security Settings window

Taking ownership of a resource

You can change the owner of a resource and its permissions in the Advanced Security Settings window. When a user account owns a file or folder, that account holds the key to that resource and can lock out non-administrative users.

By default, the owner of a file or folder is the user account that originally created it. However, ownership can be transferred to other users or groups as necessary. For example, if someone who is responsible for a shared folder leaves the organization, his replacement can be provided with ownership rights to that resource and pick up those responsibilities.

Only administrators, authorized users, and backup operators can take away ownership of a resource from another account. In addition, administrators and the current owner of a resource can assign ownership of a resource to another account.

To change the ownership of a resource, complete the following steps:

1. Open the Advanced Security Settings window (Figure 10-19).
2. Next to the name of the existing Owner, tap or click Change.
3. Provide the name of the user or group to whom ownership should be assigned.

4. When the owner information is changed, Windows asks whether you want to Replace Owner On Subcontainers And Objects. If you want to take ownership of every object beneath the selected item, select this check box. If you want to change ownership of the selected item only, make sure the check box is clear.

5. Tap or click the OK button.

> **NOTE USE CAUTION WHEN TAKING OWNERSHIP OF A RESOURCE**
>
> Although changing ownership on user-created files and folders is generally safe, be very careful when attempting to change or take ownership of system files, including those in the Windows and Program Files folders. File and folder ownership is a part of how Windows 8 determines which accounts are allowed to perform certain functions. Changing ownership of system files can have unpredictable consequences that might not always be positive.

Resolving permissions conflicts

If you've been reading carefully, you might have noticed that two sets of permissions are at play when you create a shared folder on a Windows 8–based computer and then access that shared folder over the network.

When you first access the share over the network, you're subjected to the share permissions. Then, each file and folder inside the share has NTFS permissions that must be respected.

But what happens when there is a conflict? For example, what happens when a user accesses a share that has read-only permissions but that user has full control NTFS permissions to the data in the shared folder?

In the case of a conflict between share and NTFS permissions, *the most restrictive permissions are respected.* In the preceding scenario, the access would be read-only when connecting to that read-only share even though the user has full control rights in NTFS.

> **REAL WORLD KEEPING THINGS SIMPLE WITH ONE SET OF PERMISSIONS**
>
> In the real world, administrators generally want to worry about just one set of permissions. This keeps things simple. Many administrators opt to provide Full Control or Read/Write permissions on shared folders and then use just NTFS permissions to limit what users can do. In this way, administrators can be certain that a user's access to certain folders is always limited, whether that folder is accessed from the network or directly from the desktop. Remember, NTFS permissions are always in effect, regardless of the location from which the user accesses the information. Shared permissions, however, are not applied when a user accesses a file or folder directly from the computer that is housing that file or folder.

Lesson summary

- There are a number of ways to access the Network and Sharing Center in Windows 8.
- NTFS permissions operate on the local system and protect it.
- Share permissions manage the kind of connections that can be made to the shared resource.
- When share and NTFS permissions conflict, the most restrictive set of permissions applies.
- When multiple sets of NTFS permissions are applied to a single object, the permissions are cumulative.
- A Deny permission always overrides an Allow permission.
- Inheritance is a method by which NTFS permissions flow down to subfolders and files.

Lesson review

Answer the following questions to test your knowledge of the information in this lesson. You can find the answers to these questions and explanations of why each answer choice is correct or incorrect in the "Answers" section at the end of this chapter.

1. A user has complained that he cannot save files to the shared folder that you created for him. Upon checking the NTFS permissions on the folder, you find that the user has Full Control permissions. What else could be the cause?

   A. NTFS inheritance is disabled.

   B. Share permissions are set to Read.

   C. The user does not have NTFS Modify permissions.

   D. The user is not the owner of the resource in question.

2. How can you most easily determine the permissions a user has to a file or folder?

   A. Use the Effective Access tab in Advanced Security settings.

   B. Allow the user to take ownership of the file or folder.

   C. Assign the user account to the Local Administrators group on the server.

   D. Keep track of permission assignments in Microsoft Excel.

3. How can you change the ownership of a folder and all the objects inside that folder?

   A. When sharing a file, ownership is transferred to the accounts provided access.

   B. An authorized user must proactively change ownership and remember to select the Replace Owner On Subcontainers And Objects check box.

   C. An authorized user must proactively change ownership and remember to clear the Replace Owner On Subcontainers And Objects check box.

   D. An administrator must grant the user Change Ownership rights.

Lesson 2: Sharing printers

Even though the price of printers has decreased significantly over the past few years, printers remain an expensive investment, especially when you add color printing and other features into the mix. As with files and folders, you can share printers in Windows 8 and limit who can print to certain devices.

After this lesson, you will be able to:

- Share a printer with other users.
- Limit access to those who need to use the device.

Estimated lesson time: 20 minutes

REAL WORLD **NO PRINTER? NO PROBLEM.**

If you don't have a printer to use for this lesson, you can gain access to the concepts by installing a fake printer, which is what has been done for the examples in this chapter. The printer used in this lesson is the Bullzip PDF Printer. (Use Bing to find the download site.) After it is installed, the Bullzip PDF Printer looks and acts like an actual printer. However, when jobs are sent to it, a window opens asking for the name of an output file. After the name is provided, Bullzip prints the document to a PDF file. For the examples in this lesson, it is assumed that you have some kind of printer to use.

Configuring shared printers

Sharing printers on the network is an easy task that doesn't take much time. You just need to think about whom you want to access your printer and which permissions are available.

To share a printer, complete the following steps:

1. Open Control Panel.
2. Change to Large Icons or Small Icons view.
3. Select Devices And Printers.
4. Locate the printer you want to share.
5. Press and hold or right-click the printer and choose Printer Properties.
6. Select the Sharing tab (Figure 10-20).
7. Select the Share This Printer check box.
8. Provide a name for the printer in the Share Name text box.
9. Tap or click OK.

FIGURE 10-20 The Sharing tab in the My Printer Properties dialog box

Other users can now connect to this printer and print to it just as if it were attached to their own computer.

REAL WORLD **UNDERSTANDING DRIVER ISSUES**

Many administrators consider printers to be frustrating devices to work with, often for good reason. Printers are among the most visible devices on the network because people use them constantly, and when they're not working, people's work can come to a standstill. As you mix different versions of Windows in the environment, the printing situation can get even a bit trickier because different versions of Windows sometimes require you to load different versions of drivers on the print server. For example, if you share a printer on your Windows 8 desktop, that Windows 8 desktop has become a de facto print server. If a 32-bit Windows XP user connects to that shared printer, he might not be able to use the 64-bit Windows 8 drivers that you loaded.

If users are experiencing trouble printing to a Windows 8 shared printer, either load the appropriate drivers locally to the user's machine or open the Printer Sharing tab in Windows 8 and tap or click the Additional Drivers button for more guidance.

Configuring printing permissions

Sometimes, however, you don't want to share your printer. Perhaps, for example, you have an expensive color printer that is authorized for use by only certain people. You might find it necessary to implement restrictions on the ability to print to such devices. To set permissions on a printer, complete the following steps:

1. Open Control Panel and select Printers.

2. Locate the printer you want to share.

3. Press and hold or right-click the printer and choose Printer Properties.

4. Select the Security tab, as shown in Figure 10-21.

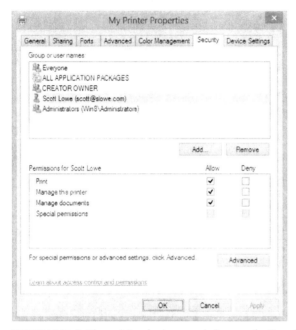

FIGURE 10-21 Setting printer sharing permissions on the Security tab in the My Printer Properties dialog box

5. Tap or click the Add button and select the user or group to which you'd like to grant printing permissions.

6. Select the appropriate printing permissions for the selected user or group. The available permissions are described in Table 10-5.

TABLE 10-5 Printing permissions

Permission name	Description (folder)
Print	The selected user or group has the rights to send documents to the printer to be printed. By default, everyone can print to the printer if she knows how to connect to it.
Manage the printer	The selected user or group has the rights to send documents to the printer to be printed. In addition, the selected user or group can fully manage the printer. This management capability allows pausing and restarting the printer, changing spooler settings, sharing the printer with others, modifying printer permissions, and changing other printer properties.
Manage documents	The selected user or group has the rights to manage the print queue. This involves cancelling and reordering print jobs.
Special permissions	There are no printer-specific special permissions.

 Quick check

- Which printer permission allows a user to modify and delete print jobs?

Quick check answer

- **Manage documents**

Lesson summary

- Windows 8 includes the ability to share printers on the network so that others in the organization can use them.
- You can restrict printers so that only authorized individuals can access them.

Lesson review

Answer the following questions to test your knowledge of the information in this lesson. You can find the answers to these questions and explanations of why each answer choice is correct or incorrect in the "Answers" section at the end of this chapter.

1. A user with whom you've shared your printer wants to be able to manage all the jobs to the printer. Which rights does she require?

    A. Print

    B. Manage the printer

    C. Manage documents

    D. Special permissions

2. A user with whom you've shared your printer wants to be able to manage the physical printer settings. Which rights does he require?

   A. Print

   B. Manage the printer

   C. Manage documents

   D. Special permissions

3. A user has accidentally changed a printer's settings. To avoid this situation, what minimal rights does the user need to be able to print but not have further access?

   A. Print

   B. Manage the printer

   C. Manage documents

   D. Special permissions

Practice exercises

In these exercises, you practice the techniques you learned in this lesson for sharing resources in Windows 8.

Exercise 1: Enable file sharing for a network adapter in your lab server

In this exercise, you make sure that your server is ready to begin sharing resources on the network. You can accomplish this from either the Windows 8 interface or from the Network and Sharing Center.

Exercise 2: Test each other

In this exercise, find a friend with a Windows 8–based computer and test connectivity.

Suggested practice exercises

The following suggested practices are designed to give you more opportunities to practice what you've learned and to help you successfully master the lessons presented in this chapter.

- **Exercise 1** Practice setting the various permissions at your disposal and watch how they can affect access to various resources. Make sure to use a variety of accounts in your testing.

- **Exercise 2** Practice what you can and can't do with various levels of rights to printers.

Answers

This section contains the answers to the lesson review questions in this chapter.

Lesson 1

1. **Correct answer: B**

   A. **Incorrect:** Full Control is an NTFS permission that provides unfettered access to files and folders.

   B. **Correct:** The share permission of Read Only will prevent the user from making changes. When NTFS and share permissions overlap, the most restrictive permission wins.

   C. **Incorrect:** Because the user has NTFS Full Control, the addition of the Modify right is not necessary.

   D. **Incorrect:** Ownership doesn't affect access in this way.

2. **Correct answer: A**

   A. **Correct:** This tab makes it very easy to determine which rights, if any, belong to the specified user.

   B. **Incorrect:** The file ownership does not matter in this case.

   C. **Incorrect:** Local group membership does not matter in this case.

   D. **Incorrect:** Using Excel to track user rights is inappropriate in the long term.

3. **Correct answer: B**

   A. **Incorrect:** File sharing and resource ownership are not related to each other.

   B. **Correct:** An authorized user must proactively change ownership and remember to select the Replace Owner On Subcontainers And Objects check box.

   C. **Incorrect:** Failure to select the Replace Owner On Subcontainers And Objects check box will result in ownership now flowing down the resource hierarchy.

   D. **Incorrect:** There is no NTFS Change Ownership right.

Lesson 2

1. **Correct answer: C**

   A. **Incorrect:** The Print permission enables a user to print.

   B. **Incorrect:** The Manage the printer permission enables a user to manage the physical printer settings but not to manage print jobs.

   C. **Correct:** The Manage documents right enables a user to control print jobs destined for a particular printer.

   D. **Incorrect:** Special permissions are not used with printers.

2. **Correct answer: B**

    A. **Incorrect:** The Print permission enables a user to print.

    B. **Correct:** The Manage the printer permission enables a user to manage the physical printer settings but not to manage print jobs.

    C. **Incorrect:** The Manage documents permission enables a user to control print jobs destined for a particular printer, but the user cannot manage the printer settings.

    D. **Incorrect:** Special rights are not used with printers.

3. **Correct answer: A**

    A. **Correct:** The Print permission enables a user to print.

    B. **Incorrect:** The Manage the printer permission enables a user to manage the physical printer settings.

    C. **Incorrect:** The Manage documents permission enables a user to control print jobs destined for a particular printer.

    D. **Incorrect:** Special rights are not used with printers.

CHAPTER 11

File system and storage management

ile systems and storage are two concepts that many take for granted. The disks just spin up and the permissions ensure the proper access to files on the disks. This chapter focuses on these items to help you understand the tools and techniques available for managing them.

Lessons in this chapter:

Before you begin

Before proceeding with this chapter, you should:

- Know the difference between Share and NTFS permissions.
- Be familiar with managing disks and partitions in a Windows environment.
- Have access to an external USB hard drive for the Storage Spaces lesson.

Lesson 1: Managing disks and storage

Using Windows requires you to store information on some type of media. Storing information on a disk might seem like a basic function of computing; however, sometimes you will need to manage the disks and other storage media on which your data resides to ensure accessibility. This lesson examines the tools and techniques available for managing disks and storage in Windows 8.

After this lesson, you will be able to:

■ Use tools included with Windows to ensure continued functionality of storage.

■ Perform maintenance on disks within your Windows environment.

■ Create and manage disk space quotas within Windows.

Estimated lesson time: 60 minutes

Using disk management

The concept of disk management has been useful in understanding how disks are used for several versions of Microsoft Windows, and Windows 8 is no exception. You can open the Disk Management utility by one of three ways:

■ Searching for Disk Management and then tapping or clicking Create And Format Hard Disk Partitions

■ Selecting it from the Storage section of the computer management console

■ Adding it to a custom Microsoft Management Console (MMC) (discussed in Chapter 9, "Working with remote management tools")

The Disk Management utility provides an overview of all the disks within a computer, as shown in Figure 11-1.

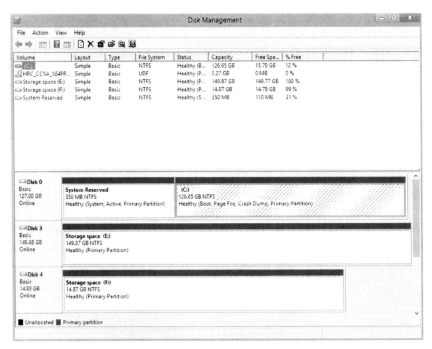

FIGURE 11-1 Disk Management console

The Disk Management snap-in has two main sections in the results pane. The top section shows a list view of the physical and logical disks installed in a computer. The bottom section shows a graphical representation of the disks in the computer and any *partitions* or logical disks they contain. Both sections of the window display the same information; only the format is different.

In addition to determining the types of disks or volumes your computer contains, the Disk Management console displays the following information:

- **Capacity**   The maximum size of the disk
- **Free Space**   The amount of space remaining
- **Percentage of space free**   The amount of space remaining displayed as a percentage of capacity
- **Disk Type**   The type of disk: basic or dynamic
- **File System**   The file system used to format the disk
- **Status**   The overall health of the disk and which roles this partition has

Disk types

A basic disk is the most common type of disk Windows uses. This disk type can contain partitions that segregate information stored on a physical disk. Basic disks use a Master Boot Record partitioning style to maintain backward compatibility, but newer operating systems support the GUID Partition Table (GPT). On a basic disk, partitions can be extended to consume all the available free space on the same disk, but they cannot extend beyond the boundaries of that disk. Basic disks support the following actions:

- Creation and deletion of primary and extended partitions
- Creation and deletion of logical drives within an extended partition
- Formatting partitions and setting their status to active to enable them for use

A dynamic disk supports options that are not available on a basic disk, including volumes that span multiple disks and fault-tolerant volumes. In addition to these features, dynamic volumes use a database to help manage the volumes contained on a dynamic disk. Replicas of the dynamic disk database are kept on each dynamic disk, which can aid in repair of dynamic volumes.

The ability to store information in noncontiguous space that can span multiple disks can be advantageous when fault tolerance is needed. Although spreading data across disks can be helpful, the ability to configure different types of volumes can be a lifesaver for your information. Dynamic disks support the following actions:

- Creating and deleting simple, spanned, striped, mirrored, and RAID-5 volumes
- Extending a simple or spanned volume
- Removing a mirror or breaking a mirrored volume into two volumes

- Repairing RAID-5 or mirrored volumes
- Reactivating missing or offline disks

Both these disk types can be useful in different situations; however, basic disks are used most commonly for personal computers or mobile devices.

> **NOTE** **MASTER BOOT RECORD OR GLOBALLY UNIQUE IDENTIFIER PARTITIONS AVAILABLE**
>
> Partitions can use the Master Boot Record (MBR) or globally unique identifier (GUID) style. MBR partitions are selected as the default style for backward compatibility. They also allow only four primary partitions or three primary partitions and one extended partition. The partition information for an MBR partition is stored at the front of the disk in the first MB of space. The layout of information on these partitions is always contiguous.
>
> GUID-style partitions are supported in Microsoft Windows Server 2003 SP1 and later. They allow up to 128 primary partitions. Logical drives and extended partitions are not necessary with this style of partition. The GPT style also supports partition sizes larger than 2 terabytes (TB).

Partition types

Basic disks support partitions. The two types of partitions available for use on a basic disk are:

- **Primary**   This partition type can contain only one logical drive and is the required type for logical disks that start Windows; that is, the C drive.
- **Extended**   This partition type can contain multiple logical drives but cannot start Windows. Each logical partition can be assigned its own drive letter. There can be only one extended partition per physical disk.

Volume types

Dynamic disks support volumes, of which five volume types are available. Some are very similar to the partitions mentioned earlier, and some provide fault tolerance for the data stored on them:

- **Simple**   This volume type operates the same way as a primary partition on a basic disk. Simple volumes can be mirrored, but if they are extended across multiple disks, they become spanned volumes.
- **Spanned**   This volume type combines unallocated space from multiple disks into one logical volume. Up to 32 disks can be included in a spanned volume. After a spanned volume is created, no portion of it can be deleted. If you delete any part of the spanned volume, you delete the entire volume. Spanned volumes must use the NTFS file system or use an unformatted portion of the disk. They provide no fault tolerance.
- **Striped**   This volume type improves disk input/output (reads and writes) by spreading information in equal parts across multiple disks. A spanned volume uses available

free space from included disks, but a striped volume evenly distributes the information across included disks for more efficient use. This volume type offers no fault tolerance. In addition, striped volumes do not support mirroring or extension. If one disk in the stripe set fails, the entire volume fails.

- **Mirrored** This volume type provides fault tolerance by creating a volume copy on another disk. The copy is an exact duplicate of the original volume. In the event of failure of a mirrored volume, the computer can continue to function by using the other portion of the mirror.
- **RAID-5** This volume type is the most fault tolerant of all available types. RAID-5 volumes stripe data and parity across three or more disks. Parity is a value calculated to ensure that a failed volume can be rebuilt from that information plus the remaining available volumes.

Actions available by using Disk Management

In addition to displaying information about disks, partitions, and volumes, the Disk Management utility can help you manage certain aspects of these items from a single, straightforward interface. The actions available from Disk Management depend on the disk type and the partition or volume selected. The entire list of actions that can be performed on partitions or volumes is as follows:

- **Open** Selecting this option opens the partition or volume in File Explorer with no tree view.
- **Explore** Selecting this option opens the partition or volume in File Explorer with the tree view.
- **Mark Partition As Active** Selecting this option sets the status of the partition as active.
- **Change Drive Letter And Paths** Selecting this option enables you to change the drive letter or folder path to a partition.
- **Format** Selecting this option erases all information from a partition.
- **Extend Volume** Selecting this option increases the size of a volume by consuming an amount of available free space.
- **Shrink Volume** Selecting this option decreases the size of a volume by returning an amount of space to the free space pool.
- **Add Mirror** Selecting this option creates a mirror of this volume on another disk.
- **Delete Volume** Selecting this option removes the volume and all the data it contains.
- **Properties** Selecting this option displays the Disk Properties window for the selected item.
- **Help** Selecting this option displays Disk Management help.

These actions are available from the context menu (press and hold or right-click) for a volume or partition. Actions unavailable for a volume or partition appear dimmed, depending on the item selected.

An example of using the Disk Management tools discussed to this point might help you understand how the tools work. Suppose you have a virtual machine running Windows 8 to use for testing purposes. The computer has two virtual hard disks attached: one for Windows 8 and one for other documents and testing of different features for hard disks in the operating system. Because you keep a copy of the documentation being created for the tests on the second virtual hard drive, it is quickly filling up. You would like to extend the drive to add 50 percent more space to the current 500 MB size. To extend the size of the virtual machine by using Disk Management, complete the following steps:

1. Open the Start screen.
2. Search for Disk Management.
3. Select Settings from the results list.
4. Select Create And Format Hard Disk Partitions.
5. Locate the 500-MB disk you want to extend in Disk Management and select it.
6. Press and hold or right-click the volume on that disk to display the context menu.
7. Select Extend Volume from the context menu.
8. Click or tap Next to skip the Extend Volume Wizard welcome page.

> **NOTE CHANGING THE SIZE OF THE VOLUME**
> The volume will appear in the Extend Volume Wizard in the selected window with all the space available on the virtual hard disk listed as the size. You can change this by entering the amount of space you want to add in the Select The Amount Of Space In MB box.

9. Enter the amount of space by which to increase the volume. To increase the amount of space by 50 percent, enter 250 MB in the Select The Amount Of Space In MB box.
10. Tap or click Next.
11. Review the changes that will be made.
12. Tap or click Finish to complete the extension.

In addition to the actions for partitions and volumes, other actions are available only on a per-disk basis. These actions are also available in a context menu by pressing and holding or right-clicking the disk item. Disks are listed along the far-left side of the graphical portion of the Disk Management snap-in. Actions available for disks include:

- **New Spanned Volume**   Select this option to create a new spanned volume.
- **New Striped Volume**   Select this option to create a new striped volume.

- **New Mirrored Volume**   Select this option to create a new mirrored volume; remember that two disks are required for this action.
- **New RAID-5 Volume**   Select this option to create a new RAID-5 volume; a minimum of three disks are required for this action.
- **Convert To Dynamic Disk**   Select this option to convert a basic disk to a dynamic disk.
- **Convert To GPT Disk**   Select this option to change the partition style from Master Boot Record to GUID Partition Table.
- **Offline**   Select this option to set the status of the disk to offline, making it unusable by the computer.
- **Properties**   Select this option to display the device properties of the disk.
- **Help**   Select this option to display Disk Management help.

As with partition options, disk options depend on the type of disk that is selected. Options for dynamic disks appear dimmed if a basic disk is selected.

> **IMPORTANT   DYNAMIC DISKS CANNOT BE CONVERTED TO BASIC DISKS**
>
> Conversion from a basic disk to a dynamic disk is a one-way process. After a disk is dynamic, it cannot be converted back to a basic disk without being deleted first, which will cause data loss.

The Disk Management snap-in is a great tool for determining what you have. It provides an easy way to see details about all your disks at a glance. Like other snap-ins (covered in Chapter 9), Disk Management can be pointed at remote computers to examine their disks. You cannot use the same instance of Disk Management to view multiple computers at the same time; to access multiple computers, you must either add multiple instances of the Disk Management snap-in to a custom MMC or change the computer being viewed by the snap-in for each computer you are interested in viewing.

Disk Defragmenter and Disk Cleanup

Files become fragmented as they are used; as a result, they are not optimally placed on the disks within a computer as they are read and written. This fragmentation can slow performance of the system over time. Disk Defragmenter can help solve these problems and improve overall performance of both your computer and the files it contains.

Disk Cleanup is a straightforward utility aimed at helping you find the files and folders that are stored on your computer but might not need to be stored. Examples of such files are leftover software installation files and Temporary Internet Files (TIFs). Letting these files accumulate on your computer can not only cause slow performance and quickly consume disk space but also lead to fragmentation of files.

Using Disk Cleanup to perform regular maintenance

Computers, like anything else that is used for an extended period, need regular maintenance and tuning to keep them performing optimally. Disk Cleanup helps you perform these tasks efficiently.

You can access Disk Cleanup in either of the following ways:

- Search for Disk Cleanup on the Start screen, tap or click Settings, and then tap or click Free Up Disk Space By Deleting Unnecessary Files.
- Press and hold or right-click a logical disk in File Explorer on the desktop.

Both of these options display dialog boxes on the desktop. The first starts Disk Cleanup immediately, whereas the second shows the Drive Properties dialog box for the disk you selected and provides the Disk Cleanup button to launch the utility.

When Disk Cleanup begins running, it analyzes the drive against which you selected to run it to locate items that might be candidates for removal. Figure 11-2 shows the Disk Cleanup analysis process.

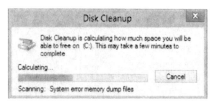

FIGURE 11-2 Analyzing the selected disk

Following initial scanning, the Disk Cleanup dialog box shown in Figure 11-3 appears. Depending on the results of the analysis, some options might be selected within the Files To Delete section of the window. The initial options for files to delete include:

- **Downloaded Program Files**   ActiveX controls and Java applets used during normal operation of some websites
- **Temporary Internet Files**   Websites and Internet content stored on your computer to speed up viewing
- **Recycle Bin**   Files you have moved to the Recycle Bin for deletion
- **Setup Log Files**   Any log files generated by application installation processes
- **System Error Memory Dump Files**   Memory dump files created by system halts and other errors
- **Temporary Files**   Information stored by programs during normal operation
- **Thumbnails**   Files that quickly display images, videos, and documents in a small preview when browsing for items
- **Per User Archived Windows Error Reports**   Files that are used for error reporting and solution checking for each user account accessing the computer

* **System Archived Windows Error Reports** Files that are used for error reporting and online solution discovery

To delete any of these groups of files, select the check box next to the group to select it for inclusion in cleanup. The Disk Cleanup utility will not affect any items not selected.

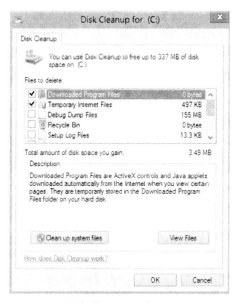

FIGURE 11-3 Disk Cleanup ready to go

In addition to the choices provided by Windows for files you might want to clean up regularly, you can clean up system files by tapping or clicking Clean Up System Files. When you select this option, additional groupings are displayed in the Files To Delete window:

* System Error Mini Dump Files
* Windows Defender

IMPORTANT **DO NOT DELETE SYSTEM FILES WITHOUT A REASON**

Deleting system files can cause data loss or problems with your computer if the files are not chosen with care. Be very careful about using Disk Cleanup to remove system files.

Any time you have made selections within Disk Cleanup to remove certain types of files, you can view the files within the groups you have selected by choosing the View Files button in the Disk Cleanup dialog box. This opens the highlighted folder in File Explorer to show you which files and folders will be deleted if that group of items is selected.

After you identify the types of files you want to include in a cleanup, you can perform a few other options from the Disk Cleanup utility. These options are found on the More Options tab of the dialog box; this tab appears only after you tap or click the Clean Up System Files button.

More Options for cleanup

On the More Options tab of the Disk Cleanup dialog box, you can remove the following items:

- Programs and features that you no longer use
- System restore points that you no longer need

Selecting the button to Clean Up Programs And Features launches the Programs and Features application by which you can remove any individual items you no longer need.

Selecting the Cleanup button in the System Restore And Shadow Copies section of the dialog box removes all the system restore points except the most recent restore point. The warning message shown in Figure 11-4 appears, and you must confirm that you want to delete the saved restore points.

> **IMPORTANT** **CONSIDER RECOVERY NEEDS BEFORE USING THIS OPTION**
>
> Select this option only if you are sure that no other restore points are needed for recovery.

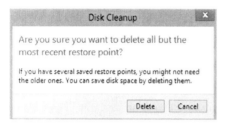

FIGURE 11-4 The Disk Cleanup dialog box, presented when choosing to clean up system restore points, as a warning and option to proceed

To remove these files, tap or click Delete in the dialog box. If you have frequently scheduled restore point snapshots, cleaning these out regularly could free up considerable storage space. The items on the More Options tab send you to other areas or delete files as soon as the options are chosen.

After you have selected all the groups of items you want to delete on the main tab of Disk Cleanup, click OK to delete the files and close the utility. If there are many files to clean out, this can take some time. On newer computers, the process will take considerably less time than it will on a computer that has not been cleaned up in some time.

Using Microsoft Drive Optimizer to organize data

Disk Defragmentation doesn't clean up files and folders on a computer as much as organize them into a more efficient layout on the disk. It does this by consolidating free space at the end of the disk and by ensuring that system files and similar files are grouped together. Doing this makes reads and writes from the disk much more efficient, providing a better overall experience for the user.

The Drive Optimizer application in Windows 8 analyzes and optimizes drives within your computer to ensure that they perform at the best level possible and are free of fragmentation. Figure 11-5 shows the Drive Optimizer.

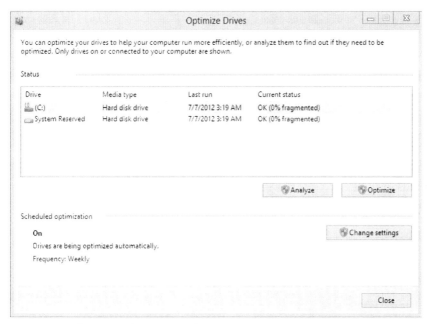

FIGURE 11-5   The Microsoft Drive Optimizer

Within the Drive Optimizer, the disks found in your computer are listed along with the type of media they use. You also see the last run time of the optimizer and the current status, which let you know whether the disks are fragmented as of the last run of the optimizer.

To determine whether a drive in your computer needs to be optimized, complete the following steps:

1. Select the drive you want to check for optimization.

2. Tap or click Analyze.

During this process, the Drive Optimizer window might flicker or disappear briefly. After the analysis is complete, the results are displayed in the same list as before but with a fresh date and time for the last run and the percentage of fragmentation found (if any).

After the analysis has completed, you can optimize your drives by completing the following steps:

1. Select the drive you want to optimize.

2. Tap or click Optimize.

You notice that the first step in optimization is to reanalyze the drive. This ensures that the optimization details are accurate before the relocation of files takes place. When the drive has been analyzed, the optimizer begins relocating files to ensure that they are placed in the best position for performance of the disk. The optimizer uses several passes to ensure the best file placement.

Sometimes, you will not be able to optimize a drive, such as in the following situations:

- Drives are in use by other applications.
- Drives are formatted with a file system other than NTFS, FAT, or FAT32.

There might also be occasions when a drive doesn't appear in the Drive Optimizer. This can indicate that the drive is not inserted into the computer (if the drive is removable) or that the drive has an error. Another utility covered later in this lesson, Check Disk (chkdsk), handles drive error checking.

You can also schedule the Drive Optimizer to analyze and optimize a computer. By default, a weekly schedule and the option for Windows to notify you if three consecutive scheduled items are missed are configured. This helps ensure that regular optimizations are performed and that they aren't being missed on portable systems that might be turned off when the schedule runs.

To modify the schedule Drive Optimizer uses, complete the following steps:

1. On the Drive Optimizer main screen, tap or click the Change Settings button under Scheduled Optimization (see Figure 11-5).

2. To change the frequency of the schedule, change the value in the Frequency drop-down list from Weekly to one of the following values:

    - Daily
    - Weekly
    - Monthly

3. To select drives to be included in scheduled optimization, tap or click Choose.

4. All drives found within the computer are selected for optimization by default (see Figure 11-6). Clear the check boxes next to any drives that should not be included.

5. To include new drives automatically, clear the Automatically Optimize New Drives check box.

6. Tap or click OK in the Optimize Drives dialog box.

7. Tap or click OK in the Optimize Drives Optimization Schedule dialog box.

This saves and configures the schedule for optimization and the drives against which the task is run.

Fragmentation can cause issues for any computer user, resulting in slow performance and frequent file and application hangs. Regular optimization of drives in a computer helps prevent issues and improves performance of a computer, extending the useful life of the device. By default, Windows 8 optimizes your drives on a weekly basis.

FIGURE 11-6 Scheduling drive optimization

Check Disk (chkdsk)

The disk optimizer and Disk Cleanup utilities provide methods to handle poorly performing disks within a computer; chkdsk (pronounced "check disk") performs disk repair to help correct problems with the drives themselves.

Chkdsk is a command-line utility designed to correct errors found in hard disks; Windows IT professionals have used it since MS-DOS. The utility previously required many of the operations it performed to be executed when the computer started. This ensured that the files chkdsk scanned would not be in use by other programs and that they could be modified or acted on by the utility.

This made a very lengthy startup process because chkdsk would run and work to repair the disk, depending on the selected options, and then Windows would start. In many cases, running chkdsk was helpful, but when weighed against the cost of startup time, it became a last resort.

Windows 8 has improved the performance of the chkdsk utility greatly. It can now perform most of its repair actions while the computer is online, avoiding the additional startup time. Table 11-1 outlines the optional command-line switches used with chkdsk.

TABLE 11-1 Chkdsk optional command-line switches

Command Line Switch	Description
Volume	Type the drive letter and a colon, mount point, or volume name to check.
Filename	Specify the files that should be checked for fragmentation (FAT or FAT32 file systems only).
/F	This switch fixes errors found on the disk.
/V	This switch displays the full path name of every file found (FAT or FAT32 only).
/R	This switch displays cleanup messages; if necessary, locates bad sectors; and recovers readable information. /F is implied when /scan is not specified on NTFS drives.
/L:size	This switch modifies the size of the log file for the operation to the specified number of kilobytes. If no size is specified, the current size is displayed (NTFS only).
/X	This switch forces a volume being scanned to dismount before being scanned if necessary. This closes all open handles to the volume.
/I	This switch checks index entries for a volume less intensely (NTFS only).
/C	This switch skips checking cycles within the folder structure (NTFS only).
/B	This switch re-evaluates clusters on the specified volume; it implies /R (NTFS only).
/scan	This switch scans the volume online (NTFS only).
/forceofflinefix	This switch disables online repair. Any items found will wait until the computer is restarted to be repaired. This requires /scan (NTFS only).
/perf	This switch uses more resources to complete a scan as quickly as possible. It requires /scan (NTFS only).
/spotfix	This switch runs spot fixes on the specified volume (NTFS only).
/sdcleanup	This switch performs garbage collection for unneeded security descriptor data; /F is implied (NTFS only).
/offlinescanandfix	This switch runs both the scan and fix operations offline.

Open a command prompt as an administrator. Run the command with no options by typing **chkdsk** on the command line; it will scan the drives in your computer and display the results. Using the utility without the /F switch executes it in read-only mode so no changes will be made to your system.

> *NOTE* **BENEFITS OF THE SPOTFIX FEATURE**
>
> Using the Spotfix feature can help correct issues on nonsystem volumes without the need to restart. This is monitored by the Action Center in Windows 8 to help ensure less downtime for a computer for maintenance.

Chkdsk runs in several phases when it executes a scan. The phases happen in the following order:

1. File system structure

2. File system indexes

3. Security descriptor

4. USN journals

First, the general *file system* is checked to ensure the absence of critical issues there. When that completes, the *indexes* for the files are checked and corrected (depending on the options). Last, the chkdsk utility examines *security descriptors*, to ensure that permissions and access objects for files are not out of order, and *USN journals*, where any changes to the volume are stored.

The scan findings are displayed in the command prompt window and provide a lot of information about what chkdsk found when it ran. Figure 11-7 shows results from a chkdsk scan.

FIGURE 11-7 Chkdsk scan data

When all the checks have been completed, the results of the process are displayed for review. Information reported includes:

- Verification of files on the disk

- Verification of file indexes

- Verification of security descriptors
- Information about total disk space available
- Total space used by files, indexes, logs, and bad sectors

Windows 8 automates many of the chkdsk operations to provide a proactive maintenance environment for your computer. The utility can be used from the command line to ensure optimal file performance, but in many cases Windows alerts you if a problem needs your attention.

The DiskPart utility

Chapter 2, "Installing and migrating to Windows 8," provides some information about the DiskPart utility, focusing on its use when installing and configuring computers running Windows 8. This section looks at the DiskPart utility in more detail, explaining the options available with DiskPart and how it might be used when performing maintenance on or troubleshooting a computer. The DiskPart utility and commands are designed to work directly with disks, volumes, and partitions. The functions provided in the Disk Management utility discussed earlier in this chapter can also be performed on the command line by using DiskPart.

When you launch DiskPart from a command line, you are prompted to allow or deny its use by User Account Control. Because DiskPart can make potentially harmful changes to your system, you are prompted to verify that it should be allowed to run. A new command prompt window opens that is running DiskPart.exe. When DiskPart is loaded, your cursor follows the DISKPART> prompt, which is shown in Figure 11-8.

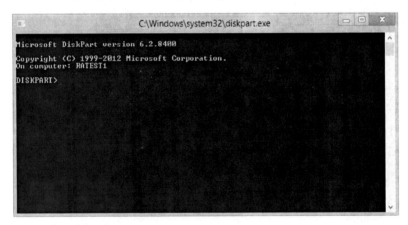

FIGURE 11-8 The DiskPart prompt

From this prompt, your command-line session can execute any of the DiskPart options and commands. Many commands, DIR for example, will produce different results within DiskPart than might appear when executing the command outside DiskPart. DIR returns a list of the commands available within the DISKPART prompt. This is shown in Figure 11-9.

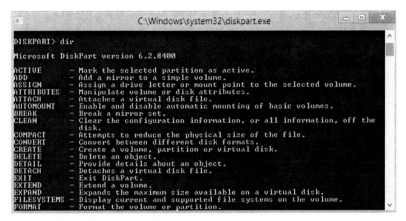

FIGURE 11-9 Executing DIR within the DiskPart prompt

Using DiskPart to manage and review existing items on your Windows 8–based computer can be a great starting point for adding or removing volumes and other potentially dangerous maneuvers.

> **NOTE** **GETTING HELP FOR COMMANDS**
>
> When working with DiskPart, help is available for all the commands by typing **help** before a command. For example, typing **Help Add** displays help items related to the Add command.

The following are the commands available in the DiskPart utility. For more information about these commands, visit *http://technet.microsoft.com/en-us/library/cc770877.aspx*.

- **Active**   Marks the selected partition as active
- **Add**   Adds a mirror to a simple volume
- **Assign**   Assigns a drive letter or mount point to the selected volume
- **Attach**   Attaches a virtual disk file
- **Attributes**   Manipulates the attributes of a disk or volume
- **Automount**   Enables or disables automatic mount for basic volumes
- **Break**   Breaks a mirror set
- **Clean**   Removes the configuration data or all data from a disk or volume
- **Compact**   Reduces the physical size of a file
- **Convert**   Converts a basic disk or volume to a dynamic disk or volume
- **Create**   Creates a partition, virtual disk, or volume
- **Delete**   Removes a partition, virtual disk, or volume
- **Detail**   Provides object details

- **Detach**   Disconnects a virtual disk file
- **Exit**   Quits DiskPart
- **Extend**   Extends a volume
- **Expand**   Expands a virtual disk file's maximum size
- **Filesystems**   Displays current and supported file systems on the selected volume
- **Format**   Formats the selected disk, partition, or volume
- **GPT**   Assigns attributes to the selected GPT partition
- **Help**   Displays help for a DiskPart command or a list of all commands
- **Import**   Imports a disk group
- **Inactive**   Sets the selected object to inactive
- **List**   Displays a list of objects
- **Merge**   Merges a child disk with its parent
- **Online**   Sets an offline object online
- **Offline**   Sets an online object offline
- **Recover**   Refreshes the state of all disks in a pack, attempts recovery on invalid disks, and resynchronizes mirrored and RAID-5 volumes
- **Rem**   Enables comment lines in scripts; takes no action on the command line
- **Remove**   Removes a drive letter or mount point
- **Repair**   Repairs a RAID-5 volume with a failed disk
- **Rescan**   Rescans the computer for new or changed disks or volumes
- **Retain**   Places a retained partition under a single volume
- **SAN**   Displays or sets the SAN policy for the currently started operating system
- **Select**   Shifts the context or focus of DiskPart to a disk, partition, volume, or other object
- **SetID**   Changes the partition type
- **Shrink**   Decreases the size of the selected volume
- **UniqueID**   Displays or sets the GUID Partition Table identifier or Master Boot Record signature of a disk

DiskPart performs a number of the same functions as the Disk Management console, providing a command-line alternative to the GUI. In addition to running operations directly at the command line, you can script DiskPart actions to automate the process of managing disks, volumes, and partitions.

Similar to the earlier example of extending the size of a volume with computer management, you can use DiskPart to shrink volumes where space might no longer be needed. For example, you added 250 MB to the documents volume earlier in this lesson. Now, you no longer need the additional space; perhaps a large number of files are no longer needed in your testing. By using DiskPart, you can reclaim this space. To do so, complete the following steps:

1. Open the Start screen.
2. Search for DiskPart.
3. Press Enter or tap or click the result returned to launch the utility.
4. Allow DiskPart when prompted for UAC by tapping or clicking Yes.
5. List the volumes available within the computer by typing **list volume** on the command line and pressing Enter.
6. From the list of volumes, select the volume to shrink by typing **select volume #** on the command line, where **#** is the number of the volume returned in the previous step. Press Enter.
7. Shrink the volume by 250 MB by typing **Shrink desired=250** on the command line and tapping or clicking Enter.
8. Type **Exit** on the command line and press Enter to close DiskPart.

> *IMPORTANT* **DISKPART MAKES CHANGES IMMEDIATELY**
>
> Shrinking volumes or partitions by using DiskPart happens almost immediately. Typing **Shrink** by itself on the command line will reduce the selected volume to the smallest available size.

 Quick check
- How can you connect to a virtual hard drive (VHD) file by using DiskPart?

Quick check answer
- The Attach command connects VHD files. Attach "x:\path to filename.vhd" attaches the virtual hard disk at that path.

Even though the DiskPart command-line tool can be scripted, it still requires you to work with one object at a time. When one operation completes, the script can move on to the next object. The following is an example of a script using DiskPart:

```
Select volume  1
Clean
Create partition primary size=300
Exit
```

This script selects volume 1 and cleans it, which removes all partitions and data from the disk. Then the script creates a 300-MB primary partition on volume 1.

To execute a script in DiskPart, type the following command:

```
diskpart -s <scriptfile>
```

Lesson summary

This lesson covered the following tools for disk management and usage:

- Using the Disk Management console
- Managing volumes, disks, and partitions by using DiskPart
- Using chkdsk
- Maximizing disk performance by using Disk Cleanup and the disk optimizer

Lesson review

Answer the following questions to test your knowledge of the information in this lesson. You can find the answers to these questions and explanations of why each answer choice is correct or incorrect in the "Answers" section at the end of this chapter.

1. A coworker called you because his computer was performing slowly, and he was not sure what was causing the issue. The performance of local reads and writes when accessing and saving documents is slow. Which utility can you use to improve overall performance of the local disk?

   A. chkdsk

   B. Disk optimizer

   C. DiskPart

   D. A new hard disk

2. Contoso uses many online applications to conduct business. Employees type orders into an online system, which requires no desktop application to be installed other than Microsoft Internet Explorer. Recently, some of the employees who have been using the online system for some time have mentioned problems getting the pages within the application to load correctly. Testing on several computers in the IT group reveals the same problem. Which utility can clean up old files stored by Internet Explorer?

   A. Recycle Bin

   B. Disk Cleanup

   C. Searching on the Start screen for files

   D. DiskPart

3. Roberto has called the help desk to ask about the new hard disk he requested for storing documents related to an accounting project. He cannot see the disk in Windows and is not sure whether it has been configured. The project is beginning the following Monday, and he would like to be sure the hard disk will be ready. Which actions

can you take to ensure that the disk is connected to the system and to expose it to Windows for Roberto? (Choose all that apply.)

A. Use computer management to view the disks connected to Roberto's computer and set the new partition online so it will appear.

B. Visit Roberto's workstation and install a new hard disk for his project data.

C. Use DiskPart to remove and reconfigure the existing partitions on Roberto's computer.

D. Use computer management to ensure that a new partition or volume has been created for use on this project.

Lesson 2: Working with file systems

Windows introduced the NTFS file system with the release of Windows NT in July 1993, and, although it has been modified, improved, and upgraded over the years, NTFS is still the primary file system for Windows today. Any data that exists for a file, from creation date to access control, is stored in the master file table within the file system as metadata. This makes accessing any data about any file much more efficient than keeping all the attributes and information with each stored file. This lesson focuses on NTFS and ways you can work with it in Windows 8.

After this lesson, you will be able to:

- Understand and use NTFS permissions.
- Manage and configure encryption.
- Audit Windows file systems.
- Enable quotas on NTFS volumes.

Estimated lesson time: 60 minutes

Security within the file system

One of the primary focuses of the NTFS file system is security. People who use Windows have at one time or another tried to open a file on the network and received an Access Denied message for that particular file. NTFS security enables administrators to ensure that only those who have permission to access certain files and locations can access them.

File system security within NTFS is an ongoing process because in many circumstances, security might need to be modified to meet the needs of an organization. The original configuration for a department's files can change over time, and NTFS must change with it.

NTFS assigns security through access control lists (ACLs); these lists contain access control entries (ACEs) that determine which entities have a certain type of access to a portion of the file system.

Access control lists can be one of two types:

- **Discretionary Access Control Lists (DACLs)**   These lists identify the entities that are allowed or denied access to a securable object within the file system.
- **System Access Control Lists (SACLs)**   These lists enable administrative logging of access attempts.

DACLs are the lists that determine whether your access to a file or folder is allowed or denied, whereas SACLs are the lists that help administrators monitor your access to those files. The use of SACLs and auditing are covered in the "Auditing access to securable objects by using SACLs" section later in this chapter.

The following example should help make DACLs a bit easier to understand.

Johanna and Mikhail are members of the operations group for City Power & Light. The operations group maintains files and folders of all the information needed to ensure that field maintenance crews and other teams have the information they need in the event of a power emergency. The operations group is a general collection of team members who help manage field maintenance teams. Operations team members must be able to read, write, and edit folders and files within the Operations folder, which lives on the City Power & Light company file server.

Other departments, such as customer care, need to view certain information regarding the field maintenance teams but do not edit it, whereas some departments might not need any access to the operations data.

With NTFS, configuring this access is easily achievable by using the built-in security provided by DACLs.

Figure 11-10 shows the default security information for the Operations folder. A few groups and other entries are added by default when a folder or file is created. These include:

- **Authenticated Users**   This group includes any users who have authenticated (signed in to) a domain in which the computer managing this object is a member, or the local computer if it is not a domain member. If access to a resource is not needed by any user account that has signed in, this group should be removed.
- **System**   This group is built in for the computer itself. The computer needs access to the objects on the system for management purposes. This group should not be removed.
- **Administrators**   This is a built-in group containing designated administrators for this computer. This group should not be removed.
- **Users**   This group includes users of the local computer or a domain in which this computer is a member and provides the members access to the object. If not all users of a computer or domain need access to this file or folder, this group should be removed.

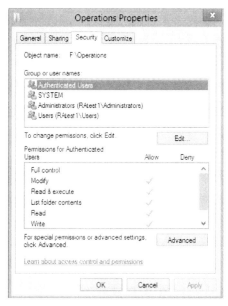

FIGURE 11-10 Security configuration for the Operations folder

Additional groups or even individual users can be added to the DACLs for any object contained within the NTFS file system. Adding and removing entries for a specific object and child objects beneath it are the basis for controlling security within the NTFS file system.

For the operations group example, Figure 11-10 shows that the Operations folder currently has only the built-in groups defined for its security.

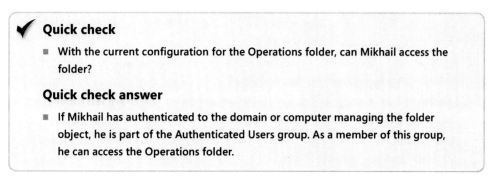

✔ **Quick check**

■ With the current configuration for the Operations folder, can Mikhail access the folder?

Quick check answer

■ If Mikhail has authenticated to the domain or computer managing the folder object, he is part of the Authenticated Users group. As a member of this group, he can access the Operations folder.

To ensure that the operations group has all the security needed to manage its departmental folder, the group would be added to the DACL for the Operations folder object. To add the operations group, complete the following steps:

1. Browse to the Operations folder.
2. Press and hold or right-click the folder.
3. Select Properties.
4. Select the Security tab.

5. Tap or click Edit.

6. In the Permissions For Operations dialog box, tap or click Add.

7. In the Select Users Or Groups dialog box, type the name of the user or group to add; in this case, type **Operations**.

> **NOTE** **LOCATIONS AND ENVIRONMENTS**
>
> Ensure that the location for the group is correct for your environment. If you are working in a domain environment, the location should be set to that of your domain.

8. Tap or click Check Names to verify the names of the groups or user accounts you have added.

9. Tap or click OK in the Select Users Or Groups dialog box.

10. To allow the ability to read, write to, and modify the Operations folder, select the check box next to Modify under the Allow column heading.

11. Tap or click OK to apply these settings to the folder and save the DACL.

> **IMPORTANT** **THE DENY PERMISSION OVERRIDES OTHER PERMISSIONS**
>
> Discretionary access lists are very specific for the Deny permission. If you specify that a group or user account is denied access to an object, that user account or members of that group will not have access to that object regardless of the permissions granted to any other groups with access to that object. If you are explicitly denied access to an object, you will not have access to the object. Use Deny permissions with caution.

Common collections of permissions make managing access to file system objects easier to understand. The common permission sets are:

- **Full Control** Allows complete access to objects, including management permissions and the ability to take ownership of an object.

- **Modify** Allows editing, visibility, and deletion of objects (assumes Read & Execute, List Folder Contents, Read, and Write permissions).

- **Read & Execute** Allows other object types such as application files to be opened or executed (assumes Read permission).

- **List Folder Contents** Allows items within folders to be viewed (assumes Read and Read & Execute permissions).

- **Read** Allows file and folder objects to be opened.

- **Write** Allows creation and editing of objects.

- **Special Permissions** Contains any combination of permissions that an administrator wants. This group of permissions is managed by clicking the Advanced button on the Security tab.

Although these groupings comprise common permission sets, you can see the entire list of available permissions by tapping or clicking the Advanced button. In the Advanced Security Settings dialog box, the currently assigned permissions for the object are displayed, as shown in Figure 11-11.

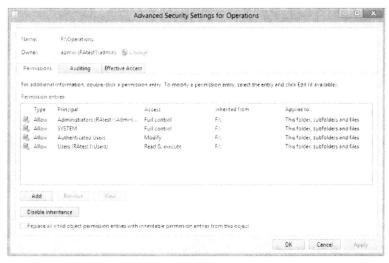

FIGURE 11-11   Advanced Security Settings

If you need to configure additional advanced permissions, tap or click the Add button in this dialog box to open the Permission Entry dialog box for the selected object. Here you can manage both basic and advanced permissions for the object. The Permission Entry dialog box is shown in Figure 11-12.

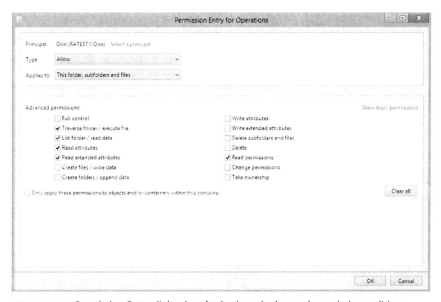

FIGURE 11-12   Permission Entry dialog box for basic and advanced permissions editing

A *principal* is a user account or group to which security and permissions can be assigned. To configure permissions from the Permission Entry dialog box, complete the following steps:

1. Tap or click the Select A Principal link at the top of the dialog box.

2. Type the account or group name with which you want to work and tap or click Check Names to verify that the account exists.

3. Tap or click OK to add the selected account or group as the security principal.

4. Select the type of permission to assign, Allow or Deny, by using the Type list.

5. Specify the objects to which this permission will apply by using the Applies To list; the following options are available for folder objects:

   - This Folder Only

   - This Folder, Subfolders, And Files

   - This Folder And Subfolders

   - This Folder And Files

   - Subfolders And Files Only

   - Subfolders Only

   - Files Only

If you are applying permissions to individual files, the Permission Entry dialog box appears slightly different. You can select either basic permissions or advanced permissions. To select permissions for files, select the check boxes for the permissions to assign. The basic permissions for files are as follows:

- Full Control

- Modify

- Read & Execute

- Read

- Write

Advanced Permissions include the following:

- Full Control

- Traverse Folder/Execute File

- List Folder/Read Data

- Read Attributes

- Read Extended Attributes

- Create Files/Write Data

- Create Folder/Append Data

- Write Attributes

- Write Extended Attributes

- Delete
- Read Permissions
- Change Permissions
- Take Ownership

In Advanced Permissions, some of these options are selected by default because advanced permissions are combined to create the basic permission sets.

> **NOTE   DOCUMENT PERMISSIONS TO AVOID POTENTIAL PROBLEMS**
>
> Working with permissions can be an interesting project. Because it is possible to isolate any user completely, including administrators, from files and folders, be very deliberate when considering permissions. Taking notes about current permissions and the permissions being assigned is a good idea until you become accustomed to working with permissions and fully understand the effect they can have on objects.

Inheritance and cumulative effectiveness

The combinations of permissions are complex. Before you consider them, think about the inheritance of permissions and the fact that permissions for user accounts and groups have a cumulative effect. This alone can be confusing.

Inheritance allows permissions to cascade downward to child objects from a parent object. For example, if the Operations folder also contains a Schedules folder and a Safety Documents folder, you could allow permissions assigned to the Operations folder to be inherited by both those child folders. This would assign the permissions from Operations to those folders and their files.

Inheritance makes assigning permissions much easier because it is not always necessary to assign permissions directly. However, relying on inheritance can produce unexpected results when accessing these objects.

Because Mikhail is a member of the operations group, he is allowed Full Control on the Operations folder by default, and he inherits the same permissions on the child objects within operations. Because he has volunteered to participate in a project with the customer service team to help ease their workload, you add him to the customer service group to allow him access to the needed materials for the project.

Customer service associates do not need access to operations and, to ensure that they do not access operations materials, the group is denied access to operations.

Removing Mikhail from the customer service group will restore the proper access to operations. This is an example of the power of the Deny permission. It takes effect regardless of other permissions an account might be assigned.

A better method for handling removal of access might be to allow no permissions to an object. This way, the security principal has no permissions and cannot access an object directly but might be granted access based on group memberships and their permission assignment.

> ✓ **Quick check**
>
> ■ When Mikhail is added to the customer service group, what access to operations files and folders will he have?
>
> **Quick check answer**
>
> ■ Mikhail will be denied access to operations because the customer service group is explicitly denied access to the Operations folder and subfolders.

Cumulative application means that all the permissions a user account or group might have are evaluated to determine the access allowed. If Maria belongs to the operations group, the schedulers group, and the human resources group, all the access permissions assigned to each of these groups will affect Maria because she is a member of each group. In addition, any permission assigned directly to her user account is evaluated.

For example, Orin is a member of the schedulers group, which can view and read items in the Operations and Schedules folders. He can view documents within the Schedules folder but cannot edit them. This group also has List Folder Contents as the only permission assigned for the Operations folder.

One of the operations managers asks Orin to help with a project for a few months. The project involves updating safety documentation for the operations team to ensure that the latest information is available. When Orin accepts this project, his account is placed in the operations safety group, which can add and remove documents from the Safety folder within Operations. The group can also change items in the Schedules folder to allow for the addition of training on new safety material.

> ✓ **Quick check**
>
> ■ After taking on this project, what access does Orin have for items in the Schedules folder?
>
> **Quick check answer**
>
> ■ Orin can edit the items in the Schedules folder because he belongs to a group that has this permission, and his account is not explicitly denied access to the folder.

Deny permissions are processed before other permissions. After that, permissions are cumulative. The overall access to items can be tricky to understand. Fortunately, a tool in the Advanced Security Settings dialog box can help. The Effective Access tab displays the permissions currently applied to the specified user account or group. This considers any access to an object, direct or inherited, and displays the cumulative permissions for a security principal on the selected object. The Effective Access tab is shown in Figure 11-13.

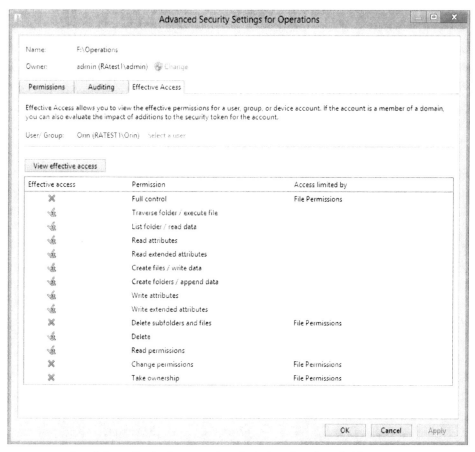

FIGURE 11-13 Permissions effective for a security principal on the selected object

Taking ownership

A security principal who has permission to take ownership of a file or folder can grant himself or herself the right to change permissions on the object in addition to having full control of the object. Taking ownership of files and folders might be necessary when the original owner of the object has left the organization and others within the organization need access to the object. Generally, taking ownership is useful for this type of recovery. The primary user of an object does not need to be the object's owner.

Understanding share-level permissions

This chapter is about NTFS and security provided by the file system, but other permissions should be mentioned because they can cause unintended results if they are not taken into consideration. Share permissions determine which user accounts or groups can access an object or group of objects over a network share. If the Share permissions are not configured, access to resources across the network might not function as needed.

> **NOTE NTFS PERMISSIONS AND SHARE-LEVEL PERMISSIONS**
>
> If you intend to manage security by using NTFS permissions and do not want to worry about share-level permissions, share-level permissions can be set to allow the Everyone group Full Control at the share level. In this way, NTFS security is the primary method for providing security. These permissions are not cumulative with NTFS permissions, but, when not configured, they can be an interesting issue to troubleshoot.

Auditing access to securable objects by using SACLs

After the security of discretionary access lists is in place, NTFS allows only those user accounts or groups with the correct permissions to access objects. However, others within an environment might attempt to access files or folders. Often, being able to review or audit these access attempts can help ensure that those within the organization who need access to an object can get it and that those who do not need access cannot get it.

For example, many organizations have documents containing personal information or human resources–related information about their employees. Outside the legal and human resources departments, not many employees need access to this information.

When you use SACLs to audit objects within an environment, entries are recorded in the Windows event logs when events occur. If Orin attempts to access files within the Human Resources folder, Windows can write that attempt to the event log. Upon review, you will see that these access attempts happened, when they happened, and which user account was involved.

> **NOTE WHEN TO AUDIT**
>
> Auditing for an object must be enabled for any actions to be logged. Consider carefully what you want to audit. Too much auditing will produce more information than is useful, whereas too little will not provide all the information necessary to monitor correctly what is occurring within your environment.

Auditing is configured in the Advanced Security Settings dialog box for an object and requires you to be an administrator or to have the appropriate permissions for the selected object to enable auditing. Figure 11-14 shows the Auditing tab of the Advanced Security Settings dialog box.

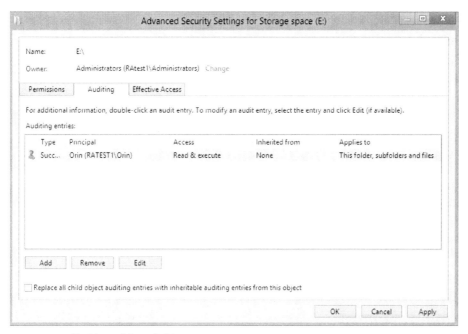

FIGURE 11-14 Enable auditing of objects

Configuring auditing is very similar in Windows 8 to configuring security permissions for an object. The only difference is that you are configuring which permissions (or actions on an object) to audit rather than access to an object. To configure auditing for an object, complete the following steps:

1. Access the Auditing tab of the Advanced Security Settings dialog box for the object to be audited.

2. Tap or click Add.

3. Select a security principal to audit.

4. Select the type of access attempts to include:

   - **All**   Records all access attempts by this security principal for this object

   - **Fail**   Records all failed attempts by this security principal to access this object

   - **Success**   Records all successful attempts by this security principal to access this object

5. Select the permissions to audit.

> *NOTE* **PERMISSIONS FOR AUDITING**
>
> When selecting permissions to include in auditing, these permissions determine the type of access that is audited for success or failure. If Read is selected, attempts to read an object will be audited for success or failure.

6. Tap or click OK to save the access control entry.

7. Tap or click OK in the Advanced Security Settings dialog box.

After security auditing has been configured for an object, Windows begins creating entries in the Security event log when conditions that meet the auditing settings are triggered.

Using auditing can be extremely helpful but, when auditing is overused, it can be difficult to manage. When you are considering auditing, keep in mind any policies put in place by your organization and work to ensure that the items audited are the items you need to know about rather than auditing everything. Many companies have policies covering auditing and access controls to ensure that they are used appropriately. This includes controls such as authorization of auditing particular information and reviewing collected information, and which information and access should be audited when particular events occur. Different events, such as litigation or investigation into employee actions internally, might require auditing to be handled differently.

Understanding Encrypting File System

Windows and NTFS provide a method for each person using a computer to encrypt his or her files, folders, and drives. Encrypting File System (EFS) is a method used to encrypt files and determine who can access the files. No administrative privileges are needed to use EFS. To enable it for a folder, complete the following steps:

1. Locate the folder in File Explorer.

2. Press and hold or right-click the folder to be encrypted.

3. Select Properties.

4. On the General tab of the Properties dialog box, tap or click Advanced.

5. Select the Encrypt Contents To Secure Data check box.

6. Tap or click OK in the Advanced Attributes dialog box.

7. Tap or click Apply in the Properties dialog box.

8. Tap or click OK.

When the folder has been encrypted, a balloon appears, reminding you to back up your encryption key for the folder. Without that key, you cannot access the files or folders that are encrypted with EFS. The encryption key is stored with your user account information in the operating system; all the files you encrypt with EFS use the same key per computer.

To back up the private key for your EFS-encrypted files, complete the following steps:

1. Open a blank Microsoft Management Console by searching for MMC on the Start screen.

2. Select File and Add/Remove Snap-In.

3. Select the Certificates snap-in and tap or click Add.

4. Select My User Account as the scope for which this snap-in will manage certificates.

5. Tap or click Finish.

6. Tap or click OK.

7. In the Console window, expand Certificates - Current User.

8. Expand Personal.

9. Select Certificates.

10. In the results pane, locate the certificate with Encrypting File System listed in the Intended Purposes column and tap or click to select it.

11. Under the actions pane for the selected certificate, select More Actions.

12. Select All Tasks.

13. Tap or click Export.

    This opens the Certificate Export Wizard. Click Next.

14. Select the Yes, Export The Private Key option and tap or click Next.

15. Select the format for the export file as Personal Information Exchange.

16. Select the option to include all certificates in the path if possible.

17. Tap or click Next.

18. Select the check box to use a password with the file.

19. Type the password.

20. Confirm the password.

21. Tap or click Next.

22. Specify the file name and path for the export and tap or click Next.

23. Review the information about the export.

24. Tap or click Finish to export the certificate and key.

25. Tap or click OK in the Export Successful dialog box.

SECURITY ALERT **KEEPING THE EFS KEY**

It is a good idea to export the EFS key to an easy-to-remember location on your computer. After the export is complete, locate the file and copy it to a location from which you can easily access the file if needed, such as a removable USB drive.

Encryption is an easy way to enable each person to secure his or her files and folders on a computer. For some, this can provide peace of mind when storing files that contain sensitive information on any computer. Remember, however, that the key file automatically decrypts files upon opening for the user who encrypted them; if others gain access to that user account, the files could be compromised.

BitLocker

Microsoft BitLocker is a whole-disk encryption method available in Windows 8 Professional and Enterprise editions. Like EFS, BitLocker encrypts files to make their access secure by the owner of the file. It differs from EFS because it works at the disk level, whereas EFS allows files to be selected and encryption applied to the folders or files. In many cases, BitLocker is easier to configure because it is enabled per disk or volume.

BitLocker is ideal for mobile devices such as laptops and tablets because the entire device can be misplaced. With BitLocker enabled on these devices, data cannot be decrypted by whomever has possession of the mobile device.

Using BitLocker requires either a Trusted Platform Module (TPM) to exist on the computer or a policy to be applied that allows BitLocker to run without TPM.

To configure BitLocker, complete the following steps:

1. From Control Panel, open BitLocker Drive Encryption.
2. Select the drive on which you would like to enable BitLocker.
3. Select the Turn On BitLocker link.

    BitLocker encrypts the volume, which might take some time.

In addition to BitLocker, Windows 8 supports BitLocker To Go, which applies BitLocker encryption to removable volumes. This makes data on removable media inaccessible without the encryption key.

NOTE **USING BITLOCKER WITHOUT TPM**

Computers and devices without TPM capabilities can also use BitLocker. To do this, Group Policy needs to be enabled to allow for additional security. Using additional authentication, such as a USB key with an encryption key stored on it, enables you to prove to Windows and BitLocker who you are and that you should be allowed access to this data. The policy needed can be found in Computer Configuration\Windows Components\BitLocker Drive Encryption\Operating System Drives\Require Additional Authentication At Startup.

Working with quotas

Working with disk quotas can provide a way to ensure that certain volumes allow each person using the computer to use only a predetermined amount of space. Consider the following example.

Fabio and Maria work for Tailspin Toys as summer interns within the marketing department. Fabio works on Mondays, Wednesdays, and Saturday mornings, whereas Maria works Tuesdays, Thursdays, and Friday afternoons, and they share the same workstation to conserve resources.

The computer Fabio and Maria use has an additional disk in it to contain their files. The disk has a maximum storage size of 1 TB and is backed up to the network every night at 10 P.M. To divide the resource evenly and ensure that one of the interns does not consume too much space, assigning quotas can allocate a certain amount of space to each intern.

You can assign quotas to entire volumes only. Each user receives an amount of storage space equal to the quota limit assigned. To configure quotas, complete the following steps:

1. Access the desktop and open File Explorer.

2. Press and hold or right-click the drive or volume on which you plan to configure quotas, and then select Properties.

3. On the Quota tab, tap or click Show Quota Settings and tap or click Yes at the UAC prompt. The Quota Settings dialog box is shown in Figure 11-15.

FIGURE 11-15 The Quota Settings dialog box, in which settings are defined

4. Select the Enable Quota Management check box to turn on quotas for the volume.

5. If you want to deny space to user accounts that exceed the quota, select the Deny Disk Space To Users Exceeding Quota Limit check box.

6. Choose one of the following options to limit storage space for new users on a volume:

   ■ Do Not Limit Disk Usage

   ■ Limit Disk Space To XX, where XX is the number of units by which to limit disk space

   When you enter a limit for a quota, you also need to choose a unit of storage for the quota. Available units are:

   ■ Kilobytes (KB)

   ■ Megabytes (MB)

   ■ Gigabytes (GB)

   ■ Terabytes (TB)

   ■ Petabytes (PB)

   ■ Exabytes (EB)

7. Choose the warning level that Windows should use for the quota.

8. Select the unit of storage for the warning.

9. If you want to use an event log for tracking quota limits, select the Log Event When A User Exceeds Their Quota Limit check box.

10. If you want to use an event log for tracking warning levels, select the Log Event When A User Exceeds Their Warning Level check box.

11. Tap or click OK to save the settings for quotas for this volume.

Now that a volume has been configured to use quotas, you can enable quotas for user accounts on the computer. To do so, from the Quotas tab of the Properties dialog box for a volume, tap or click the Enable Quotas button. The results are shown in Figure 11-16.

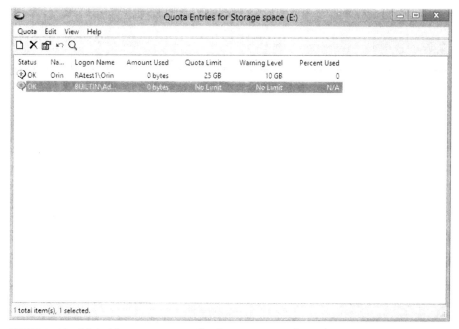

FIGURE 11-16   A list of the user accounts that have quotas configured

Working with quotas for user accounts

In the Quota Entries For Volume dialog box, you can:

- Add quotas to a user account.
- Modify the quota warning and hard limits for a selected user.
- Delete quota entries.
- Import quota entries from a file.
- Export quota entries to a file.
- Search for quota entries by user account.

When modifying quota settings for a user account, if no quota settings are configured for the volume you have selected, you cannot set the quota limit, but you can configure the warning limit.

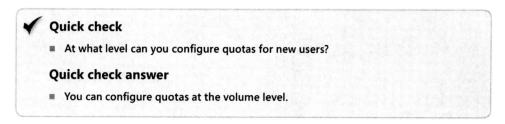

> ✔ **Quick check**
>
> - At what level can you configure quotas for new users?
>
> **Quick check answer**
>
> - You can configure quotas at the volume level.

Using quotas can help you efficiently manage storage available to a group of people. Working with quotas helps keep individuals from consuming all the available storage space by allocating only a certain portion of the space to each person.

Lesson summary

- Use disk quotas to control storage consumption.
- Keep information secure by using BitLocker on laptops and portable disks to ensure only authorized access to information.
- Use auditing as company policy allows to monitor access to resources in an environment.
- Use Share and NTFS permissions to control access to resources in an environment.

Lesson review

Answer the following questions to test your knowledge of the information in this lesson. You can find the answers to these questions and explanations of why each answer choice is correct or incorrect in the "Answers" section at the end of this chapter.

1. You are a network administrator for Tailspin Toys, and one of the department managers, Jorge, has contacted you because he can no longer access files within the New Projects folder. His access to these files was working as recently as two days ago. What actions can you take to correct this issue and restore Jorge's access to the New Projects folder?

    A. Review the permissions of the New Projects folder to ensure that Jorge has access. Then review the groups that have access to the folder and the membership within these groups to ensure that Jorge is not a member of any groups that have been denied access.

    B. Re-create Jorge's user account and reassign the permissions.

    C. Rename Jorge's user account to remove permissions.

    D. Rename the New Projects folder to reset all access permissions.

2. You are implementing an upgraded storage solution for your organization. The management team wants to ensure not only that all employees receive a 10-GB allotment of storage space for their documents but also that they cannot exceed this limit. How can you ensure that the management team's requirements are met?

    A. Enable auditing on the disk or volume containing the user directories.

    B. Enable quotas with a maximum limit of 10 GB on the volume containing user directories before moving any data to the environment.

    C. Configure encryption on the files for each user and back up the private key to ensure that directory sizes remain within the acceptable limit.

    D. Configure individual volumes for each employee that are 10 GB in size.

3. Your manager is leaving for a trip to see other locations within your organization and wants to be sure that all his data on the laptop he is taking with him is encrypted so it cannot be read by others who might ask to use his computer while in the office. Which settings can you enable to ensure that the files are protected?

   A. Ensure that all the files that need to be secured are kept in a single location within the manager's user profile.

   B. Configure EFS encryption while your manager is signed in to the computer and back up the EFS key to an external disk right away.

   C. Ask your manager to save all files to a USB disk because that ensures that no files are stored on the computer.

   D. Configure BitLocker on your manager's laptop to secure data on the computer.

Lesson 3: Introducing Storage Spaces

Microsoft has introduced another exciting feature into Windows 8 and Server 2012, called *Storage Spaces*. This lesson discusses Storage Spaces in Windows 8, explaining what it does, how it works, and how to set it up.

After this lesson, you will be able to:

- Understand how Storage Spaces works.
- Create storage spaces by using removable media.
- Manage storage spaces across computers running Windows 8.

Estimated lesson time: 45 minutes

What is Storage Spaces?

Storage Spaces is the new storage virtualization and management technology Microsoft has developed. The concept of Storage Spaces has been around for quite some time; Windows Home Server used Drive Extender to make external storage manageable within Windows Home Server, and Storage Spaces takes a cue from this technology.

The idea behind Storage Spaces is to allow nonidentical disks to be managed as a single array by Windows. This reduces the need for companies to purchase traditional and expensive storage arrays to grow their storage infrastructure or add extra storage for a project. Instead, an organization can purchase a set of disks in an enclosure, referred to as just a bunch of disks, or JBOD, and connect them to Windows. When connected, a storage pool can be created to work with all those disks. From the pool of disks, volumes are created and mounted by the operating system. Windows then manages the disk pool and volumes created from it as a traditional storage system might, removing some of the overhead and complexity from enterprise-grade storage.

In Windows 8, a storage space can be created from a collection of removable USB disks. When created, new disks can be added to the disk pool at any time, allowing the space to grow as needed. When data is saved to a volume that exists in a storage space, the information is spread across all the disks within the pool to ensure redundancy.

Creating storage spaces

To create a storage space, you first must define a disk pool. A disk pool is a collection of disks that belong to the storage space. In the disk pool, you create a storage space and volumes Windows uses. To create a disk pool and storage space, complete the following steps:

1. Search for Storage Spaces, tap or click Settings, and then tap or click Storage Spaces. Alternatively, access Control Panel, tap or click System And Security, and then tap or click Storage Spaces.

2. Tap or click Create A New Pool And Storage Space. At the User Account Control prompt, tap or click Allow.

3. Select the drives to use as part of this storage space; options can include the following:

   - Virtual Hard Disks
   - Removable USB Storage
   - Additional Internal Storage

4. After all the disks have been selected, tap or click Create Pool.

5. Enter a name for your storage space (see Figure 11-17).

Enter a name, resiliency type, and size for the storage space

Name and drive letter

Name: Storage space

Drive letter: F: ∨

Resiliency:

Resiliency type: Two-way mirror   ∨

ⓘ A two-way mirror storage space writes two copies of your data, helping to protect you from a single drive failure. A two-way mirror storage space requires at least two drives.

Size

Total pool capacity: 198   GB

Available pool capacity: 195   GB

Size (maximum):   99.2   GB   ∨

Including resiliency: 198   GB

ⓘ A storage space can be larger than the amount of available capacity in the storage pool. When you run low on capacity in the pool, you can add more drives.

Create storage space   Cancel

FIGURE 11-17 The Create A Storage Space window, in which the details of the storage space are configured

6. Select a drive letter to assign.

7. Select the Resiliency type. Options include:

   ▪ **Simple**   Requires only one drive and does not protect from any failure.

   ▪ **Two-Way Mirror**   Requires at least two disks because it stores two copies of your data to protect it from a single-drive failure.

   ▪ **Three-Way Mirror**   Writes three copies of your data across five or more drives. This type can survive a two-disk failure.

   ▪ **Parity**   Requires three or more drives and writes data with parity information across these drives. This type protects your data from a single-drive failure.

   Depending on the Resiliency type you select, the total pool capacity changes to accommodate your choice.

8. Enter the maximum size for the storage space.

   Windows calculates the maximum based on the number of disks in the pool, the available size of the disks, and the resiliency selected.

NOTE **MAXIMUM SIZE OF A STORAGE SPACE**

A storage space is a virtual representation of available space. A storage space can be thinly provisioned, which allows for additional storage to be added as needed to accommodate the growth of a storage space.

9. Tap or click Create Storage Space to apply your choices and create the space.

During the creation process, the wizard will format your storage space and attach it to Windows. After this completes, you see your storage pool and statistics about the storage spaces it contains under the Manage Storage Spaces heading in Control Panel, as shown in Figure 11-18.

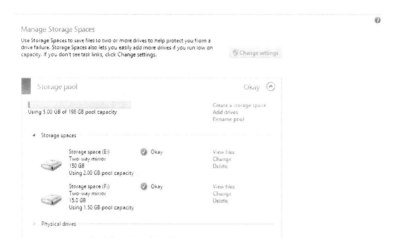

FIGURE 11-18 Manage Storage Spaces window

Storage virtualization makes this work

The storage presented to Windows as part of a storage space is a virtual representation of physical disks. This can be confusing, but it works similarly to logical disks and partitions within a disk, which were discussed in Lesson 1, "Managing disks and storage." The biggest difference is that Windows virtualizes the disk itself, so one pool of storage can contain several physical disks.

When disks are added to a pool, Windows considers these disks to be a single storage entity. The entire amount of space across all physical disks becomes available, minus any space needed to accommodate the resiliency settings chosen. Storage spaces are created on top of that pool of aggregated storage. Because they are created across multiple disks, they can provide improved performance and recoverability by adding more disks to the pool.

When a space is created and a drive letter assigned, Windows 8 sees this drive as one volume and writes data to it as though it was one disk. The work is done behind the scenes to manage the logical disk pool and physical disks included in it.

Benefits of Storage Spaces

The biggest benefit of Storage Spaces is data recoverability and the ability of a properly configured storage space to survive disk failure within the pool. Cost and affordability are also big benefits for those intending to increase the capacity of their storage without buying expensive and specialized equipment.

An additional benefit of this configuration is metadata recording. When a disk pool is created across disks and a storage space built on that pool, metadata about the disk pool and the storage space are written to all member disks. In this way, the storage space can survive a system failure.

For example, suppose you have configured a storage space by using a disk pool of two USB removable drives. After the space has been in use for some time, you get a new laptop because there is money in the budget for one. When Windows 8 is configured on the new laptop, you can connect the USB disks to the computer, and the storage space you created earlier, along with the disk pool configuration and any data stored on the space, is ready to use very quickly. This is possible because of the metadata written to any disks used in creating a storage space.

Storage Spaces is an affordable method for enabling both organizations and individuals to increase their capacity as needed for a relatively small price tag. Keep in mind that this feature is not a replacement for good backup and recovery solutions. No matter where your data is stored, it should be backed up as frequently as necessary to meet your company's requirements.

Lesson summary

- Create disk pools to contain the storage space.
- Configure resiliency across multiple disks for the storage space.
- Understand that Storage Spaces uses metadata to keep all information intact.

Lesson review

Answer the following questions to test your knowledge of the information in this lesson. You can find the answers to these questions and explanations of why each answer choice is correct or incorrect in the "Answers" section at the end of this chapter.

1. Your boss is headed on safari for a month in Africa and has asked whether there is a good way to ensure that he can store the photos he takes on vacation on his Windows 8–based notebook for later editing. Because you have worked on this laptop before, you know it has a good internal hard disk, but that keeping only one copy of

data might be risky. You want to recommend configuring a storage space. What is the minimum number of disks you should suggest he purchase to provide the best redundancy with the fewest disks?

A. Four disks

B. Two disks

C. One disk

D. Forty-two disks

2. Anna, one of your coworkers, has been curious about Storage Spaces since discovering it in Control Panel on her Windows 8–based computer. To try out the feature, Anna configured a disk pool and storage space on a few USB removable disks she had. Now that things are working better than she expected, she is curious about metadata. What does metadata enable a storage space to do?

A. Because metadata exists for both the storage space and the disk pool on each disk used to create the disk pool, it can aid in searching documents stored on the space.

B. Because metadata exists for both the storage space and the disk pool on each disk used to create the disk pool, it enables disk pools and spaces from other computers to behave as a contiguous space when attached to a new computer capable of using Storage Spaces.

C. Metadata makes the storage space more resilient and less prone to failure.

D. Metadata optimizes the storage space and makes it less prone to fragmentation.

Practice exercises

Managing storage in Windows is a bigger part of managing a Windows environment than you might think. The exercises in this practice use storage optimization tools in Windows 8 and Storage Spaces.

Exercise 1: Use disk optimizer

In this exercise, you work with the disk optimizer to schedule regular maintenance on the disks in your computer. Understanding disk optimization can help you keep your computer functioning at satisfactory levels well into the future.

1. Open the disk optimizer.

2. Select Change Settings.

3. Select the Run On A Schedule check box.

4. In the Frequency list, select the most appropriate option for your computer.

5. Select the Notify Me If Three Consecutive Scheduled Runs Are Missed check box.

6. Choose the disks to include by clicking the Choose button.

7. Include the Operating System disk.

8. Select Automatic Optimization Of New Drives.

9. Tap or click OK.

10. Tap or click OK in the Optimize Drives dialog box.

11. Tap or click Close in the Optimize Drives dialog box to close the disk optimizer.

Exercise 2: Configure Storage Spaces

Storage Spaces is the exciting new tool in Windows storage and storage management. Because this new feature will be around for some time, it is included here to increase your overall understanding of Storage Spaces.

1. Open the Storage Spaces Control Panel application.

2. Create a new storage space on an existing pool by choosing the option under Storage Pool.

3. Select a drive letter and type a name for the new storage space.

4. Choose the appropriate resiliency settings for your storage space.

5. Enter the necessary size after reviewing the recommended values.

   Question: When creating a storage space, can the maximum size be greater than the amount of physical storage available?

   Answer: Yes. Because the storage space is a virtual disk, the size of the disk can exceed the size of the disk pool. Remember that as the physical storage runs low, new storage must be added to the disk pool.

6. Tap or click Create Storage Space.

Suggested practice exercises

The following additional practice exercises are designed to give you more opportunities to practice what you've learned and to help you successfully master the lessons presented in this chapter. To complete the suggested practice exercises, you need at least two removable USB hard drives. They do not need to be large.

- **Exercise 1**   Create a storage space on a disk pool built on removable disks. Move the disks to another computer to ensure that the storage space can survive a system failure.

- **Exercise 2**   Using chkdsk, find and repair any errors on your computer's primary disk. Were any reboot requirements needed to complete the task?

Answers

This section contains the answers to the lesson review questions in this chapter.

Lesson 1

1. **Correct answer: B**

   A. **Incorrect:** Chkdsk looks for errors on the disk; it does not provide performance improvements only.

   B. **Correct:** Disk optimizer helps defragment your computer's drives and organize files in an optimal way to improve performance.

   C. **Incorrect:** DiskPart manages partitions, disks, and volumes; it does not work with performance tuning.

   D. **Incorrect:** Although a new hard disk might improve performance, it does not provide optimizations to improve the functionality of the computer other than increasing overall storage space.

2. **Correct answer: B**

   A. **Incorrect:** Recycle Bin is just a place to store deleted items until they can be permanently removed.

   B. **Correct:** Disk Cleanup can help remove many files that can cause performance issues on a computer, including temporary Internet files.

   C. **Incorrect:** To locate individual files for removal, even by using the search function, can be extremely time-consuming. Using available utilities expedites the process.

   D. **Incorrect:** DiskPart enables deletion of an entire partition or volume, not just of the temporary Internet files.

3. **Correct answers: A and D**

   A. **Correct:** Disk Management can help you perform many actions related to the disks within a computer. Because it can connect to local and remote computers, it is the most appropriate choice.

   B. **Incorrect:** Because the data should be stored somewhere it can be backed up and tested, installing local hardware in the computer would not be an optimal solution.

   C. **Incorrect:** DiskPart can remove and configure partitions but cannot connect remotely to Roberto's computer without the use of another tool.

   D. **Correct:** Using computer management to ensure that the volumes or partitions exist will also help Roberto access the disk.

Lesson 2

1. **Correct answer: A**

   A. **Correct:** Making sure that Jorge has all the permissions he needs is the best way to ensure access, but checking to ensure that he is not explicitly denied access is also a good step.

   B. **Incorrect:** Re-creating Jorge's user account would require additional work to reassign the permissions needed for the New Projects folder and all other permissions that his user account had.

   C. **Incorrect:** Renaming Jorge's account would not change the security identifier for the object. This would have no effect on the permissions assigned to the object.

   D. **Incorrect:** Renaming the folder does not modify its permissions or change security.

2. **Correct answer: B**

   A. **Incorrect:** Enabling auditing reveals which accounts are using which objects and permissions to access those objects.

   B. **Correct:** Using quotas for all the user accounts that will be receiving space on the new storage ensures that each employee receives only 10 GB of disk space.

   C. **Incorrect:** Encrypting the files ensures that no other people can access them but does not ensure that the directory does not grow past 10 GB.

   D. **Incorrect:** Creating individual volumes would require a great deal of maintenance and administrative effort to ensure that each employee received his or her storage space.

3. **Correct answer: D**

   A. **Incorrect:** Profile folders are secured, but anyone with administrator permissions on the local machine or even in the domain environment can access the files.

   B. **Incorrect:** Encrypting the file and backing up the private key is the best way to ensure that only the employees who need to see a file are able to see it.

   C. **Incorrect:** Although saving all files to a USB disk might help with an offline backup, the documents stored on the USB disk are not encrypted and are kept only for that user account.

   D. **Correct:** Configuring BitLocker on the computer ensures that all information stored on the device is encrypted. This eliminates the need to locate and encrypt all files and folders your manager uses.

Lesson 3

1. Correct answer: B

    A. **Incorrect:** Although you can use a single disk to create a pool and a storage space, this provides no redundancy to ensure that the photographs are safe during the trip.

    B. **Correct:** Two disks will provide resiliency and survive a failure of one of the disks. When a replacement disk is added to the pool, the storage space can be rebuilt from the remaining information.

    C. **Incorrect:** Although more disks always provide better resiliency for data, the fewest disks needed is two.

    D. **Incorrect:** Although more disks always provide better resiliency for data, the fewest disks needed is two.

2. Correct answer: B

    A. **Incorrect:** Metadata ensures that all disks in the pool can determine that they were used in a disk pool. Metadata does not handle searching for files within a storage space, however.

    B. **Correct:** Being able to attach disks belonging to a disk pool to another Windows 8–based computer and continue using the pool and information it contains without re-creating the storage space is possible because of the metadata written to each disk within the pool.

    C. **Incorrect:** Although metadata helps with usability, it does not directly affect storage space resiliency for the disks themselves. Metadata can help the storage spaces survive a computer failure but not a disk failure directly.

    D. **Incorrect:** Metadata does not handle disk optimization of a storage space.

CHAPTER 12

Administering authentication and authorization

The Microsoft Windows operating system has long been the platform of businesses because it is easy to use overall. It provides a consistent experience for most individuals and, by using built-in tools, enables the organization to know which employees are using its systems and when. For any organization, controlling who has access to systems and how much access is an ongoing concern. This chapter covers two primary areas associated with Windows security:

- **Authentication**   The process of proving your identity to Windows
- **Authorization**   The process of providing access to resources that you are authorized to use

Lessons in this chapter:

Before you begin

To complete the practice exercises in this chapter, you need:

- A general understanding of the reasons authentication and authorization exist in the Windows operating system.
- Access to a USB smart card reader and a USB or built-in biometric scanner for some of the elements of this chapter.

Lesson 1: Determining who's who through authentication

Authentication is built into the Windows operating system. Whether the user is in the office and signing in to a workstation that connects to a corporate domain or in his or her kitchen using a laptop, Windows authenticates the user attempting to access the system. The simple act of signing in informs Windows of who the user is. This lesson looks at the methods available for handling authentication in Windows 8.

After this lesson, you will be able to:

- Authenticate your user account to Windows 8 in both domain and nondomain environments.
- Use alternate authentication methods.
- Understand the use of certificates as authenticators.

Estimated lesson time: 55 minutes

What is authentication and what does it do?

Authentication, in a general sense, is a way for an entity to verify who you are when you use a service. For example, when you travel, you often use photo identification to verify your identity. Similarly, when you access an automated teller machine (ATM), your bank card information and personal identification number (PIN) verify that you can access your account.

Windows uses authentication to prove that the people using a computer system are who they claim to be. Usually users do this by providing a user name and a password to the system for verification. If either of these is incorrect or does not exist, the user is denied access to the system.

> *MORE INFO* **ADDITIONAL RESOURCES**
>
> You can find more information about authentication at *http://technet.microsoft.com/en-us /library/cc780469(v=WS.10).aspx*.

How does Windows authenticate users accessing the system?

Windows can authenticate a user account in several ways to prove the identity of the person at the keyboard; these include:

- User name and password.
- Smart cards.
- Certificates.
- Biometric authentication.

Windows asks you to click a picture or perform another action to sign in, such as pressing Ctrl+Alt+Delete. You then type a user name and password or select another means of authentication to prove your identity to Windows. After you provide these credentials, Windows checks your credentials either locally or against an Active Directory domain controller to ensure that the credentials exist and are valid. If both of these are verified, your user account is allowed access to the computer, and a desktop is created and displayed. Figure 12-1 shows the initial sign-in screen, prompting the user to press Ctrl+Alt+Delete.

Press Ctrl+Alt+Delete to sign in.

11:41
Saturday, August 4

FIGURE 12-1 Windows sign-in prompt

If the credentials provided are incorrect or do not exist, Windows displays a message explaining that the provided items are invalid. You are given an opportunity to enter your credentials again. Depending on the configuration of security policies, the credentials can be locked out after a specified number of attempts; this can prevent or deter malicious use or unwanted access to resources, but Windows does not require this configuration for authentication. Figure 12-2 displays an invalid sign-in attempt.

admin

The password is incorrect. Try again.

OK

FIGURE 12-2 Invalid sign-in attempt

User name and password-based authentication

The most common method of authenticating users is by user names and passwords. Windows 8 can use two possible types of user name and password credentials:

- Domain-based authentication (Active Directory domains in Windows environments)
- Security account manager database authentication

When an employee signs in to a computer joined to a domain, Windows passes the request to a domain controller, which checks the credentials provided against the domain's list of user accounts. In Active Directory environments, this is handled by Kerberos, which verifies the provided credentials and determines whether the sign-in should be allowed. *Kerberos* is a standard authentication protocol Windows (and other operating systems) uses to identify users during the sign-in process. If the credentials are correct, Kerberos provides resources to the account that allow it to access resources within a domain. This enables an authenticated user within the domain to access any resources for which he or she is authorized throughout the domain.

For example, Fernando is a user in the shipping department at Tailspin Toys. When he arrives at his desk in the morning, the first thing he does is sign in to Windows. Tailspin Toys uses standard user name and password authentication; Fernando enters his user name and password. When he clicks OK, the local Windows-based computer passes these credentials to a domain controller within the environment. When the domain controller receives the request, it checks the credentials against the Active Directory database. This includes:

- Making sure the account exists.
- Distributing an encrypted ticket and hashing the account password for access to other resources in the domain.
- Checking the age of the password, if enforced.
- Ensuring that the user account is not locked out for exceeding the number of sign-in attempts allowed by the organization's security policy.

After these items have been verified, Kerberos returns a ticket for the user account. This ticket allows the user to access any resource that exists within the domain and for which the account is authorized without further proof of identity. Fernando can then access the printer down the hall from his desk and his email without further sign-ins. This is sometimes referred to as single sign-on (SSO).

If the sign-in attempt does not succeed, perhaps Fernando's password recently changed, and he has misspelled or forgotten it. When Fernando attempts to sign in, Kerberos uses the Key Distribution Center to issue a ticket for this sign-in. If the user account can decrypt the ticket and passes preauthentication checks for the provided username, the authentication passes. Providing the wrong password would not allow the information to be decrypted when it is returned and would cause the sign-in to fail. When the credentials fail to pass verification, Windows displays a message telling Fernando that the information provided was incorrect.

Using a user name and password combination is the default sign-in method in Windows 8; however, configuration settings can make this method more secure. Some of these options include:

- Password expiration
- Password length requirements
- Password complexity requirements
- Minimum and maximum password age configuration
- Password history retention

Windows local accounts allow passwords up to 256 characters in length; your organization might have policies that impose restrictions on that limit.

Password settings for a local computer are specified in the local computer policy, as shown in Figure 12-3. To start the Local Computer Policy snap-in, complete the following steps:

1. Select the Settings charm.
2. Select Control Panel.
3. Tap or click the System and Security category.
4. Tap or click Administrative Tools.
5. Select Local Security Policy.

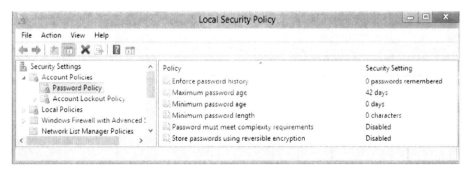

FIGURE 12-3 Configuring passwords for the local computer

You can configure the following password settings:

- **Minimum and maximum password age**   Using these two settings, as the administrator you can specify the minimum and maximum age for a password. The Minimum Password Age determines the smallest amount of time, in days, that a password must exist before it can be changed. The default is 42 days if the policy is enabled. The Maximum Password Age specifies the number of days that a password can exist before it expires and Windows requires the user to change the password.

- **Password length requirements**   The Minimum Password Length setting enables you to determine how many characters long a password must be. The maximum length is 256 characters.

- **Password complexity requirements**   This option enables you to require combinations of characters in a password. For example, you can require that passwords include uppercase and lowercase letters, that they be alphanumeric, or even that they include special characters.

- **Password expiration**   This option works with the password age requirements. When a password is set to expire, it will expire after it reaches the maximum age. You can also set a password never to expire, which disables the minimum and maximum age requirements.

- **Password history retention**   Windows can remember a designated number of previous passwords. With this setting enabled, users within your organization will have to generate unique passwords each time they change their password until they have surpassed the number of passwords remembered. For example, if this setting is configured to remember three passwords, then on the fourth password change, the original password could be used again.

These settings exist to help you make passwords a more secure authentication method. Because many organizations might not choose to invest in other authentication technologies, the user name and password sign-in should be capable of providing as secure a method as possible for authentication.

> **SECURITY ALERT   EDUCATE USERS ON SECURING PASSWORDS**
>
> Often, imposing strict and strange password complexity requirements on users will cause them to write down their password. This information is often stored under the keyboard or in a top desk drawer, and is therefore easily accessible to anyone in the building. One way to avoid this practice is to educate users about how the password is intended to work. You can also encourage users to use a pass phrase instead of a singular word with misspellings. Using a phrase related to a user's hobby or something the user enjoys can provide more secure passwords than you might think. For more information about creating strong passwords, visit *http://technet.microsoft.com/en-us/library/cc784090(v=WS.10).aspx*.

Smart card authentication

A *smart card* is a hardware token that contains certificates that prove the identity of the person using a device. Using a smart card authentication requires an organization to provide each user with a smart card, which can be tied to an identification badge or other item, and to attach a smart card reader to each computer within the environment.

When a smart card is used for sign-in, the user initiates a sign-in request and inserts the smart card into the available reader. The card is checked, and a prompt for a PIN appears. When the user enters the PIN, Windows begins the authentication process just as it does when a user name and password are used for authentication. Smart cards provide two-factor authentication to Windows. That is, the user must have two things to sign in successfully: the physical smart card and the PIN associated with the smart card. If a user does not have both these items, authentication will not succeed.

This type of authentication is similar to the type used to prove an identity at an ATM. To access an account by using the machine, you must have the physical access card to swipe in the machine and the PIN associated with the card.

Smart cards are more secure than user names and passwords because they provide an element that cannot be guessed. For example, if an organization uses the naming convention of first initial, last name (such as pfischer for Peter Fischer) when creating user names, other employees, or anyone who knows this convention, can guess that Peter Fischer's user name is pfischer. Then that person can attempt to guess his password.

If the organization uses a smart card configuration for user authentication, Peter Fischer will have a card to swipe at sign-in and, after swiping his card, he will then be asked for his PIN. If someone other than Peter attempts to sign in as Peter, he or she will not be able to sign in without Peter's smart card and PIN.

> **NOTE OTHER USES FOR SMART CARDS**
>
> In addition to providing Windows authentication, smart cards can be used for other purposes such as unlocking doors and recording hours worked by swiping into an attendance system.

Others in your organization are probably familiar with smart card technology because an ATM machine uses similar technology. You might be able to recommend the use of smart cards in other areas of the organization such as the company cafeteria to purchase meals and other items. Many do not treat their computer credentials with the same level of security as their ATM card, so deploying a smart-card system is a good idea because each employee has access to information the organization requires to conduct its business.

With the use of the Internet and other technologies increasing every day, implementing better security measures and educating an organization about the benefits of these measures can both help the IT organization monitor security better and help users become more conscious of security.

Before configuring smart cards for the workstation, ensure that a Public Key policy exists within your Active Directory environment. Configuring the Active Directory infrastructure is outside the scope of this book. The following scenario assumes that Active Directory is already configured correctly.

MORE INFO **ACTIVE DIRECTORY RESOURCES**

You can find an overview of Active Directory domain services at *http://technet.microsoft .com/library/hh831484* and an overview of Enterprise PKI concepts at *http://technet .microsoft.com/en-us/library/cc753754.aspx.* For a more in-depth view of Active Directory, see *Active Directory Administrator's Pocket Consultant* by William Stanek (Microsoft Press, 2008) and *Windows Server 2008 Active Directory Resource Kit* by Stand Reimer, Conan Kezema, Mike Mulcare, and Byron White (Microsoft Press, 2008).

IMPORTANT **VERIFY THAT YOU HAVE THE DEVICE DRIVER SOFTWARE**

Before attempting to configure a smart card reader or any peripheral device, ensure that you have access to the correct driver software for that device. Many Windows 7 device drivers will work with Windows 8; however, this might not be the case with Windows RT.

To configure a smart card for sign-in, you must install a certificate on the smart card. The required certificate is created by using the enrollment agent certificate template. In addition, a certification authority needs the enrollment agent and smart card sign in to be configured. This ensures that your certificate authority (CA) can provide certificates for smart cards.

To configure a smart card reader and prepare to sign in to Windows 8, complete the following steps:

1. Plug the smart card reader into your computer if you are using an external device.
2. If the device does not turn on, make sure the drivers for the device have been installed.
3. Insert a smart card into the reader.

To authenticate by using a smart card, insert the card into the reader. The sign-in screen will change to work with the smart card rather than with Ctrl+Alt+Delete. Windows will check any certificates on the card and display them. Select the valid certificate (if more than one choice appears) and enter the corresponding PIN to sign in. Windows might not prompt you to choose a certificate if only one is found on the card.

NOTE **USING CERTIFICATES TO SIGN IN**

When you sign in to a computer running Windows by using a smart card, you are actually using a specially designated certificate to perform the authentication. The PIN is similar to the private key, which tells the computer (or the server if you are signing in to a domain) that you have the necessary credentials and should be authenticated.

Other types of certificates can be used to prove the identity of a user and provide access to websites, thus reducing the chances of problems that might compromise information used on a website. Although these certificate types might not be used directly for Windows sign-in, they provide authentication to other services that you might encounter as a Windows user.

 Quick check

- True or false: Accessing resources by using a smart card–enabled sign-in provides the same security as a user name and password.

Quick check answer

- False. Because a smart card requires something you have (the smart card) and something you know (a PIN number), the sign-in process is more secure because others cannot guess a smart card. They must have it in their possession to sign in.

Biometric authentication

Another type of two-factor authentication is biometrics. This technique involves a scanner of some type, typically for a fingerprint, but possibly for a retina in extremely advanced cases.

When signing in to a computer by using biometrics, the user at the computer initiates the sign-in process and then touches the scanner. When reading the fingerprint of the individual, a one-time key is generated for the sign-in session. This is passed to the authenticating domain controller or the local computer and checked against the stored information for the user account. When the credentials are verified, the sign-in is completed, and that user's desktop appears.

Advantages of the use of biometrics can include:

- Unique access for each individual
- Greater difficulty in faking or impersonating identity
- Nothing to guess at sign-in

The implementation of this sign-in method comes with initial costs because, like smart cards, the computers within an environment need biometric scanners to process sign-in attempts. In addition, an organization must train employees so that they understand the process of using biometrics. Although a fingerprint scanner is used to sign in, the fingerprint itself is not stored with the user identification (ID) for the sign-in process. A security code or token is generated for each sign in. This code is passed as something similar to a password for actual authentication.

IMPORTANT **MANAGING FINGERPRINT-READING DEVICES**

If your fingerprint reader is a USB device, plug it into your computer and ensure that you have drivers installed before continuing. You might also need to download fingerprint management software so Windows can store the information the device collects. Windows will alert you during configuration if you need to do this.

To configure biometric sign-ins, complete the following steps:

1. Select the Settings charm.

2. Select Control Panel.

3. In Control Panel, open Biometric Devices.

4. Find the device currently installed on your computer and select Change Biometric Settings.

5. Ensure that Biometrics is turned on and that Allow Users To Log On To Windows Using Their Fingerprints is selected.

6. Tap or click Cancel if these options were already set; tap or click Save Changes if you modified them.

7. In the Biometric Devices Control Panel applet, tap or click Use Your Fingerprint With Windows.

8. Tap or click Continue.

Managing credentials in Windows 8 by using Credential Manager

As the number of computers and other connected devices increases, the number of passwords and access credentials will also increase. The Credential Manager utility with Windows 8 aids in storing all these user names, passwords, and other identities you use.

To access Credential Manager, complete the following steps:

1. Select the Settings charm.

2. Select Control Panel.

3. Tap or click the User Accounts And Family Safety category.

4. Tap or click Credential Manager.

Credential Manager can store both Windows credentials and web credentials. Credential Manager for Windows is shown in Figure 12-4.

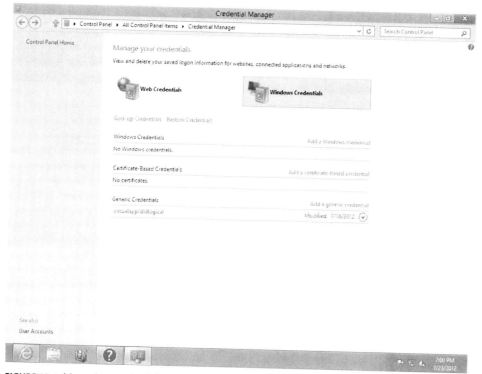

FIGURE 12-4 Managing credentials by using Credential Manager

Windows credentials are used to access servers or services on an intranet on which specific sign-in credentials can be passed by Windows when you access that resource. Three types of Windows credentials can be managed by using Credential Manager:

- **Windows credentials**   User names and passwords for specific sites and applications
- **Certificate-based credentials**   Certificate access to intranet or Internet resources, which will pass the needed sign-in information to the resource when it is accessed
- **Generic credentials**   Credentials stored for nonspecific websites, such as for social media or other items on the web

When you add Windows credentials, the operating system recognizes that a particular resource has a stored credential, and when landing on the sign-in page for that resource, Windows attempts to sign you in. Doing this reduces the number of credentials you need to remember and provides easy access to resources.

Web credentials are similar to generic Windows credentials, but they are collected credentials, and you cannot add them manually. When you browse to a website that asks you to sign in, and your web browser asks you whether you would like to save or remember the sign-in information, the information entered is stored as a web credential in the Credential Manager utility.

After the information is stored as a web credential, Windows can present the stored sign-in information to the websites that you have chosen to remember your sign-in information. However, there are some caveats to this. If the websites you have stored as web credentials change anything about their sign-in dialog box or use different tokens each time the pages are loaded (to increase security), the web credential likely will not work for automating these sign-ins.

Configuring a Microsoft account for use with Windows

As described in Chapter 2, "Installing and migrating to Windows 8," Windows 8 can use a Microsoft account as the sign-in account for Windows. Doing this provides SSO access to several Microsoft services, including Windows Live Messenger, SkyDrive, and Hotmail. However, you do not have to configure this at sign-in to use the SSO capabilities.

When you convert your local Windows account to a Microsoft account, you can access items kept on Microsoft services directly from Windows without additional sign-ins.

To convert your local account to a Microsoft account, complete the following steps:

1. Access the PC Settings charm, and then select Users.

2. Tap or click Switch To A Microsoft Account.

   Figure 12-5 shows the PC Settings screen.

FIGURE 12-5 Users information in PC Settings

3. Type your current password for the local account and tap or click Next.

4. If you already have a Microsoft account (or a Live ID), enter the email address for the account and tap or click Next.

   Windows validates your Microsoft account email address.

5. Type the password for your account and tap or click Next.

6. Type your phone number and an alternate email address and tap or click Next.

7. Tap or click Finish to convert your account.

When you have changed your local Windows 8 sign-in account to a Microsoft account, you must use your Microsoft account email and password to sign in to Windows.

Some of the applications available in Windows 8 that use Microsoft accounts include:

- **SkyDrive** Cloud-based storage

- **Outlook.com** Email

- **Photos** Photos stored within your Microsoft account

- **Calendar** Appointments stored within your account

Using a Microsoft account not only reduces the number of user names and passwords you must remember but also provides access to all your cloud-based data directly on your Windows 8–based computer. You can always switch back to a local account if you decide not to link your computer with your Microsoft account.

To change back to a local account, complete the following steps:

1. Access the Settings charm, select PC Settings, and then select Users from the navigation pane.

2. Tap or click Switch To A Local Account.

3. Enter your current (Microsoft account) password.

4. Enter a new password for the local account.

5. Confirm the new local account password.

6. Enter a password hint.

7. Tap or click Sign Out and Finish.

You will be signed out of Windows as part of this process, and the next time you sign in, you will use the new local account.

 Quick check

- **When connecting your sign-in to a Microsoft account, what is the maximum length for the password?**

Quick check answer

- **The maximum length for a Microsoft account password is 16 characters. This allows the account to work with the current cloud-based authentication these accounts use. Local account passwords can be longer.**

Logging on by using a picture password

Windows 8 supports the use of picture passwords for authentication. To create a picture password, you select a picture and associate some gestures with it that are then used to sign in to Windows.

The gestures can include the following:

* Circles
* Lines
* Taps on the screen

These short drawings on the picture you have chosen are used to create your password. After a gesture is configured, this picture password replaces the traditional password you assigned to your user account.

> **NOTE ACCESSING PHOTOS FROM ONLINE SERVICES**
>
> You can select a picture to use with your picture password from anywhere on your computer. If you choose the Photos application, you can also connect to online services such as SkyDrive to retrieve photos. When using photos from an online service, you might need to authenticate with your user name and password for the selected service to access the items.

Creating a picture password

To configure a picture password, complete the following steps:

1. Access the Settings charm, select PC Settings, and then select Users from the navigation pane.

2. Tap or click Create a Picture Password.

3. Enter the current password for your user account and tap or click OK.

   Figure 12-6 shows the picture password welcome screen.

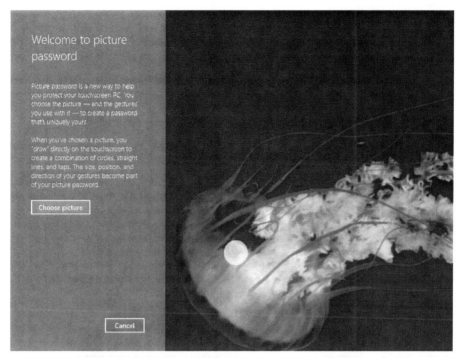

FIGURE 12-6 Creating a picture password for sign-in

4. Tap or click Choose Picture.

5. Select the photo to use for your picture password from anywhere on your computer or from online photo albums and tap or click OK.

6. After previewing the photo and dragging it to the position you want for the password, tap or click Use This Picture. If you do not want to use the selected picture, tap or click Choose New Picture.

7. Draw three gestures on the selected picture to enable it as a password.

IMPORTANT **SEQUENCE AND DIRECTION COUNT!**

Windows remembers what you draw first, second, and third and how you draw a line or a circle. You will need to use the same sequence and directionality for your gestures every time. This increases the security of a password significantly. If you want to learn the details about the security calculations, read this blog from the Windows engineering team at *http://blogs.msdn.com/b/b8/archive/2011/12/16/signing-in-with-a-picture -password.aspx*.

---

8. Redraw the same three gestures to confirm them.

9. Tap or click Finish to complete the creation of a picture password.

The next time you sign in to Windows, you must use the picture password you created.

Removing a picture password

If you have a picture password and decide you no longer want to use this type of password, you can remove it by performing the following steps:

1. Access the Settings charm, select PC Settings, and then select Users from the navigation pane.

2. Tap or click the Remove button next to Change Picture Password.

> **IMPORTANT   CHANGING YOUR PICTURE PASSWORD**
>
> At any time, you can change your picture password. To change the picture and gestures, select Change Picture Password instead of Remove, and repeat the steps to select a picture and add gestures.

Using the picture password

Figure 12-7 shows what the sign-in screen looks like when using a picture password.

FIGURE 12-7 Signing in with a picture password and gestures

When signing in with a picture password, the picture and gestures are associated with your existing user account. If necessary, you can select Switch To Password from the sign-in screen to allow a password to be entered. After you have selected Switch To Password, the picture password will be moved under sign-in options on the sign-in screen. Selecting the picture password option will change your sign-in back to the previously configured picture password.

Although picture passwords were designed with touch screen devices in mind, they work on standard laptop or desktop installations of Windows 8.

Using a personal identification number (PIN) for authentication

Another way to shorten the sign-in process is by using a PIN. This assigns a 4-digit code to your user credentials, enabling you to sign in with just this assigned code. To create a PIN, complete the following steps:

1. Access the Settings charm, select PC Settings, and then select Users from the navigation pane.

2. Tap or click Create A PIN.

3. Enter your current password.

4. Enter a 4-digit number.

5. Re-enter the 4-digit PIN for confirmation.

6. Tap or click Finish.

When the PIN is created, you are returned to the PC Settings screen. If you want to change your PIN, click the Change PIN button or click the Remove button to remove the PIN from your account.

The next time you sign in to Windows with the user account that has a PIN assigned, it prompts you to enter a PIN rather than a password. If you would rather enter your password, click Sign-In Options on the sign-in screen to select a different method.

The sign-in options are available when alternate methods of authentication are configured for a user account. Figure 12-8 shows these options.

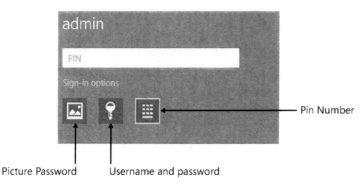

FIGURE 12-8 PIN authentication and additional sign-in options

Additional sign-in options can be useful in several situations, such as when a user signs in to a mobile device or when a user needs a simplified sign-in procedure.

Lesson summary

- Windows 8 supports several sign-in options, including picture passwords, PIN sign-in, and traditional user name and password authentication.
- When it is associated with your computer, you can use your Microsoft account to sign in to Windows and access Microsoft services.
- Using Credential Manager to maintain Windows credentials for sign-in and credentials for Internet sites can make them easier to remember and more secure.
- For even more secure access to your computer, consider using biometrics or smart cards for authentication.

Lesson review

Answer the following questions to test your knowledge of the information in this lesson. You can find the answers to these questions and explanations of why each answer choice is correct or incorrect in the "Answers" section at the end of this chapter.

1. Your organization uses Windows 8 on tablet computers in a warehouse environment to track inventory. Bill, the warehouse manager, has asked whether there is any way to simplify the password policy for his employees so they can sign in with less complex credentials while using their portable computers. How can you assist Bill without compromising security?

   A. Disable complex passwords.

   B. Enable PIN sign-ins.

   C. Remove password requirements for these users.

   D. Enable sign-in auditing for successes.

2. You have been looking for a way to manage the tremendous number of sign-in credentials for a growing number of websites and other services. In addition to user names and passwords for these sites, you would like to store certificate-based information for future use. Which built-in utility can you use to manage these credentials?

   A. Notepad

   B. Internet Explorer Favorites

   C. Credential Manager

   D. Microsoft Excel

3. You were just issued a new laptop, running Windows 8, as part of an upgrade program by your company. The new laptop has a built-in fingerprint scanner, and you wish to use that to expedite the sign-in process. Which setting needs to be configured in addition to enrolling your fingerprints to enable you to sign in by using your fingerprints?

   A. Windows Firewall must be configured to allow access.

   B. Biometrics and the Allow Users To Log On To Windows Using Their Fingerprints options must be enabled.

C. A personal identification number must be created.

D. A complex password must be configured.

Lesson 2: Managing authorization and access rights

Authorization is a user's right to access a resource. At first, it might seem that rights are the same as permissions (discussed in Chapter 11, "File system and storage management"); however, these two entities are different.

Rights are attached to user accounts and groups of user accounts, whereas *permissions* are attached to objects such as files and folders. This lesson covers authorization and access rights.

After this lesson, you will be able to:

- Manage the rights of user accounts on a computer.
- Elevate the privileges of an application.
- Manage certificates for access to resources.

Estimated lesson time: 50 minutes

> *MORE INFO* **ADDITIONAL RESOURCES**
>
> **Additional information about authorization can be found at *http://technet.microsoft.com /en-us/library/cc782880(v=WS.10).aspx.***

Getting started with user rights

After you have authenticated and signed in to a computer running Windows 8, what can you do? Typically, a desktop, Start screen, or some other piece of information starts you on the computer, but you need rights to perform certain actions. For example, suppose Oscar was hired at Contoso to work from the London office. The help desk helps provision computers for new employees and ensures that they are shipped to remote employees as soon as possible. When Oscar's computer was sent out, the time zone was still set to the local time of the office where the computer was configured. Because most employees do not need access to change the time zone, this right is disabled by default. How can Oscar modify the time zone so that his computer displays the correct system time?

Because this user right has not been assigned, you must sign in with local administrator privileges to add Oscar to the needed user rights. To assign Oscar the right to change the time zone, complete the following steps:

1. From the desktop, tap or click the Settings charm.

2. Select Control Panel, System and Security, Administrative Tools, and then Local Security Policy.

3. From the navigation pane of the Local Security Policy console, expand Local Policies and tap or click User Rights Assignment.

4. In the results pane, double-tap or double-click the Change The Time Zone policy.

5. Make a note of the users or groups defined on the Local Security Setting tab of the Properties dialog box.

6. Add Oscar's user account to the list of those allowed to modify the time zone or add the user account to one of the groups that is listed.

7. Log off the computer and have Oscar test his ability to modify the time zone.

Working in groups

Rights tend to be more effective when used in groups than when used on single user accounts. The reason for this is not technical; rather, it comes from an ease-of-administration concept. Consider the following example for why this tends to be more efficient.

If you assign rights to Oscar to perform a task, only Oscar can perform that task. If you assign rights to the help desk group to perform a task, any member of the help desk group can perform that task. In this way, as employees like Oscar come and go from the help desk group, the rights do not travel with that singular user account.

Understanding rights vs. permissions

Permissions specify which type of access to allow on an object. A folder called Operations is an object that lives on the NTFS file system. This object would have permissions assigned to it granting different types of access to different user accounts or groups.

Rights are similar to permissions, but they are applied to user accounts or groups and apply to the tasks that these user accounts (or group members) can perform on a computer. Rights define what someone is allowed to do, whereas permissions define what type of access is available for an object.

> **NOTE PERMISSIONS VS. RIGHTS**
>
> When considering permissions and rights, remember that permissions are assigned to objects that can be secured, including files, folders, and registry keys. Rights determine which tasks on a computer the specified user account can perform.

Assigning user rights

Within Windows 8, local security policy items affect what can happen on a local computer. Computers joined to an Active Directory domain process security from Active Directory before evaluating items at the local policy level. Assigning user rights is performed at both the local and domain levels.

To access user rights on a computer running Windows 8, complete the following steps:

1. Tap or click the Settings charm.

2. Select Control Panel.

3. Double-tap or double-click Administrative Tools.

4. Double-tap or double-click Local Security Policy.

5. In the left pane of the window, expand Local Policies.

6. Select User Rights Assignment.

The settings configured in User Rights Assignment allow defined tasks to be performed by the specified groups or user accounts. The available actions that can be assigned are defined in Table 12-1.

TABLE 12-1 User Rights elements that can be assigned to users or groups

Policy	Description	Groups with this privilege by default	Valid on
Access Credential Manager as trusted caller	Used by Credential Manager during backup and recovery operations. No user accounts should be assigned this privilege.	None; used by Winlogon	Workstations
Access this computer from the network	Determines which users and groups can connect to this computer over the network.	Administrators, Authenticated Users, Backup Operators, Users, Everyone	Workstations, Servers, and Domain Controllers
Act as part of the operating system	Allows a process to impersonate any user account on the system with no additional authentication.	None*	Workstations, Servers, and Domain Controllers
Add workstations to domain	Determines which user accounts or groups can add workstations to the domain.	Authenticated Users	Domain Controllers

Policy	Description	Groups with this privilege by default	Valid on
Adjust memory quotas for a process	Determines which user accounts can change the maximum memory consumption allowed for a process.	Administrators, Local Service, Network Service	Workstations, Servers, and Domain Controllers
Allow logon locally	Determines which user accounts can sign in to the computer.	On workstations/servers: Administrators, Backup Operators, Power Users, Users, Guest On domain controllers: Account Operators, Administrators, Backup Operators, Print Operators	Workstations, Servers, and Domain Controllers
Allow logon through Remote Desktop Services	Determines which user accounts can access the computer by using Remote Desktop Connections.	On workstations/servers: Administrators, Remote Desktop Users On domain controllers: Administrators	Workstations, Servers, and Domain Controllers
Back up files and directories	Determines which user accounts or groups can bypass persistent object permissions for the purposes of backing up a computer.	On workstations and servers: Administrators, Backup Operators On domain controllers: Administrators, Backup Operators, Server Operators*	Workstations, Servers, and Domain Controllers
Bypass traverse checking	Determines which user accounts can traverse directories even though the user account might not have permissions to do so on the object.	On workstations and servers: Administrators, Backup Operators, Users, Everyone, Local Service, Network Service On domain controllers: Administrators, Authenticated Users, Everyone, Local Service, Network Service, Pre–Windows 2000 Compatible Access	Workstations, Servers, and Domain Controllers
Change the system time	Determines which user accounts and groups can change the time on a computer.	On workstations and servers: Administrators, Local Service On domain controllers: Administrators, Server Operators, Local Service	Workstations, Servers, and Domain Controllers
Change the time zone	Determines which user accounts and groups can change the time zone.	Administrators, Users	Workstations, Servers, and Domain Controllers
Create a page file	Determines which user accounts or groups can call an application programming interface (API) to create a page file.	Administrators	Workstations, Servers, and Domain Controllers
Create a token object	Determines which accounts can be used by processes to create tokens used for accessing local resources.	None*	Workstations, Servers, and Domain Controllers

Policy	Description	Groups with this privilege by default	Valid on
Create global objects	Determines which user accounts can create global objects available to all sessions.	Administrators, Local Service, Network Service, Service*	Workstations, Servers, and Domain Controllers
Create permanent shared objects	Determines which accounts can be used by processes to create directory objects by using Object Manager.	None	
Create symbolic links	Determines whether a user account can create a symbolic link from the computer where the user is signed in.	Administrators	Workstations, Servers, and Domain Controllers
Debug programs	Determines which accounts can attach a debugger to any process or to the Windows kernel.	Administrators*	Workstations, Servers, and Domain Controllers
Deny access to this computer from the network	Determines which accounts are prevented from accessing the computer over the network.	Guest	Workstations, Servers, and Domain Controllers
Deny logon as a batch job	Determines which accounts are prevented from signing in as a batch job.	None	Workstations, Servers, and Domain Controllers
Deny logon as a service	Determines which service accounts are prevented from registering a process as a service.	None	Workstations, Servers, and Domain Controllers
Deny logon locally	Determines which user accounts are denied the ability to sign in locally to a computer.	Guest	Workstations, Servers, and Domain Controllers
Deny logon through Remote Desktop Services	Determines which user accounts are denied access to a computer by using Remote Desktop Services.	None	Workstations, Servers, and Domain Controllers
Enable computer and user accounts to be trusted for delegation	Determines which user accounts can set the Trusted For Delegation property on a user or a computer object.	Administrators*	Domain Controllers
Force shutdown from a remote system	Determines which accounts can shut down a computer from a remote location.	On workstations and servers: Administrators On domain controllers: Administrators, Server Operators	Workstations, Servers, and Domain Controllers
Generate security audits	Determines which accounts can be used by a process to trigger a security audit.	Local Service, Network Service	Workstations, Servers, and Domain Controllers
Impersonate a client after authentication	Allows programs running on behalf of the designated account to impersonate a client.	Administrators, Local Service, Network Service, Service	Workstations, Servers, and Domain Controllers
Increase a process working set	Determines which accounts can increase or decrease the size of a working set. (A working set defines the memory needed by a process within a given time interval.)	Users	Workstations, Servers, and Domain Controllers

Policy	Description	Groups with this privilege by default	Valid on
Increase scheduling priority	Determines which accounts can use a process with write-property access to a different process to increase the execution priority assigned to that process.	Administrators	Workstations, Servers, and Domain Controllers
Load and unload device drivers	Determines which accounts can dynamically load and unload device drivers into kernel mode. (When an application or driver runs in kernel mode, it is operating at the highest protection ring within the operating system.)	On workstations and servers: Administrators On domain controllers: Administrators, Print Operators*	Workstations, Servers, and Domain Controllers
Lock pages in memory	Determines which users can use a process to keep data in physical memory.	None	Workstations, Servers, and Domain Controllers
Log on as a batch job	Allows a user account to be signed in through a batch-queue facility. Provided for compatibility with earlier versions of Windows.	Administrators, Backup Operators	Workstations, Servers, and Domain Controllers
Log on as a service	Allows a security principal to sign in as a service.	None	Workstations, Servers, and Domain Controllers
Manage auditing and security log	Determines which accounts can specify object access auditing options for resources.	Administrators	Workstations, Servers, and Domain Controllers
Modify an object label	Determines which accounts can modify the integrity label of objects, including files, registry keys, or processes owned by other users.	None	Workstations, Servers, and Domain Controllers
Modify firmware environment values	Determines which accounts can modify the firmware environment variables stored in nonvolatile RAM. For x86 computers, the last-known good configuration is modifiable. For Itanium-based systems, boot information is stored and can be modified.	Administrators	Workstations, Servers, and Domain Controllers
Perform volume maintenance tasks	Determines which accounts can perform maintenance on a volume.	Administrators*	Workstations, Servers, and Domain Controllers
Profile single process	Determines which accounts can use performance-monitoring tools to monitor nonsystem processes.	Administrators, Power Users	Workstations, Servers, and Domain Controllers
Profile system performance	Determines which users can monitor performance of system processes.	Administrators	Workstations, Servers, and Domain Controllers
Remove computer from docking station	Determines whether an account can undock a portable computer.	Administrators, Power Users, Users	Workstations, Servers, and Domain Controllers

Policy	Description	Groups with this privilege by default	Valid on
Replace a process-level token	Determines which user accounts can call the Create Process As User() API so one service can start another service.	Network Service, Local Service	Workstations, Servers, and Domain Controllers
Restore files and directories	Determines which accounts can bypass file, directory, registry, and other persistent permissions when restoring backed-up objects.	On workstations and servers: Administrators, Backup Operators. On domain controllers: Administrators, Backup Operators, Server Operators*	Workstations, Servers, and Domain Controllers
Shut down the system	Determines which accounts, when signed in locally, can shut down the operating system.	On workstations: Administrators, Backup Operators, Users. On domain controllers: Administrators, Backup Operators, Server Operators, Print Operators	Workstations, Servers, and Domain Controllers
Synchronize directory service data	Determines which accounts can synchronize data with a directory service such as Active Directory.	None	Domain Controllers
Take ownership of files or other objects	Determines which accounts can take ownership of any securable object in the system, including Active Directory objects, files, folders, printers, and registry keys.	Administrators*	Workstations, Servers, and Domain Controllers

Although several rights can be customized, some of them have default assignments. In many cases, these default assignments will be sufficient for general computer use. Consider the needs of your organization when modifying user rights to ensure that proper access remains available.

Local Security Policy console

In addition to user rights assignment, security settings for Windows can be configured within the Local Security Policy console. Table 12-2 lists and defines the available security options in Windows 8. To access these options, select the Security Options node within the Local Policies section of the Local Security Policy console. In the table, the default configuration option is in **bold** type. Settings not configured by default are in regular type. Entries that are not configured by default will show all items for default configuration in regular type.

> *NOTE* **SECURITY OPTIONS ASSIGNED TO ITEMS**
>
> The security options available here are not assigned specifically to user accounts or groups, but they do control access to certain items on the computer.

Here are some terms that you should know that appear in the table:

- *Service principal name (SPN)* The name a client uses to identify an instance of a service uniquely

- *NT LAN Manager (NTLM)* A suite of protocols that provide authentication, integrity, and confidentiality to computer users

- *Lightweight directory access protocol (LDAP)* An application-level protocol for accessing directory service information over an Internet Protocol (IP) network

- *Symbolic links* A special file that contains a reference to another file by using an absolute or a relative path

- *BitLocker* An encryption method that encrypts entire volumes of information

- *Secure desktop* An environment displayed during user account control (UAC) elevation requests that allows only certain applications to run

- *PKU2U* A public key authentication mechanism for peer-based authentication between two user accounts

SECURITY ALERT **UNINTENDED CONSEQUENCES**

Items in Table 12-2 marked with an asterisk (*) can have unintended consequences if disabled. Items marked with a double asterisk (**) can have unintended consequences, including inaccessible accounts or computers, if enabled. Read the explanations and your organization's policies thoroughly before modifying these settings.

TABLE 12-2 Local security options

Policy	Description	Configuration Options
Accounts: Administrator account status	Determines whether the local administrator account is enabled or disabled.	Enabled or **Disabled**
Accounts: Block Microsoft accounts	Prevents users from adding new Microsoft accounts to the computer; can also prevent signing in with a Microsoft account.	Disabled Users can't add Microsoft accounts Users can't add or sign in with Microsoft accounts
Accounts: Guest account status*	Determines whether the guest account is enabled or disabled.	Enabled or **Disabled**
Accounts: Limit local account use of blank password to console logon only	Determines whether local accounts without passwords configured can sign in to the computer by using remote computers.	**Enabled** or Disabled
Accounts: Rename administrator account	Changes the name of the local administrator account.	Enter a value or **Administrator**
Accounts: Rename guest account	Changes the name of the local guest account.	Enter a value or **Guest**
Audit: Audit the access of global system objects	Determines whether access to global system objects should be audited.	Enabled or **Disabled**

Policy	Description	Configuration Options
Audit: Audit the use of backup and restore privileges	Determines whether to audit the use of all privileges, including backup and restore.	Enabled or **Disabled**
Audit: Force audit policy sub-category settings to override policy categories settings (Windows Vista or later)	Determines whether the more advanced subcategory auditing should be used.	Enabled or Disabled
Audit: Shut down system immediately if unable to log security audits**	Forces the computer to shut down if the security log is full and cannot be written to.	Enabled or **Disabled**
DCOM: Machine access restrictions in security descriptor definition language (SDDL) syntax	Determines which user accounts or groups can access the DCOM applica-tion locally or remotely; controls attack surface of the computer for DCOM applications.	Apply security permissions or **leave blank**
DCOM: Machine launch restrictions in security de-scriptor definition language (SDDL) syntax	Determines which user accounts or groups can launch DCOM applications on the computer.	Apply security permissions or **leave blank**
Devices: Allow undock with-out having to log on	Determines whether a portable com-puter can be removed from a docking station without needing the user to sign in.	**Enabled** or Disabled
Devices: Allowed to format and eject removable devices	Determines which groups of user accounts can eject and format remov-able devices.	Administrators Administrators and Power Users Administrators and Interactive Users
Devices: Prevent users from installing printer drivers	Determines whether user accounts can install printer drivers for remote print-ers but does not affect local printers or administrators.	Enabled or **Disabled**
Devices: Restrict CD-ROM access to locally logged on users only	Determines whether the CD-ROM device is available to local and remote users simultaneously.	Enabled or Disabled
Devices: Restrict floppy access to locally logged on users only	Determines whether removable floppy media is available for local and remote access simultaneously.	Enabled or Disabled
Domain controller: Allow server operators to schedule tasks	Determines whether the server opera-tors group can submit tasks by using the AT scheduling utility.	Enabled or Disabled
Domain controller: LDAP server signing requirements	Determines whether an LDAP server requires LDAP clients to negotiate with signing.	None or Require signing
Domain controller: Refuse machine account password changes	Determines whether domain control-ler computers will refuse requests by domain member computers to change computer account passwords.	Enabled or Disabled
Domain member: Digitally encrypt or sign secure chan-nel data (always)	Determines whether secure channel traffic initiated by this computer must be encrypted or signed.	**Enabled** or Disabled

Policy	Description	Configuration Options
Domain member: Digitally encrypt secure channel data (when possible)	Determines whether this computer will attempt to negotiate encryption for all secure channel traffic it initiates.	**Enabled** or Disabled
Domain member: Digitally sign secure channel data (when possible)	Determines whether this computer will attempt to negotiate signing for all secure channel traffic it initiates.	**Enabled** or Disabled
Domain member: Disable machine account password changes	Determines whether domain member computers will periodically change their passwords.	Enabled or **Disabled**
Domain member: Maximum machine account password age	Determines the maximum password age for computer accounts within a domain.	Enter number of days or **30 days**
Domain member: Require strong session key (Windows 2000 or later)	Determines whether 128-bit key strength is required for secure channel data.	**Enabled** or Disabled
Interactive logon: Display user information when session is locked	Determines what data will be displayed when an account has locked the workstation.	User display name Domain and user names User display name only Do not display any user information
Interactive logon: Do not display last user name	Determines whether the user name of the last user to sign in is displayed on the Windows sign-in screen.	Enabled or **Disabled**
Interactive logon: Do not require Ctrl+Alt+Delete	Determines whether pressing Ctrl+Alt+Delete is required when signing in.	Enabled or Disabled
Interactive logon: Machine account lockout threshold	Determines the number of failed sign-in attempts that can cause the computer to be locked out; only enforced on computers using BitLocker to encrypt system volumes.	Enter number of attempts allowed before machine account is locked out
Interactive logon: Machine inactivity limit	Determines the number of seconds after which a computer is locked.	Enter number of seconds of inactivity allowed before account is locked
Interactive logon: Message text for users attempting to log on	Enter the text to display to users signing in interactively.	Enter a value or **Empty**
Interactive logon: Message title for users attempting to log on	Enter the text to display as the title of the message box displayed to users signing in interactively.	Enter a value or **Empty**
Interactive logon: Number of previous logons to cache	Determines how many sign-ins to keep locally if a domain controller is unavailable for sign-in.	Enter a value or **10 logons**
Interactive logon: Prompt user to change password before expiration	Specifies the number of days to alert the signed-in user before the account password expires.	Enter a value or **6 days**

Policy	Description	Configuration Options
Interactive logon: Require domain controller authentication to unlock workstation	If enabled, sign-in information must be provided to unlock a computer; for domain accounts, determines whether a domain controller must be contacted to unlock the account.	Enabled or **Disabled**
Interactive logon: Require smart card	Determines whether interactive sign-ins require the use of a smart card.	Enabled or **Disabled**
Interactive logon: Smart card removal behavior	Specifies the action taken when a smart card is removed.	**No action** Lock workstation Force Sign-out Disconnect if remote desktop services session
Microsoft network client: Digitally sign communications (always)	Determines whether the SMB client component requires packet signing.	Enabled or **Disabled**
Microsoft network client: Digitally sign communications (if server agrees)	Determines whether the SMB client will attempt to negotiate packet signing.	**Enabled** or Disabled
Microsoft network client: Send unencrypted password to third-party SMB servers	If enabled, allows SMB redirector to send plaintext passwords to non-Microsoft SMB servers that do not support password encryption during authentication.	Enabled or **Disabled**
Microsoft network server: Amount of idle time required before suspending session	Specifies the amount of continuous idle time that must pass before an SMB session is suspended for inactivity.	Enter a value or **15 minutes**
Microsoft network server: Attempt S4U2Self to obtain claim information	Determines whether clients running prior versions of Windows are allowed to access file shares requiring user claims.	Default Enabled Disabled
Microsoft network server: Digitally sign communications (always)	Determines whether the SMB server component requires packet signing.	Enabled or **Disabled**
Microsoft network server: Digitally sign communications (if client agrees)	Determines whether the SMB server will negotiate packet signing if the client requests it.	Enabled or **Disabled**
Microsoft network server: Disconnect clients when logon hours expire	Determines whether SMB-connected clients should be disconnected outside their sign-in hours.	**Enabled** or Disabled
Microsoft network server: Server SPN target name validation level	Controls the level of validation a computer sharing resource performs on the SPN provided by connecting client computers.	Off Accept if provided by client Required from client
Network access: Allow anonymous SID/Name translation	Determines whether an anonymous user can request security identifier (SID) attributes for another user account.	Enabled or **Disabled**
Network access: Do not allow anonymous enumeration of SAM accounts	Determines additional permissions that will be granted for anonymous connections to the computer.	**Enabled** or Disabled

Policy	Description	Configuration Options
Network access: Do not allow anonymous enumeration of SAM accounts and shares	Determines whether anonymous enumeration of SAM accounts and shares is allowed.	Enabled or **Disabled**
Network access: Do not allow storage of passwords and credentials for network authentication	Determines whether Credential Manager saves passwords and credentials for later use after it gains domain authentication.	Enabled or **Disabled**
Network access: Let Everyone permissions apply to anonymous users	If enabled, Everyone SID and permissions are added to the anonymous user at sign-in.	Enabled or **Disabled**
Network access: Named Pipes that can be accessed anonymously	Determines which communications sessions or pipes will allow anonymous access.	Enter a value or **None**
Network access: Remotely accessible registry paths	Determines which registry paths/keys can be accessed over the network.	\System\CurrentControlSet \Control\ProductOptions \System\CurrentControlSet \Control\Server Applications \Software\Microsoft\Windows NT \CurrentVersion
Network access: Remotely accessible registry paths and subpaths	Determines which registry paths and subpaths can be accessed over the network.	\System\CurrentControlSet \Control\Print\Printers \System\CurrentControlSet \Services\Eventlog \Software\Microsoft\OLAP Server \Software\Microsoft\Windows \NT\CurrentVersion\Print \Software\Microsoft\Windows \NT\CurrentVersion\Windows \System\CurrentControlSet \Control\ContentIndex \System\CurrentControlSet \Control\Terminal Server \System\CurrentControlSet \Control\Terminal Server \UserConfig \System\CurrentControlSet \Control\Terminal Server \DefaultUserConfig \Software\Microsoft\WindowsNT \CurrentVersion\Perflib \System\CurrentControlSet \Services\SysmonLog
Network access: Restrict anonymous access to Named Pipes and Shares	Restricts anonymous access to shares and pipes to the settings.	**Enabled** or Disabled
Network access: Shares that can be accessed anonymously	Determines which network shares can be accessed by anonymous users.	Enter a value or **None**
Network access: Sharing and security model for local accounts	Determines how to authenticate network sign-ins that use local accounts.	**Classic - users authenticate as themselves** Guest only - local users authenticate as Guest
Network security: Allow local system to use computer identity for NTLM	Allows local system services set to negotiate NTLM authentication to use the local computer identity.	Enabled or Disabled

Policy	Description	Configuration Options
Network security: Allow LocalSystem Null session failback	Allows NTLM to fail back to Null session when used with the LocalSystem account.	Enabled or Disabled
Network security: Allow PKU2U authentication requests to this computer to use online identities	Prevents online identities from authenticating to domain-joined machines.	Enabled or Disabled
Network security: Configure encryption types allowed for Kerberos	Configures the encryption types used by Kerberos.	**None selected**
Network security: Do not store LAN Manager hash value on next password change	Determines whether the LAN Manager hash value for the new password is stored following a password change.	**Enabled** or Disabled
Network security: Force logoff when logon hours expire	Determines whether to disconnect user accounts connected to SMB resources outside their sign-in hours.	**Enabled** or Disabled
Network security: LAN Manager authentication level	Determines which challenge/response authentication protocol is used for network sign-ins.	Send LM & NTLM responses Send LM & NTLM - use NTLMv2 session security if negotiated Send NTLM responses only Send NTLMv2 responses only Send NTLMv2 responses - refuse LM Send NTLMv2 responses only - refuse LM and NTLM
Network security: LDAP client signing requirements	Determines the level of data signing that is requested on behalf of clients issuing LDAP BIND requests.	None **Negotiate Signing** Require Signing
Network security: Minimum session security for NTLM Security Support Provider–based (including secure Remote Procedure Call) clients	Allows the client to require negotiation of 128-bit encryption and/or NTLMv2 session security.	Require NTLMv2 session security **Require 128-bit encryption**
Network security: Minimum session security for NTLM SSP–based (including secure RPC) servers	Enables the server to require negotiation of 128-bit encryption and/or NTLMv2 session security.	Require NTLMv2 session security **Require 128-bit encryption**
Network security: Restrict NTLM: Add remote server exceptions for NTLM authentication	Enables you to create an exceptions list of servers that can be used if the Restrict NTLM: Outgoing NTLM Traffic To Remote Servers setting is enabled.	Enter values or **None**
Network security: Restrict NTLM: Add server exceptions in this domain	Enables you to create an exceptions list of servers within a domain in which NTLM can be used.	Enter values or **None**
Network security: Restrict NTLM: Audit incoming NTLM traffic	Enables you to audit incoming NTLM traffic.	Disable Enable auditing for domain accounts Enable auditing for all accounts

Policy	Description	Configuration Options
Network Security: Restrict NTLM: Audit NTLM authentication in this domain	Enables you to audit NTLM authentication in the domain from this domain controller.	Disable Enable for domain accounts to domain servers Enable for domain accounts Enable for domain servers Enable all
Network security: Restrict NTLM: Incoming NTLM traffic	Determines whether incoming NTLM traffic will be restricted.	Allow all Deny all domain accounts Deny all accounts
Network Security: Restrict NTLM: NTLM authentication in this domain	Determines whether NTLM authentication for this domain will be restricted.	Disable Deny for domain accounts to domains servers Deny for all domain accounts Deny for all domain servers Deny all
Network security: Restrict NTLM: Outgoing NTLM traffic to remote servers	Allows you to deny or audit outgoing NTLM traffic from this computer to any remote Windows Server.	Allow all Audit all Deny all
Recovery console: Allow automatic administrative logon	Determines whether the administrator password must be provided to access the recovery console.	Enabled or Disabled
Recovery console: Allow floppy copy and access to all drives and all folders.	Determines whether the SET command is available in the recovery console.	Enabled or **Disabled**
Shutdown: Allow system to be shut down without having to log on	Determines whether the computer can be shut down without requiring someone to sign in.	Enabled or **Disabled**
Shutdown: Clear virtual memory page file	Determines whether the virtual memory page file is cleared when the computer shuts down.	Enabled or **Disabled**
System cryptography: Force strong key protection for user keys stored on the computer	Determines whether private keys require a password.	User input not required when new keys are stored and used User is prompted when the key is first used User must enter password each time a key is used
System cryptography: Use FIPS-compliant algorithms for encryption, hashing, and signing	Determines whether SSL should be disabled for SSP communication and whether triple data encryption standard (3DES) and advanced encryption standard (AES) should be used.	Enabled or **Disabled**
System objects: Require case sensitivity for non-Windows subsystems	Determines whether case sensitivity is enforced for all subsystems.	**Enabled** or Disabled
System objects: Strengthen default permissions of internal system objects (for example, Symbolic Links)	Determines the strength of the default discretionary access control list (DACL) for objects.	**Enabled** or Disabled
System settings: Optional subsystems	Determines which optional subsystems can be started to support applications.	**POSIX**

Policy	Description	Configuration Options
System settings: Use certificate rules on Windows executables for software restriction policies	Determines whether digital certificates are processed when applications with an .exe file name extension are run.	Enabled or **Disabled**
User account control: Admin Approval mode for the built-in administrator account	Controls the behavior of Admin Approval mode for the built-in administrator account.	Enabled or **Disabled**
User account control: Allow UIAccess applications to prompt for elevation without using secure desktop	Controls whether User Interface Accessibility (UIAccess) programs can automatically disable the secure desktop for elevation prompting by a standard user.	Enabled or **Disabled**
User account control: Behavior of the elevation prompt for administrators in Admin Approval mode	Controls the behavior of the elevation prompt for administrators.	Elevate without prompting Prompt for credentials on the secure desktop Prompt for consent on the secure desktop Prompt for credentials Prompt for consent Prompt for consent for non-Windows binaries
User account control: Behavior of the elevation prompt for standard users	Controls the behavior of the elevation prompt for standard users.	Automatically deny elevation requests Prompt for credentials on the secure desktop Prompt for credentials
User account control: Detect application installations and prompt for elevation	Controls the behavior of the application installation detection for the computer.	**Enabled** or Disabled
User account control: Only elevate executables that are signed and validated	Enforces public key infrastructure signature checks for any interactive applications requesting elevation of privileges.	Enabled or **Disabled**
User account control: Only elevate UIAccess applications that are installed in secure locations	Controls whether applications requesting to run with a UIAccess integrity level must reside in a secure location.	**Enabled** or Disabled
User account control: Run all administrators in Admin Approval mode	Controls the behavior of UAC policy settings for the computer.	**Enabled** or Disabled
User account control: Switch to the secure desktop when prompting for elevation	Controls whether the elevation request prompt is displayed on the secure desktop or on the user's standard desktop.	**Enabled** or Disabled
User account control: Virtualize file and registry write failures to per-user location	Controls whether application write failures are redirected to predetermined registry and file system locations.	**Enabled** or Disabled

Running tasks as administrator and user account control

When working with Windows 8, it might be necessary to impersonate another user, usually the administrator account, to perform a task. Prior to user account control (UAC), many applications relied on administrative credentials and privileges to perform their tasks. Doing this enabled the applications to function unchecked and, if compromised, cause potential problems across a computer or even throughout a networked environment. UAC requires the applications to function without elevated control, unless it is specifically granted by the user who is signed in.

User account control was created to ensure that most user accounts cannot perform actions that could damage the operating system. By default, UAC is enabled and set to a moderate level, which alerts you when system-changing events happen. For example, when you try to perform an action that exceeds the privilege level of your user account, UAC presents a sign-in dialog box asking for credentials with enough privilege to complete the task. Figure 12-9 shows an example of the UAC prompt dialog box.

FIGURE 12-9 UAC alerting you of an action

The goal of UAC is to prevent users from allowing everything to run with the highest privilege possible without at least being alerted to the actions. Actions that require additional elevation will prompt the signed-in user to provide credentials with more access rights than the current user account or alert the user of actions being taken. When UAC is turned on, very few applications can perform actions without the knowledge of the person using the computer.

To determine and modify the level of universal account control on a computer, complete the following steps:

1. On the Start screen, type **UAC** and press Enter.

2. Select Settings from the search results.

3. Select Change User Account Control Settings.

    Figure 12-10 shows the UAC Settings dialog box.

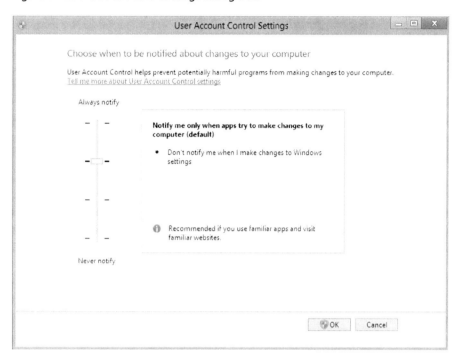

FIGURE 12-10 UAC settings configuration

4. Choose one of the following options:

    - Always notify me when:

        - Apps try to install software or make changes to my computer.

        - I make changes to Windows settings.

    - Notify me only when apps try to make changes to my computer (default).

    - Notify me only when apps try to make changes to my computer (do not dim my desktop).

    - Never notify me when:

        - Apps try to install software or make changes to my computer.

        - I make changes to Windows settings.

    If you choose the option of never being notified, you have effectively disabled UAC.

5. When you have chosen the settings that will work best for your computer, tap or click OK.

6. Restart your computer for the changes to UAC settings to take effect.

The option to dim the desktop as part of UAC helps make sure whoever is using the computer is aware of the prompt for changes. Many times with a dialog box, the first option selected or highlighted is chosen by using the Enter key, and the message presented is not reviewed. Changing the brightness of the desktop along with the dialog box will grab the user's attention. In addition, because a malicious application could produce a dialog box that looks identical to a Microsoft dialog box, the desktop is dimmed to ensure that you notice when something is modifying your computer.

Run As

Windows has supported the execution of applications or services using alternate credentials for many versions. With the introduction of UAC, the ability to elevate tasks to run as another user or as the local administrator is required when the currently signed-in user does not have the authority to perform a task.

For example, if Bob is signed in to a computer and wants to install his favorite music application, Windows will produce a prompt asking Bob for credentials with authorization to install this application. Previously, the installation would have been either denied or allowed when attempted. Bob would have needed to initiate the use of other credentials by selecting Run As from the context menu of the music application.

When selected, the task chosen to be run as administrator will be elevated to do that. This operation will prompt as needed so that a standard user account might need to provide alternate credentials. When an administrator signs in, the prompt disappears, and a dialog box in a darkened screen appears, asking whether you are sure you want to allow this level of execution. The elevated dialog box with no credential request is shown in Figure 12-11.

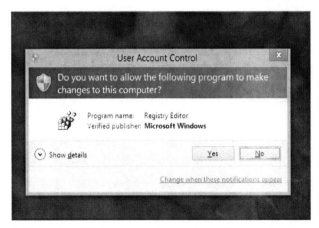

FIGURE 12-11 UAC also prompts for actions run by administrators

UAC is the result of feedback from customers at all levels. Considering how UAC operates, the prompt to confirm decisions or to provide administrative credentials to perform actions that could potentially damage the computer are steps in the right direction. These improvements, along with a certification program for applications, allow more applications to run without default administrative privilege for the primary user, which significantly decreases the odds of accidental malware installation.

 Quick check

- Which setting is the default option for UAC?

Quick check answer

- Notify me only when apps make changes to my computer.

To ensure the best security for your organization, you should make a concerted effort to leave UAC enabled at some level unless high-priority applications used in your organization cannot run with the feature enabled. It is likely that, as these applications are upgraded and new releases become available, the application's creator will begin to work UAC into the design. Because UAC is designed to help applications operate within the boundaries of the user account running them, Windows will become a more secure environment.

Using and managing certificates

In addition to using user names and passwords, smart cards, and other types of authentication or authorization methods to access resources, you can use digital certificates to ensure that the requesting party is who he claims to be. There are many types of digital certificates, some for authorization of resources (examined in detail here) and others, such as SSL or Unified Communications certificates, which verify the identity of websites to users who access them or ensure that your email client can verify the identity of the Microsoft Exchange server at your company.

How do certificates work?

Certificates use public keys to bind digital signatures to identities. Certificates are issued for identities by CAs. These servers, either within an organization or publicly available on the Internet, are trusted entities on which organizations rely to ensure the validity of the items bound to the certificates. CAs inside an organization only need to be trusted by known accounts and employees within the organization, in the case of identity certificates. Public CAs work differently, by maintaining a trusted and visible presence and charging a fee to secure identities (and other content).

When a certificate request is passed to a CA, information about the identity to which the certificate will be assigned must be provided. In many cases, this will include the following:

- Distinguished Name (DN)
- Business/Organization Name

- Department/Organizational Unit
- City/Town
- Province/Region/County/State
- Country/Region
- Email address

From the information collected during the request-generation process, a *hash*, or summary value of the collected information, is created to be submitted to the CA. The CA will use this signature to create the certificate that is bound to the identity provided.

After the certificate has been created, it can be installed on a smart card or loaded into a certificate store on a computer and used to access resources by using the certified identity. Using a certificate provides proof that this identity is valid because of the signature used to create it. Whenever the digital signature is incorrect, the identity cannot be trusted because it does not match the certificate.

Managing certificates in Windows 8

Windows has a special location called the certificate store for keeping and managing certificates. The *certificate store* is a folder containing all the certificates for a user and is managed by Certificate Manager (Certmgr). The folders displayed by Certmgr are a collection of known locations where different types of certificates are installed and managed for use by a computer. Figure 12-12 shows the certificate store in Windows 8 for the currently signed-in user account.

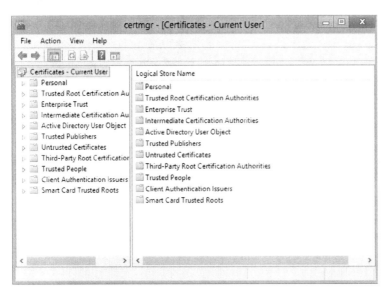

FIGURE 12-12 Certificate Manager displaying the certificate store for the current user

There are many certificate stores within Certificate Manager, including the following:

- **Personal**   Certificates with private keys known to the user
- **Trusted Root Certification Authorities**   CAs that are implicitly trusted by the user account, including all certificates in the third-party root certificates store and Microsoft
- **Enterprise Trust**   Certificate trust lists that allow self-signed certificates to be trusted
- **Intermediate Certification Authorities**   Certificates issued to subordinate (non-root) CAs
- **Active Directory User Object**   Certificates assigned to the current user's Active Directory user object and published in the directory
- **Trusted Publishers**   Certificates generated by CAs that are allowed by software restriction policies
- **Untrusted Certificates**   Certificates whose CA could not be verified or is explicitly not trusted
- **Third-Party Root Certification Authorities**   Certificates from root CAs other than those within your organization or at Microsoft
- **Trusted People**   Certificates issued to people or other entities with explicit trust
- **Client Authentication Issuers**   Certificates used by applications to authenticate to servers
- **Smart Card Trusted Roots**   Certificates obtained by root CAs for use with smart cards

Certificates can also be assigned at the computer level to allow one computer to verify another or to authenticate with a server. All certificates are managed using the Microsoft Management console; the set of stores made available to the snap-in depends on the choices made when adding the certificate snap-in. Options include the following:

- **My User Account**   Manages certificates for the signed-in (or current) user (as described previously)
- **Service Account**   Manages the certificate store for certificates assigned to service accounts
- **Computer Account**   Manages the certificate store for any certificates assigned to the computer itself

To be used, certificates obtained from a CA must be imported into a certificate store so they can be managed by the system. The purpose of the store is to organize certificates on a computer and make them easier to manage.

 Quick check

- Which certificate store would contain your personal smart card certificate?

Quick check answer

- The Smart Card Trusted Roots store.

Lesson summary

■ Permissions are assigned to objects that you want to secure, such as files and folders, whereas rights define the level of access that user accounts have to these objects.

■ UAC ensures that applications running on your computer do not rely on an administrator account and makes you aware when an application intends to make changes to your computer.

■ Certificates store information about the identity of a computer user and can be used to simplify and secure a sign-in and access to information.

Lesson review

Answer the following questions to test your knowledge of the information in this lesson. You can find the answers to these questions and explanations of why each answer choice is correct or incorrect in the "Answers" section at the end of this chapter.

1. Carmella, an employee in the sales department at Tailspin Toys, wants to install a new version of her favorite music player on her computer because there has been a recent update. When she downloads the update, a dialog box appears, asking for an administrator to sign in and allow the application to complete. She calls you because she has never seen this before and is not sure why it is appearing. Why did Carmella receive this dialog box?

   A. Because the music player is not a work-related application

   B. Because UAC is enabled, and Carmella does not have the required privileges to proceed

   C. Because the IT group has enabled auditing on the music player application

   D. Because Windows Update requires elevated credentials to complete installation

2. Janet, a new employee with your organization, is calling the help desk because she is unable to sign in to any computer within her department. All the other employees in this department have no problems signing in. Until recently, Janet has been able to sign in without a problem. Which rights should you examine to ensure that Janet can sign in?

   A. The Allow Logon Locally and Deny Logon Locally rights

   B. The Logon As A Batch Job User right

   C. The Trust User For Delegation User right

   D. Ensure that Janet's user account is not locked out

3. The owner of your company is having trouble accessing an online resource that requires a custom certificate. He tells you he has received a new certificate and downloaded the file but that the website will not work. What could be the reason the downloaded certificate file is not functioning as needed?

    A. The certificate is corrupted.

    B. The certificate has not been installed and placed in the certificate store.

    C. The certificate has expired.

    D. The computer cannot reach the website.

Practice exercises

In this chapter, you learned about authentication in Windows 8. In addition to the user name and password authentication method, Windows supports several other types of authentication. The exercises in this section will help you practice configuring these alternative methods of authentication.

Exercise 1: Configure a Microsoft account for authentication

This exercise focuses on creating and using a Microsoft account for authentication.

1. Select the Settings charm, and then select Change PC Settings.

2. Select Users from the PC Settings navigation bar.

3. Tap or click Switch To A Microsoft Account.

4. Enter your current account password.

5. Associate your Windows account with a Microsoft account.

6. Log off the computer and sign in using the associated Microsoft account.

Exercise 2: Configure a picture password and PIN for sign-in

This exercise focuses on two authentication options, a PIN and a picture password.

1. Select the Settings charm, and then select Change PC Settings.

2. Select Users from the PC Settings navigation pane.

3. Tap or click Create A PIN under Sign-In Options.

4. Assign a PIN (4-digit number) to allow the option of entering a PIN to sign in. In addition to a PIN, assign a picture password as a sign-in option.

5. From the Users screen in PC Settings, select Create A Picture Password.

6. Associate an image and gestures with your user account.

7. Log off Windows and sign in using the new picture password.

Exercise 3: Run applications with elevated privileges

This exercise uses Run As Administrator to elevate the execution of applications.

1. Locate the command prompt application.
2. Open the application without elevated privileges.
3. Notice the location of the prompt.
4. Exit the command prompt.
5. Locate the command prompt application again.
6. Execute it as the administrator.
7. Notice the location of the command prompt.
8. Exit the application.

Suggested practice exercises

The following additional practice exercises are designed to give you more opportunities to practice what you've learned and to help you successfully master the lessons presented in this chapter.

These practice exercises might require additional hardware, including a USB smart card reader and a USB fingerprint scanner.

- **Exercise 1** Configure biometric authentication for your Windows user account.
- **Exercise 2** Configure smart card authentication for your Windows user account.

Answers

This section contains answers to the lesson review questions in this chapter.

Lesson 1

1. **Correct answer: B**

    A. **Incorrect:** Disabling complex passwords can compromise security for your organization. This is not recommended.

    B. **Correct:** Enabling a PIN for the user accounts will enable streamlined sign-in for mobile devices without removing any password requirements already in place.

    C. **Incorrect:** Removing the password requirements disables any security for these users, allowing anyone to use these accounts to access the organization's resources.

    D. **Incorrect:** Auditing sign-in successes will not streamline any sign-in.

2. **Correct answer: C**

    A. **Incorrect:** Storing passwords and other sensitive information in a text file is a security risk because anyone with access to the file or knowledge of its location might be able to use the credentials stored in the file.

    B. **Incorrect:** Internet Explorer does not store credentials in the Favorites folder. This folder contains only bookmarks to websites that have been saved.

    C. **Correct:** Using Credential Manager is the best way to store sign-in information for websites that require credentials. It also enables you to store certificate-based credentials for resources.

    D. **Incorrect:** Using Microsoft Excel to manage passwords will not provide secure storage for this information.

3. **Correct answer: B**

    A. **Incorrect:** Windows Firewall does not prevent interactive sign-ins by using any method.

    B. **Correct:** The option to sign in to Windows by using biometrics must be enabled.

    C. **Incorrect:** PIN-based sign-ins are different from biometrics because they use a 4-digit code to authenticate the user; biometric sign-ins do not use a PIN.

    D. **Incorrect:** Windows does not require the user account to use a complex password to enable biometrics.

Lesson 2

1. **Correct answer: B**

   A. **Incorrect:** The business rules in place within an organization do not directly prevent applications from being installed.

   B. **Correct:** User account control requires the person who is signed in to be notified when certain events occur. In the case of an installation, if the signed-in user does not hold the required privileges to install the application, different credentials will be needed.

   C. **Incorrect:** Auditing of an application or user account access to applications does not require additional privileges.

   D. **Incorrect:** Windows Update will not specifically prompt for alternate credentials.

2. **Correct answer: A**

   A. **Correct:** Janet's user account might have been removed from the Allow Logon Locally user right or added to the Deny Logon Locally user right. This might have been the result of modification to the groups to which her user account belongs.

   B. **Incorrect:** Logon As A Batch Job does not affect interactive sign-in to the computer.

   C. **Incorrect:** Trusting the user account for delegation does not affect interactive sign-in but might have other affects that are undesirable within an environment.

   D. **Incorrect:** Although a locked-out account would prevent sign-in, the effects of this would reach beyond Janet's department.

3. **Correct answer: B**

   A. **Incorrect:** Certificate corruption would cause problems; however, in this case the owner would also be unable to install or access the downloaded certificate.

   B. **Correct:** When a certificate is installed, it is placed in the specified certificate store, which will enable both management and use of the certificate.

   C. **Incorrect:** Because the certificate is new and was recently downloaded, the chances that it has expired are very slim. The validity dates for the certificate can be checked after the certificate is installed.

   D. **Incorrect:** The owner would have been unable to download the certificate if the Internet connection on his computer had not been working.

CHAPTER 13

Managing and securing mobility

Mobility and touch are key initiatives in Windows 8, which helps bring a consistent experience to many devices. Because more mobile devices are being introduced to organizations every day, it is important for Windows administrators to consider how mobile devices are handled. Windows 8 has built-in features to help manage mobile devices and keep them performing at the standards of an organization. One of these features, Windows To Go, offers an entirely new way to use Windows and was covered in Chapter 2, "Installing and migrating to Windows 8."

Lessons in this chapter:

Before you begin

To complete the practice exercises in this chapter, you will need:

- Access to a mobile test device, such as a tablet or laptop, that runs Windows 8.
- A removable drive to configure BitLocker To Go.
- Network file shares to work with offline files.

Lesson 1: Managing BitLocker and other policy-based mobility tools

Security plays a very large role in any organization, but as the use of mobile devices increases—and with it, employees' expectation that they can work from anywhere—keeping devices secure becomes increasingly important for administrators and support staff. Using tools provided in Windows 8, mobile computing environments can remain as secure as their counterparts in the corporate office.

After this lesson, you will be able to:

- Create policies to manage offline files.
- Create policies related to power usage to manage the actions taken by a device.
- Ensure that content on mobile devices running Windows 8 is encrypted and secured with BitLocker.
- Use startup key storage.
- Configure and manage BitLocker features from the command line.

Estimated lesson time: 60 minutes

Configuring BitLocker policies

BitLocker is an encryption technology used to ensure that an entire volume is encrypted. Encrypting File System (EFS) enables encryption on specified files and folders, which allows granular control of the technology but makes management more difficult because the encrypted files or folders can be anywhere on the disk. With BitLocker, the entire volume is encrypted and requires a Trusted Platform Module (TPM) chip in the computer or an alternate method of authentication, such as an encryption key on a USB flash disk, to operate. Configuring BitLocker is covered in Chapter 11, "File system and storage management."

Using policies to configure BitLocker allows the settings to be centrally managed if the computer or device is managed by Active Directory. If the computer or device is not managed by Active Directory, the same policy settings can be applied by using the Local Group Policy Editor. Configuring the settings for a local policy uses the same concepts as configuring Group Policy in Active Directory; the difference is that the settings apply only to the local computer or to user accounts on the local computer.

If the computer joins an Active Directory domain and a conflicting setting exists within the domain, the local computer's setting will be overwritten by the settings from Active Directory.

Policy settings for BitLocker include the following:

- **Fixed Data Drives**
    - Configure Use Of Smart Cards On Fixed Data Drives
    - Deny Write Access To Fixed Drives Not Protected By BitLocker
    - Configure Use Of Hardware-Based Encryption For Fixed Data Drives
    - Enforce Drive Encryption Type On Fixed Data Drives
    - Allow Access To BitLocker-Protected Fixed Data Drives From Earlier Versions Of Windows
    - Configure Use Of Passwords For Fixed Data Drives
    - Choose How BitLocker-Protected Fixed Drives Can Be Recovered

- **Operating System Drives**
    - Allow Network Unlock At Startup
    - Allow Secure Boot For Integrity Validation
    - Require Additional Authentication At Startup
    - Require Additional Authentication At Startup (Windows Server 2008 And Windows Vista)
    - Disallow Standard Users From Changing The PIN Or Password
    - Enable Use Of BitLocker Authentication Requiring Preboot Keyboard Input On Slates
    - Allow Enhanced PINs For Startup
    - Configure Minimum PIN Length For Startup
    - Configure Use Of Hardware-Based Encryption For Operating System Drives
    - Enforce Drive Encryption Type On Operating System Drives
    - Configure Use Of Passwords For Operating System Drives
    - Choose How BitLocker-Protected Operating System Drives Can Be Recovered
    - Configure TPM Platform Validation Profile For BIOS-Based Firmware Configuration
    - Configure TPM Platform Validation Profile (Windows Vista, Windows Server 2008, Windows 7, And Windows Server 2008 R2)
    - Configure TPM Platform Validation Profile For Native Unified Extensible Firmware Interface (UEFI) Firmware Configurations
    - Reset Platform Validation Data After BitLocker Recovery
    - Use Enhanced Boot Configuration Data Validation Profile
    - Store BitLocker Recovery Information In Active Directory Domain Services (AD DS) (Windows Server 2008 And Windows Vista)
    - Choose Default Folder For Recovery Password
    - Choose How Often Users Can Recover BitLocker-Protected Drives (Windows Server 2008 And Windows Vista)
    - Choose Drive Encryption Method And Cipher Strength
    - Choose Drive Encryption Method And Cipher Strength (Windows Vista, Windows Server 2008, Windows Server 2008 R2, And Windows 7)
    - Provide The Unique Identifiers For Your Organization
    - Prevent Memory Overwrite On Restart
    - Validate Smart Card Certificate Usage Rule Compliance

NOTE **SETTINGS FOR REMOVABLE DRIVES**

The settings for removable drives (BitLocker To Go) are discussed in "Using BitLocker on removable media (BitLocker To Go)" later in this lesson.

Figure 13-1 displays the Local Group Policy Editor with the BitLocker policy objects displayed.

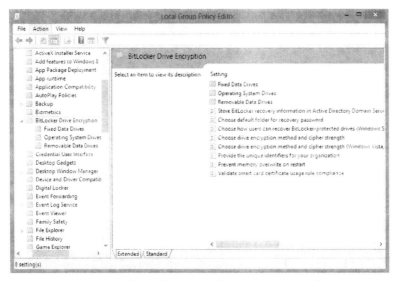

FIGURE 13-1 BitLocker configured by using policy settings to centralize management of the feature

To configure the local policy settings, complete the following steps:

1. Launch the Local Group Policy Editor by searching for gpedit.msc on the Start screen or typing **gpedit.msc** in the Run dialog box (Windows logo key+R).

2. Expand the Computer Configuration\Administrative Templates\Windows Components\ BitLocker Drive Encryption path.

3. Select the policy object you want to work with.

4. Select Enabled.

5. Review the explanation provided with the object and configure available options as needed.

6. Tap or click OK to save the changes.

Managing BitLocker at the command line

Like many other features in Windows 8, BitLocker supports command-line operations. This section describes both the Windows PowerShell cmdlets and Manage-bde.exe, which is a BitLocker command-line tool.

Manage-bde uses parameters to perform actions on specified volumes. To enable BitLocker by using Manage-bde.exe, type **manage-bde -on C:\ -recoverypassword -recoverykey F:** in an elevated command prompt or PowerShell session. This command enables BitLocker on the C drive and encrypts the content. It also prompts for a recovery password and stores the recovery key on the F disk.

Using command-line tools to work with BitLocker enables scripting of the configuration on computers within an environment. Manage-bde.exe parameters are listed in Table 13-1.

TABLE 13-1 Parameters for Manage-bde.exe

Parameter	Explanation
-status	Displays information about BitLocker-capable volumes
-on	Encrypts the selected volume and enables BitLocker
-off	Decrypts the selected volume and disables BitLocker
-pause	Suspends BitLocker encryption, decryption, or free space wipe
-resume	Continues BitLocker encryption, decryption, or free space wipe
-lock	Prevents access to BitLocker-encrypted data
-unlock	Allows access to BitLocker-encrypted data
-autounlock	Manages the capability of the BitLocker-encrypted volume to unlock automatically
-protectors	Manages protection methods for a volume
-SetIdentifier or -si	Configures the identification field for a volume
-ForceRecovery or -fr	Forces a BitLocker-protected operating system to recover on restart
-changepassword	Modifies the password for a volume
-changepin	Modifies the PIN for a volume
-changekey	Modifies the startup key for a volume
-keypackage or -kp	Creates a key package for a volume
-upgrade	Updates the BitLocker version
-WipeFreeSpace or -w	Cleans the free space on a volume
-ComputerName or -cn	Runs the commands on a remote computer
-? or /?	Displays a brief help for a specified command
-Help or -h	Displays the full help for Manage-bde

 Quick check

- **Can Manage-bde unlock a drive and provide access to its contents?**

Quick check answer

- **Yes the -unlock switch provides this functionality when a recovery key is supplied.**

Many parameters are available for the Manage-bde utility, which makes it quite scriptable and a great alternative to the GUI-based wizard, especially if an administrator needs to use the tool on multiple computers. For example, your manager will be getting a new computer running Windows 8 as part of a pilot program. He has heard about BitLocker and often travels between locations. He would like to have his computer encrypted with BitLocker as soon as possible because he is leaving on business and wants to take the computer with him. To facilitate the encryption of the hard disk, Manage-bde can enable BitLocker encryption on the computer by using the following command:

```
Manage-bde.exe -on c:\ -password -recoverykey U:
```

When this command executes, it prompts for a password and confirmation as part of the password switch. It saves the recovery key to the U drive. If this needed to be done remotely, the -computername parameter could also be specified to run the command from a remote computer, in which case the password would be specified on the system running the command.

In addition to Manage-bde.exe, some BitLocker functionality is available through Windows PowerShell cmdlets. The following cmdlets are included with Windows 8 for BitLocker:

- **Unlock-BitLocker**   Allows access to BitLocker-protected data volumes
- **Suspend-BitLocker**   Pauses BitLocker operations
- **Resume-BitLocker**   Continues BitLocker operations
- **Lock-BitLocker**   Prevents access to BitLocker-protected data volumes
- **Enable-BitLocker**   Turns BitLocker on and encrypts content
- **Disable-BitLocker**   Turns BitLocker off and decrypts content

These cmdlets perform the same functions against BitLocker as Manage-bde and can be used with Windows PowerShell to work on remote computers.

> *IMPORTANT* **WINDOWS POWERSHELL CAN BE QUITE HELPFUL**
>
> You can find help for any Windows PowerShell cmdlets by typing **help <cmdlet>**; for example, **help unlock-BitLocker**. In Windows PowerShell 3.0, only a shell of help is available on the computer. To load the complete help contents, open an administrative PowerShell session and type **update-help** to download fresh help contents.

Using BitLocker on computers without TPM

Although the Trusted Platform Module (TPM) is present on an increasing number of devices to aid with security, there are still devices in use today that do not use TPM technology. Because Windows 8 can operate on hardware that might have been provisioned for earlier versions of Windows, organizations might not purchase new laptops or, if they do purchase new laptops, they might be smaller, more portable units that do not support TPM.

In these cases, it is still possible to use BitLocker encryption to keep the information stored on mobile devices secure. The encryption key information for a BitLocker-encrypted drive will be stored on startup key storage.

Startup key storage is a storage device, usually a USB flash device, that stores the encryption key for the BitLocker configuration on a device. When the computer starts, the process asks for the USB key containing the BitLocker encryption key. After the key is provided, the computer continues to start.

To enable BitLocker on a computer without TPM, complete the following steps:

1. Launch the Local Group Policy Editor by searching for gpedit.msc on the Start screen or typing **gpedit.msc** in the Run dialog box (Windows logo key+R).

2. Expand the Computer Configuration\Administrative Templates\Windows Components\ BitLocker Drive Encryption path.

3. Select Operating System Drives.

4. Press and hold or right-click Require Additional Authentication At Startup.

5. Select Enabled.

6. Select Allow BitLocker Without A Compatible TPM.

7. Tap or click OK to save the changes.

IMPORTANT **DOCUMENT THE CHANGES**

When modifying policies such as BitLocker, it is helpful to add a comment about what has been done and the reason for the change. Since the release of Windows 7, comments have been visible when searching for policy objects. A short description can be helpful when looking for objects that have been modified.

After the settings in local Group Policy have been adjusted to allow the use of a startup key, computers without the option of TPM will be able to encrypt drives. When the policy is configured, the default options for the Group Policy Object (GPO) also enable the use of TPM, as shown in Figure 13-2. The settings do not disable it; they just allow the encryption key to be stored elsewhere.

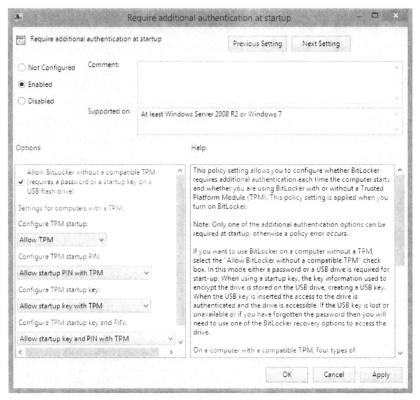

FIGURE 13-2 Configuring BitLocker to run on a device without TPM

Using BitLocker on removable media (BitLocker To Go)

Just as BitLocker for built-in drives enables data to be encrypted, BitLocker To Go focuses on removable media and encrypting data stored there. When BitLocker To Go is enabled, the entire volume is encrypted, and one key is stored on the removable media. The other portion of the pair is a password known to whomever encrypted the drive. When the drive is inserted on a computer that supports BitLocker, a password prompt appears to allow the drive to be unlocked.

Windows 8 includes the following policy settings for BitLocker for removable drives:

- Control Use Of BitLocker On Removable Drives
- Configure Use Of Smart Cards On Removable Data Drives
- Deny Write Access To Removable Drives Not Protected By BitLocker
- Configure Use Of Hardware-Based Encryption For Removable Media
- Enforce Drive Encryption Type On Removable Data Drives
- Allow Access To BitLocker-Protected Removable Data Drives From Earlier Versions Of Windows

- Configure Use Of Passwords For Removable Data Drives
- Choose How BitLocker-Protected Removable Drives Can Be Recovered

To configure the policy objects for BitLocker on removable media, complete the following steps:

1. Launch the Local Group Policy Editor by searching for gpedit.msc on the Start screen or typing **gpedit.msc** in the Run dialog box (Windows logo key+R).
2. Expand the Computer Configuration\Administrative Templates\Windows Components \BitLocker Drive Encryption\Removable Data Drives path.
3. Double-tap or double-click the policy object you want to work with.
4. Select Enabled.
5. Configure other options, if available, as needed for your organization.
6. Document the changes within the object's comments dialog box.
7. Tap or click OK to save the changes.

> *IMPORTANT* **DO NOT ENCRYPT STARTUP KEY DEVICES BY USING BITLOCKER**
>
> **Using BitLocker to encrypt a removable drive used as a startup key for a computer that does not support TPM is not supported. Because the computer requires the key from the USB drive to start Windows, but the USB drive is encrypted by BitLocker, which requires Windows to be accessed, the device will be unable to start a computer.**

Configuring policy settings for offline files

Offline files settings enable a device to continue working with files that were obtained from the network while the device is disconnected. Changes made to these files are synchronized with the network when the device is reconnected. This provides flexibility for individuals who are mobile and want to work on documents while traveling.

The following offline files policy settings are included with Windows 8:

- Subfolders Always Available Offline
- Specify Administratively Assigned Offline Files
- Configure Background Sync
- Limit Disk Space Used By Offline Files
- Non-Default Server Disconnect Actions
- Default Cache Size
- Allow Or Disallow Use Of The Offline Files Feature
- Encrypt The Offline Files Cache
- Event Logging Level
- Enable File Screens

- Files Not Cached
- Action On Server Disconnect
- Prevent Use Of Offline Files Folder
- Prohibit User Configuration Of Offline Files
- Remove "Make Available Offline" Command
- Remove "Make Available Offline" Command For These Files And Folders
- Turn Off Reminder Balloons
- Enable Transparent Caching
- At Logoff, Delete Local Copy Of User's Offline Files
- Turn On Economical Application Of Administratively Assigned Offline Files
- Reminder Balloon Frequency
- Initial Reminder Balloon Lifetime
- Configure Slow-Link Mode
- Configure Slow-Link Speed
- Synchronize All Offline Files Before Logging Off
- Synchronize All Offline Files When Logging On
- Synchronize Offline Files Before Suspend
- Enable File Synchronization On Costed Networks
- Remove "Work Offline" Command

To configure offline files policy settings, complete the following steps:

1. Launch the Local Group Policy Editor by searching for gpedit.msc on the Start screen or typing **gpedit.msc** in the Run dialog box (Windows logo key+R).

2. Expand the Computer Configuration\Administrative Templates\Network\Offline Files path.

3. Double-tap or double-click the policy object you want to work with.

4. Select Enabled.

5. Configure other options, if available, as needed for your organization.

6. Document the changes within the object's comments dialog box.

7. Tap or click OK to save the changes.

Figure 13-3 shows the configuration dialog box for the Subfolders Always Available Offline policy object.

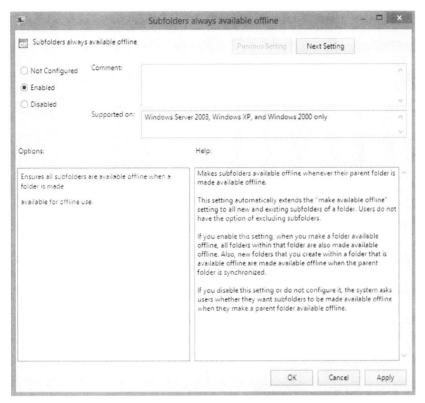

FIGURE 13-3 Policy settings to ensure that subfolders of an offline folder are also available offline

One of the best use cases for offline files, as mentioned previously, is to configure the portable devices of employees within an organization who travel some of the time or work from home some of the time. For example, the vice president of sales for Contoso travels about 100 days per year but maintains an office at Contoso and spends most of his days there when he is not traveling. When he travels, he uses time on airplanes and in hotel rooms to work. Configuring offline files allows him to have the necessary files while he is away. In addition to connecting to the corporate network through a virtual private network (VPN) or other technologies, the files taken offline are available locally without any connection to the office, making him productive even without the Internet.

Configuring offline file synchronization

When offline files are enabled, other settings also need to be configured to enable the files to synchronize. Because a number of services are available that Windows 8 can synchronize with, the settings have been placed in Control Panel under a Sync Options heading. Selecting this option displays all the items the computer can currently synchronize with. If nothing has been configured to synchronize, no items are displayed. Figure 13-4 displays the Sync Center in Windows 8.

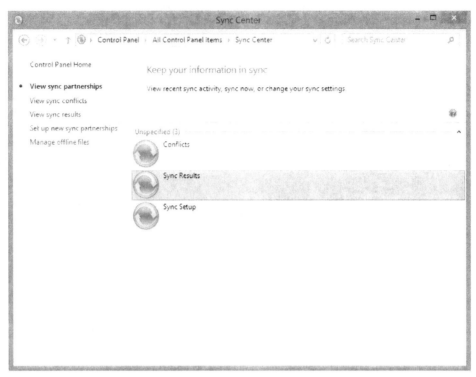

FIGURE 13-4 Managing the services or files that synchronize with a computer

Because offline files require the synchronization of items between the network and the local computer, they are also managed in Sync Center. Selecting Manage Offline Files from the navigation pane on the left side of the Sync Center displays the Offline Files dialog box shown in Figure 13-5.

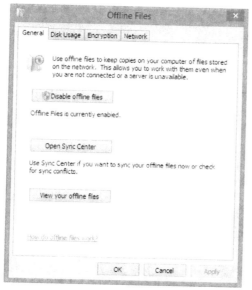

FIGURE 13-5 Configuring Offline Files

The Offline Files dialog box has the following tabs and features available for configuration:

- **General**
    - Enable (or Disable) Offline Files
    - Open Sync Center
    - View Your Offline Files
- **Disk Usage**
    - All Offline Files   Shows the amount of disk space being consumed by files available offline
    - Temporary Files   Shows the amount of disk space used by temporary files
    - Change Limits   Opens the Offline Files Disk Usage Limits dialog box, which enables disk space for offline files and temporary files to be controlled
    - Delete Temporary Files   Removes temporary files from the computer
- **Encryption**
    - Encrypt   Encrypts offline files and new files as they are taken offline
    - Decrypt   Decrypts offline files
- **Network**
    - On Slow Connections, Automatically Work Offline
    - Check For A Slow Connection Every 5 Minutes

These settings allow the files that will be available offline to be selected and managed on the remote computer. Policy settings described earlier might disable or control some of these settings when the two groups of settings are used together.

 Quick check

- Can Offline Files policies restrict which files are allowed to be available offline?

Quick check answer

- Yes, several policy settings can restrict access to the entire feature for Offline Files. Policies can also be used to specify administratively selected files and folders for use offline.

Configuring policy settings for device power

As more devices become portable or mobile and can support an operating system such as Windows 8, the amount of configuration for Windows available through policy will likely grow as new features become available. In Windows 8, a number of power management settings are available to help centrally manage the actions taken with regard to power. One useful feature can ensure that Windows restarts when certain actions are taken; for example, when the user accounts within a certain organizational unit log off. If the computer used by one of these employees is not restarted very often and some updates require a restart, this can ensure that the computer receives updates during restart.

The configurable policy options for power management include the following:

- **Button settings**
  - Select The Power Button Action (Plugged In)
  - Select The Sleep Button Action (Plugged In)
  - Select The Start Menu Power Button Action (Plugged In)
  - Select The Lid Switch Action (Plugged In)
  - Select The Power Button Action (On Battery)
  - Select The Sleep Button Action (On Battery)
  - Select The Start Menu Power Button Action (On Battery)
  - Select The Lid Switch Action (On Battery)
- **Hard disk settings**
  - Turn Off The Hard Disk (Plugged In)
  - Turn Off The Hard Disk (On Battery)
- **Notification settings**
  - Critical Battery Notification Action
  - Low Battery Notification Action

- Critical Battery Notification Level
- Turn Off Low Battery User Notification
- Low Battery Notification Level
- Reserve Battery Notification Level

- **Sleep settings**
  - Turn On The Ability For Applications To Prevent Sleep Transitions (Plugged In)
  - Turn On The Ability For Applications To Prevent Sleep Transitions (On Battery)
  - Specify The System Hibernate Timeout (Plugged In)
  - Specify The System Hibernate Timeout (On Battery)
  - Require A Password When A Computer Wakes (Plugged In)
  - Require A Password When A Computer Wakes (On Battery)
  - Specify The System Sleep Timeout (Plugged In)
  - Specify The System Sleep Timeout (On Battery)
  - Turn Off Hybrid Sleep (Plugged In)
  - Turn Off Hybrid Sleep (On Battery)
  - Allow Standby States (S1-S3) When Sleeping (Plugged In)
  - Allow Standby States (S1-S3) When Sleeping (On Battery)
  - Allow Applications To Prevent Automatic Sleep (Plugged In)
  - Allow Applications To Prevent Automatic Sleep (On Battery)
  - Specify The Unattended Sleep Timeout (Plugged In)
  - Specify The Unattended Sleep Timeout (On Battery)

- **Video and display settings**
  - Specify The Display Dim Brightness (Plugged In)
  - Specify The Display Dim Brightness (On Battery)
  - Reduce Display Brightness (Plugged In)
  - Reduce Display Brightness (On Battery)
  - Turn On Desktop Background Slideshow (Plugged In)
  - Turn On Desktop Background Slideshow (On Battery)
  - Turn Off Adaptive Display Timeout (Plugged In)
  - Turn Off Adaptive Display Timeout (On Battery)
  - Turn Off The Display (Plugged In)
  - Turn Off The Display (On Battery)
  - Specify A Current Active Power Plan
  - Select An Active Power Plan

To configure power management policy objects, complete the following steps:

1. Launch the Local Group Policy Editor by searching for gpedit.msc on the Start screen or typing **gpedit.msc** in the Run dialog box (Windows logo key+R).

2. Expand the Computer Configuration\Administrative Templates\System\Power Management path.

3. Double-tap or double-click the policy object you want to work with.

4. Select Enabled.

5. Configure other options, if available, as needed for your organization.

6. Document the changes within the object's comments dialog box.

7. Tap or click OK to save the changes for the setting.

> *MORE INFO*   **GROUP POLICY SETTINGS REFERENCE**
>
> **For more information on configuring policy and to see a Microsoft Excel document listing the policy items included with Windows 8, please visit the Group Policy Settings Reference at *https://www.microsoft.com/en-us/download/details.aspx?displaylang=en&id=25250*.**

Lesson summary

- BitLocker and BitLocker To Go both have policy settings that help provide security for mobile devices.
- Functionality is available for devices without TPM to use BitLocker.
- Configure BitLocker from the command line by using either the Manage-bde command-line tool or Windows PowerShell cmdlets.
- Windows 8 enable you to configure policy objects for offline files.
- Policy objects can be used to manage power policies for devices.

Lesson review

Answer the following questions to test your knowledge of the information in this lesson. You can find the answers to these questions and explanations of why each answer choice is correct or incorrect in the "Answers" section at the end of this chapter.

1. Steve, an accounting director for Contoso, wants to keep backup copies of the Excel workbooks he uses every day on a flash drive to ensure that he can work on them whenever necessary. When he inserts a flash drive into his computer, he receives a dialog box stating that before he can save files on the drive, it needs to be encrypted by using BitLocker. Concerned, he opens a help desk ticket about the issue. What is the reason for this message?

    A. The computer's hard disk is encrypted with BitLocker and requires special permissions to use removable media.

B. The BitLocker policy denying write access to non-BitLocker-encrypted media is enabled.

C. Windows 8 requires all removable media to be encrypted.

D. Because the removable media is not owned by the organization, it cannot be used on this computer.

2. While you are trying to enable BitLocker encryption on several netbook computers running Windows 8 that your organization uses for those who travel infrequently to give presentations, the process fails to encrypt the computer. You have enabled BitLocker on other computers without problems. What would cause BitLocker encryption to fail on the netbook computers?

A. BitLocker is not available on computers with less than 2 GB RAM installed.

B. BitLocker works only on computers that have Trusted Platform Module (TPM) capabilities.

C. The policy object for additional authentication at startup is not configured.

D. Configuring BitLocker requires the use of command-line utilities.

3. Because Tailspin Toys employs a number of remote account managers who do not work in the office every day, the IT department must ensure that the files and folders these employees need are available when they are not on the Internet. Which of the following would allow this type of access and place the least burden on employees in the office?

A. Allow the remote employees to connect to the corporate network over a VPN.

B. Require the remote employees to request documents through email.

C. Configure offline files policies for the remote workers and help them sync the files they need next time they connect to the network.

D. Configure Direct Access connections to the corporate network.

4. The help desk has been receiving complaints about computers being turned off when employees return from extended meetings or from lunch. When this happens, the employees are required to press the power button to turn their computers on to access their computers. What can be changed on these computers to prevent this from occurring?

A. Schedule the computers to restart after a period of inactivity so they are back at the logon screen when the employees return.

B. Configure each computer to use an AlwaysOn power scheme.

C. Configure power policies for all the computers in the organization to ensure the same experience on all computers.

D. Explain that the computers are not actually turned off but in a sleep state to conserve energy and allow the button pressing to continue.

Lesson 2: Working with location-based settings and connection methods

Windows 8 runs on a variety of devices, from traditional desktop and laptop computers to netbooks, ultrabooks, and tablets, making it the most mobility-ready version of Windows yet. Features including metered connection monitoring, airplane mode, and GPS availability enhance the mobility aspect of Windows 8. This lesson focuses on some of these settings, including where to find them and how to configure them.

> **After this lesson, you will be able to:**
> - Understand Wi-Fi Direct in Windows 8.
> - Manage built-in GPS settings.
> - Manage airplane mode in Windows 8.
>
> **Estimated lesson time: 35 minutes**

Connecting to devices by using Wi-Fi Direct

Computers and mobile devices have shared a connection over Bluetooth for some time, enabling wireless headsets to pair with smart phones and computers and enabling the use of wireless mice for traveling users. Windows 8 supports Bluetooth and continues to allow these types of connections. In addition, it supports a new standard of communication between devices called Wi-Fi Direct, which creates a peer-to-peer network between devices within a certain range.

Securing Wi-Fi to a device

The specification for Wi-Fi Direct lists the security as WPA-2, which uses AES 256-bit security. For most peer-to-peer networks on which Wi-Fi Direct will be used—between computer and mouse, computer and headset, and hardware-to-computer communication in general—WPA2 should be acceptably secure.

How does Windows 8 use Wi-Fi Direct?

Windows 8 has Wi-Fi Direct built in. When another device that supports Wi-Fi Direct, such as a television, appears within range, the device can be added to Windows in the same way a Bluetooth keyboard or USB scanner is added. There are no special considerations for Wi-Fi Direct (other than devices using the technology). When the device is added to Windows, in the case of the television, media on the Windows 8–based computer or device can be sent directly to the television for output.

Using airplane mode and location-based services in Windows 8

Mobile phones have a feature called airplane mode. The concept is that all the radios in the device are switched off, but the rest of the device remains on and can be used. Because the Internet is available almost anywhere and there are mobile hotspots in a number of smart phones today, airplane mode makes even more sense in Windows 8. Turning off Wi-Fi on a computer is fairly straightforward; however, note that you also disable Bluetooth, cellular, or GPS radios that might exist within the device you are carrying.

Turning on airplane mode handles all these radios at once. To enable or disable airplane mode in Windows 8, complete the following steps:

1. Select the Settings charm.

2. Select PC Settings.

3. Select Wireless in the navigation pane.

4. Toggle the Airplane Mode selector to Off to disable airplane mode or to On to enable it.

In addition to airplane mode, Windows 8 supports location-based services. This enables your applications to use your location, much the same way a smart phone might. With the location settings turned on, the experience presented in a particular application might change, depending on the location of the device.

The Weather app is a good example of one that can use location-based services. When these services are enabled for Windows and then for the Weather app, the application attempts to change the weather information displayed based on the location of the device. This can be handy for many mobile devices and applications. To configure location settings in Windows 8, complete the following steps:

1. Select the Settings charm.

2. Select PC Settings.

3. Select Privacy.

4. Toggle the Let Apps Use My Location setting on or off.

In addition to general configuration settings through the Windows GUI, location-based services can be configured in Group Policy. In the Group Policy console, expand the Computer Configuration\Administrative Templates\Windows Components\Location and Sensors path. The policy settings for Windows Location Provider include:

- Turn Off Windows Location Provider

- Turn Off Location Scripting

- Turn Off Location

- Turn Off Sensors

Disabling location and sensors data prevents applications on a computer or other device from accessing these resources.

Lesson summary

- Use Wi-Fi Direct to connect peripheral devices to each other without connecting to a network.
- Enable and disable airplane mode on mobile devices to activate and deactivate all radios in the devices.
- Manage location-based services in Windows to enable applications to provide information based on your current location.

Lesson review

Answer the following questions to test your knowledge of the information in this lesson. You can find the answers to these questions and explanations of why each answer choice is correct or incorrect in the "Answers" section at the end of this chapter.

1. Recently, an executive in your organization returned from a business trip, asking questions about the usefulness of Windows 8 on an airplane. She had been unsure whether her device was transmitting radio signals outside of wireless because she knew the device had Bluetooth. Which settings can ensure that no radio transmissions can be made?

   A. Location-based services

   B. Offline files

   C. Airplane mode

   D. Disabling location-based service providers

2. A member of your team has heard about Wi-Fi Direct and is curious about how it can be configured in Windows 8. He asks you which settings need to be modified for Wi-Fi Direct to operate with capable devices. Which settings must be configured to use Wi-Fi Direct?

   A. Wi-Fi must be enabled.

   B. Special drivers must be obtained from Microsoft.

   C. Location-based services must be turned on.

   D. None of the above.

Practice exercises

Windows 8 has a number of features that make it well suited for mobile devices while maintaining a centralized configuration by using Group Policy and local policy. The following exercises allow you to configure these features and work with them in your own environment. To complete the exercises, you need:

- A removable drive to configure BitLocker to Go.
- Network file shares to work with offline files.

Exercise 1: Configure BitLocker and BitLocker To Go

In this exercise, you configure BitLocker by using Manage-bde.exe and configure BitLocker To Go by using Windows PowerShell.

1. Open an elevated command prompt.
2. Type **manage-bde** and press Enter.
3. Use the listed commands to configure the C drive of the local computer to use BitLocker and store the key on a network drive.
4. Open an elevated Windows PowerShell session.
5. Use the enable-bitlocker cmdlet to enable BitLocker on a connected removable drive.

Exercise 2: Configure subfolder availability for offline files

In this exercise, you use policy settings to configure subfolder availability for offline files.

1. Open the Group Policy Editor.
2. Browse to the Offline Files node within Computer Configuration\Administrative Templates\Network.
3. Enable the Subfolders Always Available Offline setting.
4. Tap or click OK to save the setting.
5. Close the Group Policy Editor.

Exercise 3: Configure actions for the power button

In this exercise, you modify the actions for the power button on a device, both when the device is plugged in and when it is running on battery.

1. Open the Group Policy Editor.
2. Browse to the Power Management node in the Computer Configuration\Administrative Templates\System\ path.
3. Enable the policy setting to select actions for the power button (plugged in).
4. Specify Take No Action.

5. Tap or click OK to save the setting.

6. Enable the policy setting to select actions for the power button (on battery).

7. Specify Shut Down.

8. Tap or click OK to save the setting.

9. Close the Group Policy Editor.

Suggested practice exercises

The following additional practices are designed to give you more opportunities to practice what you've learned and to help you successfully master the lessons presented in this chapter.

- **Exercise 1**   Configure a device to connect to Windows 8 by using Wi-Fi Direct.
- **Exercise 2**   Configure Offline Files to be disallowed.
- **Exercise 3**   Configure BitLocker to work on devices without Trusted Platform Module (TPM).

Answers

This section contains the answers to the lesson review questions in this chapter.

Lesson 1

1. **Correct answer: B**

    A. **Incorrect:** BitLocker encryption does not require special permissions for use but does require a password to access encrypted data.

    B. **Correct:** A policy can be configured that requires all removable media to be BitLocker encrypted for files to be written to them. This ensures that data is kept safe regardless of the media on which it is stored.

    C. **Incorrect:** Windows 8 does not have encryption requirements by default. These are configurations that are enabled by an organization in accordance with its needs.

    D. **Incorrect:** BitLocker, by default, does not pay attention to the owner of the media; all removable media is capable of encryption by using BitLocker.

2. **Correct answer: C**

    A. **Incorrect:** BitLocker does not have a minimum RAM requirement.

    B. **Incorrect:** BitLocker uses Trusted Platform Module (TPM) by default, but this can be modified to enable computers without TPM capabilities to use BitLocker.

    C. **Correct:** Enabling the additional authentication policy setting enables the encryption key to be stored on a flash drive. Using this feature causes Windows to prompt for the key if TPM is not available.

    D. **Incorrect:** BitLocker can be configured and managed from the command line, but this is not required.

3. **Correct answer: C**

    A. **Incorrect:** A VPN connection allows access to files only when the computer is connected to the Internet.

    B. **Incorrect:** Email exchange of documents provides access that remote workers need but would put undue workload on those in the office who needed to send the files and manage the incoming modified files.

    C. **Correct:** Using offline files would enable remote workers to collect files they need while connected to the network and sync changes back to the network when they connect next.

    D. **Incorrect:** Using Direct Access requires an organization to be able to use Direct Access and requires the computer to be connected to the Internet.

4. **Correct answer: C**

   A. **Incorrect:** Although restarting the computer after a period of inactivity might in some cases prevent the computer from going to sleep, any unsaved work would be lost when the forced restart took place.

   B. **Incorrect:** AlwaysOn power schemes would prevent sleeping altogether, which solves the problem but might have both a power-cost impact and an environmental impact because of the constant power use.

   C. **Correct:** Configuring power settings for all the computers in the organization to ensure that they sleep or hibernate only at appropriate times is the best way to solve this issue.

   D. **Incorrect:** This solution might work, but it does not use configuration options within Windows to solve the issue and leaves the issue up to the employee to manage.

Lesson 2

1. **Correct answer: C**

   A. **Incorrect:** Location-based services do not prevent radio transmissions.

   B. **Incorrect:** Offline Files makes files available when there is no connection to the file location; it does not prevent access to resources.

   C. **Correct:** Airplane mode disables all radio communication in Windows 8.

   D. **Incorrect:** Disabling location-based service providers does not affect radio transmissions.

2. **Correct answer: A**

   A. **Correct:** Because Wi-Fi Direct relies on wireless, Wi-Fi must be enabled.

   B. **Incorrect:** No special drivers from Microsoft are required.

   C. **Incorrect:** Location-based services do not affect the peer-to-peer communication Wi-Fi Direct uses.

   D. **Incorrect:** Wireless must be enabled for the feature to work.

CHAPTER 14

Monitoring and maintaining Windows

As with all software products, vulnerabilities, bugs, and other problems in the Windows operating system code are discovered from time to time, and they need to be corrected. Further, third-party programs sometimes have a way of negatively affecting how your Windows-based computer operates.

Windows 8 includes a number of mechanisms to keep your computer in good health and methods to monitor even the most arcane elements of the system to ensure that everything is in good working order.

Lessons in this chapter:

Before you begin

By this point in the book, you should have a fully functioning Windows 8 system that you can use to follow along with the information in this chapter. To carry out some of the examples in this chapter, make sure your Windows 8–based computer is connected to a network that has unrestricted access to the Internet.

Lesson 1: Managing Windows Update

Ensuring that your Windows 8–based computer remains fully updated is considered a best practice by security professionals. By making sure that all new updates are installed, you're actively closing potential holes through which attackers might attempt to gain access to or otherwise exploit your computer. As a Windows desktop administrator, managing security becomes one of your critical responsibilities.

After this lesson, you will be able to:

- Configure update settings.
- Configure Windows Update policies.
- View update history.
- Roll back updates.

Estimated lesson time: 30 minutes

REAL WORLD **DON'T IGNORE WINDOWS UPDATE**

More often than not, the organizations that fail to take basic security precautions are the ones that fall victim to the increasingly sophisticated attacker. Unlike law-abiding organizations, attackers don't have to follow rules, so for them, it's an anything-goes world. Organizations must do everything they can to prevent attackers from infiltrating their environments. Perhaps one of the easiest and most basic lines of defense is to ensure that every computer is applying updates as soon as possible after an update is released.

Accessing Windows Update settings by using Control Panel

The process for configuring Windows Update in Windows 8 has not changed dramatically from the process found in earlier versions of Windows, but the new Windows 8 interface changes the method by which you access Windows Update settings. You can open Control Panel in Window 8 by using a number of methods. Control Panel is your configuration point for a computer's local Windows Update settings.

Using the Power User menu

To access Control Panel, either press and hold or right-click the lower-left corner of the desktop to open a shortcut menu that provides access to a number of system utilities, including Control Panel. Choose Control Panel. When it opens, type **Update** in the search box at the upper-right corner of the window and then choose Windows Update, as shown in Figure 14-1.

FIGURE 14-1 Using Control Panel to access Windows Update

Using the Start screen

You can also use the new Windows 8 interface to access Control Panel in two ways. First, with the Start screen open, start typing **Control Panel**. As you type, Windows narrows the options that match what you've typed and displays the results, as shown in Figure 14-2.

FIGURE 14-2 Control Panel on the Start screen

Using the Windows 8 desktop

Alternatively, from the Windows 8 desktop, access the charms by tapping one of the right-side corners of the screen or by moving your mouse pointer to one of those locations. Choose the Settings charm, tap or click Control Panel, and then open Windows Update by using the method described previously.

Regardless of your method, the goal is to open the Windows Update window, shown in Figure 14-3.

FIGURE 14-3 The Windows Update configuration window

The Windows Update window includes information about the current update configuration and status and links to tools to manage various configuration elements. In Figure 14-3, you see that this computer is currently configured to install updates automatically and that Windows looked for new updates yesterday at 10:31 P.M. If automatic updating were not enabled, the line that reads You're Set To Automatically Receive Updates would just provide the current status of updates, such as Your PC Is Up To Date.

At the bottom of the window, note the line that reads For Windows And Other Products From Microsoft Update. Windows Update is intended to address the update needs for the Windows operating system, but it also provides update services for other installed Microsoft products such as Office. You have a single point of update administration for all your supported Microsoft products.

Configuring update settings

To make changes to your existing Windows Update settings, open Windows Update and tap or click Change Settings on the left side of the screen (see Figure 14-3). This action opens the window you see in Figure 14-4, in which you can make changes to how Windows Update operates.

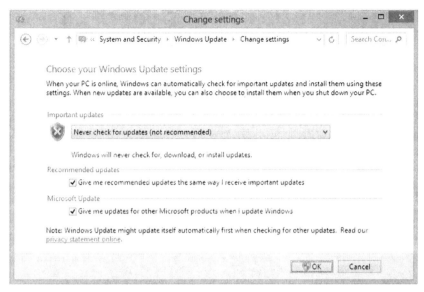

FIGURE 14-4 Changing Windows Update settings

Three classes of updates are available, each with configuration options:

- **Important Updates**   Important updates are updates that require immediate attention. These often address critical security issues that need to be corrected.

- **Recommended Updates**   Recommended updates are updates that address less critical issues such as minor bug fixes, cosmetic adjustments to a program, and functionality corrections. Select the Give Me Recommended Updates The Same Way I Receive
  Important Updates check box to configure Windows Update to handle recommended
  updates in the same manner as important updates.

- **Microsoft Update**   Windows Update can assume responsibility for updating other
  Microsoft programs. Select the Give Me Updates For Other Microsoft Products When I
  Update Windows check box to enable this capability.

REAL WORLD   **MICROSOFT UPDATE IN ACTION**

This check box exists only if you have chosen to receive updates for Windows and other
Microsoft products. By default, this is not enabled. To enable this option, complete the
following steps:

1. Open Windows Update.
2. Select Change Settings at the left side of the page.
3. On the Change Settings page shown in Figure 14-4, select the Give Me Updates For
   Other Microsoft Products When I Update Windows check box.
4. Tap or click OK.

In the Important Updates section of the Change Settings window is a drop-down menu that lists a number of options for how to handle the installation of updates on your Windows computer:

- **Install Updates Automatically (Recommended)**   As part of Windows background processing, it checks for new updates on a regular basis. If new updates are located, they will be downloaded automatically and installed without requiring further administrator intervention.

- **Download Updates But Let Me Choose Whether To Install Them**   Windows checks for and downloads new updates on a set schedule but lets you to choose whether to install them. You can choose to install all, some, one, or none of the updates that are downloaded.

- **Check For Updates But Let Me Choose Whether to Download And Install Them**   Windows looks for any new updates and offers the option to download and install each one.

- **Never Check For Updates (Not Recommended)**   Windows never checks for new updates. Further, Windows will not automatically download or install new updates.

> **REAL WORLD**   **METERED VS. UNMETERED INTERNET CONNECTIONS AND WINDOWS UPDATE**
>
> Metered Internet connections—connections you pay for by the megabyte or gigabyte—can be very expensive, particularly if Windows is downloading updates on its own in the background. Some updates—particularly full service packs—can be extremely large and might exhaust monthly bandwidth allotments. Fortunately, Windows Update is configured so that it will not download updates over a connection that is marked as metered.

Some of the options at your disposal provide you with further configuration parameters. For example, if you choose Install Updates Automatically, a link entitled Updates Will Be Automatically Installed During The Maintenance Window appears on your screen (Figure 14-5).

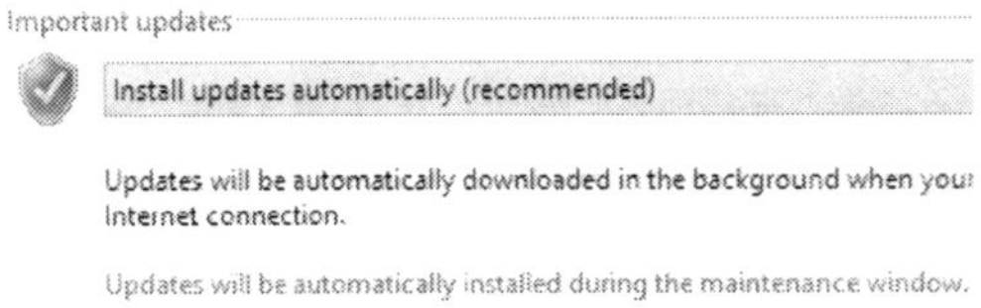

FIGURE 14-5 Additional options available when automatic updates are enabled

Tap or click this link to open the Automatic Maintenance window shown in Figure 14-6. In this window, you can change the time at which your computer performs automatic maintenance, including Windows Update.

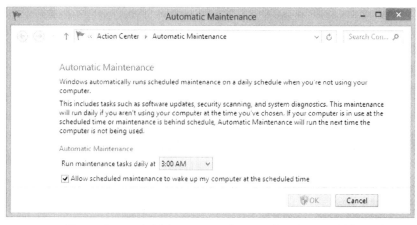

FIGURE 14-6 Change Automatic Maintenance options to adjust time at which Windows Update looks for new updates

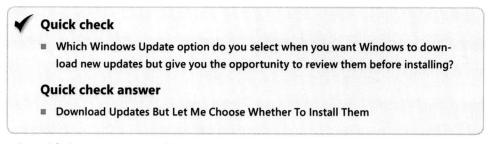

Quick check

- Which Windows Update option do you select when you want Windows to download new updates but give you the opportunity to review them before installing?

Quick check answer

- Download Updates But Let Me Choose Whether To Install Them

Identifying new updates

Windows can identify new updates in a number of ways. First, you can allow Windows to check for new updates on its own by changing Windows Update settings as discussed in the previous section. Second, you can force Windows to look for new updates by tapping or clicking the Check For Updates link in the Windows Update window. When you use this method to check for updates, the process is immediate; Windows does not wait for the automatic maintenance window to check for updates.

After Windows performs its check, the results are displayed in the Windows Update window. In Figure 14-7, you see that two important updates are available for this Windows 8 system.

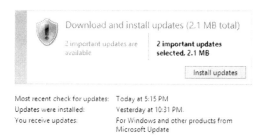

FIGURE 14-7 Windows identifying new updates that need to be installed

If you want to install all the updates, tap or click Install Updates. If you want to select which updates to install, tap or click the 2 Important Updates Are Available link. This text will vary slightly, depending on the number and types of updates that Windows Update locates.

Before you learn how to install selected updates, you need to understand how to manage updates by using the Windows 8 native interface. Eventually, the Windows 8 interface method and what you just learned will merge, so this is a good time to cover this topic.

Managing Windows Update in Windows 8 native interface

The Windows 8 native interface does not expose all the Windows Update settings that you have seen up to this point. Instead, the Windows 8 native view of Windows Update provides you with just the critical subset of Windows Update functionality that is necessary to perform updates. If you want to make changes to the way Windows Update operates, you must do so using the methods described so far in this chapter.

However, the Windows 8 native Windows Update tool does provide a subset of functionality, primarily to acquire and install updates. To access this tool, open the Settings charm from the desktop and tap or click Change PC Settings. (It's at the very bottom of the window.) In the PC Settings window, choose Windows Update, as shown in Figure 14-8.

FIGURE 14-8 Windows identifying new updates that need to be installed

On the screen shown in Figure 14-8, the 2 Important Updates information box is displayed when you tap or click See Details. It is covering the Install Updates button, but you can dismiss the details box by tapping or clicking the See Details link a second time. Tap or click the Install Update button to install all the updates Windows has identified.

If, however, you want to install just a subset of the identified updates, tap or click Choose Which Important Updates You Want To Install in the information box. This link returns you to the earlier Windows interface and to the dialog box shown in Figure 14-7. Tap or click the 2 Important Updates Are Available link. (Remember that the wording might be slightly different for your system.)

The result is a screen like the one shown in Figure 14-9. On this screen, you can see that two updates are ready to be installed. One is an update for Windows 8 itself, and the other is a definition update for the Windows Defender system protection tool.

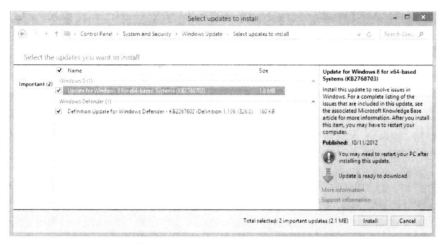

FIGURE 14-9 Windows identifying new updates that need to be installed

The update selection window provides you with information about each update that is ready to be installed. To view this information, tap or click the update you want to review. You can get additional information about an update by tapping or clicking the More Information link at the right side of the window. Clicking the link opens Internet Explorer and directs you to the Microsoft Knowledge Base article that is associated with the specific update.

To install an update, make sure that the check box next to that update is selected. When you have finished selecting the updates, tap or click the Install button. Your updates will be installed, and you'll be kept apprised of the installation progress by a progress message box, as shown in Figure 14-10.

FIGURE 14-10 Updates being installed

Viewing update history

Because updates are so important, Windows helps you keep track of the updates that you've installed or attempted to install. In addition, Windows provides the status of the installation, the importance level of the update, and the date on which the update installation was attempted. To access this information, tap or click View Update History on the Windows Update screen. The View Update History window (see Figure 14-11) displays the information. You can get full information about an update by double-tapping or double-clicking the name of the update.

FIGURE 14-11 Windows Update installation history

The information in the View Update History window is invaluable for a number of reasons. First, as an administrator, you can determine whether a particular update was applied to a system.

Second, this information provides a significant boon in system troubleshooting. In Figure 14-11, you can see that one of the updates failed. This information enables you to begin taking steps to determine the cause of the failure.

Rolling back updates

The information provided as part of the update history can help you if you find that you've deployed an update that needs to be rolled back or otherwise removed from a system.

Although updates are tested, it's not possible for Microsoft to test an update against every possible hardware and software combination. Therefore, on rare occasions, the company releases an update that creates problems for some users. If this happens to you or your users, you must take steps to remove problematic updates from Windows 8 systems to return systems to an operational state.

Updates can be uninstalled by using Programs And Features in Control Panel. If you're in Control Panel and you do not see a Programs And Features option, click the down arrow next to the View By option and choose either Large Icons or Small Icons.

This option is accessible from the View Update History window by tapping or clicking the Installed Updates link. Alternatively, you can access Programs And Features by opening Control Panel and tapping or clicking View Installed Updates in the left navigation area. The resulting Installed Updates window is shown in Figure 14-12.

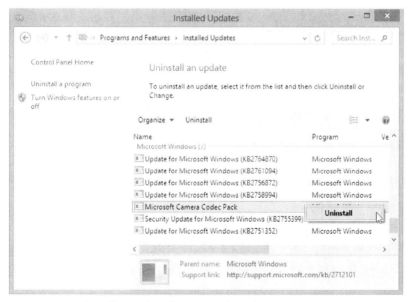

FIGURE 14-12 Uninstalling updates from Control Panel

Each listed update has the Microsoft Knowledge Base article ID listed with it. This makes it easier for you to ensure that you're removing the correct update. You can use the search box in the upper-right corner of the window to search for an update you want to remove.

> **REAL WORLD** **FINDING MICROSOFT KNOWLEDGE BASE (KB) ARTICLES**
>
> Over the years, Microsoft has amassed a great number of useful articles in its publicly accessible knowledge base system. As you can see from the information in this chapter, almost every update includes an article in the KB describing the update in detail. To locate a Knowledge Base article quickly, visit *http://support.microsoft.com/search/*. In the search box, type the Knowledge Base article ID number and press Enter. If the KB ID is not known, provide some keywords and allow the search engine to locate the KB for you.

To uninstall an update, select the update and then tap or click Uninstall or press and hold or right-click the update and choose Uninstall from the shortcut menu. Windows asks you whether you're sure you want to uninstall the update. Tap or click Yes to continue. Depending on the update you select, you might have to restart the computer.

After an update has been uninstalled, that update will show up as a required installation the next time you check for new updates. After all, the purpose of Windows Update is to find missing updates. After you remove an update, it's considered missing.

This can be fixed. When you find your list of updates that are available to install in Windows Update, you can hide updates that you want to skip so that they aren't made available for installation. To hide an update, press and hold or right-click the update and then tap or click Hide Update, as shown in Figure 14-13. From now on, the update will not be made available for installation.

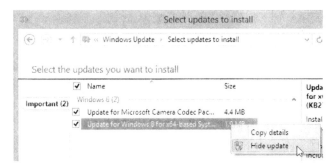

FIGURE 14-13 Hiding an update to make it unavailable for installation

If you need to install a previously hidden update, tap or click Restore Hidden Updates on the Windows Update screen. When the Restore Hidden Updates window (Figure 14-14) opens, select the updates you'd like to restore and then tap or click the Restore button.

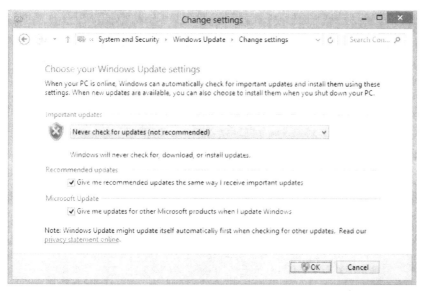

FIGURE 14-14 Restoring a previously hidden update

Configuring Windows Update policies

Unless you decide to configure every PC in your organization to download and install new updates automatically, the update process could become difficult to administer; for example, if you need to block a bad update from being installed in the environment.

This situation becomes more apparent in larger organizations, especially those with custom applications or diverse hardware. When an update breaks something, it becomes clear that policies can be helpful to block driver updates without prior administrator approval or block library updates until they have been tested against the custom app.

Further, bandwidth becomes an issue in larger organizations. Suppose, for example, that 500 desktops all try to download a service pack on the same day; the network would slow to a crawl or go offline entirely. By using centralized Group Policy and tying Windows Update to a centralized Windows Server Update Services (WSUS) server, both of these challenges can be averted.

WSUS provides for a single update download from Microsoft, which is then distributed to workstations over the internal network rather than over the Internet. In addition, WSUS provides highly granular control over the distribution of updates to ensure that the administrator has full control of the process.

WSUS is generally combined with a series of Group Policy settings. So, rather than working with Windows Update on a computer-by-computer basis, you can manage every computer's Windows Update settings from one place.

> **MORE INFO**   **WINDOWS UPDATE GROUP POLICY SETTINGS**
>
> Configuring Group Policy settings is beyond the scope of this book. However, a complete Group Policy list for Windows 8 and Windows Server 2012 is available from Microsoft. With this list, you can determine exactly which policies need to be enabled on Windows Server to enforce Windows Update settings on a Windows 8 client. You can find the list in "Group Policy Settings Reference for Windows and Windows Server," which is available for download from *https://www.microsoft.com/en-us/download/details .aspx?displaylang=en&id=25250*.

> **MORE INFO**   **WINDOWS 8 AND WINDOWS SERVER UPDATE SERVICES**
>
> A full deployment of WSUS is beyond the scope of this book, but WSUS is considered critical infrastructure in most organizations because of how easy it makes the update process. To learn more about WSUS, read the TechNet article at *http://technet.microsoft.com /en-us/library/hh852345.aspx*. In addition, make sure you read *Training Guide: Installing and Configuring Windows Server 2012* by Mitch Tulloch (Microsoft Press, 2012) (*http:// go.microsoft.com/FWLink/?Linkid=263955*).

Lesson summary

- You can use a number of settings to handle Windows Update. You can automate the entire process, or you can manage the entire process manually.
- If you apply an update that is later deemed unstable, you can uninstall that update and then hide it so the problem doesn't happen again.
- Windows updates are delivered with a number of severity levels. Critical and Important updates should receive prompt attention.
- You can change the automatic maintenance settings to meet your company's unique policies and install updates during off hours.

Lesson review

Answer the following questions to test your knowledge of the information in this lesson. You can find the answers to these questions and explanations of why each answer choice is correct or incorrect in the "Answers" section at the end of this chapter.

1. Which method is not supported for opening the Windows Update window?

    A. Accessing it through the Windows 8 native interface

    B. Accessing it by the charms and Control Panel

    C. Using the Change PC Settings option by selecting the Settings charm

    D. Accessing it directly from the Power Users menu

2. Which two steps are recommended to roll back an update that created system stability issues?

   A. Remove the update and then hide it.

   B. Remove the update and then configure Windows Update for manual installation.

   C. Remove the update and then remove Windows Update.

   D. Remove the update and then install any new updates that Windows can find.

3. How can you roll back a previously installed update?

   A. Use Programs and Features in Control Panel to remove the update.

   B. Open Windows Update, browse to View Update History, and delete an installed update.

   C. From the Windows Update configuration page, locate the update and delete it.

   D. Go to Restore Hidden Updates and choose to unhide an update.

Lesson 2: Monitoring, optimizing, and troubleshooting system health and performance

Keeping your system current is just the first line of a defense-in-depth strategy designed to thwart attackers who are intent on compromising your system. The second step involves routinely monitoring your system to ensure that it remains in a healthy state and that it is performing as expected. Although poor system performance isn't a security issue, it is a road-block that can affect the user experience just as significantly as an attack can.

Windows 8 includes a number of methods by which you can monitor, troubleshoot, and optimize your system to meet business goals. In this lesson, you learn how to use these features to keep your system in top operating condition.

After this lesson, you will be able to:

- Manage and monitor the system by using Task Manager.
- Configure and analyze event logs.
- Use Windows Action Center.
- Configure event subscriptions.
- Monitor system resources.
- Optimize networking performance.
- Optimize the desktop environment.
- Configure indexing options.

Estimated lesson time: 90 minutes

Managing and monitoring the system by using Task Manager

Windows 8 and Windows Server 2012 include a completely revamped Task Manager, which has been an effective troubleshooting tool for decades. Windows 8 Task Manager provides significantly more complete status information and information regarding the performance characteristics of Windows 8 native applications.

To access Task Manager, use one of the following methods:

- From the desktop, press and hold or right-click the taskbar and, from the shortcut menu, choose Task Manager.

- From the Power Users menu, choose Task Manager.

- From the Start screen, start typing **Task Manager** and then tap or click the Task Manager icon.

- Press Ctrl+Alt+Delete and choose Task Manager.

Regardless of the method you use, the outcome is the same; the Task Manager utility, shown in Figure 14-15, opens. To open a window like the one shown in Figure 14-15, tap or click More Details in Task Manager.

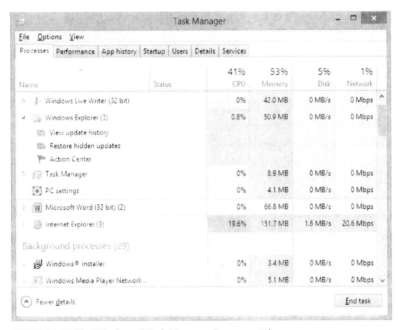

FIGURE 14-15 The Windows 8 Task Manager Processes tab

The main window of Task Manager includes elements that can aid you in your monitoring and troubleshooting efforts. Included on the screen are multiple tabs, each displaying critical system performance and resource usage information. Each of these tabs is described in this section.

Processes

The Processes tab provides you with a single location from which to view all the software running on the system, down to the application and even document or instance level. In Figure 14-15, you can see this level of detail. The Processes tab lists all the actual Windows applications that are running on the target system. If an application is running more than one instance of itself—for example, if you have more than one Word document open—an arrow appears next to the application. Select the arrow to expand the application list and display the individual instances that are running for the selected app. Figure 14-15 shows Windows Explorer expanded and three Windows Explorer instances running, each with a different purpose.

The information on this tab is important. You can view exactly how much of the system resources a particular application is using, although this information is available only at the actual app level, not at the instance level. The displayed information is a real-time snapshot and changes as circumstances change.

In general, Windows 8 system resources are divided into the following categories, each of which is shown in a column on the Processes tab:

- **CPU** The CPU metric displays the percentage of system processor resources currently dedicated to servicing this application. If an application is sitting idle due to a small workload, this might be zero even when the application is running.

- **Memory** The memory column displays the amount of system RAM dedicated to the application. System RAM is often one of the most limiting factors in system performance, so watch this one if you or one of your users is experiencing system troubles.

- **Disk** In the context of Task Manager, the Disk metric does not display how much storage space is being consumed by an application. Instead, this metric provides insight into a second critical, storage-related metric: transfer speed. This column of information outlines how much information is being transferred to and from the disk.

- **Network** Although today's networks are generally extremely fast, network resources remain a source of contention at times. In years past, a computer might be able to get through an entire day without accessing the network, but today's modern systems and applications are quite network-centric. In Task Manager, Windows details how much network capacity is dedicated to each app.

At the top of each resource column, you can see the total commitment level for each individual resource. As commitment levels reach sustained high levels, system performance can begin to suffer.

ENDING A PROCESS

The Processes tab is useful when you're attempting to correct system performance or some other issue. For example, if a user reports that her computer is running very slowly, you can open Task Manager and quickly see whether any process is using a large percentage of the CPU. If so, discontinuing that process might be necessary. This is known as ending the process or ending the task.

To end a process in Windows, complete the following steps:

1. Use Task Manager to identify the process you want to end.

2. Press and hold or right-click the task in question.

3. From the resulting shortcut menu, choose End Task.

Windows does not warn you that you're about to end a process; it just carries out your request and ends the task.

> **IMPORTANT** **BE CAREFUL WHAT YOU END**
>
> Although generally you can safely end most application processes without affecting the stability of the system, be cautious when you end system background processes. Ending these processes can destabilize the system, and you might need to restart.
>
> Further, even though system stability might not be affected by ending an application process, you might lose data by doing so. When you end an application process, you aren't provided an opportunity to save your work. Save early and save often but also be careful as you end processes.

Performance

On the Performance tab, you can get more high-level information quickly about the operation of the system. In Figure 14-16, note that you can switch between the four major resource areas and see how those resources are currently being used. In the figure, the CPU information is displayed. Out of 2.59 GHz of available processing power, this Windows 8 PC is currently using about 36 percent of the total available CPU.

In addition to current performance statistics, you see deep information about the overall capabilities of the processor. In this example, the computer has a single processor with dual cores, and hardware virtualization extensions are enabled.

The Performance tab also gives you information about memory, disk performance, and the network, just as you saw on the Processes tab. However, as is the case with the CPU information, you can glean a lot more information here than you can on the Processes tab.

The Memory option displays the current usage of the system's total memory. This system has 3.1 GB assigned, 1.6 GB of which is in use. This tab also provides you with information about paged and non-paged memory. Given the importance of RAM on a Windows 8 system, being able to obtain detailed statistics for how it's used can be invaluable in troubleshooting efforts. If you're seeing RAM usage consistently exceeding 90 percent, you might need to consider adding more RAM to the computer.

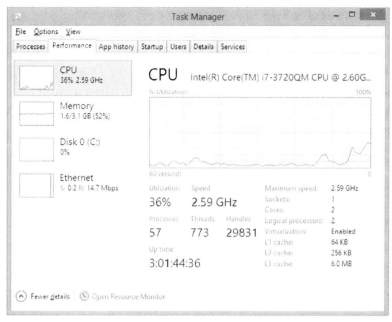

FIGURE 14-16 The Windows 8 Task Manager Performance tab

The Disk option displays the current statistics for the various disk drives that are installed in the Windows 8–based computer, including:

- **Active Time** This metric shows the percentage of time the disk is actually active. The higher the number, the harder the disk is working. If this statistic is constantly high, consider adding additional disks to the computer to alleviate the burden.

- **Average Response Time** From a performance standpoint, average response time is the most critical metric for you to track. This key metric tells you immediately whether you're having disk-based performance issues that could be affecting the user experience. In general, if you see constant values exceeding 20 to 25 ms in this field, that's cause for concern. Other factors can affect this metric, but response time is key in determining how the system is operating.

- **Read Speed** This metric displays the speed at which the system is reading data from storage.

- **Write Speed** This metric displays the speed at which the system is sending data to storage to be written.

- **Capacity/Formatted** The capacity and formatted fields display the total size of the disk and the size of the disk after it's been formatted. Some disks use different mathematical computations to determine post-formatting capacity.

- **System Disk**   Is the disk a system disk? If so, it requires careful monitoring.

- **Page File**   Does the disk host the system's paging file? The disk that holds the paging file might require a little more performance if memory conditions become low and the system starts paging to disk.

- **Transfer Rate**   The graph in the middle of the window displays the total speed at which data is being transferred between the computer and the disk.

Finally, the Ethernet option displays basic information about how the network is operating. A graph displays current network usage, and counters at the bottom of the window display the amount of data that has been sent or received using this adapter.

Your Windows 8–based computer might have slightly different items on the Performance tab. For example, if you have multiple disks or multiple network adapters, you will also see information for those additional devices.

App history

App history is a new concept in Windows 8 and was introduced to provide administrators with insight into how Windows 8 native applications are running. The App History tab is shown in Figure 14-17.

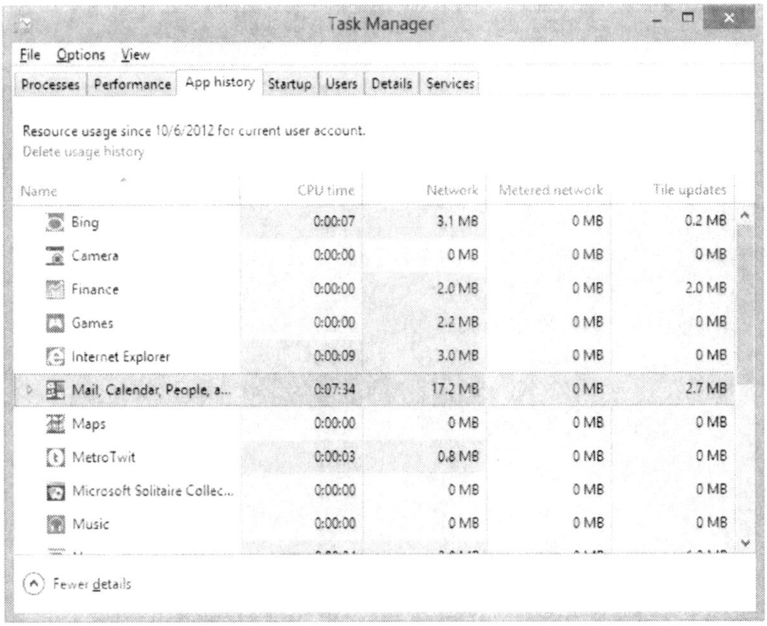

FIGURE 14-17 The Windows 8 Task Manager App History tab

For each Windows 8 native app, Windows captures four data points:

- **CPU Time**   Displays the amount of processor time this app or group of apps has consumed since the date at the top of the window and for the current user account.

- **Network**   Displays the total amount of network traffic that has been generated by this app.

- **Metered Network**   Displays the amount of data that has been transmitted over a network connection if the app has had to consume resources using a metered network.

- **Tile Updates**   Displays the amount of bandwidth needed to perform tile updates. As you watch the Start screen in Windows 8, notice that the individual tiles change as new information comes in. Those updates require network bandwidth.

SWITCHING TO A WINDOWS 8 NATIVE APP

While you're using Task Manager, you can quickly switch to one of your Windows 8 native apps. To do so, complete the following steps:

1. In Task Manager, identify the app you want to run.

2. Press and hold or right-click the app.

3. Choose Switch To.

Windows switches to that app.

DELETING APP USAGE HISTORY

The statistics you see on the App History tab reflect usage from a particular date. You might want to clear usage history periodically. For example, you might want to reset usage history on the same day that your monthly data plan from your cellular provider resets. By doing so, you can track the amount of metered data usage you're experiencing more carefully and easily so that you don't accidentally overrun your monthly data limit and incur significant charges.

Follow these steps to delete usage history:

1. Start Task Manager.

2. Switch to the App History tab.

3. Tap or click Delete Usage History.

This process is immediate. Usage information is reset with no further prompts or warnings.

Startup

The Startup tab helps you optimize your system. It lists the various programs that are configured to start automatically when the system starts. The more programs on the list, the longer it takes the computer to become fully available to the user at start time.

In Figure 14-18, you can see the Startup tab. The impact column is the most important one here. Startup items that have a high impact are the slowest to load. To make your system start a bit faster, you can optimize the start process by selecting items in this window and then tapping or clicking the Disable button. Repeat the process for each startup service you want to disable.

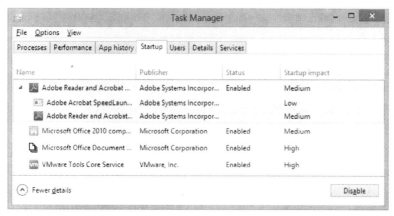

FIGURE 14-18 The Windows 8 Task Manager Startup tab

Generally, it's safe to disable startup items. Many items are installed in the startup area to make the associated program run faster when you use it. However, some items should not be disabled; these include services that help the system operate fully. In Figure 14-18, you saw that the sample computer was running the VMware Tools Core Service. This is a startup item that would not be disabled because the system depends on this service.

Disabling items at startup helps the computer start faster. You just need to be careful about what you choose to disable.

> **MORE INFO   MSCONFIG**
>
> The Startup tab is a new addition to Windows 8 that helps you keep your system opti-
> mized. However, an earlier tool remains in Windows 8 that can help you configure startup
> items. Many administrators are familiar with MSconfig, discussed in Chapter 15, "System
> protection and recovery."

Users

The Users tab is similar to the Processes tab. It displays almost identical information, but it does so on a per-user basis, so you can view all the processes that are associated with a particular user. It's just another way to view what is happening on a Windows 8 PC.

As is possible from the other tabs, you can press and hold or right-click any of the listed processes to manage that process, which includes ending the process and opening its Properties page.

Details

If you've managed previous versions of Windows and used Task Manager in those versions, the Details tab (Figure 14-19) will be familiar to you. This tab displays information similar to the Processes tab but does so in a more advanced way and provides some additional context about the process.

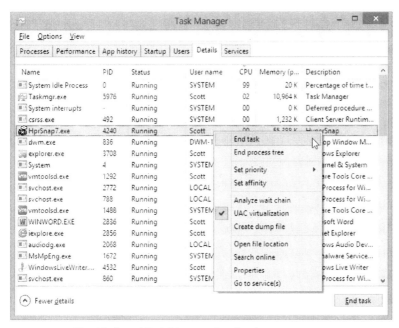

FIGURE 14-19 The Windows 8 Task Manager Details tab

The Details tab exposes significant functionality that enables administrators to exert good control over processes on the computer. As was possible from the Processes window, you can end tasks from this tab, but you can also do much more.

ENSURING LICENSING COMPLIANCE THROUGH AFFINITY SETTINGS

Some software titles, including those designed for desktop systems, carry with them strict per-processor or per-core licensing terms. That is, when you buy the license for the software, that license is tied to a particular physical processor.

By default, when Windows runs a program, it doesn't care which processor runs it. It just assigns the program to the first available processor. By using the Details tab, you can change this behavior.

To change application affinity settings, complete the following steps:

1. Start Task Manager.

2. Open the Details tab.

3. Press and hold or right-click the application.

4. From the shortcut menu, choose Set Affinity.

5. When the Processor Affinity window opens, choose which processor should be responsible for running the program.

6. Tap or click OK.

Services

Just about every task in Windows depends on a service of some kind. The Windows 8 Task Manager Services tab is shown in Figure 14-20. A service is an executable program that performs a very specific function on the Windows-based computer. In general, services are applications that do not require any user intervention and operate silently in the background, performing critical functions upon which running applications rely.

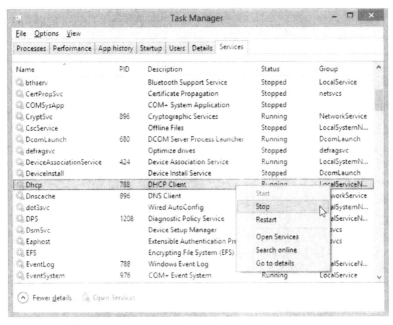

FIGURE 14-20 The Windows 8 Task Manager Services tab

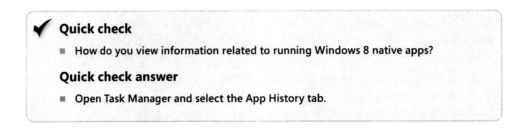

Quick check

■ How do you view information related to running Windows 8 native apps?

Quick check answer

■ Open Task Manager and select the App History tab.

Using Windows Action Center

In Figure 14-21, note the flag with the little red X on it. You might see a similar flag on your own Windows 8 system, with or without the red X. This flag denotes the current status of the machine as viewed by the Windows Action Center.

FIGURE 14-21 A Windows Action Center notification

Windows Action Center is intended to provide you, at a glance, with real-time insight into the current health of your computer from a security perspective. The Windows Action Center watches a number of critical system elements in an effort to provide you with coherent, actionable information. Among the sources the Windows Action Center uses are:

- Windows Update
- Windows Firewall
- User account control (UAC) settings
- Virus protection (or lack thereof)
- File history

These sources continually report their status to Windows Action Center. When something is amiss, Windows Action Center notifies you so that you can decide whether corrective action is warranted.

To view Windows Action Center, complete the following steps:

1. Tap or click the flag icon in the notification area of the taskbar on the desktop.
2. From the shortcut menu, choose Open Action Center to open the Action Center window shown in Figure 14-22.

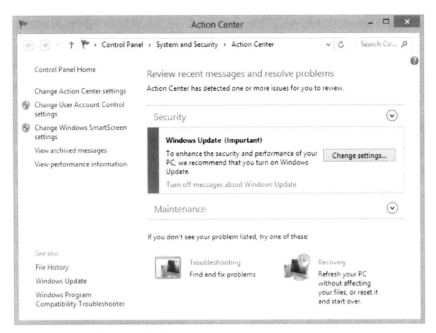

FIGURE 14-22 Windows 8 Action Center

3. You can change how the Action Center behaves by clicking or tapping Change Action Center Settings in the navigation area at the left side of the window.

4. When the screen shown in Figure 14-23 opens, choose which services should be configured to send messages to the Action Center and then click the OK button.

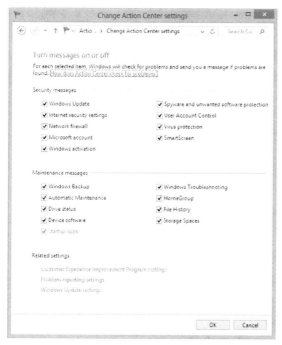

FIGURE 14-23 The Windows 8 Action Center settings

From within the Action Center, you can take specific actions to address the issues that are identified as risks. The various actions, such as configuring Windows Update, are described in other sections of this book.

Configuring and analyzing event logs

The operating system and many applications use the event log in Windows to record various activities. The event log is a busy place; it's not uncommon to see hundreds or thousands of new entries written to the various Windows event logs, depending on what is happening with the computer.

Events in Windows 8 are catalogued and configured by Event Viewer. You can open it by using either of the following methods:

- **Power Users menu**   Open the Power Users menu (press and hold or right-click the lower-left corner of the screen) and choose Event Viewer.
- **Start screen**   The Event Viewer is part of the Windows administrative tools. Open the Start screen and either select or search for Event Viewer.

Event Viewer is shown in Figure 14-24.

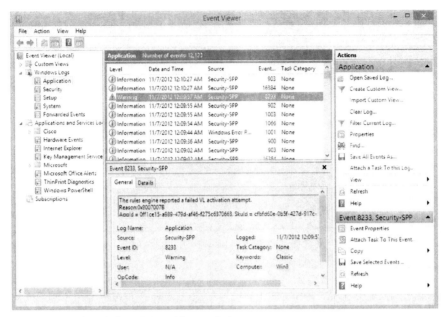

FIGURE 14-24 The Windows 8 Event Viewer window

The Event Viewer window is divided into a number of discrete panes. The leftmost pane provides the primary navigation for Event Viewer. From here, you can choose which event logs you want to view or configure.

After you select the event log you want to view, the related events are displayed in the middle pane. When you select an event in the list of events, the details for that event appear below the list.

The rightmost pane is the Actions pane, which lists all the actions that you can take with regard to the selected event log and specific event. You have a number of options within each of the event logs.

First, event logs can fill up. Each log is preconfigured with a limit. By default, when that limit is reached, Windows starts to overwrite the oldest log entries with newer ones. If you want to change this behavior, complete the following steps:

1. Open Event Viewer.

2. Select the event log you'd like to reconfigure. Each event log is configured separately.

3. From the Actions pane, tap or click Properties to open the Log Properties page, as shown in Figure 14-25.

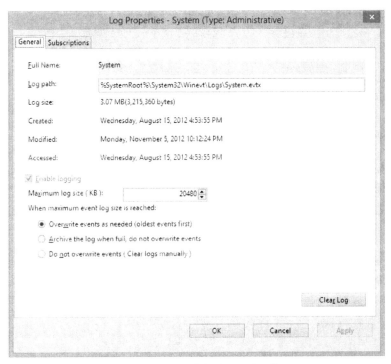

FIGURE 14-25 The Log Properties page of the System log file

4. Choose the behavior you want for how full log files should be handled:

- Overwrite Events As Needed (Oldest Events First) This is the default behavior.

- Archive The Log When Full, Do Not Overwrite Events Save the log file when it fills up so that older items are preserved.

- Do Not Overwrite Events (Clear Logs Manually) This option requires constant administrator intervention. Log files must be cleared manually before new events can be written to a full log.

5. Tap or click the OK button.

If a log fills up or you just want to clear the log's contents, tap or click the Clear Log button on the log's Properties page.

You can also increase the amount of disk space dedicated to the log file by adjusting the Maximum Log Size (KB) field shown in Figure 14-25.

Filtering events

Suppose a user contacts you with a complaint about a program she needs that won't operate, but the last time she tried to run it was a couple of days ago. Since that time, Windows has probably written hundreds of new entries to the event log. You can filter the event log based on a number of factors.

To filter an event log, open Event Viewer, select the log, and then tap or click Filter Current Log in the Actions pane. This opens a screen (Figure 14-26) from which you can filter the current log.

To filter by date, click the down arrow in the Logged field. You can choose from a number of predefined time ranges, or you can choose a specific time range. After you do so, only events from your selected range are displayed.

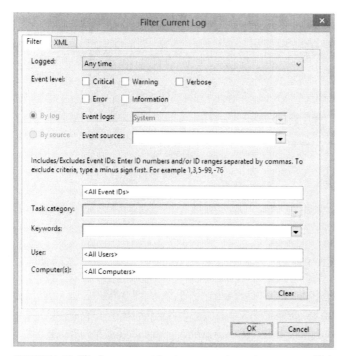

FIGURE 14-26 Filtering an event log to narrow down the amount of information you see

After you've decided what you want to view, you must interpret what you're looking at. Every log entry includes several kinds of information, including:

- **Level** The severity of the item.
  - Critical   These are the most severe kinds of items written to the event log, and they require attention. For example, if your system fails for what appears to be no reason, a critical error will be written to the event log. Although that alone won't fix the situation, it aids you in your troubleshooting efforts because you might be able to identify a pattern of behavior that helps you determine the cause of the problem.
  - Error   An error isn't as severe as a critical event, but it still requires attention. An error can be the result of a program not loading properly at startup, for example. Errors can create system stability issues if ignored.
  - Warning   A warning is written to the event log when the system thinks that an administrator needs to know about a particular situation. In most cases, warnings

don't result in system stability issues, but they might require attention at some point.

- **Information** In general, informational events are just that—informational. They are written to the event log just to inform you that something took place, but they are rarely associated with an error.
- **Audit Failure** You see this in the security log; it indicates a sign-in failure.
- **Audit Success** You also see this in the security log; it indicates a sign-in success.

- **Date and Time** The date and time that Windows experienced the issue that resulted in the log entry.

- **Source** The source of the event log entry. This could be the name of a program component, a full program, or some component of the system.

- **Event ID** Every event has an event ID. Sometimes you can use this to help identify the event and find solutions.

- **Task Category** This field is used primarily by the Security log. It identifies the kind of task that was taking place, such as sign-in, sign-out, and so on.

Saving events to an archive

Some events call for an administrator to archive system log files immediately for analysis. For example, if your organization suffers a security breach, you might be asked to salvage log files from one or more Windows 8–based computers so that they can undergo forensic analysis to determine the source of the breach.

To save the full contents of a log file to a separate location, complete the following steps:

1. Open the Event Viewer.
2. Select the event log that you need to archive.
3. From the Actions pane, tap or click Save All Events As.
4. When prompted, provide a location at which the log file should be saved.
5. Tap or click the Save button.

Monitoring system resources by using Performance Monitor

For monitoring system performance, nothing is better than the Performance Monitor tool. Built into Windows from the beginning, the Performance Monitor tool enables administrators to glean deep insight into how even the most granular aspects of the computer are running. By using Performance Monitor, administrators can create processes that continually monitor specific system statistics to watch those resources.

To open Performance Monitor, start typing **Performance Monitor** on the Start screen and, when Windows narrows down your search selection, tap or click Performance Monitor.

Alternatively, run Performance Monitor from the Power User menu or tap or click Run on the Start screen, type **perfmon**, and then tap or click OK.

When you first open the tool, there's not a lot to see, although if you expand Monitoring Tools and select Performance Monitor, Windows starts monitoring one system metric: percent processor time (Figure 14-27).

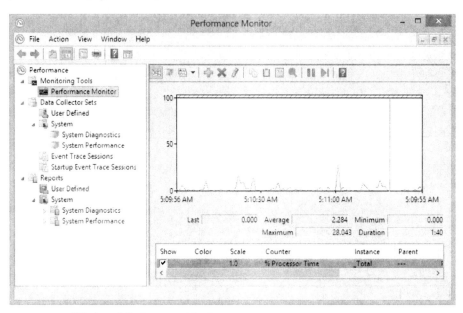

FIGURE 14-27 Windows 8 Performance Monitor

For the system being monitored in Figure 14-27, only a single metric is being monitored. Although monitoring system processor performance is an important activity, you can monitor much more.

To add data elements to the graph, complete the following steps:

1. Open the Performance Monitor tool.

2. Expand Monitoring Tools.

3. Choose Performance Monitor.

4. From the menu above the graph, tap or click the green plus icon that appears above the graph.

   This opens the Add Counters window shown in Figure 14-28.

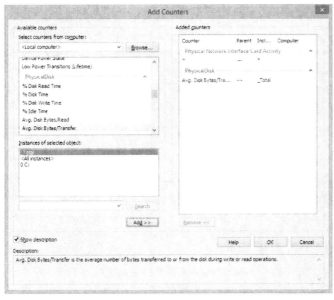

FIGURE 14-28 Adding counters to the Performance Monitor graph

5. From the Available Counters box, choose the performance metric you'd like to track.

6. Tap or click the Add button to move the counter to the Added Counters list.

7. Repeat steps 5 and 6 for additional counters, if desired.

8. When you're finished, tap or click the OK button.

You might be surprised at the sheer number of counters that are available for your use. Hundreds of counters are divided into dozens of categories. You can monitor even the most granular system elements, which makes the Performance Monitor tool ideal for troubleshooting performance-related system issues.

> **TIP EXPLORE PERFORMANCE MONITOR IN DETAIL**
>
> If you're interested in learning about how your Windows 8–based computer really works, one of the best tools you can use to do that is Performance Monitor. You can see all the elements the system is capable of monitoring. By perusing the various counters at your disposal, you can see exactly how your computer sees various values. As time goes on and you learn more about these counters and how your Windows-based computer operates, you can troubleshoot more quickly any problems that might arise.

While you're looking for performance counters to add to your graph, select the Show Description check box. This will help you understand exactly what the counter tracks.

For some counters, multiple instances of the counter are available, such as when there is more than one of a certain device. For example, if you have more than one hard disk drive in your computer, you would see each drive listed separately. As a result, if you suspect you're having a problem with just one of the drives, you can monitor just that drive without viewing statistics from the other drive.

Performing system diagnostics by using Performance Monitor

Even though you can take the time to go through individual performance counters to decide what you want to monitor, Windows provides you with a fast way to gather dozens of critical performance elements. After the information is gathered, Windows displays the results of the system diagnostic into an easily readable report. The full system diagnostic relies on more than just performance counters to work its magic. It's configured to pull all kinds of information from various parts of the system.

To run a full system diagnostic, complete the following steps:

1. Open the Performance Monitor tool.

2. Expand Data Collector Sets and then choose System.

3. Select System Diagnostics.

   A number of items appear in the right side of the window. If you double-tap or double-click one of the items, you can see how Windows plans to gather the information necessary to satisfy the tool's needs. In the example in Figure 14-29, Windows browses a registry key to determine UAC status.

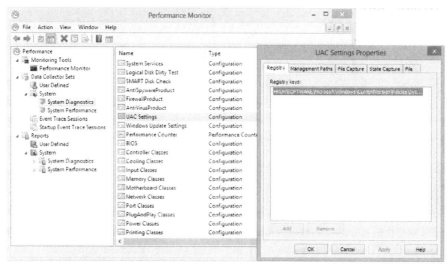

FIGURE 14-29 A look at the source of one of the System Diagnostics data points

4. Press and hold or right-click System Diagnostics in the navigation pane.

   From the shortcut menu, choose Start to start a data collector process, using default settings. Allow the data collector to run for as long as you like. The longer it runs, the more information it will collect.

5. Press and hold or right-click System Diagnostics and choose Stop. A new report associated with your data collection efforts will be created.

6. Expand Reports, System, and System Diagnostics in the navigation pane.

7. Select the new report. It will be displayed in the main window, as shown in Figure 14-30.

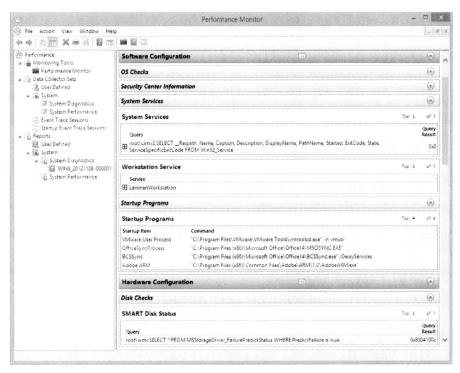

FIGURE 14-30 The results of the system diagnostics process

The report that is generated is comprehensive. It provides you with a lot of the information you need to identify and enables you to correct potential system performance issues and optimize your system.

Lesson summary

- Windows Action Center provides you with real-time insight into the current health of your computer from a security perspective. Filter events in Event Viewer to focus on those that require action.

- Save events to an archive in case you need to refer to them later.

- Use Task Manager to monitor almost all aspects of Windows 8.

- Use Task Manager to end running programs that might be causing system stability issues.

Lesson review

Answer the following questions to test your knowledge of the information in this lesson. You can find the answers to these questions and explanations of why each answer choice is correct or incorrect in the "Answers" section at the end of this chapter.

1. How can you end a process in Windows?

    A. Use Control Panel to end the running process.

    B. In Task Manager, open the Details tab and end the process.

    C. In Task Manager, open the App History tab and end the process.

    D. Use the Services tab in Task Manager to end the process.

2. Which is the default log file configuration in Windows 8?

    A. Overwrite Events As Needed (Oldest Events First)

    B. Archive The Log When Full, Do Not Overwrite Events

    C. Do Not Overwrite Events (Clear Logs Manually)

    D. There is no default log file configuration; each is configured manually.

3. How can you change the items that appear in Windows Action Center?

    A. From the Action Center, click or tap Change Action Center Settings in the navigation area at the left side of the window.

    B. Use Programs And Features in Control Panel to make configuration changes to Action Center settings.

    C. Open Windows Update settings to adjust Action Center settings.

    D. Use Task Manager to modify the information displayed in the Action Center.

Practice exercises

In these exercises, you apply what you've learned about working with Windows Update and monitoring tools.

Exercise 1: Enable automatic updates on your computer

In this exercise, you instruct Windows to download and install new updates automatically at 5:00 A.M.

1. Adjust Windows Update settings.

2. Change the time at which updates are applied.

Exercise 2: Manually end a process in Windows

In this exercise, you end a running process.

1. Start the WordPad app (a basic editing tool that comes with Windows).
2. Open Task Manager.
3. Find the WordPad app and end the process.
4. Repeat Steps 1 and 2, but this time end the process from the Details tab.

Exercise 3: Create an event log filter

In this exercise, you filter an event log on a certain date range.

1. Open Event Viewer.
2. Create a filter to view events in the System log from just the past two weeks.

Suggested practice exercises

The following additional practices are designed to give you more opportunities to practice what you've learned and to help you successfully master the lessons presented in this chapter.

- **Exercise 1**   Run the System Diagnostics report and carefully review the information.
- **Exercise 2**   Practice creating new counters and adding them to a Performance Monitor chart.
- **Exercise 3**   Remove a previously installed Windows update.

Answers

This section contains the answers to the lesson review questions in this chapter.

Lesson 1

1. **Correct answer: D**

   A. **Incorrect:** Windows updates are accessible through the Windows 8 native interface by tapping or clicking the Settings charm, choosing Change PC Settings, and then selecting Windows Update.

   B. **Incorrect:** Windows updates are accessible by opening Control Panel from the Settings charm.

   C. **Incorrect:** Windows updates are accessible through the Windows 8 native interface by tapping or clicking the Settings charm, choosing Change PC Settings, and then selecting Windows Update.

   D. **Correct:** There is no direct option on the Power Users menu for Windows Update.

2. **Correct answer: A**

   A. **Correct:** Removing the update and then hiding it adds it to a list of updates that should not be installed.

   B. **Incorrect:** Removing the update and then configuring Windows Update for manual installation would prevent new updates from being downloaded and installed automatically.

   C. **Incorrect:** You cannot remove Windows Update.

   D. **Incorrect:** Removing the update and then installing any new updates Windows finds will result in the removed update being reinstalled.

3. **Correct answer: A**

   A. **Correct:** Open the Programs And Features page in Control Panel and delete the update.

   B. **Incorrect:** View Update History is a read-only update repository.

   C. **Incorrect:** Individual updates are not listed on the Windows Update configuration page.

   D. **Incorrect:** Restore Hidden Updates is used to view updates that were previously hidden to prevent installation.

Lesson 2

1. **Correct answer: B**

   A. **Incorrect:** Processes are not managed directly from Control Panel.

   B. **Correct:** You can end a process by opening the Details tab in Task Manager.

C. **Incorrect:** App History does not enable you to end tasks, only to view information.

D. **Incorrect:** The Services tab is used to manage services.

2. **Correct answer: C**

A. **Correct:** Overwrite Events As Needed (Oldest Events First) is the default log file configuration.

B. **Incorrect:** Archive The Log When Full, Do Not Overwrite Events.

C. **Incorrect:** Do Not Overwrite Events (Clear Logs Manually).

D. **Incorrect:** Each log file has a default configuration.

3. **Correct answer: A**

A. **Correct:** From Windows Action Center, tap or click Change Action Center Settings in the navigation area at the left side of the window.

B. **Incorrect:** Use Programs And Features in Control Panel to add and remove programs.

C. **Incorrect:** Windows Update settings are used to manage patches, not to adjust Windows Action Center settings.

D. **Incorrect:** Task Manager is used to watch the system's performance, not to manage Windows Action Center settings.

CHAPTER 15

System protection and recovery

B ecause your data changes constantly, and the computers that maintain the data that runs your organization change almost as quickly, understanding how to protect and recover that data can save you time in an emergency. This chapter covers recoverability, protection, and details you need to know to put your computers back online as quickly as possible.

> **REAL WORLD BACKUP AND RECOVERY ARE FACTS OF LIFE**
>
> **Files are usually the most important when they are gone. This fact seems to pop up often. Office workers everywhere are quick to brush off potential problems as long as things appear to be working, but when a needed file is missing, it might as well be the most important document in the history of documents. Take great care in backup and recovery planning and education to help your colleagues understand the importance of backup, recovery, and testing to avoid crises in the future.**

Lessons in this chapter:

Before you begin

To complete the practice exercises in this chapter, you need the following:

- An understanding of the basics of backing up and recovering computers and data
- Experience with some of the tools and features used for backup and restoration, including:
  - System Restore
  - MSConfig
- A removable USB drive or a network share
- An external hard disk

Lesson 1: Working with backup and restoration

Computers are the tools you use as an IT professional to keep your organization working as efficiently as possible. Sometimes, these machines fail or need replacement. In an emergency, the files you are able to back up are only as useful as the files you can restore from backup. This lesson walks through backup and restoration in Windows 8 by using built-in tools and utilities.

After this lesson, you will be able to:

■ Perform a backup and restoration of a computer running Windows 8.

■ Use System Restore to recover system settings.

■ Back up files and folders on demand and on schedule.

■ Quickly recover previous versions of files and folders.

Estimated lesson time: 75 minutes

Backing up Windows 8

Many organizations today have data spread around the globe, from big corporate data centers with various levels of backup and offsite storage to laptops the sales force carry, which might not be backed up regularly, if at all. By using tools built into Windows, you can ensure that the organization's information is safe in case of an emergency.

Windows has included a backup utility for several versions that enables you to ensure that data stored on a computer can be backed up and recovered without the need for third-party utilities.

To back up your Windows 8–based computer completely, you must configure Windows Backup. To do so and create a backup job, complete the following steps:

1. From the desktop, select the Settings charm and then select Control Panel.

2. Select Windows 7 File Recovery.

3. Tap or click Set Up Backup.

4. Wait for Windows Backup to start.

5. Select A Removable Disk or select Save On A Network. It is recommended that you store backup data on an external disk.

6. If you are saving to a network, enter the Universal Naming Convention (UNC) path to the share where your data will be stored and do the following:

   A. Enter the necessary credentials for the resource.

   B. Tap or click OK to continue configuring Windows Backup.

7. If you use removable media, select the removable disk listed in the Setup Backup dialog box and tap or click Next.

8. If the media to which you want to save your backup is not listed, plug the media into the computer, tap or click Refresh, select one of the following backup options, and then tap or click Next:

   ■ **Let Windows Choose (recommended)** This option retains data from common libraries, the desktop, and default Windows folders. In addition, a system image is taken to enable full system restores if the computer stops working.

   ■ **Let Me Choose** This option enables you to select the folders and locations to include in the backup and to choose whether to include a system image.

9. Review your backup settings:

   ■ To modify backup settings, tap or click the Back button in the top-left corner of the Backup dialog box.

   ■ To modify the backup schedule, tap or click Change Schedule in the middle of the Backup dialog box.

10. When you are satisfied with the configured settings, tap or click Save Settings And Run Backup to begin taking your first backup. While the backup is running, the Windows 7 File Recovery Wizard displays the progress of the operation, as shown in Figure 15-1.

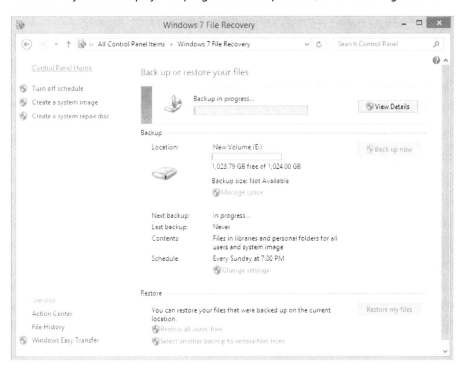

FIGURE 15-1 Backup progress

Creating additional images

You might want to create an updated system image backup of a computer without modifying the regular backup schedule or options. For example, when the marketing department purchases updated versions of graphics applications, you might consider creating an updated system image with the new versions. This way, if there is a problem in the future that is not related to the installation, the computer can be restored and the graphics application will be restored with it, thus reducing the need for additional installations to ensure that the affected computer is running properly.

To create a system image, complete the following steps:

1. From Control Panel, select Windows 7 File Recovery.

2. From the navigation pane on the left, select Create A System Image.

3. In the Create A System Image Wizard, specify from the following options where to store the image:

   - **On A Hard Disk**   Select a hard drive on which to create the image.

   - **On One Or More DVDs**   Specify the DVD drive containing blank media on which to write the image; you will be prompted to insert additional media as needed.

   - **On A Network Location**   Specify the UNC path to a share to store your image.

4. Tap or click Next when you have selected the location for the image.

5. Select the drives you want to include in the system image and click Next.

6. Review the options you selected and click Start Backup to create the image.

While the image is being created, Windows displays the progress bar shown in Figure 15-1.

Protecting files and data by using File History

Windows 8 has another new feature, File History, to make backing up your personal settings easier than in the past. Its aim is to provide an easy-to-configure tool for backing up your Windows 8 files and data. The folders included in File History backups by default are:

- Libraries

- Desktop

- Contacts

- Favorites
- Microsoft SkyDrive

If you have files or folders you want backed up, you can add them to one of your existing libraries or create a new library. To configure File History, complete the following steps:

1. From the desktop, select the Settings charm, tap or click Control Panel, and then tap or click File History.

   When the application opens, it tries to detect removable drives to use when storing backups. If none are found, you can choose a network location and specify a UNC path where backups can be stored.

2. If you will be configuring removable media to store your data, select the drive you want to use and tap or click Turn On. File History is shown in Figure 15-2.

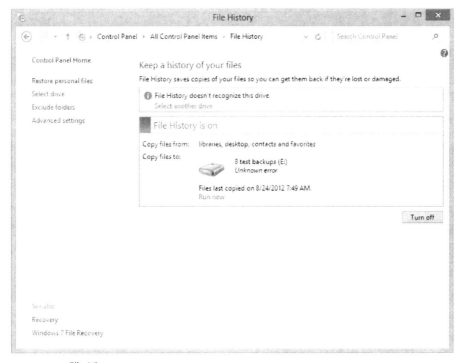

FIGURE 15-2 File History

When File History is turned on, the wizard copies items from the default locations to the drive you have selected. The initial copy process takes a bit longer than subsequent copies to complete.

Excluding items from File History

If you want to exclude certain folders or libraries from File History backups, click the Exclude Folders link in the left pane of the File History window, as shown in Figure 15-2. This opens the Exclude Folders window, which is shown in Figure 15-3.

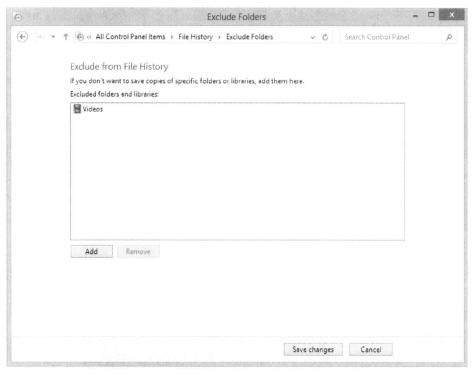

FIGURE 15-3 Excluding folders from File History backups

To exclude a folder, complete the following steps:

1. In the Exclude Folders window, tap or click Add.

2. Navigate to a folder or library and select it for exclusion.

3. Tap or click Select Folder.

4. Tap or click Save Changes. The selected folders or libraries will not be included in File History backups.

> **NOTE CONSIDER CAREFULLY WHAT TO BACK UP AND WHAT TO EXCLUDE**
> Carefully consider files to be excluded. Although these settings can always be modified to include files that have previously been excluded, until this is done, File History will not back up excluded files.

Offline caching is a method used to store a portion of the information, typically saved to a network drive or online resource, on your local computer for faster access.

In addition to drive choices and folders to exclude, you can configure the following advanced settings:

- **Save Copies Of Files** Specifies how often the files will be saved. Every Hour is the default.

- **Size Of Offline Cache** Specifies the amount of disk space that Windows should use to cache File History data offline.

- **Keep Saved Versions** Specifies the length of time Windows should keep versions of files that File History has saved.

After you have configured these settings as appropriate for your computer, tap or click Save Changes to store the configuration.

 Quick check

- **What is the default backup schedule for Windows 8?**

Quick check answer

- **The default schedule for backup is Sunday at 7:00 P.M., and the schedule runs weekly.**

Restoring files, folders, and entire computers

Backing up a computer's files helps you feel secure, knowing that your data—from photos of your family to documents covering a large corporate merger—is safe. However, you per-form backups to restore your data in the event of an emergency. The restoration capabili-ties available in Windows 8 are much more advanced than previous versions of Windows, so restores can include a just few files and folders rather than requiring the restoration of entire computers.

Performing a restoration of only certain files or folders that have been backed up (for example, the items included in a File History backup) can save time and productivity if a document is lost, moved, deleted, or becomes corrupted.

To recover items from a File History backup, complete the following steps:

1. From the desktop, select the Settings charm and then select Control Panel.
2. Open File History.
3. From the navigation pane, select Restore Personal Files.
4. The most recent copies of items that have been backed up are displayed in the Home - File History dialog box shown in Figure 15-4. If the files you need to recover are in a different version of the backup, tap or click the left or right arrow in the center of the bottom of the dialog box to switch to the previous or next version of the backup, respectively.

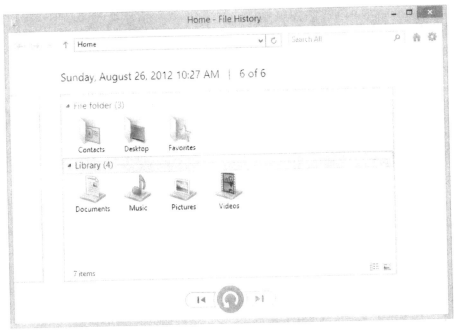

FIGURE 15-4 Choosing an item to recover from File History

5. When you have located the files you need to restore, highlight them and click the center button at the bottom of the dialog box to restore the files to their original location.

   In addition to restoring the items to their original location, you can select the items and then press and hold or right-click them to access the following additional options:

   ■ **Preview**   Displays the items contained in the backup.

   ■ **Restore**   Performs a restoration of the items to their original location.

   ■ **Restore To**   Performs a restoration after you specify where you want the files restored. This option is helpful when you want to compare documents to keep multiple versions of a file on hand.

   When you have selected a restore option (and the restore location if using Restore To), the object is copied from the backup, and its location is displayed in Windows Explorer.

6. Close the Home - File History window.

REAL WORLD RECOVERING FILES FOR EVERYONE

Recovering individual files is much easier in Windows 8 than by using Previous Versions in earlier versions of Windows, so you might want to alert your coworkers to the idea of self-service restoration. The File History option can be a great time saver for both employees who need help and the IT support staff providing the help because it enables the person missing a file to locate it and restore it with little effort. Doing this can reduce help desk calls about missing files and their recovery from other backup media.

Restoring an entire computer

Sometimes, just getting a few files back is not enough to solve a problem. Accidents happen, and the occasional recovery becomes necessary. Using images for backup and recovery has been available as part of Windows since Windows 7.

System image recovery options depend on your computer's configuration. If you are using only Windows 8 and have no other operating systems on your computer, just pressing F8 to access the menu during startup will present the options you need. If your computer can start multiple operating systems, you must select the operating system to start and then press F8 to access the menu.

When you see the Advanced Boot Options screen, complete the following steps to recover your computer from a system image:

1. Select Repair Your Computer.
2. Choose the appropriate keyboard layout and tap or click Next.
3. Enter your user name and password and tap or click OK.
4. Select System Image Recovery from the Recovery Options menu.
5. Choose a target operating system for the System Image Recovery.

   Windows scans for system images on the computer and selects the images it finds. If no images are found, a dialog box appears to inform you that no images were found. If you see this, tap or click Cancel to select the image yourself.

6. Select the location of the image. If it is on DVD media, insert the DVD and select the image.
7. If you need more options, click the Advanced button to enable driver installation for other devices or to access a network location containing the image.
8. Select the image needed for the restoration and tap or click Next.
9. Select the backup you want to use from the available backups list and tap or click Next.

10. Select additional options, including:

- **Format And Repartition Disks** Erases all data from your computer and realigns the disks according to the layout used in the image.

- **Install Drivers** Enables you to install additional drivers during the imaging process.

- **Advanced** Presents two additional options. You can either restart the computer after the restoration is complete or automatically check and update disk error information.

11. Include the options you want to use and tap or click Next.

12. Review the options you have selected and tap or click Finish to begin the restoration.

A progress bar appears during the process. The total time of the recovery varies, depending on the size of your computer's hard disks and the amount of data contained in the image. When the computer restarts, it will be restored to the date and time selected.

In some cases, restoring a computer from a system image can be the fastest method available to restore the computer to a functional state. For example, an employee in the customer service department calls because his computer, which has few applications installed on it, is performing slowly. He explains that several windows pop up throughout the day, asking him to download and install an antivirus application he has never heard of. He wants to know what he should do.

Because investigating the malware might take more time than is available, you decide to restore the computer from a previously created image, making note of both the information about the malware displayed in the pop-ups and the version of antimalware definitions currently installed on the computer.

> **REAL WORLD BACKUP AS GOOD AS RESTORE**
>
> When deciding which information to back up, keep in mind that the data might perform very well and appear to be available for use in case of emergency, but when you must use that backup, the information might be corrupted or unusable. Performing regular test restorations of information that has been backed up is the only way to determine whether the information that has been captured by backup will prove useful for something as simple as a missing file or as mission critical as a disaster recovery operation.

Using System Restore for less invasive troubleshooting

Completely removing everything from your computer and restoring your computer to a previous image periodically can keep your computer performing well for a very long time, but there are less extreme methods for recovering computers that are not working as they should. System Restore is a program included with Windows by which you can recover files after certain operations without harming your data on the computer.

For example, if a user installs a copy of Microsoft Office 2010 on his computer and something goes wrong during this process, the applications might not work properly—if the installation even completes. System Restore can roll back changes made to system files and attempt the installation again or decide not to install Micosoft Office.

Understanding how System Restore works

System Restore relies on snapshots of a computer that are taken before (and sometimes after) major events. A major event could be software or driver installation or a scheduled restore point snapshot configured by an administrator.

After the application is enabled and has snapshots from which to select, System Restore can roll back changes to the point in time of the selected snapshot. When the process is complete, the computer has no trace of the applications or settings that were installed following that restore point.

Configuring System Restore

To use System Restore in Windows 8, it must be enabled for a volume. To access System Restore, complete the following steps:

1. Open the System Properties dialog box by selecting System from Control Panel or by searching for "system restore" on the Start screen.

2. Select the System Protection tab, shown in Figure 15-5.

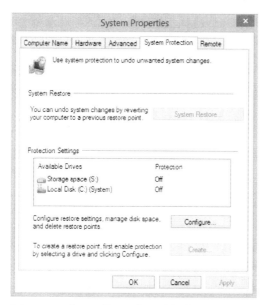

FIGURE 15-5 System Protection tab in System Properties

3. Tap or click the Configure button to access and modify the options for System Restore, including:

   ■ Turning system protection on or off.

   ■ Setting the amount of disk space that System Restore should use for snapshots.

   ■ Deleting restore points.

Creating restore points

Windows automatically creates snapshots before application installations or Windows update applications, just in case there are problems. You can also create a snapshot manually by completing the following steps:

1. On the System Protection tab of the System Properties dialog box (Figure 15-5), select the Create button.

2. Enter a description for the snapshot.

3. Tap or click Create.

4. Tap or click Close after the restore point is created.

Using System Restore

After the restore points are created, they can be used to recover a computer to a point in time or to undo changes made following a restore point. To perform a system restore, complete the following steps:

1. Open the System Properties dialog box.

2. Select the System Protection tab (Figure 15-5).

3. Tap or click the System Restore button.

4. Tap or click Next on the welcome screen of the System Restore Wizard.

5. Select the restore point you would like to use by highlighting it in the list of restore points.

   If the restore point you need is not listed, select the Show More Restore Points check box to see more options.

   If you are unsure which applications might be affected by a restore operation, click Scan For Affected Programs while a restore point is selected to list programs that might not work correctly if this restore is performed and programs that were added since the last restore point, which will be removed.

6. Tap or click Next to review the options selected.

7. Tap or click Finish to begin the restore process.

8. Tap or click Yes to acknowledge the prompt and continue or tap or click No to cancel the restore.

9. Your computer will restart during the system restore process.

Following the restoration and restart of the system, a dialog box appears to inform you that the restore completed or did not complete.

10. Tap or click OK to close the dialog box.

System Restore is an efficient way to roll back changes that were made to system files during troubleshooting, application installation, or the Windows update process. Using this method can save more time than performing a full computer restoration using a system image or installation media.

Two new methods of restoration and recovery

Windows 8 includes two additional methods for recovering a computer that have not been in previous versions of Windows:

- **Refresh**   Changes PC settings back to the default state without affecting Windows Store apps, personal files, or personalization settings. Applications from other websites or disc installations will be removed. When you select this option, Windows tells you what will happen, as shown in Figure 15-6.

FIGURE 15-6   What happens during a refresh

- **Reset**   All personal files and personalization settings will be removed. Windows settings will be restored to their default values, as shown in Figure 15-7.

FIGURE 15-7 What happens during a reset

Making your computer like new again by using Refresh

In some instances, cleaning up a computer and removing applications or files that are no longer needed can help improve performance. Microsoft has created Refresh to ease this process. Using a new computer is often a very different experience from using a computer that is holding many temporary files and downloaded items because the older or more used system might seem slower than the new computer. To refresh your computer, complete the following steps:

1. Open the Start screen and search for Refresh. Select the Settings charm and choose Refresh Your PC or PC Settings.

2. On the Refresh Your PC welcome screen (Figure 15-6), read the proposed changes and tap or click Next.

3. Wait while the refresh process is prepared.

4. Tap or click Refresh to begin the process.

   Windows begins the refresh and configures updates and settings changes. When this portion of the process completes, the computer restarts. Windows displays a progress counter for the refresh process, shown in Figure 15-8. Following this restart, devices are configured for use. Windows restarts again.

   The refresh process returns the computer to the default settings but keeps your personalization settings, files, and Windows Store applications.

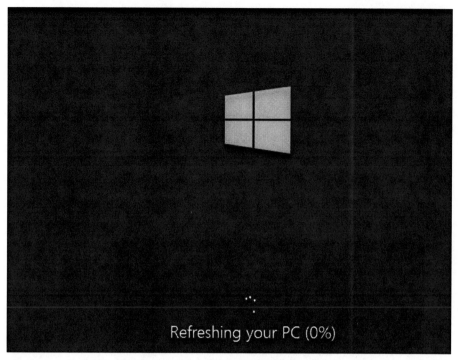

FIGURE 15-8 Refresh progress

When the refresh process doesn't go far enough

Refreshing a computer to restore it to the original configuration without losing customizations is useful, but sometimes it is necessary to go all the way back to the out-of-the-box configuration. Suppose you have been testing Windows 8 on a computer for a few months and running a few development applications on the system to get an idea of how they will perform. When the test period for these applications is over, you must make a decision about whether they will work well for your organization. This is a good time to restore your computer to the manufacturer's original configuration.

Another situation in which resetting your computer might be best is if the computer has suffered a malware infection. Although fixes and cleanups are available for troubleshooting, a simple reinstallation might make the process easier. To perform a reset of Windows 8, complete the following steps:

1. From the Start screen, search for "remove everything." Select Settings and then tap or click Remove Everything And Reinstall Windows.

2. Tap or click Next on the Reset Your PC welcome screen.

3. Wait for the reset to prepare.

4. If your computer has more than one available drive, select the drives to reset:

  ▪ Only the drive on which Windows is installed

  ▪ All drives detected on the computer

5. Specify whether the reset process should clean the drive fully by choosing one of the following:

  ▪ **Just Remove My Files**   Removes only the current user's files; takes a few moments

  ▪ **Fully Clean The Drive**   Removes all files from the disk and takes considerably longer

6. To begin the reset process, tap or click Reset.

  Windows restarts to begin the process; it displays a progress screen, as shown in Figure 15-9, to show the progress of the operation.

FIGURE 15-9   Reset progress

Both these procedures, Refresh and Reset, take from one hour to four or more hours, depending on the size of the volumes in the computer and other hardware. The process itself, however, is mostly automated after you have answered some questions about how you want to handle your files and settings. These two features decrease the time needed to clean up a Windows PC and free considerable time for other tasks.

Using File History and other backup and recovery techniques on computers within your environment can not only reduce administrative workload by reducing the number of file recoveries needed from other media but also serve as a way to educate others in your organization about the importance of data recovery. Helping your coworkers locate missing files by themselves rather than waiting for someone at the help desk to retrieve something from the last tape backup can be very empowering for employees. In some cases, the capability to help themselves is all people want.

 Quick check

■ Which recovery method should you use when you want to keep personal settings but change Windows to the default settings?

Quick check answer

■ Use Refresh to restore Windows files to their original state; it does not modify or remove Windows Store applications or personal files and folders. Applications installed from external media will be removed. During the process, a list of removed applications will be stored on your desktop.

Lesson summary

■ Create backups and restore files by using File History.

■ Build system images to create full and complete copies of a computer.

■ Use System Restore to roll back changes to a computer.

■ Refresh a computer to remove customizations.

■ Reset a computer to return to the original manufacturer's configuration.

Lesson review

Answer the following questions to test your knowledge of the information in this lesson. You can find the answers to these questions and explanations of why each answer choice is correct or incorrect in the "Answers" section at the end of this chapter.

1. Your organization's CEO says that her computer has been infected with a virus. She and her assistant have been working to return the computer to a functional state but are making little progress. She has stated that she is not worried about the data and just wants the computer to work again. Which Windows recovery solution would you recommend to meet the needs and requirements of the CEO? (Choose all that apply.)

   A. A computer refresh

   B. A computer reset

   C. System Restore to a date before the infection

   D. Starting the computer in safe mode

2. Because Windows 8 has straightforward backup and recovery procedures for files and folders, you have been training your coworkers to recover their own files within your organization. An employee from the accounting office calls because she has lost the budget spreadsheet she has been working on for the past three days. Because she has

just received Windows 8 and has not yet attended any training sessions, which recovery solution should you walk her through?

A. System Restore

B. System image restoration

C. File History to locate an earlier version of the file

D. The steps required to reset her computer

3. An executive in the sales department has been leaving messages for you all day. He claims that he cannot access his email following the installation of Microsoft Office 2010 that he performed over the weekend. The installation appeared to finish, but he thinks that there was an error message during the process; however, he cannot remember. Which recovery process can you help him use to remove the installation of Microsoft Office 2010?

A. System image recovery

B. System Restore

C. PC Refresh

D. Starting Windows by using the Last Known Good Configuration

Lesson 2: Advanced settings and features for Windows recovery

The techniques covered in the previous lesson are great tools for repairing a computer, but sometimes more advanced options might be necessary to correct a problem. This lesson discusses some of these advanced tools and how to use them.

After this lesson, you will be able to:

- Use MSConfig to manage startup processes and services.
- Recover from a failed driver installation.
- Use Task Manager to determine which applications are configured to launch at startup.

Estimated lesson time: 75 minutes

MSConfig

The Microsoft Configuration utility (MSConfig), shown in Figure 15-10, has been included in several versions of the Windows operating system. It helps you work through problems with services or applications that do not start properly, and it helps you remove items from the startup menu to ease the troubleshooting process.

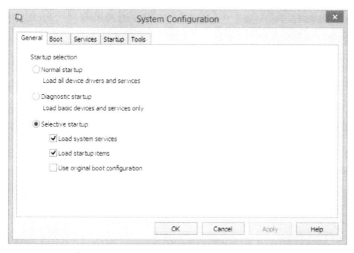

FIGURE 15-10 The system configuration options of the MSConfig utility

Each of the tabs in the MSConfig application covers a different aspect of the Windows operating system. These tabs (and their options) include:

- **General** This tab covers the following startup options for the computer:
    - Normal Startup Loads all drivers and services when the computer starts
    - Diagnostic Startup Loads only basic drivers and services
    - Selective Startup Loads system services and startup items or uses the original boot configuration
- **Boot** This tab enables you to configure the startup menu; select one of the following startup modes: Safe Boot, Minimal, Alternative Shell, Active Directory Repair, or Network. Other options on this tab are:
    - No GUI Boot Starts Windows with the graphical user interface (GUI) disabled.
    - Boot Log Logs all items during the startup process.
    - Base Video Uses the lowest or most basic video configuration.
    - OS Boot Information Displays startup information for the operating system.
    - Timeout Specifies the number of seconds any startup menu options will be displayed; default is 30 seconds.
    - Make All Boot Settings Permanent Saves the chosen selections to Windows, allowing them to be used on each successive startup.
- **Services** This tab displays all the services that can start with Windows. Clearing the check box for a service disables the service at startup. Select the Disable All Services or Enable All Services buttons to apply a choice to all services. The option to hide all Microsoft services removes any Microsoft services from view and protects them from Enable All or Disable All.

- **Startup** This tab has no options; these settings have been moved to Task Manager.
- **Tools** This tab displays a list of tools that might be useful in troubleshooting. Select a tool from the list and tap or click the Launch button to start that tool.

Task Manager Startup

The Startup tab of Task Manager shows any items that are currently configured to start with Windows. In addition, it provides the status and startup impact of any listed applications. This gives you an idea of what the application does when starting up. The Task Manager Startup tab is shown in Figure 15-11.

FIGURE 15-11 The Task Manager Startup tab

Selecting an item listed on the Startup tab and clicking the Disable button will prevent that item from starting the next time Windows starts.

Recovering from a bad driver installation

Microsoft includes a large number of device drivers with each new release of Windows. Sometimes, however, devices are released after Windows has been shipped, or the hardware manufacturers have added other technical functions to their own drivers that operate better than the driver included with Windows. For example, monitors have manufacturer-written drivers that provide functionality beyond what Windows provides. Windows might provide some of the basic features that enable the monitor to display output, but it seldom provides extended resolutions the device is capable of using. Refresh rate is also usually set to a standard value if no driver is installed.

> **IMPORTANT   MICROSOFT CERTIFIES HARDWARE FOR WINDOWS**
>
> To help ensure that manufacturers meet certain criteria for their devices and that their drivers are included in Windows Update, Microsoft has a certification program for drivers. Using Windows Update to select drivers enables IT professionals to receive a more stable and tested release than the latest version from the manufacturer.

Windows operates correctly using its own standard values, but you might need the additional features the manufacturer included for a certain scenario.

Sometimes drivers exhibit problems with execution and stop functioning correctly. When this occurs, you will want to be familiar with the driver rollback functionality.

Using *driver rollback* enables you to quickly recover failed installations if a device does not function following a driver update. You can roll back device drivers to previously installed versions. To make these changes, complete the following steps:

1. Open Control Panel.
2. Select Update Device Drivers.
3. Locate the device on which you want to roll back drivers.
4. Press and hold or right-click the device and then select Properties.
5. Select the Driver tab and then tap or click Roll Back Driver.

    Windows will roll back the new driver to the previously installed version.
6. When the operation completes, tap or click the Device Properties dialog box.
7. Close the Device Manager window.
8. Close Control Panel.

Lesson summary

- Roll back drivers that are not properly installed or functioning.
- Use MSConfig to modify the startup status of applications and services.
- Recover Windows by using Advanced Startup Options.

Lesson review

Answer the following questions to test your knowledge of the information in this lesson. You can find the answers to these questions and explanations of why each answer choice is correct or incorrect in the "Answers" section at the end of this chapter.

1. A coworker in your organization's finance department calls because her Windows 8–based computer is failing during the startup process. She mentions that the computer had been working until that morning with no problems. Which of the following options can you try to restore this computer to working order?

   A. MSConfig

   B. Last Known Good Configuration

   C. The Task Manager Startup tab

   D. Safe mode

2. You have been having trouble determining why an application continually displays an error message when the computer starts. You want to see whether particular services being started with the operating system are causing the problem. How can you selectively start services in Windows?

   A. Use MSConfig to disable all non-Microsoft services.

   B. Use Windows Task Manager to disable all non-Microsoft services.

   C. Use MSConfig to edit the startup menu options used when starting Windows.

   D. Use Windows Task Manager to edit the startup menu options used when starting Windows.

3. Your boss purchased a new webcam to use during a meeting taking place later that day. After plugging in the webcam, she notices that Windows has detected the camera and notices no issues with the hardware. Because the camera came with a CD including drivers and software for the camera, your boss installs the drivers to make sure the camera works. Starting the camera produces an error about driver incompatibility. What can you do to help your boss correct the issues with her new webcam?

   A. Perform a driver update to get a newer version of the webcam's driver.

   B. Perform a driver rollback to remove the last installed driver for the device.

   C. Remove the camera and reinstall it.

   D. Use MSConfig to disable the drivers for the webcam.

Lesson 3: Advanced recovery and restoration options

This chapter focuses on backup and recovery and methods for repairing computers running Windows 8. This lesson focuses on the advanced options for recovery.

After this lesson, you will be able to:

- Use system repair and recovery discs to repair Windows 8.
- Access advanced startup options in Windows.

Estimated lesson time: 35 minutes

Creating a system repair or recovery disc

A Windows repair disc is a handy tool to have just in case you encounter issues with Windows 8 that might require media, including corrupted or missing system files or even a computer refresh. System repair discs enable you to start an unresponsive computer and use utilities and tools to fix problems with your Windows installation.

> *IMPORTANT* **RECOVERY MEDIA SIZE**
>
> **Any media used for recovery must be at least 256 MB in size.**

To create a Windows 8 system repair disc, complete the following steps:

1. Navigate to Control Panel.
2. Tap or click Recovery.
3. Tap or click Create A Recovery Drive.
4. In the Recovery Drive Wizard, tap or click Next.
5. Select the USB drive you want to use for the system repair disk, and then tap or click Next. On the Create The Recovery Drive page, click Create.
6. When the system recovery drive is ready, tap or click Finish.
7. To use the repair media that has been created, restart your computer with the repair media inserted.
8. When the system restarts, select the keyboard layout/language to be used.

> *NOTE* **SELECTION OF RESET OR REFRESH OPTIONS**
>
> **Selecting Refresh Your PC cleans up Windows files on the computer without affecting your files. Selecting Reset Your PC removes all your data and reinstalls Windows on your computer.**

Selecting Advanced options from the PC Settings page provides the following tools:

- System Restore
- System Image Recovery
- Automatic Repair
- Command Prompt

The advanced recovery utilities are designed to facilitate troubleshooting computers running Windows 8. Some of the tools are designed to replace Windows on your computer, similar to installing Windows from a USB drive or DVD. The Automatic Repair tool can diagnose issues that prevent Windows from starting.

> *NOTE* **ACCESSING RECOVERY TOOLS**
>
> **You can also use the Windows 8 installation media to access the recovery tools contained on a repair disc.**

Using Windows Recovery Environment

Windows includes a recovery method built on the pre-installation version of Windows (Windows PE) that is used when a computer does not start. In the event of a startup problem, your Windows PC automatically restarts in Windows Recovery Environment (Windows RE) to run the startup repair tool to help diagnose the problem with the startup process.

Windows 8 Recovery Environment is an excellent set of troubleshooting tools that can provide efficient solutions to help a client computer function again. For example, a user from the marketing department opens a support ticket because her computer is "acting up." You see that the computer appears to be stuck in a restart loop. Using a system recovery disk (or the Windows 8 media), you start Windows RE to troubleshoot the problem further. Because the issue appears to be startup related and has been occurring for only a short time, selecting Automatic Repair might be the only step needed to start this computer successfully. If the computer continues to fail at startup, a system refresh or reset, as mentioned previously, is also available from Windows RE and could remedy the problem.

 Quick check

■ Which tools available in Windows RE can roll back a computer to a previous state, perhaps before an application installation occurred?

Quick check answer

■ System Restore

Windows RE can also be accessed by completing the following steps:

1. Open the Settings charm and select Change PC Settings.

2. Select General from the navigation pane.

3. In Advanced Startup, select Restart Now.

4. From the Choose An Option page, shown in Figure 15-12, select Troubleshoot.

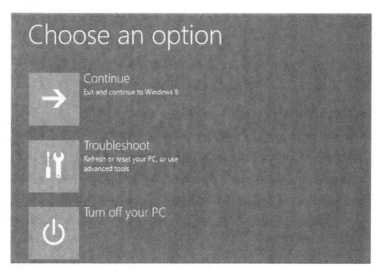

FIGURE 15-12 Advanced startup options

5. On the Troubleshoot page, shown in Figure 15-13, select Advanced Options. On the Advanced Options page, select Startup Settings, and then tap or click Restart.

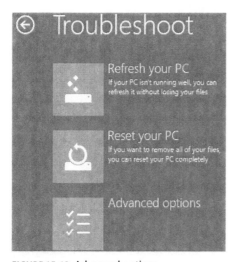

FIGURE 15-13 Advanced options

This restarts the computer and opens the Startup Settings menu, from which you can perform the following actions:

▪ Enable Debugging

▪ Enable Boot Logging

▪ Enable Safe Mode

▪ Enable Safe Mode With Networking

- Enable Safe Mode With Command Prompt
- Disable Driver Signature Enforcement
- Disable Early Launch Anti-Malware Protection
- Disable Automatic Restart After Failure

> **NOTE BEGINNING AGAIN**
>
> You have one additional option to access the recovery console: press F10 and select Launch Recovery Environment. This causes Windows to restart and open at the beginning of the Advanced Startup menu, enabling you to begin the startup option selection process from the beginning.

> **REAL WORLD DISABLING RESTART AFTER A FAILURE**
>
> Sometimes, you will want to disable the option to have Windows 8 restart following a failure. Allowing Windows to restart and attempt automatic recovery of a problem the first or second time a failure occurs can be a great time saver; however, if the failure continues to occur, disable automatic restart so that you can investigate the messages or patterns that occur during the failure.

The advanced tools available in Windows 8 are intended to correct issues and help avoid interruptions in normal work on your computer. Windows 8 has integrated a number of these tools into a more graphical experience than prior versions of Windows, thus providing a more uniform experience for both the users and the IT staff supporting them.

Lesson summary

- Create a recovery drive by using USB or optical media.
- Access the recovery options from a running Windows operating system.
- Use Automatic Repair to troubleshoot startup issues with Windows 8.

Lesson review

Answer the following questions to test your knowledge of the information in this lesson. You can find the answers to these questions and explanations of why each answer choice is correct or incorrect in the "Answers" section at the end of this chapter.

1. Your computer has not been performing optimally, and you are unable to determine what the issue might be. Which option can you use to access advanced options for troubleshooting issues?

    A. Select Advanced Startup Options from the PC Settings menu.

    B. Start Windows in safe mode.

    C.   Reset Windows to the Last Known Good Configuration.

    D.   Reformat your computer and reinstall Windows.

2.   Windows 8 provides advanced options to speed up the recovery process for your computer. Which options can be used to perform recovery steps in Windows 8? (Choose all that apply.)

    A.   Refresh

    B.   Restart

    C.   Reset

    D.   Last Known Good Configuration

3.   You are creating some recovery media for your Windows 8–based computer by using the Recovery Drive Wizard. What is the minimum size the media must have available to be used for recovery purposes?

    A.   2,048 MB

    B.   1,024 MB

    C.   512 MB

    D.   256 MB

Practice exercises

In the exercises in this section, you perform backup and recovery of files and entire computers by using both standard and advanced options.

Exercise 1: Back up files in Windows 8

In this exercise, you back up files on your computer by using File History.

1.   Open Control Panel.

2.   Select File History.

3.   Choose a backup location.

4.   Create a File History backup.

Exercise 2: Recover files by using File History

In this exercise, you recover the files backed up in Exercise 1.

1.   Open Control Panel.

2.   Select File History.

3.   Locate the files you backed up in the previous exercise.

4.   Check one of the files to ensure that it is correct.

5.   Restore the file to an alternate location.

Exercise 3: Bring your computer back to new with a reset

In this exercise, you reset your computer to its original state.

1. Open PC Settings.

2. Select the option to remove everything and reinstall Windows.

3. Perform a computer reset.

Exercise 4: Use Advanced Startup to troubleshoot problems with Windows 8

In this exercise, you start your computer by using Advanced Startup.

1. Open PC Settings.

2. Select the option to open the Advanced Startup menu.

3. Navigate to the Troubleshoot option.

4. Restart your computer to access the Startup Settings menu.

Suggested practice exercises

The following practice exercises are designed to give you more opportunities to practice what you've learned and to help you successfully master the lessons presented in this chapter.

Exercise 1 requires an external hard disk. If you do not have an external hard disk, skip this exercise and continue on to Exercise 2 or Exercise 3.

■ **Exercise 1** Configure recovery media by using a removable external hard disk, and then use the media to recover your computer.

■ **Exercise 2** Manually create a system restore point for your computer, and then modify the computer in some way (perhaps by installing a new application) and test a system restore to that restore point.

■ **Exercise 3** Use MSConfig to disable all non-Microsoft services on your computer. Restart and make sure none of the additional services have started. Add these third-party services back, one at a time.

Answers

This section contains the answers to the lesson review questions in this chapter.

Lesson 1

1.   **Correct answers: A and B**

   A.   **Correct:** Because the problem appears to be related to Windows files, the CEO might be able to recover the computer without compromising her personal data by performing a refresh.

   B.   **Correct:** Using a computer reset will bring the computer back to its out-of-the-box state, removing all personal data and restoring Windows to a like-new configuration.

   C.   **Incorrect:** Because the system restore might not solve the problem in one attempt, it does not meet the CEO's requirements to restore the computer to a working state as quickly as possible.

   D.   **Incorrect:** Starting the computer in safe mode is not enabled in Windows 8 by default. In addition, this would be a troubleshooting step that might not solve the problem right away.

2.   **Correct answer: C**

   A.   **Incorrect:** System Restore would roll back system changes only and not personal files.

   B.   **Incorrect:** System image restoration would not recover the personal files created since the image was created.

   C.   **Correct:** The File History method accomplishes the task of restoring the missing file and serves as a precursor to training, covering this and other features available in Windows 8.

   D.   **Incorrect:** Resetting the computer would remove all other personal documents from the computer rather than recovering the missing documents.

3.   **Correct answer: B**

   A.   **Incorrect:** System image recovery is an advanced recovery option that would remove all information from the computer and restore the versions of Windows and applications that were installed on the computer when the image was created.

   B.   **Correct:** System Restore would enable the user to roll the computer back to the state it was in before the Office 2010 installation occurred. This way, the installation could be retried without too much effort.

   C.   **Incorrect:** PC Refresh would return the operating system to an out-of-the-box state without affecting personal files. Even though the applications from media that were installed would be removed, the time needed to refresh a computer might be longer than necessary to solve this problem.

D. **Incorrect:** Using Last Known Good Configuration restores the settings that worked the last time Windows started successfully. This does not take into account applications that do not start or that function improperly.

Lesson 2

1. **Correct answer: B**

   A. **Incorrect:** MSConfig is used to enable or disable different services and startup options during the startup process for the next start. Although it can permanently change startup options, it is not used to restore previous settings.

   B. **Correct:** Last Known Good Configuration restores the settings that last worked correctly for your computer and attempts to start. If a previous configuration change caused the problem, replacing the setting with its previous value can help correct the problem.

   C. **Incorrect:** The Task Manager Startup tab displays the applications that are configured to start with Windows. Only applications installed on a computer can be added to or removed from starting by using this method. Windows settings are not affected.

   D. **Incorrect:** Safe mode is not enabled as a startup option in Windows 8. To enable this mode, you must modify the start menu by using MSConfig to add the option to start in safe mode.

2. **Correct answer: A**

   A. **Correct:** Using MSConfig to disable all non-Microsoft services enables you to start services selectively with Windows, and it displays only the non-Microsoft services to provide an idea of the third-party services that are currently starting with the operating system.

   B. **Incorrect:** You cannot disable services from Task Manager. MSConfig is the utility that performs this action.

   C. **Incorrect:** Editing the startup menu enables you to modify choices available when starting Windows, but it will not enable you to configure the services that start with Windows.

   D. **Incorrect:** Windows Task Manager cannot edit the startup menu used when starting Windows.

3. **Correct answer: B**

   A. **Incorrect:** Although performing a driver update might enable Windows to locate other drivers, those drivers might not be newer than the drivers already loaded.

   B. **Correct:** Rolling back the device driver to the original one provided by Windows will likely correct the problem because the drivers included on the disc that came with the camera might not be optimized for Windows 8.

C.	**Incorrect:** Removing the device might not remove the driver installed from the CD that came with the camera.

D.	**Incorrect:** MSConfig cannot be used to disable or remove device drivers.

Lesson 3

1.	**Correct answer: A**

A.	**Correct:** The Advanced Startup options selection in PC Settings will restart your computer into the Advanced Options menu.

B.	**Incorrect:** Starting Windows in safe mode will not correct startup issues with your computer.

C.	**Incorrect:** Restarting to the Last Known Good Configuration might correct issues with your computer, but it is not specific to startup issues and provides a rollback only to the last working settings.

D.	**Incorrect:** Reformatting the computer requires more administrative effort than needed to correct the individual problem.

2.	**Correct answers: A and C**

A.	**Correct:** Refresh repairs problems with Windows files but does not affect your personal files.

B.	**Incorrect:** Restart will not repair issues with the operating system.

C.	**Correct:** Reset removes your personal data and reconfigures Windows to the original configuration.

D.	**Incorrect:** Last Known Good Configuration just reapplies the last settings that worked successfully.

3.	**Correct answer: D**

A.	**Incorrect:** 2,048 MB is larger than the minimum size needed for recovery media.

B.	**Incorrect:** 1,024 MB is larger than the minimum size needed for recovery media.

C.	**Incorrect:** 512 MB is larger than the minimum size needed for recovery media.

D.	**Correct:** 256 MB is the minimum media size needed for recovery media.

Index

About the authors

 SCOTT LOWE is the founder and managing consultant of the 1610 Group, a strategic and tactical IT consulting firm based in the Midwest. Scott has been in the IT field for almost 20 years and spent 10 of those years as chief intelligence officer (CIO) for various organizations. Scott is also a micro-analyst for Wikibon and an *InformationWeek Analytics* contributor. In addition, Scott has also written thousands of articles and blog postings and regularly contributes to such sites as TechRepublic, Wikibon, and Virtualizationadmin.com. He's also either authored or co-authored four books and is the creator of 10 video training courses for TrainSignal. You can follow Scott on Twitter at @otherscottlowe.

 DEREK SCHAULAND is a Microsoft MVP with 15 years of experience in technical support and Microsoft Systems Administration. He has been writing for various electronic and print publications for the past 10 years to help others learn about technology and expand his own knowledge along the way.

In addition to blogging, Derek co-founded Tech On Tap Training Series, a nonprofit organization to promote networking among IT professionals and assist them in meeting and learning from organizations of all sizes in the information technology industry.

 RICK VANOVER is a product strategy specialist for Veeam Software, based in Columbus, Ohio. Rick's passion for challenges led to his commitment to communicate technologies and educate others at all levels, engaging those new to virtualization as well as those who are experts.

As a popular blogger, podcaster, and active member of the virtualization community, Rick builds relationships and spreads excitement about virtualization technologies. Before becoming the go-to guy for virtualization questions, Rick was in systems administration and IT management. His certifications include MCITP, vExpert, and VCP. Follow Rick on Twitter at @RickVanover.

Training Guide: *Configuring Windows 8* and Exam 70-687

This book is designed to help build and advance your job-role expertise. In addition, it covers some of the topics and skills related to Microsoft Certification Exam 70-687, and may be useful as a complementary study resource. Note: This book is not designed to cover all exam topics; see chart below. If you are preparing for the exam, use additional materials such as *Exam Ref 70-687: Configuring Windows 8* (978-0-7356-7392-2) to help bolster your readiness in conjunction with real-world experience.

EXAM OBJECTIVES/SKILLS	SEE TOPIC-RELATED COVERAGE HERE
INSTALL AND UPGRADE TO WINDOWS 8	
Evaluate hardware readiness and compatibility.	Chapter 1, Lesson 2
Install Windows 8.	Chapter 2, Lesson 1, Lesson 3
Migrate and configure user data.	Chapter 2, Lesson 2
CONFIGURE HARDWARE AND APPLICATIONS	
Configure devices and device drivers.	Chapter 3
Install and configure desktop applications.	Chapter 4, Lesson 1
Install and configure Windows Store applications.	Chapter 4, Lesson 2
Control access to local hardware and applications.	Chapter 4, Lesson 2
Configure Internet Explorer.	Chapter 5
Configure Hyper-V.	Chapter 6
CONFIGURE NETWORK CONNECTIVITY	
Configure IP settings.	Chapter 7, Lesson 1. See "Configuring IP settings."
Configure networking settings.	Chapter 7, Lesson 1
Configure and maintain network security.	Chapter 7; Chapter 8
Configure remote management.	Chapter 9
CONFIGURE ACCESS TO RESOURCES	
Configure shared resources.	Chapter 10
Configure file and folder access.	Chapter 10; Chapter 11, Lesson 1, Lesson 2
Configure local security settings.	Chapter 11, Lesson 2
Configure authentication and authorization.	Chapter 12

CONFIGURE REMOTE ACCESS AND MOBILITY	
Configure remote connections.	Chapter 9, Lesson 1, Lesson 2
Configure mobility options.	Chapter 1; Chapter 13
Configure security for mobile devices.	Chapter 1; Chapter 3, Lesson 3; Chapter 13

MONITOR AND MAINTAIN WINDOWS CLIENTS	
Configure and manage updates.	Chapter 3; Chapter 14, Lesson 1
Manage local storage.	Chapter 11, Lesson 3
Monitor system performance.	Chapter 14, Lesson 2

CONFIGURE BACKUP AND RECOVERY OPTIONS	
Configure backup.	Chapter 15, Lesson 1
Configure system recovery options.	Chapter 15
Configure file recovery options.	Chapter 15

For complete information on Exam 70-687, go to *http://www.microsoft.com/learning/en/us/exam.aspx?ID=70-687*. And for more information on Microsoft certifications, go to *www.microsoft.com/learning*.

What do you think of this book?

We want to hear from you!
To participate in a brief online survey, please visit:

microsoft.com/learning/booksurvey

Tell us how well this book meets your needs—what works effectively, and what we can do better. Your feedback will help us continually improve our books and learning resources for you.

Thank you in advance for your input!

CPSIA information can be obtained at www.ICGtesting.com
Printed in the USA
LVOW111714230413

330561LV00005B/197/P